NON-LEAGUE FOOTBALL TABLES 1889-2005

EDITOR
Michael Robinson

British Library Cataloguing in Publication Data
A catalogue record for this book is available from the British Library

ISBN 1-86223-125-7

Printed by The Cromwell Press

FOREWORD

In selecting the Leagues to be included in this fourth edition of Non-League Football Tables we have again chosen those forming the pinnacle of the Non-League Football Pyramid, i.e. The Football Conference and it's three direct feeders.

In addition we have once more included the briefly-lived Football Alliance which became, effectively, the 2nd Division of the Football League in 1892 together with four Midland area leagues. In future editions we expect to continue to include leagues for other parts of the country.

Furthermore, as league sponsors change frequently, we have not used sponsored names (eg. Rymans League) other than in an indicative way on the cover.

We are indebted to Mick Blakeman for providing tables for the four Midland area Leagues included in this edition of the book.

CONTENTS

FOOTBALL ALLIANCE

1889-90

Sheffield Wednesday	22	15	2	5	70	39	32
Bootle	22	13	2	7	66	39	28
Sunderland Albion	21	12	2	7	64	39	28
Grimsby Town	22	12	2	8	58	47	26
Crewe Alexandra	22	11	2	9	68	59	24
Darwen	22	10	2	10	70	75	22
Birmingham St George	21	9	3	9	62	49	21
Newton Heath	22	9	2	11	40	44	20
Walsall Town Swifts	22	8	3	11	44	59	19
Small Heath	22	6	5	11	44	67	17
Nottingham Forest	22	6	5	11	31	62	17
Long Eaton Rangers	22	4	2	16	35	73	10

Sunderland Albion record includes 2 points awarded when Birmingham St George refused to fulfil a fixture which the Alliance committee had ordered to be replayed.

1890-91

Stoke	22	13	7	2	57	39	33
Sunderland Albion	22	12	6	4	69	28	30
Grimsby Town	22	11	5	6	43	27	27
Birmingham St George	22	12	2	8	64	62	26
Nottingham Forest	22	9	7	6	66	39	25
Darwen	22	10	3	9	64	59	23
Walsall Town Swifts	22	9	3	10	34	61	21
Crewe Alexandra	22	8	4	10	59	67	20
Newton Heath	22	7	3	12	37	55	17
Small Heath	22	7	2	13	58	66	16
Bootle	22	3	7	12	40	61	13
Sheffield Wednesday	22	4	5	13	39	66	13

1891-92

Nottingham Forest	22	14	5	3	59	22	33
Newton Heath	22	12	7	3	69	33	31
Small Heath	22	12	5	5	53	36	29
Sheffield Wednesday	22	12	4	6	65	35	28
Burton Swifts	22	12	2	8	54	52	26
Grimsby Town	22	6	6	10	40	39	18
Crewe Alexandra	22	7	4	11	44	49	18
Ardwick	22	6	6	10	39	51	18
Bootle	22	8	2	12	42	64	18
Lincoln City	22	6	5	11	37	65	17
Walsall Town Swifts	22	6	3	13	33	59	15
Birmingham St George	22	5	3	14	34	64	13

SOUTHERN LEAGUE

1894-95

First Division

Millwall Athletic	16	12	4	0	68	19	28
Luton Town	16	9	4	3	36	22	22
Southampton St Mary's	16	9	2	5	34	25	20
Ilford	16	6	3	7	26	40	15
Reading	16	6	2	8	33	38	14
Chatham	16	4	5	7	22	25	13
Royal Ordnance Factories	16	3	6	7	20	30	12
Clapton	16	5	1	10	22	38	11
Swindon Town	16	4	1	11	24	48	9

Second Division

New Brompton	12	11	0	1	57	10	22
Sheppey United	12	6	1	5	25	23	13
Old St Stephen's	12	6	0	6	26	26	12
Uxbridge	12	4	3	5	14	20	11
Bromley	12	4	1	7	23	30	9
Chesham	13	3	3	6	20	42	9
Maidenhead	12	2	4	6	19	33	8

1895-96

First Division

Millwall Athletic	18	16	1	1	75	16	33
Luton Town	18	13	1	4	68	14	27
Southampton St Mary's	18	12	0	6	44	23	24
Reading	18	11	1	6	45	38	23
Chatham	18	9	2	7	43	45	20
New Brompton	18	7	4	7	30	37	18
Swindon Town	18	6	4	8	38	41	16
Clapton	18	4	2	12	30	67	10
Royal Ordnance Factories	18	3	3	12	23	44	9
Ilford	18	0	0	18	10	81	0

Second Division

Wolverton L & NW Railway	16	13	1	2	43	10	27
Sheppey United	16	11	3	2	60	19	25
1st Scots Guards	16	8	5	3	37	22	21
Uxbridge	16	9	1	6	28	23	19
Old St Stephen's	16	6	3	7	34	21	15
Guildford	16	7	1	8	29	41	15
Maidenhead	16	4	1	11	20	49	9
Chesham	16	2	3	11	15	48	7
Bromley	16	2	2	12	16	49	6

1896-97

First Division

Southampton St Mary's	20	15	5	0	63	18	35
Millwall Athletic	20	13	5	2	63	24	31
Chatham	20	13	1	6	54	29	27
Tottenham Hotspur	20	9	4	7	43	29	22
Gravesend United	20	9	4	7	35	34	22
Swindon Town	20	8	3	9	33	37	19
Reading	20	8	3	9	31	49	19
New Brompton	20	7	2	11	32	42	16
Northfleet	20	5	4	11	24	46	14
Sheppey United	20	5	1	14	34	47	11
Wolverton L & NW Railway	20	2	0	18	17	74	4

Second Division

Dartford	24	16	4	4	83	19	36
Royal Engineers Training Battalion	24	11	9	4	49	37	31
Freemantle	24	12	4	8	58	40	28
Uxbridge	24	11	5	8	62	37	27
Wycombe Wanderers	24	10	6	8	37	54	26
Chesham	24	11	3	10	41	55	25
Southall	24	9	6	9	55	52	24
1st Scot Guards	24	9	6	9	49	50	24
West Herts	24	11	1	12	41	49	23
Warmley (Bristol)	24	10	2	12	44	43	22
Old St Stephen's	24	5	7	12	36	52	17
Maidenhead	24	4	8	12	33	64	16
1st Coldstream Guards	24	3	6	15	30	66	12

1897-98

First Division

Southampton	22	18	1	3	53	18	37
Bristol City	22	13	7	2	67	33	33
Tottenham Hotspur	22	12	4	6	52	31	28
Chatham	22	12	4	6	50	34	28
Reading	22	8	7	7	39	31	23
New Brompton	22	9	4	9	37	37	22
Sheppey United	22	10	1	11	40	49	21
Gravesend United	22	7	6	9	28	39	20
Millwall Athletic	22	8	2	12	48	45	18
Swindon Town	22	7	2	13	36	48	16
Northfleet	22	4	3	15	29	60	11
Wolverton L & NW Railway	22	3	1	18	28	82	7

Second Division

Royal Artillery (Portsmouth)	22	19	1	2	75	22	39
Warmley (Bristol)	22	19	0	3	108	15	38
West Herts	22	11	6	5	50	48	28
Uxbridge	22	11	2	9	39	57	24
St Albans	22	9	5	8	47	41	23
Dartford	22	11	0	11	68	55	22
Southall	22	8	2	12	49	61	18
Chesham	22	8	2	12	38	48	18
Olsd St Stephen's	22	7	2	13	47	66	16
Wycombe Wanderers	22	7	2	13	37	55	16
Maidenhead	22	4	4	14	27	81	12
Royal Engineers Training Battalion	22	4	2	16	26	62	10

1898-99

First Division

Southampton	24	15	5	4	54	24	35
Bristol City	24	15	3	6	55	12	33
Millwall Athletic	24	12	6	6	59	35	30
Chatham	24	10	8	6	32	23	28
Reading	24	9	8	7	31	24	26
New Brompton	24	10	5	9	38	30	25
Tottenham Hotspur	24	10	4	10	40	36	24
Bedminster	24	10	4	10	35	39	24
Swindon Town	24	9	5	10	43	49	23
Brighton United	24	9	2	13	37	48	20
Gravesend United	24	7	5	12	42	52	19
Sheppey United	24	5	3	16	23	53	13
Royal Artillery (Portsmouth)	24	4	4	16	17	60	12

Second Division (London Section)

Thames Ironworks	22	19	1	2	64	16	39
Wolverton L & NW Railway	22	13	4	5	88	43	30
Watford	22	14	2	6	62	35	30
Brentford	22	11	3	8	59	39	25
Wycombe Wanderers	22	10	2	10	55	57	22
Southall	22	11	0	11	44	55	22
Chesham	22	9	2	11	45	62	20
St Albans	22	8	3	11	45	59	19
Shepherds Bush	22	7	3	12	37	53	17
Fulham	22	6	4	12	36	44	16
Uxbridge	22	7	2	13	29	48	16
Maidenhead	22	3	2	17	33	86	8

Second Division (South West Section)

Cowes	10	10	0	0	58	8	20
Ryde	10	7	0	3	30	11	14
Freemantle	10	4	1	5	18	31	9
Sandown	10	4	0	6	20	29	8
Eastleigh	10	2	1	7	17	37	5
Andover	10	2	0	8	14	41	4

1899-1900

First Division

Tottenham Hotspur	28	20	4	4	67	26	44
Portsmouth	28	20	1	7	58	27	41
Southampton	28	17	1	10	70	33	35
Reading	28	15	2	11	41	28	32
Swindon Town	28	15	2	11	50	42	32
Bedminster	28	13	2	13	44	45	28
Millwall Athletic	28	12	3	13	36	37	27
Queens Park Rangers	28	12	2	14	49	57	26
Bristol City	28	9	7	12	43	47	25
Bristol Rovers	28	11	3	14	46	55	25
New Brompton	28	9	6	13	39	49	24
Gravesend United	28	10	4	14	38	54	24
Chatham	28	10	3	15	38	58	23
Thames Ironworks	28	8	5	15	30	45	21
Sheppey United	28	3	7	18	24	66	13

Second Division

Watford	20	14	2	4	57	25	30
Fulham	20	10	4	6	44	23	24
Chesham Town	20	11	2	7	43	37	24
Wolverton L & NW Railway	20	9	6	5	46	36	24
Grays United	20	8	6	6	63	29	22
Shepherds Bush	20	9	4	7	45	37	22
Dartford	20	8	3	9	36	44	19
Wycombe Wanderers	20	8	3	9	35	50	19
Brentford	20	5	7	8	31	48	17
Southall	20	6	3	11	21	44	15
Maidenhead	20	1	2	17	16	64	4

1900-01

First Division

Southampton	28	18	5	5	58	26	41
Bristol City	28	17	5	6	54	27	39
Portsmouth	28	17	4	7	56	32	38
Millwall Athletic	28	17	2	9	55	32	36
Tottenham Hotspur	28	16	4	8	55	33	36
West Ham United	28	14	5	9	40	28	33
Bristol Rovers	28	14	4	10	46	35	32
Queens Park Rangers	28	11	4	13	43	48	26
Reading	28	8	8	12	24	25	24
Luton Town	28	11	2	15	43	49	24
Kettering	28	7	9	12	33	46	23
New Brompton	28	7	5	16	34	51	19
Gravesend United	28	6	7	15	32	85	19
Watford	28	6	4	18	24	52	16
Swindon Town	28	3	8	17	19	47	14

Second Division

Brentford	16	14	2	0	63	11	30
Grays United	16	12	2	2	62	12	26
Sheppey United	16	8	1	7	44	26	17
Shepherds Bush	16	8	1	7	30	30	17
Fulham	16	8	0	8	38	26	16
Chesham Town	16	5	1	10	26	39	11
Maidenhead	16	4	1	11	21	49	9
Wycombe Wanderers	16	4	1	11	23	68	9
Southall	16	4	1	11	22	68	9

1901-02

First Division

Portsmouth	30	20	7	3	67	24	47
Tottenham Hotspur	30	18	6	6	61	22	42
Southampton	30	18	6	6	71	28	42
West Ham United	30	17	6	7	45	28	40
Reading	30	16	7	7	57	24	39
Millwall Athletic	30	13	6	11	48	31	32
Luton Town	30	11	10	9	31	35	32
Kettering	30	12	5	13	44	39	29
Bristol Rovers	30	12	5	13	43	39	29
New Brompton	30	10	7	13	39	38	27
Northampton	30	11	5	14	53	64	27
Queens Park Rangers	30	8	7	15	34	56	23
Watford	30	9	4	17	36	60	22
Wellingborough	30	9	4	17	34	75	22
Brentford	30	7	6	17	34	61	20
Swindon Town	30	2	3	25	17	93	7

Second Division

Fulham	16	13	0	3	51	19	26
Grays United	16	12	1	3	49	14	25
Brighton & Hove Albion	16	11	0	5	34	17	22
Wycombe Wanderers	16	7	3	6	36	30	17
West Hampstead	16	6	4	6	39	29	16
Shepherds Bush	16	6	1	9	31	31	13
Southall	16	5	2	9	28	52	12
Maidenhead	16	3	1	12	23	59	7
Chesham Town	16	2	2	12	24	64	6

1902-03

First Division

Southampton	30	20	8	2	83	20	48
Reading	30	19	7	4	72	30	45
Portsmouth	30	17	7	6	69	32	41
Tottenham Hotspur	30	14	7	9	47	31	35
Bristol Rovers	30	13	8	9	46	34	34
New Brompton	30	11	11	8	37	35	33
Millwall Athletic	30	14	3	13	52	37	31
Northampton Town	30	12	6	12	39	48	30
Queens Park Rangers	30	11	6	13	34	42	28
West Ham United	30	9	10	11	35	49	28
Luton Town	30	10	7	13	43	44	27
Swindon Town	30	10	7	13	38	46	27
Kettering	30	8	11	11	33	40	27
Wellingborough	30	11	3	16	36	56	25
Watford	30	6	4	20	35	87	16
Brentford	30	2	1	27	16	84	5

Second Division

Fulham	10	7	1	2	27	7	15
Brighton & Hove Albion	10	7	1	2	34	11	15
Grays United	10	7	0	3	28	12	14
Wycombe Wanderers	10	3	3	4	13	19	9
Chesham Town	10	2	1	7	9	37	5
Southall	10	1	0	9	10	35	2

1903-04

First Division

Southampton	34	22	6	6	75	30	50
Tottenham Hotspur	34	16	11	7	54	37	43
Bristol Rovers	34	17	8	9	66	42	42
Portsmouth	34	17	8	9	41	38	42
Queens Park Rangers	34	15	11	8	53	37	41
Reading	34	14	13	7	48	35	41
Millwall	34	16	8	10	64	42	40
Luton Town	34	14	12	8	38	33	40
Plymouth Argyle	34	13	10	11	44	34	36
Swindon Town	34	10	11	13	30	42	31
Fulham	34	9	12	13	33	34	30
West Ham United	34	10	7	17	38	43	27
Brentford	34	9	9	16	34	48	27
Wellingborough	34	11	5	18	44	63	27
Northampton Town	34	10	7	17	36	69	27
New Brompton	34	6	13	15	26	43	25
Brighton & Hove Albion	34	6	12	16	45	79	24
Kettering	34	6	7	21	30	78	19

Second Division

Watford	20	18	2	0	70	15	38
Portsmouth Reserves	20	15	2	3	85	25	32
Millwall Reserves	20	9	4	7	35	39	22
Southampton Reserves	20	9	3	8	59	35	21
Grays United	20	9	3	8	25	55	21
Fulham Reserves	20	8	4	8	40	34	20
Swindon Town Reserves	20	8	3	9	50	44	19
Reading Reserves	20	8	2	10	43	42	18
Wycombe Wanderers	20	5	5	10	29	64	15
Southall	20	4	2	14	25	62	10
Chesham Town	20	1	2	17	19	65	4

1904-05

First Division

Bristol Rovers	34	20	8	6	74	36	48
Reading	34	18	7	9	57	38	43
Southampton	34	18	7	9	54	40	43
Plymouth Argyle	34	18	5	11	57	39	41
Tottenham Hotspur	34	15	8	11	53	34	38
Fulham	34	14	10	10	46	34	38
Queens Park Rangers	34	14	8	12	51	46	36
Portsmouth	34	16	4	14	61	56	36
New Brompton	34	11	11	12	40	41	33
West Ham United	34	12	8	14	48	42	32
Brighton & Hove Albion	34	13	6	15	44	45	32
Northampton Town	34	12	8	14	43	54	32
Watford	34	14	3	17	41	44	31
Brentford	34	10	9	15	33	38	29
Millwall	34	11	7	16	38	47	29
Swindon Town	34	12	5	17	41	59	29
Luton Town	34	12	3	19	45	54	27
Wellingborough	34	5	3	26	25	104	13

Second Division

Fulham Reserves	22	16	4	2	78	25	36
Portsmouth Reserves	22	14	2	6	75	28	30
Swindon Town Reserves	22	12	3	7	54	47	27
Grays United	22	11	3	8	61	40	25
Southampton Reserves	22	10	5	7	52	35	25
Brighton & Hove Albion	22	9	3	10	48	49	21
West Ham United Reserves	22	8	5	9	45	47	21
Clapton Orient	22	7	7	8	47	56	21
Watford Reserves	22	5	6	11	30	62	16
Southall	22	7	2	13	31	66	16
Wycombe Wanderers	22	6	2	14	37	70	14
Reading Reserves	22	4	4	14	24	57	12

1905-06

First Division

Fulham	34	19	12	3	44	15	50
Southampton	34	19	7	8	58	39	45
Portsmouth	34	17	9	8	61	35	43
Luton Town	34	17	7	10	64	40	41
Tottenham Hotspur	34	16	7	11	46	29	39
Plymouth Argyle	34	16	7	11	52	33	39
Norwich City	34	13	10	11	46	38	36
Bristol Rovers	34	15	5	14	56	56	35
Brentford	34	14	7	13	43	52	35
Reading	34	12	9	13	53	46	33
West Ham United	34	14	5	15	42	39	33
Millwall	34	11	11	12	38	41	33
Queens Park Rangers	34	12	7	15	58	44	31
Watford	34	8	10	16	38	57	26
Swindon Town	34	8	9	17	31	52	25
Brighton & Hove Albion	34	9	7	18	30	55	25
New Brompton	34	7	8	19	20	62	22
Northampton Town	34	8	5	21	32	79	21

Second Division

Crystal Palace	24	19	4	1	66	14	42
Leyton	24	16	6	2	61	18	38
Portsmouth Reserves	24	12	8	4	52	24	32
Fulham Reserves	24	11	6	7	52	39	28
Southampton Reserves	24	7	9	8	39	41	23
Southern United	24	8	7	9	45	49	23
St Leonard's United	24	9	4	11	54	50	22
Watford Reserves	24	8	5	11	43	47	21
West Ham United Reserves	24	7	5	12	46	48	19
Grays United	24	8	3	13	24	77	19
Reading Reserves	24	6	5	13	36	49	15
Swindon Town Reserves	24	5	5	14	36	51	15
Wycombe Wanderers	24	5	3	16	36	83	13

1906-07

First Division

Fulham	38	20	13	5	58	32	53
Portsmouth	38	22	7	9	64	36	51
Brighton & Hove Albion	38	18	9	11	53	43	45
Luton Town	38	18	9	11	52	52	45
West Ham United	38	15	14	9	60	41	44
Tottenham Hotspur	38	17	9	12	63	45	43
Millwall	38	18	6	14	71	50	42
Norwich City	38	15	12	11	57	48	42
Watford	38	13	16	9	46	43	42
Brentford	38	17	8	13	57	56	42
Southampton	38	13	9	16	49	56	35
Reading	38	14	6	18	57	47	34
Leyton	38	11	12	15	38	60	34
Bristol Rovers	38	12	9	17	55	54	33
Plymouth Argyle	38	10	13	15	43	50	33
New Brompton	38	12	9	17	47	59	33
Swindon Town	38	11	11	16	43	54	33
Queens Park Rangers	38	11	10	17	47	55	32
Crystal Palace	38	8	9	21	46	66	25
Northampton Town	38	5	9	24	29	88	19

Second Division

Southend United	22	14	5	3	58	23	33
West Ham United Reserves	22	14	3	5	64	30	31
Portsmouth Reserves	22	11	6	5	53	24	28
Fulham Reserves	22	11	4	7	47	32	26
Hastings & St Leonards	21	10	4	7	46	31	24
Tunbridge Wells Rangers	22	10	1	11	46	36	21
Salisbury City	22	9	2	11	40	42	20
Southampton Reserves	22	8	2	12	37	56	18
Swindon Town Reserves	22	7	3	12	35	43	17
Reading Reserves	22	6	4	12	32	47	16
Royal Engineers (Aldershot)	21	5	4	12	27	58	14
Wycombe Wanderers	22	4	6	12	28	68	14

The match between Tunbridge Wells Rangers and Royal Engineers (Aldershot) was not completed.

1907-08

First Division

Queens Park Rangers	38	21	9	8	82	57	51
Plymouth Argyle	38	19	11	8	50	31	49
Millwall	38	19	8	11	49	32	46
Crystal Palace	38	17	10	11	54	51	44
Swindon Town	38	16	10	12	55	40	42
Bristol Rovers	38	16	10	12	59	56	42
Tottenham Hotspur	38	17	7	14	59	48	41
Northampton Town	38	15	11	12	50	41	41
Portsmouth	38	17	6	15	63	52	40
West Ham United	38	15	10	13	47	48	40
Southampton	38	16	6	16	51	60	38
Reading	38	15	6	17	55	50	36
Bradford Park Avenue	38	12	12	14	53	54	36
Watford	38	12	10	16	47	49	34
Brentford	38	14	5	19	49	52	33
Norwich City	38	12	9	17	46	49	33
Brighton & Hove Albion	38	12	8	18	46	59	32
Luton Town	38	12	6	20	33	56	30
Leyton	38	8	11	19	51	73	27
New Brompton	38	9	7	22	44	75	25

Second Division

Southend	18	13	3	2	47	16	29
Portsmouth Reserves	18	10	5	3	39	22	25
Croydon Common	18	10	3	5	35	25	23
Hastings & St Leonard's	18	10	2	6	43	29	22
Southampton Reserves	18	7	4	7	54	46	18
Tunbridge Wells Rangers	18	7	3	8	42	38	17
Salisbury City	18	6	4	8	35	46	16
Swindon Town Reserves	18	5	5	8	36	40	15
Brighton & Hove Albion Reserves	18	4	4	10	34	47	12
Wycombe Wanderers	18	1	1	16	16	72	3

1908-09

First Division

Northampton Town	40	25	5	10	90	45	55
Swindon Town	40	22	5	13	96	55	49
Southampton	40	19	10	11	67	58	48
Portsmouth	40	18	10	12	68	60	46
Bristol Rovers	40	17	9	14	60	63	43
Exeter City	40	18	6	16	56	65	42
New Brompton	40	17	7	16	48	59	41
Reading	40	11	18	11	60	57	40
Luton Town	40	17	6	17	59	60	40
Plymouth Argyle	40	15	10	15	46	47	40
Millwall	40	16	6	18	59	61	38
Southend United	40	14	10	16	52	54	38
Leyton	40	15	8	17	52	55	38
Watford	40	14	9	17	51	64	37
Queens Park Rangers	40	12	12	16	52	50	36
Crystal Palace	40	12	12	16	62	62	36
West Ham United	40	16	4	20	56	60	36
Brighton & Hove Albion	40	14	7	19	60	61	35
Norwich City	40	12	11	17	59	75	35
Coventry City	40	15	4	21	64	91	34
Brentford	40	13	7	20	59	74	33

Second Division

Croydon Common	12	10	0	2	67	14	20
Hastings & St Leonard's	12	8	1	3	42	18	17
Depot Battalion Royal Engineers	12	8	1	3	23	22	17
2nd Grenadier Guards	12	5	0	7	21	33	10
South Farnborough Athletic	12	2	4	6	20	39	8
Salisbury City	12	3	1	8	24	36	7
Chesham Town	12	2	1	9	17	52	5

1909-10

First Division

Brighton & Hove Albion	42	23	13	6	69	28	59
Swindon Town	42	22	10	10	92	46	54
Queens Park Rangers	42	19	13	10	56	47	51
Northampton Town	42	22	4	16	90	44	48
Southampton	42	16	16	10	64	55	48
Portsmouth	42	20	7	15	70	63	47
Crystal Palace	42	20	6	16	69	50	46
Coventry City	42	19	8	15	71	60	46
West Ham United	42	15	15	12	69	56	45
Leyton	42	16	11	15	60	46	43
Plymouth Argyle	42	16	11	15	61	54	43
New Brompton	42	19	5	18	76	74	43
Bristol Rovers	42	16	10	16	37	48	42
Brentford	42	16	9	17	50	58	41
Luton Town	42	15	11	16	72	92	41
Millwall	42	15	7	20	45	59	37
Norwich City	42	13	9	20	59	78	35
Exeter City	42	14	6	22	60	69	34
Watford	42	10	13	19	51	76	33
Southend United	42	12	9	21	51	90	33
Croydon Common	42	13	5	24	52	96	31
Reading	42	7	10	25	38	73	24

Second Division - Section A

Stoke	10	10	0	0	48	9	20
Ton Pentre	10	4	2	4	17	21	10
Merthyr Town	9	4	1	4	16	21	9
Salisbury City	8	2	1	5	7	18	5
Burton United	6	2	0	4	8	21	4
Aberdare	7	1	0	6	6	11	2

Second Division - Section B

Hastings & St Leonard's	9	6	3	0	26	11	15
Kettering	10	6	0	4	34	19	12
Chesham Town	10	5	2	3	25	25	12
Peterborough City	10	4	2	4	16	23	10
South Farnborough Athletic	10	4	1	5	23	19	9
Romford	9	0	0	9	7	33	0

1910-11

First Divison

Swindon Town	38	24	5	9	80	31	53
Northampton Town	38	18	12	8	54	27	48
Brighton & Hove Albion	38	20	8	10	58	35	48
Crystal Palace	38	17	13	8	55	48	47
West Ham United	38	17	11	10	63	46	45
Queens Park Rangers	38	13	14	11	52	41	40
Leyton	38	16	8	14	57	52	40
Plymouth Argyle	38	15	9	14	54	55	39
Luton Town	38	15	8	15	67	63	38
Norwich City	38	15	8	15	46	48	38
Coventry City	38	16	6	16	65	68	38
Brentford	38	14	9	15	41	42	37
Exeter City	38	14	9	15	51	53	37
Watford	38	13	9	16	49	65	35
Millwall	38	11	9	18	42	54	31
Bristol Rovers	38	10	10	18	42	55	30
Southampton	38	11	8	19	42	67	30
New Brompton	38	11	8	19	34	65	30
Southend United	38	10	9	19	47	64	29
Portsmouth	38	8	11	19	34	53	27

Second Division

Reading	22	16	3	3	55	11	35
Stoke	22	17	1	4	72	21	35
Merthyr Town	22	15	3	4	52	22	33
Cardiff City	22	12	4	6	48	29	28
Croydon Common	22	11	3	8	61	26	25
Treharris	22	10	3	9	38	31	23
Aberdare	22	9	5	8	38	33	23
Ton Pentre	22	10	3	9	44	40	23
Walsall	22	7	4	11	37	41	18
Kettering	22	6	1	15	34	68	13
Chesham Town	22	1	3	18	16	93	5
Salisbury City	22	0	3	19	16	92	3

1911-12

First Division

Queens Park Rangers	38	21	11	6	59	35	53
Plymouth Argyle	38	23	6	9	63	31	52
Northampton Town	38	22	7	9	82	41	51
Swindon Town	38	21	6	11	82	50	48
Brighton & Hove Albion	38	19	9	10	73	35	47
Coventry City	38	17	8	13	66	54	42
Crystal Palace	38	15	10	13	70	46	40
Millwall	38	15	10	13	60	57	40
Watford	38	13	10	15	56	68	36
Stoke	38	13	10	15	51	63	36
Reading	38	11	14	13	43	69	36
Norwich City	38	10	14	14	40	60	34
West Ham United	38	13	7	18	64	69	33
Brentford	38	12	9	17	60	65	33
Exeter City	38	11	11	16	48	62	33
Southampton	38	10	11	17	46	63	31
Bristol Rovers	38	9	13	16	41	62	31
New Brompton	38	11	9	18	35	72	31
Luton Town	38	9	10	19	49	61	28
Leyton	38	7	11	20	27	62	25

Second Division

Merthyr Town	26	19	3	4	60	14	41
Portsmouth	26	19	3	4	73	20	41
Cardiff City	26	15	4	7	55	26	34
Southend United	26	16	1	9	73	24	33
Pontypridd	26	13	6	7	39	24	32
Ton Pentre	26	12	3	11	56	45	27
Walsall	26	13	1	11	44	41	27
Treharris	26	11	5	10	44	47	27
Aberdare	26	10	3	13	39	44	23
Kettering	26	11	0	15	37	62	22
Croydon Common	26	8	2	15	43	45	18
Mardy	26	6	6	12	37	51	18
Cwm Albion	26	5	1	16	27	70	11
Chesham Town	26	1	0	25	18	131	2

1912-13

First Divison

Plymouth Argyle	38	27	6	10	77	36	50
Swindon Town	38	20	8	10	66	41	48
West Ham United	38	18	12	8	66	43	48
Queens Park Rangers	38	18	10	10	46	35	43
Crystal Palace	38	17	11	10	55	58	45
Millwall	38	19	7	12	62	43	45
Exeter City	38	18	8	12	48	44	44
Reading	38	17	8	13	59	55	42
Brighton & Hove Albion	38	13	12	13	48	47	38
Northampton Town	38	12	12	14	61	48	36
Portsmouth	38	14	8	16	41	49	36
Merthyr Town	38	12	12	14	42	60	36
Coventry City	38	13	8	17	53	59	34
Watford	38	12	10	16	43	50	34
Gillingham	38	12	10	16	36	53	34
Bristol Rovers	38	12	9	17	55	64	33
Southampton	38	10	11	17	40	72	31
Norwich City	38	10	9	19	39	50	29
Brentford	38	11	5	22	42	55	27
Stoke	38	10	4	24	39	75	24

Second Division

Cardiff City	24	18	5	1	54	15	41
Southend United	24	14	6	4	43	23	34
Swansea Town	24	12	7	5	29	23	31
Croydon Common	24	13	4	7	51	29	30
Luton Town	24	13	4	7	52	39	30
Llanelly	24	9	6	9	33	39	24
Pontypridd	24	6	11	7	30	28	23
Mid Rhondda	24	9	4	11	33	31	22
Aberdare	24	8	6	10	38	40	22
Newport County	24	7	5	12	29	36	19
Mardy	24	6	3	15	38	38	15
Treharris	24	5	2	17	18	60	12
Ton Pentre	24	3	3	18	22	69	9

1913-14

First Division

Swindon Town	38	21	8	9	81	41	50
Crystal Palace	38	17	16	5	60	32	50
Northampton Town	38	14	19	5	50	37	47
Reading	38	17	10	11	43	36	44
Plymouth Argyle	38	15	13	10	46	42	43
West Ham United	38	15	12	11	61	60	42
Brighton & Hove Albion	38	15	12	11	43	45	42
Queens Park Rangers	38	16	9	13	45	43	41
Portsmouth	38	14	12	12	57	48	40
Cardiff City	38	13	12	13	46	42	38
Southampton	38	15	7	16	55	54	37
Exeter City	38	10	16	12	39	38	36
Gillingham	38	13	9	16	48	49	35
Norwich City	38	9	17	12	49	51	35
Millwall	38	11	12	15	51	56	34
Southend Unied	38	10	12	16	41	66	32
Bristol Rovers	38	10	11	17	46	67	31
Watford	38	10	9	19	50	56	29
Merthyr Town	38	9	10	19	38	61	28
Coventry City	38	6	14	18	43	68	26

Second Division

Croydon Common	30	23	5	2	76	14	51
Luton Town	30	24	3	3	92	22	51
Brentford	30	20	4	6	80	18	44
Swansea Town	30	20	4	6	66	23	44
Stoke	30	19	2	9	71	34	40
Newport County	30	14	8	8	49	38	36
Mid Rhondda	30	13	7	10	55	37	33
Pontypridd	30	14	5	11	43	38	33
Llanelly	30	12	4	14	45	39	28
Barry	30	9	8	13	44	70	26
Abertillery	30	8	4	18	44	57	20
Ton Pentre	30	8	4	18	33	61	20
Mardy	30	6	6	18	30	60	18
Caerphilly	30	4	7	19	21	103	15
Aberdare	30	4	5	21	33	87	13
Treharris	30	2	4	24	19	106	8

1914-15

First Division

Watford	38	22	8	8	68	46	52
Reading	38	21	7	10	68	43	49
Cardiff City	38	22	4	12	72	38	48
West Ham United	38	18	9	11	58	47	45
Northampton Town	38	16	11	11	56	51	43
Southampton	38	19	5	14	78	74	43
Portsmouth	38	16	10	12	54	42	42
Millwall	38	16	10	12	50	51	42
Swindon Town	38	15	11	12	77	59	41
Brighton & Hove Albion	38	16	7	15	46	47	39
Exeter City	38	15	8	15	50	41	38
Queens Park Rangers	38	13	12	13	55	56	38
Norwich City	38	11	14	13	53	56	36
Luton Town	38	13	8	17	61	73	34
Crystal Palace	38	13	8	17	47	61	34
Bristol Rovers	38	14	3	21	53	75	31
Plymouth Argyle	38	8	14	16	51	61	30
Southend United	38	10	8	20	44	64	28
Croydon Common	38	9	9	20	47	63	27
Gillingham	38	6	8	24	43	82	20

Second Division

Stoke	24	17	4	3	62	15	38
Stalybridge Celtic	24	17	3	4	47	22	37
Merthyr Town	24	15	5	4	46	20	35
Swansea Town	24	16	1	7	48	21	33
Coventry City	24	13	2	9	56	33	28
Ton Pentre	24	11	6	7	42	43	28
Brentford	24	8	7	9	35	45	23
Llanelly	24	10	1	13	39	32	21
Barry	24	6	5	13	30	35	17
Newport County	24	7	3	14	27	42	17
Pontypridd	24	5	6	13	31	58	16
Mid Rhondda	24	3	6	15	17	40	12
Ebbw Vale	24	3	1	20	23	88	7

1919-20

First Division

Portsmouth	42	23	12	7	73	27	58
Watford	42	26	6	10	69	42	58
Crystal Palace	42	22	12	8	69	43	56
Cardiff City	42	18	17	7	70	43	53
Plymouth Argyle	42	20	10	12	57	29	50
Queens Park Rangers	42	18	10	14	62	50	46
Reading	42	16	13	13	51	43	45
Southampton	42	18	8	16	72	63	44
Swansea Town	42	16	11	15	53	45	43
Exeter City	42	17	9	16	57	51	43
Southend United	42	13	17	12	46	48	43
Norwich City	42	15	11	16	64	57	41
Swindon Town	42	17	7	18	65	68	41
Millwall	42	14	12	16	52	55	40
Brentford	42	15	10	17	52	59	40
Brighton & Hove Albion	42	14	8	20	60	72	36
Bristol Rovers	42	11	13	18	61	78	35
Newport County	42	13	7	22	45	70	33
Northampton Town	42	12	9	21	64	103	33
Luton Town	42	10	10	22	51	76	30
Merthyr Town	42	9	11	22	47	78	29
Gillingham	42	10	7	25	34	74	27

Second Division

Mid Rhondda	20	17	3	0	79	10	37
Ton Pentre	20	12	7	1	50	14	31
Llanelly	20	10	5	5	47	30	25
Pontypridd	20	10	3	7	33	29	23
Ebbw Vale	20	7	7	6	38	40	21
Barry	20	7	5	8	32	27	19
Mardy	20	7	5	8	29	30	19
Abertillery	20	6	5	9	29	40	17
Porth Athletic	20	4	4	12	30	74	12
Aberaman Athletic	20	4	3	13	28	48	11
Caerphilly	20	1	3	16	20	74	5

1920-21

English Section

Brighton & Hove Albion Reserves	24	16	3	5	65	29	35
Portsmouth Reserves	24	13	7	4	44	20	33
Millwall Reserves	24	12	4	8	46	24	28
Southampton Reserves	24	10	7	7	53	35	27
Boscombe	24	10	6	8	25	40	26
Reading Reserves	24	11	3	10	41	34	25
Luton Town Reserves	24	8	8	8	38	35	24
Charlton Athletic	24	8	8	8	41	41	24
Watford Reserves	24	9	4	11	43	45	22
Norwich City Reserves	24	7	7	10	31	39	21
Gillingham Reserves	24	6	5	13	32	47	17
Chatham	24	5	6	13	24	47	16
Thornycrofts	24	4	6	14	29	74	14

Welsh Section

Barry	20	13	4	3	35	12	30
Aberdare Athletic	20	12	3	5	29	23	27
Ebbw Vale	20	10	5	5	34	23	25
Pontypridd	20	10	3	7	34	23	23
Mid Rhondda	20	10	3	7	26	18	23
Abertillery Town	20	8	5	7	35	24	21
Ton Pentre	20	7	5	8	32	34	19
Aberaman Athletic	20	5	7	8	30	33	17
Llanelly	20	7	2	11	28	46	16
Mardy	20	2	6	12	18	39	10
Porth Athletic	20	3	3	14	28	54	9

1921-22

English Section

Plymouth Argyle Reserves	36	22	5	9	91	38	49
Bristol City Reserves	36	18	8	10	73	50	44
Portsmouth Reserves	36	17	10	9	63	41	44
Southampton Reserves	36	19	5	12	70	47	43
Gillingham Reserves	36	17	9	10	65	47	43
Charlton Athletic Reserves	36	18	6	12	69	54	42
Boscombe	36	17	5	14	38	55	39
Luton Town Reserves	36	17	4	15	50	54	38
Watford Reserves	36	15	7	14	65	53	37
Brighton & Hove Albion Reserves	36	12	13	11	60	52	37
Bath City	36	16	5	15	55	53	37
Swindon Town Reserves	36	14	7	15	59	46	35
Bristol Rovers Reserves	36	13	7	16	50	82	33
Millwall Reserves	36	13	4	19	49	53	30
Reading Reserves	36	11	7	18	46	59	29
Exeter City Reserves	36	10	9	17	42	63	29
Guildford United	36	11	6	19	44	56	28
Norwich City Reserves	36	10	6	20	47	86	26
Southend United Reserves	36	9	3	24	47	92	21

Welsh Section

Ebbw Vale	16	11	3	2	33	11	25
Ton Pentre	16	9	4	3	35	14	22
Aberaman Athletic	16	7	5	4	25	19	19
Porth Athletic	16	6	6	4	31	20	18
Pontypridd	16	7	4	5	28	19	18
Swansea Town Reserves	16	7	4	5	24	17	18
Barry	16	3	3	10	14	35	9
Abertillery Town	16	3	2	11	21	45	8
Mardy	16	2	3	11	14	43	7

1922-23

English Section

Bristol City Reserves	38	24	5	9	84	39	53
Boscombe	38	22	7	9	67	34	51
Portsmouth Reserves	38	23	3	12	93	51	49
Bristol Rovers Reserves	38	20	8	10	59	41	48
Plymouth Argyle Reserves	38	20	7	11	74	41	47
Torquay United	38	18	8	12	63	38	44
Brighton & Hove Albion Reserves	38	20	3	15	95	60	43
Luton Town Reserves	38	16	11	11	67	56	43
Southend United Reserves	38	18	6	14	69	68	42
Southampton Reserves	38	18	5	15	65	54	41
Millwall Reserves	38	15	10	13	61	55	40
Coventry City Reserves	38	15	8	15	56	61	38
Guildford Town Reserves	38	15	7	16	65	59	37
Swindon Town Reserves	38	13	6	19	54	73	32
Bath City	38	10	8	20	44	71	28
Watford Reserves	38	11	6	21	34	79	28
Yeovil & Petters United	38	10	6	22	56	104	26
Norwich City Reserves	38	9	7	22	42	68	25
Exeter City Reserves	38	10	5	23	43	81	25
Reading Reserves	38	7	6	25	43	95	20

Welsh Section

Ebbw Vale	12	6	5	1	22	15	17
Aberaman Athletic	12	7	2	3	30	19	16
Swansea Town Reserves	12	6	2	4	25	14	14
Pontypridd	12	6	2	4	18	18	14
Barry	12	4	3	5	15	11	11
Bridgend Town	12	4	2	6	15	21	10
Porth Athletic	12	0	2	10	18	24	2

1923-24

Eastern Section

Peterborough & Fletton United	30	20	2	8	54	31	42
Leicester City Reserves	30	19	3	8	72	30	41
Southampton Reserves	30	18	5	7	60	36	41
Millwall Reserves	30	18	3	9	56	38	39
Portsmouth Reserves	30	16	2	12	66	37	34
Brighton & Hove Albion Reserves	30	13	7	10	55	42	33
Norwich City Reserves	30	13	6	11	46	34	32
Folkestone	30	12	5	13	61	51	29
Coventry City Reserves	30	10	8	12	39	4	28
Watford Reserves	30	11	6	13	36	48	28
Reading Reserves	30	11	6	13	32	43	28
Northampton Town Reserves	30	9	10	11	32	47	28
Luton Town Reserves	30	10	7	13	40	49	27
Guildford United	30	7	5	18	38	72	19
Kettering	30	5	8	17	30	67	18
Bournemouth Reserves	30	4	5	21	40	85	13

Western Section

Yeovil & Petters United	34	25	3	6	71	30	53
Plymouth Argyle Reserves	34	21	5	8	74	37	47
Pontypridd	34	19	8	7	81	44	46
Torquay United	34	19	7	8	59	25	45
Bristol City Reserves	34	17	9	8	63	39	43
Swansea Town Reserves	34	19	5	10	62	38	43
Bristol Rovers Reserves	34	17	6	11	69	43	40
Cardiff City Reserves	34	15	4	15	55	31	34
Exeter City Reserves	34	11	11	12	48	47	33
Weymouth	34	15	3	16	48	60	33
Llanelly	34	14	5	15	47	62	33
Swindon Town Reserves	34	11	6	17	36	60	28
Bridgend Town	34	11	5	18	57	72	27
Newport County Reserves	34	10	7	17	57	79	27
Ebbw Vale	34	8	8	18	38	62	24
Bath City	34	6	9	19	32	71	21
Barry	34	6	7	21	36	74	19
Aberaman Athletic	34	6	4	24	41	87	16

1924-25

Eastern Section

Southampton Reserves	32	17	10	5	65	30	44
Kettering Town	32	17	6	9	67	39	40
Brighton & Hove Albion Reserves	32	15	10	7	68	42	40
Millwall Reserves	32	15	10	7	65	48	40
Peterborough & Fletton United	32	15	9	8	56	29	39
Bournemouth Reserves	32	15	9	8	66	48	39
Leicester City Reserves	32	15	7	10	61	45	37
Portsmouth Reserves	32	15	7	10	51	40	37
Folkestone	32	13	11	8	55	46	37
Norwich City Reserves	32	13	8	11	65	58	34
Coventry City Reserves	32	12	9	11	51	41	33
Luton Town Reserves	32	15	2	15	48	63	32
Northampton Town Reserves	32	10	5	17	38	59	25
Watford Reserves	32	7	7	18	44	71	21
Nuneaton Town	32	8	2	22	37	62	18
Reading Reserves	32	8	1	23	38	87	17
Guildford United	32	4	3	25	40	107	11

Western Section

Swansea Town Reserves	38	25	4	9	73	26	54
Plymouth Argyle Reserves	38	22	10	6	97	35	54
Pontypridd	38	24	4	10	81	39	52
Bridgend Town	38	20	11	7	74	52	51
Mid Rhondda United	38	21	6	11	79	48	48
Weymouth	38	21	4	13	77	50	46
Cardiff City Reserves	38	18	6	14	56	44	42
Newport County Reserves	38	17	8	13	71	60	42
Swindon Town Reserves	38	17	8	13	48	46	42
Bristol City Reserves	38	18	5	15	51	43	41
Yeovil & Petters United	38	15	10	13	49	50	40
Exeter City Reserves	38	16	6	16	78	55	38
Taunton Unied	38	15	6	17	55	51	36
Bristol Rovers Reserves	38	13	6	19	45	50	32
Torquay United	38	9	11	18	41	73	29
Llanelly	38	6	12	20	49	94	24
Ebbw Vale	38	9	6	23	40	91	24
Bath City	38	8	8	22	28	85	24
Barry	38	8	6	24	38	82	22
Aberaman Athletic	38	6	7	25	39	95	19

1925-26

Eastern Section

Millwall Reserves	34	24	6	4	106	37	54
Leicester City Reserves	34	23	2	9	105	60	48
Brighton & Hove Albion Reserves	34	21	4	9	105	69	46
Kettering Town	34	19	5	10	98	68	43
Peterborough & Fletton United	34	19	3	12	76	62	41
Portsmouth Reserves	34	17	5	12	76	67	39
Norwich City Reserves	34	17	4	13	85	90	38
Bournemouth Reserves	34	15	7	12	76	67	37
Southampton Reserves	34	14	7	13	65	72	35
Fulham Reserves	34	13	6	15	86	77	32
Grays Thurrock United	34	13	5	16	63	77	31
Guildford United	34	11	8	15	71	87	30
Watford Reserves	34	12	2	20	62	94	26
Luton Town Reserves	34	11	3	20	70	78	25
Folkestone	34	9	6	19	67	93	24
Reading Reserves	34	10	3	21	58	84	23
Coventry City Reserves	34	9	5	20	54	93	23
Nuneaton Town	34	7	3	24	61	113	17

Western Section

Plymouth Argyle Reserves	26	20	1	5	67	31	41
Bristol City Reserves	26	16	4	6	48	28	36
Bristol Rovers Reserves	26	13	4	9	51	35	30
Swindon Town Reserves	26	13	4	9	57	40	30
Ebbw Vale	26	13	3	10	60	46	29
Torquay United	26	12	5	9	59	46	29
Yeovil & Petters United	26	9	8	9	43	48	26
Mid Rhondda	26	12	1	13	47	49	25
Weymouth	26	10	3	13	64	60	23
Exeter City Reserves	26	8	5	13	40	49	21
Barry	26	8	4	14	47	55	20
Taunton United	26	9	2	15	44	60	20
Pontypridd	26	7	5	14	44	77	19
Bath City	26	7	1	18	38	86	15

1926-27

Eastern Section

Brighton & Hove Albion Reserves	32	21	6	5	86	47	48
Peterborough & Fletton United	32	18	9	5	80	39	45
Portsmouth Reserves	32	19	6	7	95	65	44
Kettering Town	32	15	10	7	66	41	40
Millwall Reserves	32	16	5	11	67	56	37
Bournemouth Reserves	32	14	6	12	69	64	34
Norwich City Reserves	32	14	5	13	79	74	33
Dartford	32	13	7	12	60	71	33
Reading Reserves	32	12	8	12	75	79	32
Luton Town Reserves	32	10	11	11	75	70	1
Leicester City Reserves	32	12	5	15	94	72	29
Watford Reserves	32	10	8	14	74	84	28
Southampton Reserves	32	10	6	16	57	77	26
Poole	32	9	6	17	55	86	24
Grays Thurrock United	32	10	3	19	49	66	23
Guildford United	32	6	7	19	57	106	19
Folkestone	32	7	4	21	57	98	18

Western Section

Torquay United	26	17	4	5	63	30	38
Bristol City Reserves	26	14	10	2	77	37	38
Plymouth Argyle Reserves	26	15	4	7	56	38	34
Ebbw Vale	26	14	2	10	67	45	30
Bristol Rovers Reserves	26	12	4	10	51	43	28
Swindon Town Reserves	26	11	5	10	60	57	27
Barry	26	11	4	11	65	50	26
Essex City Reserves	26	10	6	10	62	49	26
Weymouth	26	12	2	12	48	65	26
Newport County Reserves	26	9	6	11	57	53	24
Bath City	26	7	9	10	44	52	23
Yeovil & Petters United	26	9	5	12	49	66	23
Taunton United	26	4	4	18	36	83	12
Mid Rhondda United	26	2	5	19	22	89	9

1927-28

Easter Section

Kettering Town	34	23	6	5	90	39	52
Peterborough & Fletton United	34	21	3	10	73	43	45
Northfleet United	34	17	7	10	83	54	41
Brighton & Hove Albion Reserves	34	20	0	14	90	63	40
Norwich City Reserves	34	17	6	11	69	69	40
Southampton Reserves	34	16	7	11	92	70	39
Aldershot Town	34	17	5	12	85	66	39
Sittingbourne	34	16	5	13	64	70	37
Millwall Reserves	34	15	6	13	66	59	36
Poole	34	15	5	14	69	84	35
Folkestone	34	12	6	16	71	91	30
Guildford City	34	12	5	17	65	89	29
Dartford	34	12	4	18	46	49	28
Gillingham Reserves	34	10	7	17	72	84	27
Sheppey United	34	11	3	20	57	87	25
Chatham	34	10	4	20	49	70	24
Grays Thurrock United	34	10	3	21	48	88	23
Bournemouth Reserves	34	9	4	21	48	62	22

Western Section

Bristol City Reserves	30	20	3	7	95	51	43
Exeter City Reserves	30	18	4	8	104	56	40
Bristol Rovers Reserves	30	16	3	11	80	64	35
Plymouth Argyle Reserves	30	16	2	12	88	53	34
Newport County Reserves	30	13	8	9	99	70	34
Ebbw Vale	30	15	3	12	67	74	33
Swindon Town Reserves	30	13	4	13	80	74	30
Aberdare & Aberaman	30	12	6	12	62	68	30
Yeovil & Petters United	30	11	7	12	64	57	29
Torquay United Reserves	30	11	6	13	51	67	28
Bath City	30	12	3	15	64	68	27
Taunton Town	30	11	5	14	60	65	27
Weymouth	30	10	6	14	50	83	26
Merthyr Town Reserves	30	9	4	17	50	77	22
Barry	30	8	6	16	45	87	22
Mid Rhondda United	30	7	6	17	36	81	20

1928-29

Eastern Section

Kettering Town	36	24	4	8	96	46	52
Peterborough & Fletton United	36	21	5	10	86	44	47
Brighton & Hove Albion Reserves	36	19	9	8	91	56	47
Millwall Reserves	36	21	4	11	90	67	46
Bournemouth Reserves	36	20	5	11	82	58	45
Aldershot Town	36	18	5	13	68	52	41
Sheppey United	36	17	7	12	58	58	41
Folkestone	36	17	6	13	83	80	40
Northfleet United	36	17	4	15	87	65	38
Gillingham Reserves	36	15	8	13	68	70	38
Guildford City	36	13	11	12	85	78	37
Southampton Reserves	36	14	6	16	86	79	34
Poole	36	13	8	15	62	66	34
Thames Association	36	13	5	18	67	74	31
Dartford	36	10	6	20	55	106	26
Chatham	36	8	8	20	47	81	24
Sittingbourne	36	11	1	24	59	98	23
Norwich City Reserves	36	8	6	22	48	96	22
Grays Thurrock United	36	6	6	24	47	91	18

Western Section

Plymouth Argyle Reserves	26	15	6	5	69	27	36
Newport County Reserves	26	15	2	9	64	58	32
Bristol Rovers Reserves	26	14	3	9	54	45	31
Bristol City Reserves	26	14	2	10	70	46	30
Torquay United Reserves	26	13	4	9	52	42	30
Bath City	26	13	4	9	43	59	30
Exeter City Reserves	26	11	6	9	69	53	28
Lovells Athletic	26	11	6	9	54	48	28
Swindon Town Reserves	26	11	5	10	68	74	27
Yeovil & Petters United	26	11	2	13	49	57	24
Taunton Town	26	9	5	12	58	66	23
Ebbw Vale	26	9	5	12	56	66	23
Barry	26	6	3	17	38	66	15
Merthyr Town Reserves	26	3	1	22	37	92	7

1929-30

Eastern Section

Aldershot Town	32	21	6	5	84	39	48
Millwall Reserves	32	21	3	8	75	56	45
Thames Association	32	17	6	9	80	60	40
Peterborough & Fletton United	32	18	3	11	66	39	39
Northampton Town Reserves	32	17	4	11	86	60	38
Southampton Reserves	32	14	7	11	73	62	35
Sheppey United	32	15	5	12	76	69	35
Kettering Town	32	13	7	12	70	69	33
Dartford	32	14	5	13	57	59	33
Norwich City Reserves	32	14	3	15	69	69	31
Guildford City	32	13	2	17	65	97	28
Bournemouth Reserves	32	10	7	15	59	63	27
Brighton & Hove Albion Reserves	32	12	2	18	56	79	26
Folkestone	32	13	0	19	56	82	26
Sittingbourne	32	10	5	17	55	59	25
Northfleet United	32	6	7	19	53	77	19
Grays Thurrock United	32	7	2	23	54	101	16

Western Section

Bath City	28	16	6	6	85	52	38
Bristol Rovers Reserves	28	16	4	8	66	64	35
Taunton Town	28	14	7	7	50	40	35
Barry	28	15	3	10	65	55	33
Yeovil & Petters United	28	12	7	9	63	47	31
Plymouth Argyle Reserves	28	14	3	11	68	52	31
Newport County Reserves	28	13	4	11	68	76	30
Lovells Athletic	28	13	2	13	59	57	28
Exeter City Reserves	28	11	6	11	49	54	28
Bristol City Reserves	28	11	5	12	59	63	27
Swindon Town Reserves	28	10	6	12	69	67	26
Torquay United Reserves	28	10	6	12	76	77	26
Llanelly	28	10	4	14	55	52	24
Ebbw Vale	28	5	6	17	52	97	16
Merthyr Town Reserves	28	5	1	22	48	93	11

1930-31

Eastern Section

Dartford	16	9	5	2	39	18	23
Aldershot Town	16	10	3	3	50	28	23
Norwich City Reserves	16	9	1	6	47	38	19
Peterborough & Fletton United	16	6	5	5	35	29	17
Thames Association Reserves	16	7	2	7	38	31	16
Millwall Reserves	16	7	0	9	47	40	14
Folkestone	16	4	3	9	31	46	11
Guildford City	16	5	1	10	28	53	11
Sheppey United	16	4	2	10	31	63	10

Western Section

Exeter City Reserves	22	15	2	5	59	28	32
Llanelly	22	10	8	4	72	39	28
Merthyr Town	22	12	3	7	62	49	27
Plymouth Argyle Reserves	22	12	2	8	55	34	26
Bath City	22	10	6	6	47	39	26
Torquay United Reserves	22	9	5	8	66	49	23
Swindon Town Reserves	22	7	7	8	48	52	21
Bristol Rovers Reserves	22	7	6	9	58	64	20
Barry	22	7	5	10	29	39	19
Taunton Town	22	5	7	10	36	62	17
Newport County Reserves	22	6	2	14	36	66	14
Ebbw Vale	22	5	1	16	32	79	11

1931-32

Eastern Section

Dartford	18	12	3	3	53	18	27
Folkestone	18	12	2	4	58	27	26
Guildford City	18	11	1	6	33	24	23
Norwich City Reserves	18	9	2	7	46	33	20
Millwall Reserves	18	9	2	7	41	39	20
Tunbridge Wells Rangers	18	7	5	6	23	25	19
Bournemouth Reserves	18	6	4	8	43	61	16
Peterborough & Fletton United	18	4	5	9	28	29	13
Aldershot Town	18	3	5	10	17	30	11
Sheppey United	18	2	1	15	16	72	5

Western Section

Yeovil & Petters United	24	16	4	4	65	31	36
Plymouth Argyle Reserves	24	15	5	4	81	31	35
Bath City	24	12	7	5	50	33	31
Llanelly	24	12	4	8	65	46	28
Taunton Town	24	13	2	9	53	58	28
Newport County Reserves	24	10	6	8	70	51	26
Exeter City Reserves	24	9	7	8	59	43	25
Merthyr Town	24	9	4	11	66	73	22
Bristol Rovers Reserves	24	8	4	12	54	47	20
Swindon Town Reserves	24	8	4	12	54	95	20
Barry	24	7	3	14	58	76	17
Torquay United Reserves	24	5	6	13	43	66	16
Ebbw Vale	24	3	2	19	34	102	8

1932-33

Eastern Section

Norwich City Reserves	14	9	2	3	34	22	20
Dartford	14	8	2	4	26	23	18
Folkestone	14	7	1	6	35	32	15
Bournemouth Reserves	14	5	4	5	36	33	14
Tunbridge Wells Rangers	14	5	2	7	23	24	12
Guildford City	14	5	2	7	22	28	12
Millwall Reserves	14	5	1	8	27	31	11
Aldershot Reserves	14	3	4	7	24	34	10

Western Section

Bath City	20	13	4	3	62	34	30
Exeter City Reserves	20	12	3	5	62	46	27
Torquay United Reserves	20	12	1	7	56	37	25
Plymouth Argyle Reserves	20	11	2	7	68	38	24
Yeovil & Petters United	20	11	2	7	59	44	24
Llanelly	20	10	2	8	53	33	22
Bristol Rovers Reserves	20	7	3	10	53	65	17
Newport County Reserves	20	6	4	10	42	55	16
Merthyr Tydfil	20	7	1	12	39	58	15
Barry	20	3	4	13	30	72	10
Taunton Town	20	4	2	14	21	63	10

1933-34

Eastern Section

Norwich City Reserves	16	9	4	3	41	15	22
Margate	16	8	3	5	23	20	19
Millwall Reserves	16	7	4	5	28	28	18
Clapton Orient Reserves	16	8	1	7	33	34	17
Bournemouth Reserves	16	6	3	7	28	30	15
Tunbridge Wells Rangers	16	6	2	8	25	36	14
Folkestone	16	5	3	8	26	26	13
Guildford City	16	5	3	8	27	33	13
Dartford	16	4	5	7	15	24	13

Western Section

Plymouth Argyle Reserves	20	13	6	1	62	22	32
Bristol Rovers Reserves	20	14	3	3	56	27	31
Bath City	20	11	3	6	43	25	25
Torquay United Reserves	20	9	4	7	54	36	22
Yeovil & Petters United	20	10	1	9	35	39	21
Exeter City Reserves	20	8	3	9	54	47	19
Merthyr Town	20	8	2	10	39	50	18
Llanelly	20	8	1	11	25	39	17
Barry	20	4	5	11	37	64	13
Newport County Reserves	20	4	3	13	36	54	11
Taunton Town	20	5	1	14	27	65	11

Central Section

Plymouth Argyle Reserves	18	16	1	1	47	14	33
Clapton Orient Reserves	18	9	3	6	35	25	21
Norwich City Reserves	18	8	4	6	41	27	20
Yeovil & Petters United	18	7	4	7	34	38	18
Bath City	18	7	3	8	31	36	17
Dartford	18	6	4	8	28	26	16
Tunbridge Wells Rangers	18	7	1	10	26	37	15
Llanelly	18	6	2	10	28	39	14
Folkestone	18	6	1	11	30	41	13
Guildford City	18	6	1	11	28	45	13

1934-35

Eastern Section

Norwich City Reserves	18	12	1	5	52	21	25
Dartford	18	8	6	4	36	22	22
Margate	18	7	6	7	38	30	20
Bournemouth Reserves	18	8	3	8	34	26	19
Guildford City	18	7	5	6	41	34	19
Aldershot Reserves	18	7	3	8	29	43	17
Folkestone	18	5	6	7	30	39	16
Tunbridge Wells Rangers	18	6	4	8	32	56	16
Clapton Orient Reserves	18	5	4	9	33	35	14
Millwall Reserves	18	3	6	9	26	45	12

Western Section

Yeovil & Petters United	16	11	2	3	49	18	24
Newport County Reserves	16	8	5	3	45	29	21
Plymouth Argyle Reserves	16	7	5	4	40	24	19
Exeter City Reserves	16	7	2	7	38	32	16
Bath City	16	6	4	6	35	32	16
Bristol Rovers Reserves	16	5	5	6	33	37	15
Barry	16	6	3	7	30	40	15
Torquay United Reserves	16	5	3	8	24	29	13
Taunton Town	16	1	3	12	13	66	5

Central Section

Folkestone	20	11	4	5	43	31	26
Guildford City	20	11	4	5	43	39	26
Plymouth Argyle Reserves	20	6	9	5	40	28	21
Torquay United Reserves	20	7	6	7	34	35	20
Bristol Rovers Reserves	20	8	4	8	38	46	20
Margate	20	8	3	9	40	34	19
Dartford	20	8	3	9	43	38	19
Aldershot Reserves	20	8	3	9	33	44	19
Tunbridge Wells Rangers	20	8	2	10	33	37	18
Yeovil & Petters United	20	8	1	11	45	51	17
Bath City	20	6	3	11	34	43	15

1935-36

Eastern Section

Margate	18	13	2	3	49	16	28
Folkestone	18	11	3	4	46	23	25
Dartford	18	9	3	6	47	25	21
Tunbridge Wells Rangers	18	9	1	8	26	41	19
Clapton Orient Reserves	18	7	4	7	39	31	18
Millwall Reserves	18	7	3	8	42	39	17
Norwich City Reserves	18	8	0	10	39	38	16
Guildford City	18	6	3	9	32	52	15
Aldershot Reserves	18	6	1	11	24	45	13
Bournemouth Reserves	18	3	2	13	25	59	8

Western Section

Plymouth Argyle Reserves	16	12	3	1	51	18	27
Bristol Rovers Reserves	16	8	3	5	35	30	19
Newport County Reserves	16	8	3	5	29	30	19
Torquay United Reserves	16	7	1	8	25	28	15
Bath City	16	5	5	6	18	26	15
Cheltenham Town	16	6	2	8	32	28	14
Yeovil & Petters United	16	5	3	8	31	35	13
Barry	16	5	2	9	29	41	12
Exeter City Reserves	16	4	2	10	24	38	10

Central Section

Margate	20	14	3	3	57	18	31
Bristol Rovers Reserves	20	13	1	6	51	37	27
Plymouth Argyle Reserves	20	12	2	6	53	32	26
Aldershot Reserves	20	9	4	7	37	37	22
Folkestone	20	9	3	8	51	36	21
Tunbridge Wells Rangers	20	7	4	9	40	41	18
Dartford	20	7	3	10	34	42	17
Guildford City	20	7	3	10	33	47	17
Cheltenham Town	20	5	5	10	32	45	15
Bath City	20	5	5	10	34	52	15
Yeovil & Petters United	20	3	5	12	40	75	11

1936-37

Ipswich Town	30	19	8	3	68	35	46
Norwich City Reserves	30	18	5	7	70	35	41
Folkestone	30	17	4	9	71	62	38
Margate	30	15	4	11	64	49	34
Guildford City	30	15	4	11	54	60	34
Bath City	30	14	5	11	65	55	33
Yeovil & Petters United	30	15	3	12	77	69	33
Plymouth Argyle Reserves	30	11	8	11	64	58	30
Newport County Reserves	30	11	8	11	72	68	30
Barry	30	12	4	14	58	72	28
Cheltenham Town	30	10	4	16	61	70	24
Dartford	30	9	5	16	41	55	23
Exeter City Reserves	30	8	7	15	57	78	23
Tunbridge Wells Rangers	30	8	6	16	62	64	22
Torquay United Reserves	30	8	5	17	46	76	21
Aldershot Reserves	30	7	6	17	47	74	20

Midweek Section

Margate	18	12	1	5	48	24	25
Bath City	18	10	5	3	38	28	25
Norwich City Reserves	18	9	5	4	44	27	23
Folkestone	18	7	6	5	32	36	20
Millwall Reserves	18	8	3	7	44	47	19
Portsmouth Reserves	18	6	5	7	40	27	17
Tunbridge Wells Rangers	18	5	4	9	30	41	14
Aldershot Reserves	18	6	2	10	20	30	14
Guildford City	18	3	6	9	24	36	12
Dartford	18	4	3	11	19	43	11

1937-38

Guildford City	34	22	5	7	94	60	49
Plymouth Argyle Reserves	34	18	9	7	98	58	45
Ipswich Town	34	19	6	9	89	54	44
Yeovil & Petters United	34	14	14	6	72	45	42
Norwich City Reserves	34	15	11	8	77	55	41
Colchester United	34	15	8	11	90	58	38
Bristol Rovers Reserves	34	14	8	12	63	62	36
Swindon Town Reserves	34	14	7	13	70	76	35
Tunbridge Wells Rangers	34	14	6	14	68	74	34
Aldershot Reserves	34	10	12	12	42	55	32
Cheltenham Town	34	13	5	16	72	68	31
Exeter City Reserves	34	13	5	16	71	75	31
Dartford	34	9	11	14	51	70	29
Bath City	34	9	9	16	45	65	27
Folkestone	34	10	6	18	58	82	26
Newport County Reserves	34	10	6	18	56	86	26
Barry	34	8	7	19	50	88	23
Torquay United Reserves	34	8	7	19	46	81	23

Midweek Section

Millwall Reserves	18	13	3	2	59	21	29
Colchester United	18	13	1	4	42	23	27
Aldershot Reserves	18	11	3	4	38	29	25
Norwich City Reserves	18	9	1	8	45	39	19
Portsmouth Reserves	18	5	5	8	31	30	15
Dartford	18	6	3	9	32	35	15
Folkestone	18	6	3	9	34	38	15
Tunbridge Wells Rangers	18	5	4	9	28	36	14
Bath City	18	5	3	10	27	45	13
Guildford City	18	4	0	14	21	61	8

1938-39

Colchester United	44	31	5	8	110	37	67
Guildford City	44	30	6	8	126	52	66
Gillingham	44	29	6	9	104	57	64
Plymouth Argyle Reserves	44	26	5	13	128	63	57
Yeovil & Petters United	44	22	10	12	85	70	54
Arsenal Reserves	44	21	9	14	92	57	51
Cardiff City Reserves	44	24	3	17	105	72	51
Tunbridge Wells Rangers	44	22	6	16	93	76	50
Norwich City Reserves	44	23	4	17	86	76	50
Chelmsford City	44	18	8	18	74	73	44
Bath City	44	16	12	16	58	74	44
Barry	44	18	7	19	76	90	43
Cheltenham Town	44	16	9	19	76	105	41
Ipswich Town Reserves	44	14	12	18	64	76	40
Worcester City	44	13	14	17	72	90	40
Folkestone	44	16	6	22	74	85	38
Newport County Reserves	44	13	10	21	74	108	36
Exeter City Reserves	44	12	9	23	51	107	33
Torquay United Reserves	44	12	8	24	53	89	32
Swindon Town Reserves	44	11	9	24	66	101	31
Aldershot Reserves	44	12	6	26	69	92	30
Bristol Rovers Reserves	44	9	11	24	66	85	29
Dartford	44	8	5	31	53	119	21

Midweek Section

Tunbridge Wells Rangers	16	8	7	1	37	18	23
Colchester United	16	9	2	5	36	21	20
Norwich City Reserves	16	7	4	5	40	26	18
Millwall Reserves	16	7	4	5	33	23	18
Portsmouth Reserves	16	5	4	7	21	29	14
Guildford City	16	4	6	6	24	39	14
Aldershot Reserves	16	4	5	7	22	25	13
Folkestone	16	4	5	7	24	35	13
Dartford	16	4	3	9	24	45	11

1939-40

Eastern Section

Chelmsford City	7	5	0	2	29	9	10
Guildford City	8	4	1	3	26	13	9
Tunbridge Wells Rangers	7	2	3	2	21	16	7
Dartford	7	2	1	4	17	30	5
Norwich City Reserves	7	2	1	4	9	34	5

Western Section

	P	W	D	L	F	A	Pts
Lovells Athletic	14	11	1	2	53	22	23
Worcester City	14	9	2	3	55	30	20
Hereford United	14	8	0	6	45	31	16
Yeovil & Petters United	14	7	2	5	30	24	16
Gloucester City	14	5	0	9	35	49	10
Barry	14	4	1	9	31	56	9
Cheltenham Town	13	3	2	8	21	38	8
Bath City	13	3	2	8	21	41	8

1945-46

	P	W	D	L	F	A	Pts
Chelmsford City	18	15	1	2	66	23	34
Hereford United	20	13	3	4	59	31	29
Bath City	20	12	2	6	62	32	26
Cheltenham Town	18	9	1	8	35	54	22
Barry Town	20	8	4	8	42	42	20
Yeovil & Petters United	18	7	1	10	57	52	18
Worcester City	20	8	2	10	60	58	18
Colchester United	20	7	3	10	29	47	17
Bedford Town	16	4	1	11	30	49	15
Swindon Town Reserves	18	4	3	11	36	65	14
Cardiff City Reserves	20	4	5	11	39	60	13

1946-47

	P	W	D	L	F	A	Pts
Gillingham	31	20	6	5	103	45	47
Guildford City	32	21	4	7	86	39	46
Merthyr Tydfil	31	21	2	8	104	37	45
Yeovil Town	32	19	6	7	100	49	44
Chelmsford City	31	17	3	11	90	60	38
Gravesend & Northfleet	32	17	4	11	82	58	38
Barry Town	30	14	6	10	89	61	36
Colchester United	31	15	4	12	65	60	35
Cheltenham Town	31	14	3	14	68	75	32
Millwall	24	8	5	11	59	57	29
Dartford	32	10	5	17	71	100	25
Bedford Town	32	8	8	16	63	98	24
Hereford United	32	8	7	17	37	85	23
Worcester City	31	8	5	18	55	90	22
Exeter City Reserves	32	10	2	20	69	126	22
Bath City	32	7	7	18	52	93	21
Gloucester City	32	8	1	23	57	120	17

1947-48

	P	W	D	L	F	A	Pts
Merthyr Tydfil	34	23	7	4	84	38	53
Gillingham	34	21	5	8	81	43	47
Worcester City	34	21	3	10	74	45	45
Colchester United	34	17	10	7	88	41	44
Hereford United	34	16	10	8	77	53	42
Lovells Athletic	34	17	6	11	74	50	40
Exeter City Reserves	34	15	7	12	65	57	37
Yeovil Town	34	12	11	11	56	50	35
Chelmsford City	34	14	7	13	62	58	35
Cheltenham Town	34	13	9	12	71	71	35
Bath City	34	12	8	14	55	62	32
Barry Town	34	10	9	15	60	70	29
Gravesend & Northfleet	34	11	6	17	52	81	28
Guildford City	34	11	4	19	69	74	26
Dartford	34	10	6	18	35	62	26
Gloucester City	34	8	6	20	45	78	22
Torquay United Reserves	34	6	9	19	43	95	21
Bedford Town	34	6	3	25	41	104	15

1948-49

	P	W	D	L	F	A	Pts
Gillingham	42	26	10	6	104	48	62
Chelmsford City	42	27	7	8	115	64	61
Merthyr Tydfil	42	26	8	8	133	54	60
Colchester United	42	21	10	11	94	61	52
Worcester City	42	22	7	13	87	56	51
Dartford	42	21	9	12	73	53	51
Gravesend & Northfleet	42	20	9	13	60	46	49
Yeovil Town	42	19	9	14	90	53	47
Cheltenham Town	42	19	9	14	71	64	47
Kidderminster Harriers	42	19	6	17	77	96	44
Exeter City Reserves	42	18	7	17	83	73	43
Hereford United	42	17	6	19	83	84	40
Bath City	42	15	8	19	72	87	38
Hastings United	42	14	10	18	69	93	38
Torquay United Reserves	42	15	7	20	73	93	37
Lovells Athletic	42	14	8	20	73	74	36
Guildford City	42	12	12	18	58	85	36
Gloucester City	42	12	10	20	78	100	34
Barry Town	42	12	10	20	55	95	34
Tonbridge	42	9	7	26	54	105	25
Chingford Town	42	6	9	27	43	94	21
Bedford Town	42	5	8	29	32	101	18

1949-50

	P	W	D	L	F	A	Pts
Merthyr Tydfil	46	34	3	9	143	62	71
Colchester United	46	31	9	6	109	51	71
Yeovil Town	46	29	7	10	104	45	65
Chelmsford City	46	26	9	11	121	64	61
Gillingham	46	23	9	14	92	61	55
Dartford	46	20	9	17	70	65	49
Worcester City	46	21	7	18	85	80	49
Guildford City	46	18	11	17	79	73	47
Weymouth	46	19	9	18	80	81	47
Barry Town	46	18	10	18	78	72	46
Exeter City Reserves	46	16	14	16	73	83	46
Lovells Athletic	46	17	10	19	86	78	44
Tonbridge	46	16	12	18	65	76	44
Hastings United	46	17	8	21	92	450	42
Gravesend & Northfleet	46	16	9	21	88	81	41
Torquay United Reserves	46	14	12	20	80	89	40
Bath City	46	16	7	23	61	78	39
Gloucester City	46	14	11	21	72	101	39
Hereford United	46	15	8	23	74	76	38
Cheltenham Town	46	13	11	22	75	96	37
Headington United	46	15	7	24	72	97	37
Bedford Town	46	12	11	23	63	79	35
Kidderminster Harriers	46	12	11	23	64	108	35
Chingford Town	46	10	6	30	63	151	26

1950-51

	P	W	D	L	F	A	Pts
Merthyr Tydfil	44	29	8	7	156	66	66
Hereford United	44	27	7	10	110	69	61
Guildford City	44	23	8	13	88	60	54
Chelmsford City	44	21	12	11	84	58	54
Llanelly	44	19	13	12	89	73	51
Cheltenham Town	44	21	8	15	91	61	50
Headington United	44	18	11	15	84	83	47
Torquay United Reserves	44	20	6	18	93	79	46
Exeter City Reserves	44	16	12	16	90	94	44
Weymouth	44	16	12	16	82	88	44
Tonbridge	44	16	12	16	79	87	44
Gloucester City	44	16	11	17	81	76	43
Yeovil Town	44	13	15	16	72	72	41
Worcester City	44	15	11	18	69	78	41
Bath City	44	15	10	19	66	73	40
Dartford	44	14	11	19	61	70	39
Bedford Town	44	15	9	20	64	94	39
Gravesend & Northfleet	44	12	14	18	65	83	38
Kettering Town	44	13	11	20	87	87	37
Lovells Athletic	44	12	13	19	81	93	37
Kidderminster Harriers	44	13	9	22	58	103	35
Barry Town	44	13	7	24	54	104	33
Hastings United	44	11	6	27	91	143	28

1951-52

Merthyr Tydfil	42	27	6	9	128	60	60
Weymouth	42	22	13	7	81	42	57
Kidderminster Harriers	42	22	10	10	70	40	54
Guildford City	42	18	16	8	66	47	52
Hereford United	42	21	9	12	80	59	51
Worcester City	42	23	4	15	86	73	50
Kettering Town	42	18	10	14	83	56	46
Lovells Athletic	42	18	10	14	87	68	46
Gloucester City	42	19	8	15	68	55	46
Bath City	42	19	6	17	75	67	44
Headington United	42	16	11	15	55	53	43
Bedford Town	42	16	10	16	75	64	42
Barry Town	42	18	6	18	84	89	42
Chelmsford City	42	15	10	17	67	80	40
Dartford	42	15	9	18	63	65	39
Tonbridge	42	15	6	21	63	84	36
Yeovil Town	42	12	11	19	56	76	35
Cheltenham Town	42	15	4	23	59	85	34
Exeter City Reserves	42	13	7	22	76	106	33
Llanelly	42	13	6	23	70	111	32
Gravesend & Northfleet	42	12	7	23	68	88	31
Hastings United	42	3	5	34	41	131	11

1952-53

Headington United	42	23	12	7	93	50	58
Merthyr Tydfil	42	25	8	9	117	66	58
Bedford Town	42	24	8	10	91	61	56
Kettering Town	42	23	8	11	88	50	54
Bath City	42	22	10	10	71	46	54
Worcester City	42	20	11	11	100	66	51
Llanelly	42	21	9	12	95	72	51
Barry Town	42	22	3	17	89	69	47
Gravesend & Northfleet	42	19	7	16	83	76	45
Gloucester City	42	17	9	16	50	78	43
Guildford City	42	17	8	17	64	60	42
Hastings United	42	18	5	19	75	66	41
Cheltenham Town	42	15	11	16	70	89	41
Weymouth	42	15	10	17	70	75	40
Hereford United	42	17	5	20	76	73	39
Tonbridge	42	12	9	21	62	88	33
Lovells Athletic	42	12	8	22	68	81	32
Yeovil Town	42	11	10	21	75	99	32
Chelmsford City	42	12	7	23	58	92	31
Exeter City Reserves	42	13	4	25	71	94	30
Kidderminster Harriers	42	12	5	25	54	85	29
Dartford	42	6	5	31	40	121	17

1953-54

Merthyr Tydfil	42	27	8	7	97	55	62
Headington United	42	22	9	11	68	43	53
Yeovil Town	42	20	8	14	87	76	48
Bath City	42	17	12	13	73	67	46
Kidderminster Harriers	42	18	9	15	62	59	45
Weymouth	42	18	8	16	83	72	44
Barry Town	42	17	9	16	108	91	43
Bedford Town	42	19	5	18	80	84	43
Gloucester City	42	16	11	15	69	77	43
Hastings United	42	16	10	16	73	67	42
Kettering Town	42	15	12	15	65	63	42
Hereford United	42	16	9	17	66	62	41
Llanelly	42	16	9	17	80	85	41
Guildford City	42	15	11	16	56	60	41
Gravesend & Northfleet	42	16	8	18	76	77	40
Worcester City	42	17	6	19	66	71	40
Lovells Athletic	42	14	11	17	62	60	39
Tonbridge	42	15	9	18	85	91	39
Chelmsford City	42	14	10	18	67	71	38
Exeter City Reserves	42	11	13	18	61	72	35
Cheltenham Town	42	11	12	19	56	83	34
Dartford	42	6	13	23	42	89	25

1954-55

Yeovil Town	42	23	9	10	105	66	55
Weymouth	42	24	7	11	105	84	55
Hastings United	42	21	9	12	94	60	51
Cheltenham Town	42	21	8	13	85	72	50
Guildford City	42	20	8	14	72	59	48
Worcester City	42	19	10	13	80	73	48
Barry Town	42	16	15	11	82	87	47
Gloucester City	42	16	13	13	66	54	45
Bath City	42	18	9	15	73	80	45
Headington Town	42	18	7	17	82	62	43
Kidderminster Harriers	42	18	7	17	84	86	43
Merthyr Tydfil	42	17	8	17	97	94	42
Exeter City Reserves	42	19	4	19	67	78	42
Lovells Athletic	42	15	11	16	71	68	41
Kettering Town	42	15	11	16	70	69	41
Hereford United	42	17	5	20	91	72	39
Llanelly	42	16	7	19	78	81	39
Bedford Town	42	16	3	23	75	103	35
Tonbridge	42	11	8	23	68	91	30
Dartford	42	9	12	21	55	76	30
Chelmsford City	42	11	6	25	73	111	28
Gravesend & Northfleet	42	9	9	24	62	97	27

1955-56

Guildford City	42	26	8	8	74	34	60
Cheltenham Town	42	25	6	11	82	53	56
Yeovil Town	42	23	9	10	98	55	55
Bedford Town	42	21	9	12	99	69	51
Dartford	42	20	9	13	78	62	49
Weymouth	42	19	10	13	83	63	48
Gloucester City	42	19	9	14	72	60	47
Lovells Athletic	42	19	9	14	91	78	47
Chelmsford City	42	18	10	14	67	55	46
Kettering Town	42	16	11	15	105	86	43
Exeter City Reserves	42	17	9	16	75	76	43
Gravesend & Northfleet	42	17	8	17	79	75	42
Hereford United	42	17	7	18	90	90	41
Hastings United	42	15	10	17	90	76	40
Headington United	42	17	6	19	82	86	40
Kidderminster Harriers	42	14	7	21	86	108	35
Llanelly	42	14	6	22	64	98	34
Barry Town	42	11	11	20	91	108	33
Worcester City	42	12	9	21	66	83	33
Tonbridge	42	11	11	20	53	74	33
Merthyr Tydfil	42	7	10	25	52	127	24
Bath City	42	7	10	25	43	107	24

1956-57

Kettering Town	42	28	10	4	106	47	66
Bedford Town	42	25	8	9	89	52	58
Weymouth	42	22	10	10	92	71	54
Cheltenham Town	42	19	15	8	73	46	53
Gravesend & Northfleet	42	21	11	10	74	58	53
Lovells Athletic	42	21	7	14	99	84	49
Guildford City	42	18	11	13	68	49	47
Hereford United	42	19	8	15	96	60	46
Headington United	42	19	7	16	64	61	45
Gloucester City	42	18	8	16	74	72	44
Hastings United	42	17	9	16	70	58	43
Worcester City	42	16	10	16	81	80	42
Dartford	42	16	10	16	79	88	42
Chelmsford City	42	16	9	17	73	85	41
Tonbridge	42	14	12	16	74	65	40
Yeovil Town	42	14	11	17	83	85	39
Bath City	42	15	8	19	56	78	38
Exeter City Reserves	42	10	10	22	52	89	30
Merthyr Tydfil	42	9	11	22	72	95	29
Barry Town	42	6	11	25	39	84	23
Kidderminster Harriers	42	7	10	25	60	83	20
Llanelly	42	5	8	29	39	123	18

1957-58

Gravesend & Northfleet	42	27	5	10	109	71	59
Bedford Town	42	25	7	10	112	64	57
Chelmsford City	42	24	9	9	93	57	57
Weymouth	42	25	5	12	90	61	55
Worcester City	42	23	7	12	95	59	53
Cheltenham Town	42	21	10	11	115	66	52
Hereford United	42	21	6	15	79	56	48
Kettering Town	42	18	9	15	99	76	45
Headington Town	42	18	7	17	90	83	43
Poole Town	42	17	9	16	82	81	43
Hasting United	42	13	15	14	78	77	41
Gloucester City	42	17	7	18	70	70	41
Yeovil Town	42	16	9	17	70	84	41
Dartford	42	14	9	19	66	92	37
Lovells Athletic	42	15	6	21	60	83	36
Bath City	42	13	9	20	65	64	35
Guildford City	42	12	10	20	58	92	34
Tonbridge	42	16	7	22	77	100	33
Exeter City Reserves	42	12	8	22	60	94	32
Barry Town	42	11	9	22	72	101	31
Kidderminster Harriers	42	10	10	22	60	101	30
Merthyr Tydfil	42	9	3	30	69	137	21

1958-59

North-Western Zone

Hereford United	34	22	5	7	80	37	49
Kettering Town	34	20	7	7	83	63	47
Boston United	34	18	8	8	73	47	44
Cheltenham Town	34	20	4	10	65	47	44
Worcester City	34	19	4	11	74	47	42
Bath City	34	17	5	12	89	62	39
Wellington Town	34	15	9	10	74	58	39
Nuneaton Borough	34	17	5	12	76	66	39
Wisbech Town	34	16	5	13	77	54	37
Headington United	34	16	3	15	76	61	35
Barry Town	34	15	5	14	64	67	35
Merthyr Tydfil	34	16	3	15	54	59	35
Gloucester City	34	12	6	16	50	65	30
Corby Town	34	10	8	16	59	79	28
Lovells Athletic	34	10	3	21	51	70	23
Rugby Town	34	7	6	21	45	93	20
Kidderminster Harriers	34	7	3	24	42	94	17
Burton Albion	34	3	3	28	41	104	9

South-Eastern Zone

Bedford Town	32	21	6	5	90	41	48
Gravesend & Northfleet	32	21	2	9	79	54	44
Dartford	32	20	3	9	77	41	43
Yeovil Town	32	17	8	7	60	41	42
Weymouth	32	13	11	8	61	43	37
Chelmsford City	32	12	12	8	74	53	36
King's Lynn	32	14	5	13	70	63	33
Poole Town	32	12	8	12	60	65	32
Cambridge City	32	12	7	13	61	54	31
Hastings United	32	13	5	14	60	59	31
Tonbridge	32	14	3	15	51	59	31
Cambridge United	32	11	8	13	55	77	30
Trowbridge Town	32	12	4	16	53	75	28
Exeter City Reserves	32	7	12	13	47	71	26
Guildford City	11	7	6	19	45	67	20
Clacton Town	32	6	7	19	44	81	19
Yiewsley	32	3	7	22	36	78	13

1959-60

Premier Division

Bath City	42	32	3	7	116	50	67
Headington United	42	23	8	11	78	61	54
Weymouth	42	22	9	11	93	69	53
Cheltenham Town	42	21	6	15	82	68	48
Cambridge City	42	18	11	13	81	72	47
Chelmsford Town	42	19	7	16	90	70	45
Bedford Town	42	21	3	18	97	85	45
King's Lynn	42	17	11	14	89	78	45
Boston United	42	17	10	15	83	80	44
Wisbech Town	42	17	10	15	81	84	44
Yeovil Town	42	17	8	17	81	73	42
Hereford United	42	15	12	15	70	74	42
Tonbridge	42	16	8	18	79	73	40
Hastings United	42	16	8	18	63	77	40
Wellington Town	42	13	11	18	63	78	37
Dartford	42	15	7	20	64	82	37
Gravesend & Northfleet	42	14	8	20	69	84	36
Worcester City	42	13	10	19	72	89	36
Nuneaton Borough	42	11	11	20	64	78	33
Barry Town	42	14	5	23	78	103	33
Poole Town	42	10	8	24	69	96	28
Kettering Town	42	9	10	23	60	90	28

First Division

Clacton Town	42	27	5	10	106	69	59
Romford	42	21	11	10	65	40	53
Folkestone Town	42	23	5	14	93	71	51
Exeter City Reserves	42	23	3	16	85	62	49
Guildford City	42	19	9	14	79	56	47
Sittingbourne	42	20	7	15	66	55	47
Margate	42	20	6	16	88	77	46
Trowbridge Town	42	18	9	15	90	78	45
Cambridge United	42	18	9	15	71	72	45
Yiewsley	42	17	10	15	83	69	44
Bexleyheath & Welling	42	16	11	15	85	77	43
Merthyr Tydfil	42	16	10	16	63	65	42
Ramsgate Athletic	42	16	8	18	83	84	40
Ashford Town	42	14	12	16	61	70	40
Tunbridge Wells United	42	17	5	20	77	73	39
Hinckley Athletic	42	14	8	20	62	75	36
Gloucester City	42	13	9	20	56	84	35
Dover	42	14	6	22	59	85	34
Kidderminster Harriers	42	14	6	22	59	97	34
Corby Town	42	15	3	24	75	91	33
Burton Albion	42	11	10	21	52	79	32
Rugby Town	42	10	11	21	67	91	31

1960-61

Premier Division

Oxford United	42	27	10	5	104	43	64
Chelmsford City	42	23	11	8	91	55	57
Yeovil Town	42	23	9	10	109	54	55
Hereford United	42	21	10	11	83	67	52
Weymouth	42	21	9	12	78	63	51
Bath City	42	18	14	10	74	52	50
Cambridge City	42	16	12	14	101	71	44
Wellington Town	42	17	9	16	66	68	43
Bedford Town	42	18	7	17	94	97	43
Folkestone Town	42	18	7	17	75	86	43
King's Lynn	42	13	16	13	68	66	42
Worcester City	42	15	11	16	69	69	41
Clacton Town	42	15	11	16	82	83	41
Romford	42	13	15	14	66	69	41
Guildford City	42	14	11	17	65	62	39
Tonbridge	42	16	6	20	79	85	38
Cheltenham Town	42	15	7	20	81	81	37
Gravesend & Northfleet	42	15	7	20	75	101	37
Dartford	42	13	11	18	57	90	37
Hastings United	42	8	9	25	60	100	25
Wisbech Town	42	9	6	27	58	112	24
Boston United	42	6	8	28	62	123	20

Oxford United were previously known as Headington United.

First Division

Kettering Town	40	26	7	7	100	55	59
Cambridge United	40	25	5	10	100	53	55
Bexleyheath & Welling	40	22	8	10	93	46	52
Merthyr Tydfil	40	23	6	11	88	65	52
Sittingbourne	40	21	10	9	77	63	52
Hinckley Athletic	40	17	13	10	74	59	47
Ramsgate Athletic	40	19	7	14	77	56	45
Rugby Town	40	18	9	13	89	71	45
Corby Town	40	16	10	14	82	73	42
Poole Town	40	18	5	17	71	65	41
Barry Town	40	16	9	15	65	74	41
Yiewsley	40	17	7	16	65	76	41
Trowbridge Town	40	14	10	16	71	73	38
Ashford Town	40	14	8	18	61	67	36
Margate	40	11	12	17	62	75	34
Dover	40	12	7	21	67	74	31
Canterbury City	40	10	10	20	52	75	30
Nuneaton Borough	40	11	7	22	60	91	29
Burton Albion	40	12	4	24	63	85	28
Tunbridge Wells United	40	8	5	27	56	115	21
Gloucester City	40	7	7	26	40	102	21

1961-62

Premier Division

Oxford United	42	28	5	9	118	46	61
Bath City	42	25	7	10	102	70	57
Guildford City	42	24	8	10	79	49	56
Yeovil Town	42	23	8	11	97	59	54
Chelmsford City	42	19	12	11	74	60	50
Weymouth	42	20	7	15	80	64	47
Kettering Town	42	21	5	16	90	84	47
Hereford United	42	21	2	19	81	68	44
Cambridge City	42	18	8	16	70	71	44
Bexleyheath & Welling	42	19	5	18	69	75	43
Romford	42	15	9	18	63	70	39
Cambridge United	42	13	12	17	76	78	38
Wellington United	42	14	10	18	75	78	38
Gravesend & Northfleet	42	17	4	21	59	92	38
Bedford Town	42	16	5	21	73	79	37
Worcester City	42	15	7	20	51	64	37
Merthyr Tydfil	42	13	11	18	62	80	37
Clacton Town	42	13	10	19	74	91	36
Tonbridge	42	10	14	18	71	92	34
King's Lynn	42	12	8	22	59	74	32
Folkestone Town	42	12	6	24	64	103	30
Cheltenham	42	9	7	26	48	86	25

First Division

Wisbech Town	38	21	11	6	76	42	53
Poole Town	38	23	6	9	81	47	52
Dartford	38	21	8	9	89	50	50
Rugby Town	38	20	9	9	82	49	49
Margate	38	20	6	12	73	55	46
Corby Town	38	19	6	13	82	60	44
Sittingbourne	38	16	12	10	69	51	44
Dover	38	19	6	13	66	55	44
Yiewsley	38	18	6	14	64	51	42
Barry Town	38	14	11	13	55	51	39
Ashford Town	38	14	11	13	66	70	39
Hinckley Athletic	38	15	8	15	75	65	38
Burton Albion	38	16	5	17	70	79	37
Nuneaton Borough	38	12	12	14	63	69	36
Tunbridge Wells United	38	12	7	19	60	85	31
Canterbury City	38	11	8	19	60	82	30
Ramsgate Athletic	38	10	9	19	48	70	29
Trowbridge Town	38	9	9	20	45	69	27
Gloucester City	38	6	4	28	46	104	16
Hastings United	38	5	4	29	45	115	14

1962-63

Premier Division

Cambridge City	40	25	6	9	99	64	56
Cambridge United	40	23	7	10	74	50	53
Weymouth	40	20	11	9	82	43	51
Guildford City	40	20	11	9	70	50	51
Kettering Town	40	22	7	11	66	49	51
Wellington Town	40	19	9	12	71	49	47
Dartford	40	19	9	12	61	54	47
Chelmsford City	40	18	10	12	63	50	46
Bedford Town	40	18	8	14	61	45	44
Bath City	40	18	6	16	58	56	42
Yeovil Town	40	15	10	15	64	54	40
Romford	40	14	11	15	73	68	39
Bexleyheath & Welling	40	13	11	16	55	63	37
Hereford United	40	14	7	19	56	66	35
Merthyr Tydfil	40	15	4	21	54	71	34
Rugby Town	40	14	5	21	65	76	33
Wisbech Town	40	15	3	22	64	84	33
Worcester City	40	12	9	19	47	65	33
Poole Town	40	10	12	18	54	66	32
Gravesend & Northfleet	40	10	3	27	62	91	23
Clacton Town	40	3	7	30	50	135	13

First Division

Margate	38	21	13	4	86	47	55
Hinckley Athletic	38	22	9	7	66	38	53
Hastings United	38	22	8	8	86	36	52
Nuneaton Borough	38	21	10	7	82	41	52
Tonbridge	38	22	8	8	81	51	52
Dover	38	22	7	9	78	56	51
Corby Town	38	19	8	11	79	50	46
King's Lynn	38	19	7	15	76	66	45
Cheltenham Town	38	18	7	13	83	52	43
Folkestone Town	38	15	10	13	79	57	40
Canterbury City	38	14	8	16	42	56	36
Yiewsley	38	11	10	17	63	71	32
Ramsgate Athletic	38	12	7	19	58	82	31
Trowbridge Town	38	11	9	18	50	81	31
Burton Albion	38	10	10	18	48	76	30
Gloucester City	38	9	11	18	42	78	29
Sittingbourne	38	12	3	23	56	75	27
Ashford Town	38	9	6	23	58	76	24
Barry Town	38	6	5	27	35	75	17
Tunbridge Wells United	38	6	2	30	43	118	14

1963-64

Premier Division

Yeovil Town	42	29	5	8	93	36	63
Chelmsford City	42	26	7	9	99	55	59
Bath City	42	24	9	9	88	51	57
Guildford City	42	21	9	12	90	55	51
Romford	42	20	9	13	71	58	49
Hastings United	42	20	8	14	75	61	48
Weymouth	42	20	7	15	65	53	47
Bedford Town	42	19	9	14	71	68	47
Cambridge United	42	17	9	16	92	77	43
Cambridge City	42	17	9	16	76	70	43
Wisbech Town	42	17	8	17	64	68	42
Bexley United	42	16	10	16	70	77	42
Dartford	42	16	8	18	56	71	40
Worcester City	42	12	15	15	70	74	39
Nuneaton Borough	42	15	8	19	58	61	38
Rugby Town	42	15	8	19	68	86	38
Margate	42	12	13	17	68	81	37
Wellington Town	42	12	9	21	73	85	33
Merthyr Tydfil	42	12	8	22	69	108	32
Hereford United	42	12	7	23	58	86	31
Kettering Town	42	10	5	27	49	89	25
Hinckley Athletic	42	7	6	29	51	104	20

First Division

Folkestone Town	42	28	7	7	82	38	63
King's Lynn	42	28	5	9	94	44	61
Cheltenham Town	42	25	10	7	92	49	60
Tonbridge	42	24	11	7	98	54	59
Corby town	42	24	7	11	114	56	55
Stevenage Town	42	21	6	15	70	59	48
Ashford Town	42	19	9	14	73	57	47
Burton Albion	42	19	8	15	76	70	46
Poole Town	42	17	11	14	75	61	45
Dover	42	18	9	15	86	75	45
Canterbury City	42	16	12	14	66	66	44
Crawley Town	42	20	2	20	81	71	42
Trowbridge Town	42	16	9	17	71	78	41
Clacton Town	42	19	1	22	76	88	39
Gloucester City	42	17	4	21	88	89	38
Yiewsley	42	15	8	19	63	77	38
Sittingbourne	42	15	8	19	52	70	38
Ramsgate Athletic	42	13	9	20	57	55	35
Tunbridge Wells Rangers	42	10	8	24	47	89	28
Gravesend & Northfleet	42	7	9	26	43	96	23
Deal Town	42	5	7	30	48	106	17
Barry Town	42	3	6	33	33	137	12

1964-65

Premier Division

Weymouth	42	24	8	10	99	50	56
Guildford City	42	21	12	9	73	49	54
Worcester City	42	22	6	14	100	62	50
Yeovil Town	42	18	14	10	76	55	50
Chelmsford City	42	21	8	13	86	77	50
Margate	42	20	9	13	88	79	49
Dartford	42	17	11	14	74	64	45
Nuneaton Borough	42	19	7	16	57	55	45
Cambridge United	42	16	11	15	78	66	43
Bedford Town	42	17	9	16	66	70	43
Cambridge City	42	16	9	17	72	69	41
Cheltenham Town	42	15	11	16	72	78	41
Folkestone Town	42	17	7	18	72	79	41
Romford	42	17	7	18	61	70	41
King's Lynn	42	13	13	16	56	79	39
Tonbridge	42	10	16	16	66	75	36
Wellington Town	42	13	10	19	63	78	36
Rugby Town	42	15	6	21	71	98	36
Wisbech Town	42	14	6	22	75	91	34
Bexley United	42	14	5	23	67	74	33
Hastings United	42	9	14	19	58	86	32
Bath City	42	13	3	26	60	86	29

First Division

Hereford United	42	34	4	4	124	39	72
Wimbledon	42	24	13	5	108	52	61
Poole Town	42	26	6	10	92	56	58
Corby Town	42	24	7	11	88	55	55
Stevenage Town	42	19	13	10	83	43	51
Hillingdon Borough	42	21	7	14	105	63	49
Crawley Town	42	22	5	15	83	52	49
Merthyr Tydfil	42	20	9	13	75	59	49
Gloucester City	42	19	10	13	68	65	48
Burton Albion	42	20	7	15	83	75	47
Canterbury City	42	13	16	13	73	53	42
Kettering Town	42	14	13	15	74	64	41
Ramsgate Athletic	42	16	8	18	51	59	40
Dover	42	14	10	18	54	59	38
Hinckley Athletic	42	13	9	20	56	81	35
Trowbridge Town	42	13	5	24	68	106	31
Ashford Town	42	11	8	23	60	98	30
Barry Town	42	11	7	24	47	103	29
Deal Town	42	7	13	22	61	127	27
Tunbridge Wells Rangers	42	10	6	26	51	107	26
Gravesend & Northfleet	42	9	7	26	57	101	25
Sittingbourne	42	8	5	29	58	103	21

1965-66

Premier Division

Weymouth	42	22	13	7	70	35	57
Chelmsford City	42	21	12	9	74	50	54
Hereford United	42	21	10	11	81	49	52
Bedford Town	42	23	6	13	80	57	52
Wimbledon	42	20	10	12	80	47	50
Cambridge City	42	19	11	12	67	52	49
Romford	42	21	7	14	87	72	49
Worcester City	42	20	8	14	69	54	48
Yeovil Town	42	17	11	14	91	70	45
Cambridge United	42	18	9	15	72	64	45
King's Lynn	42	18	7	17	75	72	43
Corby Town	42	16	9	17	66	73	41
Wellington Town	42	13	13	16	65	70	39
Nuneaton Borough	42	15	8	19	66	74	38
Folkestone Town	42	14	9	19	53	75	37
Guildford City	42	14	8	20	70	84	36
Poole Town	42	14	7	21	61	75	35
Cheltenham Town	42	13	9	20	69	99	35
Dartford	42	13	7	22	62	69	33
Rugby Town	42	11	10	21	67	95	32
Tonbridge	42	11	6	25	63	101	28
Margate	42	8	10	24	66	111	26

First Division

Barnet	46	30	9	7	114	49	69
Hillingdon Borough	46	27	10	9	101	46	64
Burton Albion	46	28	8	10	121	60	64
Bath City	46	25	13	8	88	50	63
Hastings United	46	25	10	11	104	59	60
Wisbech Town	46	25	9	12	98	54	59
Canterbury City	46	25	8	13	89	66	58
Stevenage Town	46	23	9	14	86	49	55
Kettering Town	46	22	9	15	77	74	53
Merthyr Tydfil	46	22	6	18	95	68	50
Dunstable Town	46	15	14	17	76	72	44
Crawley Town	46	17	10	19	72	71	44
Bexley United	46	20	4	22	65	71	44
Trowbridge Town	46	16	11	19	79	81	43
Dover	46	17	8	21	59	62	42
Barry Town	46	16	10	20	72	94	42
Gravesend & Northfleet	46	16	9	21	84	86	41
Gloucester City	46	14	12	20	75	98	40
Sittingbourne	46	11	12	23	77	121	34
Ramsgate Athletic	46	9	15	22	35	76	33
Hinckley Athletic	46	10	12	24	59	93	32
Tunbridge Wells Rangers	46	12	8	26	47	88	32
Ashford Town	46	9	10	27	44	92	28
Deal Town	46	3	4	39	29	165	10

1966-67

Premier Division

Romford	42	22	8	12	80	60	52
Nuneaton Borough	42	21	9	12	82	54	51
Weymouth	42	18	14	10	64	40	50
Wimbledon	42	19	11	12	88	60	49
Barnet	42	18	13	11	86	66	49
Guildford City	42	19	10	13	65	51	48
Wellington Town	42	20	7	15	70	67	47
Cambridge United	42	16	13	13	75	67	45
Chelmsford City	42	15	15	12	66	59	45
Hereford United	42	16	12	14	79	61	44
King's Lynn	42	15	14	13	78	72	44
Cambridge City	42	15	13	14	66	70	43
Cheltenham Town	42	16	11	15	60	71	43
Yeovil Town	42	14	14	14	66	72	42
Burton Albion	42	17	5	20	63	71	39
Corby Town	42	15	9	18	60	75	39
Poole Town	42	14	11	17	52	65	39
Hillingdon Borough	42	11	13	18	49	70	35
Bath City	42	11	12	19	51	74	34
Worcester City	42	11	8	23	59	79	30
Bedford Town	42	8	13	21	54	72	29
Folkestone Town	42	6	15	21	44	81	27

First Division

Team	P	W	D	L	F	A	Pts
Dover	46	29	12	5	92	35	70
Margate	46	31	7	8	127	54	69
Stevenage Town	46	29	8	9	90	32	66
Hastings United	46	25	16	5	89	45	66
Kettering Town	46	27	9	10	105	62	63
Canterbury City	46	26	8	12	81	48	60
Ramsgate Athletic	46	23	8	15	79	62	54
Dartford	46	19	15	12	92	67	53
Tonbridge	46	21	10	15	91	69	52
Trowbridge Town	46	20	12	14	73	60	52
Ashford Town	46	18	8	20	74	68	44
Merthyr Tydfil	46	17	9	20	81	71	43
Gloucester City	46	18	6	22	69	83	42
Canterbury City	46	17	8	21	57	75	42
Wisbech Town	46	16	9	21	87	93	41
Bexley United	46	13	15	18	53	69	41
Banbury United	46	13	14	19	88	100	40
Rugby Town	46	15	7	24	57	77	37
Dunstable Town	46	14	6	26	55	87	34
Barry Town	46	11	11	24	62	89	33
Gravesend & Northfleet	46	11	9	26	63	106	31
Hinckley United	46	10	8	28	44	100	28
Tunbridge Wells Rangers	46	4	15	27	31	96	23
Sittingbourne	46	5	10	31	44	136	20

1967-68

Premier Division

Team	P	W	D	L	F	A	Pts
Chelmsford City	42	25	7	10	85	50	57
Wimbledon	42	24	7	11	85	47	55
Cambridge United	42	20	13	9	73	42	53
Cheltenham Town	42	23	7	12	97	67	53
Guildford City	42	18	13	11	56	43	49
Romford	42	20	8	14	72	60	48
Barnet	42	20	8	14	81	71	48
Margate	42	19	8	15	80	71	46
Wellington Town	42	16	13	13	70	66	45
Hillingdon Borough	42	18	9	15	53	54	45
King's Lynn	42	18	8	16	66	57	44
Yeovil Town	42	16	12	14	45	43	44
Weymouth	42	17	8	17	65	62	42
Hereford United	42	17	7	18	58	62	41
Nuneaton Borough	42	13	14	15	62	64	40
Dover	42	17	6	19	54	56	40
Poole Town	42	13	10	19	55	74	36
Stevenage Town	42	13	9	20	57	75	35
Burton Albion	42	14	6	22	51	73	34
Corby Town	42	7	13	22	40	77	27
Cambridge City	42	10	6	26	51	81	26
Hastings United	42	4	8	30	33	94	16

First Division

Team	P	W	D	L	F	A	Pts
Worcester City	42	23	14	5	92	35	60
Kettering Town	42	24	10	8	88	40	58
Bedford Town	42	24	7	11	101	40	55
Rugby Town	42	20	15	7	72	44	55
Dartford	42	23	9	10	70	48	55
Bath City	42	21	12	9	78	51	54
Banbury United	42	22	9	11	79	59	53
Ramsgate Athletic	42	22	7	13	70	37	51
Merthyr Tydfil	42	18	13	11	80	66	49
Tonbridge	42	18	9	15	76	71	45
Canterbury City	42	16	11	15	66	63	43
Ashford Town	42	18	6	18	73	78	42
Brentwood Town	42	16	9	17	63	73	41
Bexley United	42	12	13	17	56	64	37
Trowbridge Town	42	12	11	19	64	70	35
Gloucester City	42	12	9	21	54	68	33
Wisbech Town	42	11	10	21	43	78	32
Crawley Town	42	10	8	24	54	85	28
Folkestone Town	42	10	7	25	49	80	27
Dunstable Town	42	8	10	24	44	94	26
Barry Town	42	7	12	23	36	81	26
Gravesend & Northfleet	42	6	7	29	28	112	19

1968-69

Premier Division

Team	P	W	D	L	F	A	Pts
Cambridge United	42	27	5	10	72	39	59
Hillingdon Borough	42	24	10	8	68	47	58
Wimbledon	42	21	12	9	66	48	54
King's Lynn	42	20	9	13	68	60	49
Worcester City	42	19	11	12	53	47	49
Romford	42	18	12	12	58	52	48
Weymouth	42	16	15	11	52	41	47
Yeovil Town	42	16	13	13	52	50	45
Kettering Town	42	18	8	16	51	55	44
Dover	42	17	9	16	66	61	43
Nuneaton Borough	42	17	7	18	74	58	41
Barnet	42	15	10	17	72	66	40
Chelmsford City	42	17	6	19	56	58	40
Hereford United	42	15	9	18	68	62	39
Telford United	42	14	10	18	62	61	38
Poole Town	42	16	6	20	75	76	38
Burton Albion	42	16	5	21	55	71	37
Margate	42	14	7	21	79	90	35
Cheltenham Town	42	15	5	22	55	64	35
Bedford Town	42	11	12	19	46	63	34
Rugby Town	42	10	6	26	38	83	26
Guildford City	42	7	11	24	41	73	25

First Division

Team	P	W	D	L	F	A	Pts
Brentwood Town	42	26	12	4	44	37	64
Bath City	42	26	10	6	96	40	62
Gloucester City	42	25	9	8	100	53	59
Crawley Town	42	21	13	8	65	32	55
Corby Town	42	22	6	14	81	65	50
Dartford	42	20	8	14	79	51	48
Ramsgate Athletic	42	19	9	14	72	57	47
Salisbury	42	20	6	16	69	52	46
Cambridge City	42	18	10	14	73	63	46
Banbury United	42	16	12	14	67	72	44
Trowbridge Town	42	15	8	19	70	60	44
Folkestone Town	42	19	5	18	53	59	43
Canterbury City	42	17	7	18	67	63	41
Ashford Town	42	16	8	18	72	73	40
Bexley United	42	15	9	18	62	75	39
Hastings United	42	15	9	18	58	69	39
Wisbech Town	42	11	13	18	57	70	35
Dunstable Town	42	14	6	22	73	99	34
Merthyr Tydfil	42	10	7	25	49	101	27
Barry Town	42	8	10	24	39	78	26
Gravesend & Northfleet	42	8	9	25	51	79	25
Tonbridge	42	2	6	34	36	137	10

1969-70

Premier Division

Team	P	W	D	L	F	A	Pts
Cambridge United	42	26	6	10	86	49	58
Yeovil Town	42	25	7	10	78	48	57
Chelmsford City	42	20	11	11	76	58	51
Weymouth	42	18	14	10	59	37	50
Wimbledon	42	19	12	11	64	52	50
Hillingdon Borough	42	19	12	11	56	50	50
Barnet	42	16	15	11	71	54	47
Telford United	42	18	10	14	61	62	46
Brentwood Town	42	16	13	13	61	38	45
Hereford United	42	18	9	15	74	65	45
Bath City	42	18	8	16	66	53	44
King's Lynn	42	16	11	15	72	68	43
Margate	42	17	8	17	70	64	42
Dover	42	15	10	17	51	50	40
Kettering Town	42	18	3	21	64	75	39
Worcester City	42	14	10	18	35	44	38
Romford	42	13	11	18	52	74	37
Poole Town	42	8	19	15	48	57	35
Gloucester City	42	12	9	21	53	73	33
Nuneaton Borough	42	11	10	21	52	74	32
Crawley Town	42	6	15	21	53	101	27
Burton Albion	42	3	9	30	24	82	15

First Division

Bedford Town	42	26	9	7	93	37	61
Cambridge City	42	26	8	8	104	43	60
Dartford	42	24	11	7	33	46	58
Ashford Town	42	19	15	8	71	43	53
Rugby Town	42	20	10	12	82	66	50
Trowbridge Town	42	20	8	14	72	65	48
Hastings United	42	18	11	13	67	51	47
Guildford City	42	19	9	14	68	58	54
Cheltenham Town	42	20	5	17	78	81	45
Canterbury City	42	15	13	14	61	57	43
Corby Town	42	14	15	13	58	53	43
Folkestone Town	42	19	5	18	57	55	43
Ramsgate Athletic	42	14	13	15	53	57	41
Salisbury	42	13	13	16	48	53	39
Gravesend & Northfleet	42	13	11	18	62	71	37
Bexley United	42	10	11	21	58	76	31
Dunstable Town	42	11	9	22	52	82	31
Merthyr Tydfil	42	9	11	22	40	80	29
Barry Town	42	11	6	25	39	76	28
Wisbech Town	42	8	9	25	58	116	25
Tonbridge	42	4	10	28	46	101	18

1970-71

Premier Division

Yeovil Town	42	25	7	10	66	31	57
Cambridge City	42	22	11	9	67	38	55
Romford	42	23	9	10	63	42	55
Hereford United	42	23	8	11	71	53	54
Chelmsford City	42	20	11	11	61	32	51
Barnet	42	18	14	10	69	49	50
Bedford Town	42	20	10	12	62	46	50
Wimbledon	42	20	8	14	72	54	48
Worcester City	42	20	8	14	61	46	48
Weymouth	42	14	16	12	64	48	44
Dartford	42	15	12	15	53	51	42
Dover	42	16	9	17	64	63	41
Margate	42	15	10	17	64	70	40
Hillingdon Borough	42	17	6	19	61	68	40
Bath City	42	13	12	17	48	68	38
Nuneaton Borough	42	12	12	18	43	66	36
Telford United	42	13	8	21	64	70	34
Poole Town	42	14	6	22	57	75	34
King's Lynn	42	11	7	24	44	67	29
Ashford Town	42	8	13	21	52	86	29
Kettering Town	42	8	11	23	48	84	27
Gloucester City	42	6	10	26	34	81	21

First Division

Guildford City	38	22	10	6	76	36	54
Merthyr Tydfil	38	19	12	7	52	33	50
Gravesend & Northfleet	38	19	10	9	74	42	48
Folkestone	38	20	8	10	83	53	48
Burton Albion	38	19	10	9	56	37	48
Rugby Town	38	17	14	7	58	40	48
Ramsgate Athletic	38	20	5	13	83	54	45
Trowbridge Town	38	19	7	12	78	55	45
Bexley United	38	17	11	10	57	45	45
Crawley Town	38	15	11	12	84	68	41
Hastings United	38	13	12	13	51	50	38
Banbury United	38	13	11	14	58	53	37
Corby Town	38	14	8	16	57	60	36
Salisbury	38	13	7	18	56	60	33
Cheltenham Town	38	8	15	15	44	58	31
Stevenage Athletic	38	12	7	19	55	79	21
Tonbridge	38	8	8	22	48	83	24
Barry Town	38	9	6	23	35	82	24
Dunstable Town	38	8	4	26	32	81	20
Canterbury City	38	5	4	29	37	105	14

1971-72

Premier Division

Chelmsford City	42	28	6	8	109	46	62
Hereford United	42	24	12	6	68	30	60
Dover	42	20	11	11	67	45	51
Barnet	42	21	7	14	80	57	49
Dartford	42	20	8	14	75	68	48
Weymouth	42	21	5	16	69	43	47
Yeovil Town	42	18	11	13	67	51	47
Hillingdon Borough	42	20	6	16	64	58	46
Margate	42	19	8	15	74	68	46
Wimbledon	42	19	7	16	75	64	45
Romford	42	16	13	13	54	49	45
Guildford City	42	20	5	17	71	65	45
Telford United	42	18	7	17	83	68	43
Nuneaton Borough	42	16	10	16	46	47	42
Bedford Town	42	16	9	17	59	66	41
Worcester City	42	17	7	18	46	57	41
Cambridge City	42	12	14	16	68	71	38
Folkestone	42	14	7	21	58	64	35
Poole Town	42	9	11	22	43	72	29
Bath City	42	11	4	27	45	86	26
Merthyr Tydfil	42	7	8	27	29	93	22
Gravesend & Northfleet	42	5	6	31	30	110	16

First Division (North)

Kettering Town	34	23	6	5	70	27	52
Burton Albion	34	18	13	3	58	27	49
Cheltenham Town	34	20	4	10	72	51	44
Rugby Town	34	18	7	9	52	36	43
Wellingborough Town	34	15	10	9	73	44	40
Stourbridge	34	13	14	7	59	42	40
King's Lynn	34	14	11	9	62	45	39
Corby Town	34	15	9	10	47	35	39
Ilkeston Town	34	14	11	9	44	38	39
Banbury United	34	14	5	15	54	46	33
Bury Town	34	14	5	15	47	44	33
Wealdstone	34	14	5	15	51	58	33
Lockheed Leamington	34	15	3	16	41	52	33
Gloucester City	34	8	8	18	46	61	24
Stevenage Athletic	34	8	8	18	41	69	24
Bletchley	34	7	7	20	36	70	21
Dunstable Town	34	5	7	22	29	75	17
Barry Town	34	1	7	26	22	84	9

First Division (South)

Waterlooville	30	15	9	6	40	22	39
Ramsgate Athletic	30	14	11	5	42	27	39
Maidstone United	30	14	10	6	48	28	38
Crawley Town	30	15	5	10	67	55	35
Metropolitan Police	30	15	3	12	48	41	33
Tonbridge	30	12	9	9	37	34	33
Bexley United	30	14	4	12	52	46	32
Basingstoke Town	30	14	4	12	37	36	32
Andover	30	11	9	10	32	34	31
Ashford Town	30	12	4	14	43	48	28
Salisbury	30	10	7	13	45	44	27
Winchester City	30	10	7	13	40	47	27
Hastings United	30	10	7	13	28	42	27
Trowbridge Town	30	8	7	15	41	49	23
Canterbury City	30	7	8	15	39	56	22
Woodford Town	30	4	6	20	22	52	14

1972-73

Premier Division

Kettering Town	42	20	17	5	74	44	57
Yeovil Town	42	21	14	7	67	61	56
Dover	42	23	9	10	61	68	55
Chelmsford City	42	23	7	12	75	43	53
Worcester City	42	20	13	9	68	47	53
Weymouth	42	20	12	10	72	51	52
Margate	42	17	15	10	80	60	49
Bedford Town	42	16	15	11	43	36	47
Nuneaton Borough	42	16	14	12	51	41	46
Telford United	42	12	20	10	57	47	44
Cambridge City	42	14	15	13	64	53	43
Wimbledon	42	14	14	14	50	50	42
Barnet	42	15	11	16	60	59	41
Romford	42	17	5	20	51	65	39
Hillingdon Borough	42	16	6	20	52	58	38
Dartford	42	12	11	19	49	63	35
Folkestone	42	11	11	20	41	72	33
Guildford City	42	10	11	21	59	84	31
Ramsgate	42	9	13	20	35	61	31
Poole Town	42	10	10	22	50	88	30
Burton Albion	42	9	7	26	43	81	25
Waterlooville	42	4	16	22	33	63	24

First Division (North)

Grantham	42	29	8	5	113	41	66
Atherstone Town	42	23	11	8	82	48	57
Cheltenham Town	42	24	8	10	87	47	56
Rugby Town	42	20	10	12	60	47	50
Kidderminster Harriers	42	19	12	11	67	56	50
Merthyr Tydfil	42	17	12	13	51	40	46
Corby Town	42	14	16	12	62	56	44
Stourbridge	42	16	11	15	70	64	43
Gloucester City	42	18	7	17	55	64	43
Bromsgrove Rovers	42	17	8	17	63	54	42
Redditch United	42	18	6	18	58	59	42
Banbury United	42	18	5	19	60	53	41
Wellingborough Town	42	17	7	18	58	71	41
King's Lynn	42	14	12	16	45	49	40
Lockheed Leamington	42	13	12	17	51	58	38
Enderby Town	42	12	14	16	50	61	38
Stevenage Athletic	42	12	13	17	50	63	37
Tamworth	42	14	8	20	45	65	36
Bury Town	42	13	9	20	52	69	35
Barry Town	42	11	10	21	45	71	32
Ilkeston Town	42	9	6	27	35	68	24
Bedworth United	42	10	3	29	42	94	23

First Division (South)

Maidstone United	42	25	12	5	90	38	62
Tonbridge	42	26	7	9	70	44	59
Ashford Town	42	24	7	11	90	40	55
Bideford	42	19	14	9	70	43	52
Minehead	42	20	12	10	65	47	52
Gravesend & Northfleet	42	22	7	13	81	55	51
Bath City	42	18	11	13	56	54	47
Wealdstone	42	16	12	14	81	61	44
Bletchley Town	42	14	13	15	54	51	41
Hastings United	42	14	13	15	53	53	41
Andover	42	15	11	16	62	70	41
Canterbury City	42	14	12	16	51	59	40
Basingstoke Town	42	14	12	16	48	57	40
Crawley Town	42	14	11	17	59	76	39
Metropolitan Police	42	15	8	19	82	75	38
Trowbridge Town	42	15	8	19	65	77	38
Bexley United	42	12	14	16	54	64	38
Salisbury	42	14	10	18	49	60	38
Bognor Regis Town	42	12	9	21	41	66	33
Dorchester Town	42	10	12	20	47	73	32
Winchester City	42	7	11	24	41	79	25
Dunstable Town	42	4	10	28	38	105	18

1973-74

Premier Division

Dartford	42	22	13	7	67	37	57
Grantham	42	18	13	11	70	49	49
Chelmsford City	42	19	10	13	62	49	48
Kettering Town	42	16	16	10	62	51	48
Maidstone United	42	16	14	12	54	43	46
Yeovil Town	42	13	20	9	45	39	46
Weymouth	42	19	7	16	60	41	45
Barnet	42	18	9	15	55	46	45
Nuneaton Borough	42	13	19	10	54	47	45
Cambridge City	42	15	12	15	45	54	42
Atherstone Town	42	16	9	17	61	59	41
Wimbledon	42	15	11	16	50	56	41
Telford United	42	12	16	14	51	57	40
Dover	42	11	17	14	41	46	39
Tonbridge	42	12	15	15	38	45	39
Romford	42	11	17	14	39	52	39
Margate	42	15	8	19	56	63	38
Guildford City	42	13	11	18	48	67	37
Worcester City	42	11	14	17	53	67	36
Bedford Town	42	11	14	17	38	51	36
Folkestone	42	11	12	19	56	65	34
Hillingdon Borough	42	9	15	18	44	65	33

First Division (North)

Stourbridge	42	29	11	2	103	36	69
Burton Albion	42	27	9	6	88	32	63
Cheltenham Town	42	24	9	10	75	51	56
AP Leamington	42	21	12	9	82	45	54
Enderby Town	42	19	14	9	60	36	52
Witney Town	42	20	10	12	69	55	50
Stevenage Athletic	42	19	11	12	65	46	49
Banbury United	42	19	11	12	69	57	49
King's Lynn	42	19	10	13	65	50	48
Kidderminster Harriers	42	15	14	13	67	53	44
Merthyr Tydfil	42	16	12	14	70	61	44
Redditch United	42	14	11	17	56	73	39
Bromsgrove Rovers	42	14	10	18	54	61	38
Bedworth United	42	14	10	18	50	77	38
Tamworth	42	13	11	18	42	51	37
Corby Town	42	12	11	19	40	57	35
Bletchley Town	42	10	15	17	47	71	35
Barry Town	42	10	8	24	53	85	29
Bury Town	42	10	6	26	57	84	26
Gloucester City	42	10	6	26	52	81	26
Wellingborough Town	42	7	9	26	42	87	23
Dunstable Town	42	5	11	26	26	83	21

First Division (South)

Wealdstone	38	26	7	5	75	35	59
Bath City	38	20	8	10	55	34	48
Waterlooville	38	16	15	7	55	38	47
Minehead	38	16	15	7	69	52	47
Bideford	38	17	12	9	61	51	46
Poole Town	38	18	9	11	67	47	45
Bexley United	38	18	7	13	50	42	43
Hastings United	38	16	9	13	45	36	41
Basingstoke Town	38	14	11	13	55	44	39
Gravesend & Northfleet	38	13	13	12	58	52	39
Bognor Regis Town	38	13	12	13	48	54	38
Ashford Town	38	14	8	16	41	42	36
Ramsgate	38	13	9	16	46	44	35
Dorchester Town	38	10	13	15	40	48	33
Canterbury City	38	9	12	17	37	46	30
Trowbridge Town	38	8	14	16	44	61	30
Salisbury	38	10	9	19	40	60	29
Metropolitan Police	38	9	11	18	37	61	29
Andover	38	11	3	24	38	70	25
Crawley Town	38	6	9	23	35	79	21

1974-75

Premier Division

Wimbledon	42	25	7	10	63	33	57
Nuneaton Borough	42	23	8	11	56	37	54
Yeovil Town	42	21	9	12	64	34	51
Kettering Town	42	20	10	12	73	41	50
Burton Albion	42	18	13	11	54	48	49
Bath City	42	20	8	14	63	50	48
Margate	42	17	12	13	64	64	46
Wealdstone	42	17	11	14	62	61	45
Telford United	42	16	13	13	55	56	45
Chelmsford City	42	16	12	14	62	51	44
Grantham	42	16	11	15	70	62	43
Dover	42	15	13	14	43	53	43
Maidstone United	42	15	12	15	52	50	42
Atherstone Town	42	14	14	14	48	53	42
Weymouth	42	13	13	16	66	58	39
Stourbridge	42	13	12	17	56	70	38
Cambridge	42	11	14	17	51	56	36
Tonbridge	42	11	12	19	44	66	34
Romford	42	10	13	19	46	62	33
Dartford	42	9	13	20	52	70	31
Barnet	42	10	9	23	44	76	29
Guildford & Dorking United	42	10	5	27	45	82	25

First Division (North)

Bedford Town	42	28	9	5	85	33	65
Dunstable Town	42	25	8	9	105	61	58
AP Leamington	42	25	7	10	68	48	57
Redditch United	42	22	12	8	76	40	56
Worcester City	42	24	8	10	84	50	56
Cheltenham Town	42	21	9	12	72	53	51
Tamworth	42	21	8	13	74	53	50
King's Lynn	42	19	10	13	71	64	48
Enderby Town	42	17	12	13	61	48	46
Banbury United	42	18	10	14	52	51	46
Stevenage Athletic	42	16	13	13	62	48	45
Bromsgrove Rovers	42	18	9	15	63	52	45
Merthyr Tydfil	42	11	15	16	53	64	37
Witney Town	42	16	4	22	57	76	36
Corby Town	42	11	13	18	60	57	35
Kidderminster Harriers	42	12	11	19	50	66	35
Gloucester City	42	13	8	21	55	75	34
Wellingborough Town	42	9	13	20	42	61	31
Barry Town	42	10	10	22	49	73	30
Bedworth United	42	9	9	24	60	91	27
Milton Keynes City	42	7	5	30	48	100	19
Bury Town	42	5	7	30	36	119	17

First Division (South)

Gravesend & Northfleet	38	24	12	2	70	30	60
Hillingdon Borough	38	22	8	8	87	45	52
Minehead	38	21	9	8	74	33	51
Ramsgate	38	19	11	8	70	37	49
Bexley United	38	19	7	12	61	44	45
Waterlooville	38	17	11	10	67	49	45
Ashford Town	38	16	12	10	64	55	44
Basingstoke Town	38	16	11	11	64	50	43
Canterbury City	38	16	9	13	54	43	41
Hastings United	38	13	14	11	54	45	40
Poole Town	38	11	13	14	50	60	35
Metropolitan Police	38	11	13	14	54	66	35
Folkestone & Shepway	38	10	14	14	53	57	34
Andover	38	12	8	18	52	71	32
Bognor Regis Town	38	10	11	17	49	64	31
Salisbury	38	9	11	18	45	66	29
Trowbridge Town	38	10	9	19	48	76	29
Bideford	38	10	8	20	40	71	28
Dorchester Town	38	8	10	20	40	63	26
Crawley Town	38	3	5	30	31	102	11

1975-76

Premier Division

Wimbledon	42	26	10	6	74	29	62
Yeovil Town	42	21	12	9	68	35	54
Atherstone Town	42	18	15	9	56	55	51
Maidstone United	42	17	16	9	52	39	50
Nuneaton Borough	42	16	18	8	41	33	50
Gravesend & Northfleet	42	16	18	8	49	47	50
Grantham	42	15	14	13	56	47	44
Dunstable Town	42	17	9	16	52	43	43
Bedford Town	42	13	17	12	55	51	43
Burton Albion	42	17	9	16	52	53	43
Margate	42	15	12	15	62	60	42
Hillingdon Borough	42	13	14	15	61	54	40
Telford United	42	14	12	16	54	51	40
Chelmsford City	42	13	14	15	52	57	40
Kettering Town	42	11	17	14	48	52	39
Bath City	42	11	16	15	62	57	38
Weymouth	42	13	9	20	51	67	35
Dover	42	8	18	16	51	60	34
Wealdstone	42	12	9	21	61	82	33
Tonbridge AFC	42	11	11	20	45	70	33
Cambridge City	42	8	15	19	41	67	31
Stourbridge	42	10	9	23	38	72	29

First Division (North)

Redditch United	42	29	11	2	101	39	69
AP Leamington	42	27	10	5	85	31	64
Witney Town	42	24	9	9	66	40	57
Worcester City	42	24	8	10	90	49	56
Cheltenham Town	42	20	10	12	87	55	50
Barry Town	42	19	10	13	52	47	48
King's Lynn	42	17	14	11	52	48	48
Tamworth	42	18	11	13	65	43	47
Barnet	42	15	12	15	56	56	42
Oswestry Town	42	16	8	18	63	71	40
Enderby Town	42	16	6	20	48	51	38
Banbury United	42	15	8	19	58	67	38
Merthyr Tydfil	42	11	15	16	59	67	37
Bromsgrove Rovers	42	13	11	18	49	65	37
Milton Keynes City	42	15	6	21	51	63	36
Bury Town	42	12	11	19	52	72	35
Gloucester City	42	13	9	20	49	78	35
Kidderminster Harriers	42	13	8	21	54	70	34
Bedworth United	42	8	18	16	41	66	34
Corby Town	42	11	10	21	50	65	32
Wellingborough Town	42	9	11	22	42	68	29
Stevenage Athletic	42	6	6	30	46	105	18

First Division (South)

Minehead	38	27	8	3	102	35	62
Dartford	38	26	4	8	84	46	56
Romford	38	21	9	8	66	37	51
Salisbury	38	17	11	10	73	53	45
Hastings United	38	15	15	8	67	51	45
Poole United	38	20	2	16	57	57	42
Bexley United	38	14	13	11	62	53	41
Waterlooville	38	13	13	12	62	54	39
Basingstoke Town	38	13	12	13	69	71	38
Ashford Town	38	14	8	16	67	73	36
Canterbury City	38	11	13	14	53	60	35
Folkestone & Shepway	38	10	14	14	36	51	34
Metropolitan Police	38	9	14	15	46	58	32
Trowbridge Town	38	11	10	17	48	75	32
Guildford & Dorking United	38	9	13	16	43	50	31
Bognor Regis Town	38	6	17	15	44	72	29
Ramsgate	38	9	10	19	57	76	28
Crawley Town	38	9	10	19	46	66	28
Andover	38	9	10	19	42	62	28
Dorchester Town	38	11	6	21	45	69	28

1976-77

Premier Division

Wimbledon	42	28	7	7	64	22	63
Minehead	42	23	12	7	73	39	58
Kettering Town	42	20	16	6	66	46	56
Bath City	42	20	15	7	51	30	55
Nuneaton Borough	42	20	11	11	52	35	51
Bedford Town	42	17	14	11	54	47	48
Yeovil Town	42	15	16	11	54	42	46
Dover	42	13	16	13	46	43	42
Grantham	42	14	12	16	55	50	40
Maidstone United	42	13	14	15	46	50	40
Gravesend & Northfleet	42	13	13	16	38	43	39
AP Leamington	42	12	15	15	44	53	39
Redditch United	42	12	14	16	45	54	38
Wealdstone	42	13	12	17	54	66	38
Hillingdon Borough	42	14	10	18	45	59	38
Atherstone Town	42	14	9	19	41	49	37
Weymouth	42	16	5	21	53	73	37
Dartford	42	13	10	19	52	57	36
Telford United	42	11	12	19	36	50	34
Chelmsford City	42	9	13	20	56	68	31
Burton Albion	42	10	10	22	41	52	30
Margate	42	9	10	23	47	85	28

First Division (North)

Worcester City	38	32	5	1	97	22	69
Cheltenham Town	38	23	8	7	85	35	54
Witney Town	38	21	8	9	48	31	50
Bromsgrove Rovers	38	20	8	10	61	37	48
Barry Town	38	19	8	11	62	45	46
Cambridge City	38	17	10	11	68	43	44
Stourbridge	38	17	9	12	48	35	43
Kidderminster Harriers	38	17	6	15	74	65	40
Banbury United	38	15	10	13	51	47	40
Gloucester City	38	18	4	16	70	81	40
Enderby Town	38	15	9	14	50	44	39
King's Lynn	38	13	11	14	47	53	37
Corby Town	38	11	13	14	56	64	35
Tamworth	38	11	13	14	49	58	35
Merthyr Tydfil	38	12	6	20	60	69	30
Oswestry Town	38	8	10	20	30	60	26
Wellingborough Town	38	8	7	23	37	73	23
Dunstable	38	7	7	24	38	84	21
Bedworth United	38	5	10	23	28	68	20
Milton Keynes City	38	7	6	25	31	76	20

First Division (South)

Barnet	34	23	8	3	65	25	54
Hastings United	34	18	11	5	47	18	47
Waterlooville	34	19	6	9	50	25	44
Dorchester Town	34	16	11	7	48	30	43
Salisbury	34	15	11	8	57	39	41
Romford	34	18	5	11	47	32	41
Poole Town	34	17	7	10	40	35	41
Trowbridge Town	34	15	8	11	47	39	38
Crawley Town	34	14	9	11	53	42	37
Folkestone & Shepway	34	12	11	11	39	42	35
Basingstoke Town	34	12	10	12	51	43	34
Canterbury City	34	6	16	12	36	46	28
Bognor Regis Town	34	9	9	16	33	50	27
Tonbridge AFC	34	9	9	16	33	50	27
Metropolitan Police	34	5	12	17	37	61	22
Andover	34	4	11	19	17	49	19
Ashford Town	34	5	8	21	32	65	18
Aylesbury United	34	5	6	23	27	68	16

1977-78

Premier Division

Bath City	42	22	18	2	83	32	62
Weymouth	42	21	16	5	64	36	58
Maidstone United	42	20	11	11	59	41	51
Worcester City	42	20	11	11	67	50	51
Gravesend & Northfleet	42	19	11	12	57	42	49
Kettering Town	42	18	11	13	58	48	47
Barnet	42	18	11	13	63	58	47
Wealdstone	42	16	14	12	54	48	46
Telford United	42	17	11	14	52	45	45
Nuneaton Borough	42	15	14	13	38	36	44
Dartford	42	14	15	13	57	65	43
Yeovil Town	42	14	14	14	57	49	42
Hastings United	42	15	9	18	49	60	39
Cheltenham Town	42	12	14	16	43	52	38
Hillingdon Borough	42	13	9	20	45	54	35
Atherstone Town	42	10	15	17	41	56	35
Redditch United	42	15	5	22	40	55	35
AP Leamington	42	11	13	18	34	57	35
Minehead	42	11	12	19	43	48	34
Dover	42	9	13	20	41	63	31
Bedford Town	42	8	13	21	51	75	29
Grantham	42	11	6	25	40	66	28

First Division (North)

Witney Town	38	20	15	3	54	27	55
Bridgend Town	38	20	9	9	59	45	49
Burton Albion	38	17	11	10	48	32	45
Enderby Town	38	17	10	11	59	44	44
Bromsgrove Rovers	38	16	12	10	56	41	44
Banbury United	38	17	10	11	52	47	44
Kidderminster Harriers	38	16	11	11	58	41	43
Merthyr Tydfil	38	18	6	14	85	62	42
Cambridge City	38	14	12	12	56	45	40
Barry Town	38	14	11	13	58	48	39
Wellingborough Town	38	11	15	12	47	43	37
King's Lynn	38	12	13	13	55	55	37
Gloucester City	38	14	8	16	68	75	36
Corby Town	38	9	17	12	46	48	35
Dunstable Town	38	11	13	14	49	59	35
Stourbridge	38	9	15	14	52	53	33
Tamworth	38	10	11	17	37	48	31
Bedworth United	38	8	14	16	36	58	30
Milton Keynes City	38	5	11	22	26	74	21
Oswestry Town	38	6	8	24	29	85	20

First Division (South)

Margate	38	24	10	4	92	32	58
Dorchester Town	38	23	10	5	67	31	56
Salisbury	38	21	10	7	60	27	52
Waterlooville	38	19	13	6	66	36	51
Romford	38	17	15	6	58	37	49
Aylesbury United	38	20	7	11	56	42	47
Trowbridge Town	38	16	11	11	65	59	43
Chelmsford City	38	15	11	12	58	46	41
Folkestone & Shepway	38	16	9	13	64	56	41
Taunton Town	38	15	10	13	57	54	40
Addlestone	38	14	10	14	57	60	38
Crawley Town	38	14	9	15	61	60	37
Basingstoke Town	38	11	11	16	44	50	33
Tonbridge AFC	38	13	5	20	64	77	31
Ashford Town	38	9	13	16	39	60	31
Hounslow	38	10	10	18	43	62	30
Bognor Regis Town	38	9	8	21	52	69	26
Poole Town	38	8	10	20	43	68	26
Andover	38	4	12	22	30	68	20
Canterbury City	38	2	6	30	31	113	10

1978-79

Premier Division

Worcester City	42	27	11	4	92	33	65
Kettering Town	42	27	7	8	109	43	61
Telford United	42	22	10	10	60	39	54
Maidstone United	42	18	18	6	55	35	54
Bath City	42	17	19	6	59	41	53
Weymouth	42	18	15	9	71	51	51
AP Leamington	42	19	11	12	65	53	49
Redditch United	42	19	10	13	70	57	48
Yeovil Town	42	15	16	11	59	49	46
Witney Town	42	17	10	15	53	52	44
Nuneaton Borough	42	13	17	12	59	50	43
Gravesend & Northfleet	42	15	12	15	56	55	42
Barnet	42	16	10	16	52	64	42
Hillingdon Borough	42	12	16	14	50	41	40
Wealdstone	42	12	12	18	51	59	36
Atherstone Town	42	9	17	16	46	65	35
Dartford	42	10	14	18	40	56	34
Cheltenham Town	42	11	10	21	38	72	32
Margate	42	10	9	23	44	75	29
Dorchester Town	42	7	11	24	46	86	25
Hastings United	42	5	13	24	37	85	23
Bridgend Town	42	6	6	30	39	90	18

First Division (North)

Grantham	38	21	10	7	70	45	52
Merthyr Tydfil	38	22	7	9	90	53	51
Alvechurch	38	20	10	8	70	42	50
Bedford Town	38	19	9	10	74	49	47
King's Lynn	38	17	11	10	57	46	45
Oswestry Town	38	18	8	12	63	43	44
Gloucester City	38	18	8	12	76	59	44
Burton Albion	38	16	10	12	51	40	42
Kidderminster Harriers	38	13	14	11	70	60	40
Bedworth United	38	13	14	11	41	34	40
Tamworth	38	15	8	15	47	45	38
Stourbridge	38	15	7	16	64	61	37
Barry Town	38	14	9	15	51	53	37
Enderby Town	38	14	8	16	46	55	36
Banbury United	38	10	13	15	42	58	33
Wellingborough Town	38	13	6	19	50	71	32
Cambridge City	38	9	9	20	37	62	27
Bromsgrove Rovers	38	6	14	18	33	61	26
Milton Keynes City	38	7	9	22	37	87	23
Corby Town	38	5	6	27	40	85	16

First Division (South)

Dover	40	28	9	3	88	20	65
Folkestone & Shepway	40	22	6	12	84	50	50
Gosport Borough	40	19	11	10	62	47	49
Chelmsford City	40	20	7	13	65	61	47
Minehead	40	16	13	11	58	39	45
Poole Town	40	15	15	10	48	44	45
Hounslow	40	16	12	12	56	45	44
Waterlooville	40	17	10	13	52	43	44
Trowbridge Town	40	15	12	13	65	61	42
Aylesbury United	40	16	9	15	54	52	41
Taunton Town	40	16	9	15	53	51	41
Bognor Regis Town	40	17	7	16	58	58	41
Dunstable	40	18	4	18	57	55	40
Tonbridge AFC	40	15	10	15	43	47	40
Salisbury	40	13	10	17	47	51	36
Basingstoke Town	40	12	11	17	49	62	35
Addlestone	40	12	9	19	56	64	33
Andover	40	12	6	22	47	69	30
Ashford Town	40	10	10	20	28	53	30
Crawley Town	40	9	9	22	44	75	27
Canterbury City	40	6	3	31	31	98	15

1979-80

Midland Division

Bridgend Town	42	28	6	8	85	39	62
Minehead	42	22	15	5	70	42	59
Bedford Town	42	20	12	10	71	42	52
Kidderminster Harriers	42	23	6	13	81	59	52
Merthyr Tydfil	42	20	11	11	70	47	51
Enderby Town	42	21	8	13	62	50	50
Stourbridge	42	19	11	12	67	49	49
Alvechurch	42	17	14	11	78	60	48
Trowbridge Town	42	19	9	14	62	61	47
Bromsgrove Rovers	42	18	10	14	67	56	46
Barry Town	42	15	12	15	64	58	42
King's Lynn	42	15	11	16	48	55	41
Banbury United	42	13	14	15	56	56	40
Taunton Town	42	16	8	18	55	62	40
Witney Town	42	10	19	13	43	45	39
Bedworth United	42	12	15	15	40	42	39
Milton Keynes City	42	15	7	20	46	59	37
Gloucester City	42	10	14	18	55	68	32
Cheltenham Town	42	13	5	24	49	70	31
Wellingborough Town	42	9	7	26	54	106	25
Cambridge City	42	6	9	27	30	73	21
Corby Town	42	5	9	28	40	94	19

Southern Division

Dorchester Town	46	25	12	9	81	53	62
Aylesbury United	46	25	11	10	73	40	61
Dover	46	22	13	11	78	47	57
Gosport Borough	46	21	15	10	70	50	57
Dartford	46	21	14	11	66	45	56
Bognor Regis Town	46	20	15	11	66	38	55
Hillingdon Borough	46	19	16	11	64	41	54
Dunstable	46	17	19	10	93	64	53
Addlestone	46	20	13	13	72	57	53
Hastings United	46	19	15	12	74	65	53
Fareham Town	46	16	16	14	61	53	48
Waterlooville	46	17	12	17	67	64	46
Andover	46	16	13	17	65	65	45
Poole Town	46	16	13	17	49	64	45
Canterbury City	46	15	15	17	56	60	44
Hounslow	46	14	14	17	44	57	43
Margate	46	17	8	21	51	62	42
Folkestone & Shepway	46	14	11	21	54	63	39
Ashford Town	46	12	14	20	54	71	38
Crawley Town	46	13	11	22	55	72	37
Chelmsford City	46	9	18	19	47	69	36
Basingstoke Town	46	9	15	22	48	79	33
Salisbury	46	10	12	24	47	59	32
Tonbridge AFC	46	3	9	34	30	128	15

1980-81

Midland Division

Alvechurch	42	26	9	7	76	40	61
Bedford Town	42	25	11	6	63	32	61
Trowbridge Town	42	24	9	9	69	39	57
Kidderminster Harriers	42	23	9	10	67	41	55
Barry Town	42	21	9	12	60	40	51
Stourbridge	42	17	16	9	75	49	50
Enderby Town	42	21	8	13	71	47	50
Cheltenham Town	42	18	12	12	70	59	48
Bromsgrove Rovers	42	19	9	14	65	50	47
Corby Town	42	19	7	16	69	58	45
Bridgend Town	42	19	7	16	74	64	45
Minehead	42	19	7	16	54	60	45
Gloucester City	42	19	6	17	82	72	44
Merthyr Tydfil	42	15	12	15	60	50	42
Bedworth United	42	14	12	16	49	46	40
Banbury United	42	11	11	20	51	65	33
Taunton Town	42	10	9	23	48	68	29
Cambridge City	42	8	12	22	46	87	28
Witney Town	42	9	9	24	44	65	27
Wellingborough Town	42	10	7	25	43	91	27
Redditch United	42	11	4	27	54	92	26
Milton Keynes City	42	3	7	32	28	103	13

Southern Division

Dartford	46	26	14	6	76	39	66
Bognor Regis Town	46	25	13	8	95	43	63
Hastings United	46	24	14	8	87	43	62
Gosport Borough	46	24	12	10	84	52	60
Waterlooville	46	19	21	6	67	50	59
Dorchester Town	46	21	13	12	84	56	55
Dover	46	22	10	14	70	50	54
Poole Town	46	19	14	13	70	56	52
Addlestone & Weybridge	46	21	9	16	66	57	51
Dunstable	46	19	13	14	73	68	51
Aylesbury United	46	20	10	16	66	60	50
Hounslow	46	17	13	16	65	55	47
Hillingdon Borough	46	16	15	15	50	49	47
Basingstoke Town	46	16	14	16	69	58	46
Crawley Town	46	18	4	24	64	78	40
Ashford Town	46	12	15	19	55	76	39
Tonbridge AFC	46	12	15	19	44	68	39
Chelmsford City	46	13	12	21	54	78	38
Canterbury City	46	12	13	21	40	59	37
Salisbury	46	14	8	24	57	76	36
Folkestone	46	11	11	24	47	65	33
Margate	46	11	7	28	65	117	29
Fareham Town	46	5	18	23	31	73	28
Andover	46	6	10	30	41	94	22

1981-82

Midland Division

Nuneaton Borough	42	27	11	4	88	32	65
Alvechurch	42	26	10	6	79	34	62
Kidderminster Harriers	42	22	12	8	71	40	56
Stourbridge	42	21	10	11	69	47	52
Gloucester City	42	21	9	12	64	48	51
Bedworth United	42	20	10	12	59	40	50
Enderby Town	42	20	10	12	79	66	50
Witney Town	42	19	8	15	71	49	46
Barry Town	42	16	14	12	59	46	46
Corby Town	42	19	8	15	70	59	46
Merthyr Tydfil	42	16	12	14	63	54	44
Wellingborough Town	42	15	12	15	50	45	42
Bridgend Town	42	13	13	16	50	62	39
Bromsgrove Rovers	42	15	8	19	57	63	38
Bedford Town	42	12	13	17	45	54	37
Cheltenham Town	42	11	14	17	65	68	36
Taunton Town	42	12	8	22	46	76	32
Banbury United	42	11	8	23	63	91	30
Minehead	42	12	6	24	38	69	30
Cambridge City	42	10	8	24	38	80	28
Milton Keynes City	42	6	11	25	34	70	23
Redditch United	42	8	5	29	37	103	21

Southern Division

Wealdstone	46	32	8	6	100	32	72
Hastings United	46	31	9	6	79	34	71
Dorchester Town	46	21	18	7	76	41	60
Gosport Borough	46	26	8	12	76	45	60
Fareham Town	46	20	14	12	58	48	54
Poole Town	46	19	15	12	92	63	53
Waterlooville	46	22	9	15	75	53	53
Welling United	46	19	13	14	70	48	51
Addlestone & Weybridge	46	17	17	12	71	53	51
Chelmsford City	46	20	11	15	64	53	51
Aylesbury United	46	19	12	15	79	61	50
Basingstoke Town	46	18	12	16	75	61	48
Dover	46	19	8	19	61	63	46
Ashford Town	46	16	14	16	52	56	46
Tonbridge AFC	46	19	7	20	62	70	45
Dunstable	46	18	8	20	63	68	44
Salisbury	46	16	10	20	64	81	42
Hounslow	46	15	11	20	59	83	41
Hillingdon Borough	46	14	10	22	46	58	38
Canterbury City	46	10	16	20	49	78	36
Crawley Town	46	9	12	25	46	81	30
Folkestone	46	10	6	30	49	101	26
Andover	46	4	11	31	39	100	19
Thanet United	46	5	7	34	37	110	17

1982-83

Premier Division

AP Leamington	38	25	4	9	78	50	79
Kidderminster Harriers	38	23	7	8	69	40	76
Welling United	38	21	6	11	63	40	69
Chelmsford City	38	16	11	11	57	40	59
Bedworth United	38	16	11	11	47	39	59
Dartford	38	16	8	14	48	38	56
Gosport Borough	38	14	13	11	47	43	55
Fareham Town	38	16	7	15	73	82	55
Dorchester Town	38	14	12	12	52	50	54
Gravesend & Northfleet	38	14	12	12	49	50	54
Gloucester City	38	13	12	13	61	57	51
Witney Town	38	12	13	13	60	48	47
Alvechurch	38	13	8	17	60	66	47
Stourbridge	38	12	11	15	48	54	47
Corby Town	38	12	11	15	58	67	47
Hastings United	38	11	11	16	48	61	44
Enderby Town	38	11	9	18	44	62	42
Waterlooville	38	10	9	19	62	83	39
Poole Town	38	9	9	20	57	73	36
Addlestone & Weybridge	38	5	10	23	24	62	25

Midland Division

Cheltenham Town	32	22	5	5	65	29	71
Sutton Coldfield Town	32	21	7	4	62	24	70
Forest Green Rovers	32	21	3	8	68	32	66
Merthyr Tydfil	32	17	7	8	64	45	58
Willenhall Town	32	17	6	9	74	49	57
Oldbury United	32	16	6	10	52	49	54
Banbury United	32	15	3	14	59	55	48
Bridgend Town	32	12	11	9	46	37	47
Wellingborough Town	32	13	7	12	49	37	46
Bromsgrove Rovers	32	13	5	14	47	47	44
Dudley Town	32	12	7	13	40	45	43
Bridgwater Town	32	12	6	14	42	43	42
Aylesbury United	32	12	5	15	37	51	41
Redditch United	32	8	6	18	51	73	30
Taunton Town	32	5	7	20	30	64	22
Minehead	32	5	7	20	24	62	22
Milton Keynes City	32	0	4	28	22	90	4

Southern Division

Fisher Athletic	34	23	5	6	79	34	74
Folkestone	34	22	6	6	79	41	72
RS Southampton	34	21	7	6	66	30	70
Dunstable	34	19	5	10	57	39	62
Hillingdon Borough	34	14	11	9	41	30	53
Salisbury	34	14	10	10	59	49	52
Crawley Town	34	14	9	11	51	43	51
Ashford Town	34	13	10	11	51	41	49
Tonbridge AFC	34	14	5	15	57	57	47
Hounslow	34	11	12	11	46	47	45
Canterbury City	34	12	9	13	52	63	45
Cambridge City	34	12	5	17	56	63	41
Dover	34	11	7	16	35	52	40
Thanet United	34	10	5	19	30	61	35
Basingstoke Town	34	8	10	16	37	56	34
Woodford Town	34	6	9	19	29	57	27
Andover	34	6	8	20	28	53	26
Erith & Belvedere	34	5	9	20	26	62	24

1983-84

Premier Division

Team	P	W	D	L	F	A	Pts
Dartford	38	23	9	6	67	32	78
Fisher Athletic	38	22	9	7	80	42	75
Chelmsford City	38	19	9	10	67	45	66
Gravesend & Northfleet	38	18	9	11	50	38	63
Witney Town	38	18	6	14	75	50	60
King's Lynn	38	18	6	14	42	45	60
Folkestone	38	16	9	13	60	56	57
Cheltenham Town	38	16	7	15	63	56	55
Gloucester City	38	13	15	10	55	50	54
Hastings United	38	15	9	14	55	57	54
Bedworth United	38	15	9	14	51	55	54
Welling United	38	15	7	16	61	61	52
AP Leamington	38	14	9	15	73	83	51
Corby Town	38	12	14	12	55	54	50
Fareham Town	38	13	11	14	65	70	50
Alvechurch	38	12	12	14	56	62	48
Sutton Coldfield Town	38	10	14	14	49	53	44
Gosport Borough	38	6	15	17	31	64	33
Dorchester Town	38	4	8	26	40	69	20
Stourbridge	38	4	7	27	30	82	19

Midland Division

Team	P	W	D	L	F	A	Pts
Willenhall Town	38	27	4	7	100	44	85
Shepshed Charterhouse	38	25	5	8	88	37	80
Bromsgrove Rovers	38	20	8	10	73	43	68
Dudley Town	38	18	13	7	71	43	67
Aylesbury United	38	17	15	6	62	35	66
Moor Green	38	18	12	8	63	44	66
Rushden Town	38	17	12	9	68	42	63
Merthyr Tydfil	38	18	8	12	63	44	62
Redditch United	38	17	9	12	67	67	60
VS Rugby	38	15	12	11	68	51	57
Forest Green Rovers	38	15	12	11	67	51	57
Bridgnorth Town	38	16	9	13	64	52	57
Leicester United	38	12	9	17	58	58	45
Oldbury United	38	10	13	15	53	51	43
Coventry Sporting	38	11	7	20	40	67	40
Bridgwater Town	38	10	8	20	39	65	38
Wellingborough Town	38	7	9	22	43	80	30
Banbury United	38	6	11	21	37	78	29
Milton Keynes City	38	3	9	26	31	110	18
Tamworth	38	2	7	29	25	118	13

Southern Division

Team	P	W	D	L	F	A	Pts
RS Southampton	38	26	6	6	83	35	84
Crawley Town	38	22	9	7	68	28	75
Basingstoke Town	38	20	9	9	54	36	69
Tonbridge AFC	38	20	9	9	61	44	69
Addlestone & Weybridge	38	19	11	8	58	34	68
Poole Town	38	20	7	11	68	42	67
Hillingdon Borough	38	18	11	9	43	20	65
Ashford Town	38	19	5	14	65	47	62
Salisbury	38	17	8	13	61	48	59
Cambridge City	38	13	9	16	43	53	48
Canterbury City	38	12	9	17	44	52	45
Waterlooville	38	12	9	17	56	69	45
Dover Athletic	38	12	9	17	51	74	45
Chatham Town	38	11	10	17	46	56	43
Andover	38	12	6	20	35	54	42
Erith & Belvedere	38	11	9	18	43	68	42
Dunstable	38	10	8	20	38	65	38
Thanet United	38	9	8	21	40	65	35
Woodford Town	38	7	8	23	30	69	29
Hounslow	38	4	12	22	30	58	24

1984-85

Premier Division

Team	P	W	D	L	F	A	Pts
Cheltenham Town	38	24	5	9	83	41	77
King's Lynn	38	23	6	9	73	48	75
Crawley Town	38	22	8	8	76	52	74
Willenhall Town	38	20	8	10	57	38	68
RS Southampton	38	21	4	13	76	52	67
Welling United	38	18	11	9	55	38	65
Folkestone	38	19	6	13	70	54	63
Fisher Athletic	38	19	5	14	67	57	62
Chelmsford City	38	17	10	11	52	50	61
Shepshed Charterhouse	38	18	5	15	67	50	59
Corby Town	38	15	6	17	56	54	51
Bedworth United	38	14	8	16	48	52	50
Gravesend & Northfleet	38	12	12	14	46	46	48
Fareham Town	38	13	8	17	52	55	47
Alvechurch	38	11	7	20	53	59	40
Hastings United	38	11	7	20	46	71	40
Witney Town	38	9	12	17	51	58	39
Gloucester City	38	10	6	22	49	74	36
Trowbridge	38	10	5	23	45	83	35
AP Leamington	38	2	5	31	22	112	11

Midland Division

Team	P	W	D	L	F	A	Pts
Dudley Town	34	21	8	5	70	36	71
Aylesbury United	34	20	7	7	62	30	67
Hednesford Town	34	18	7	9	58	42	61
Moor Green	34	17	9	8	63	43	60
VS Rugby	34	17	9	8	59	41	60
Bromsgrove Rovers	34	16	10	8	53	42	58
Stourbridge	34	15	11	8	52	45	56
Redditch United	34	12	11	11	68	57	47
Sutton Coldfield Town	34	13	6	15	50	56	45
Bridgnorth Town	34	13	5	16	67	65	44
Coventry Sporting	34	11	9	14	45	52	42
Merthyr Tydfil	34	10	11	13	43	46	41
Rushden Town	34	10	7	17	42	52	37
Forest Green Rovers	34	9	10	15	49	65	37
Wellingborough Town	34	10	7	17	39	63	37
Oldbury United	34	10	6	18	52	66	36
Banbury United	34	9	5	20	33	59	32
Leicester United	34	3	6	25	17	62	15

Southern Division

Team	P	W	D	L	F	A	Pts
Basingstoke Town	38	24	9	5	61	22	81
Gosport Borough	38	22	6	10	78	41	72
Poole Town	38	20	12	6	69	38	72
Hillingdon	38	19	10	9	51	23	67
Thanet United	38	19	9	10	63	47	66
Salisbury	38	19	5	14	55	54	62
Sheppey United	38	18	6	14	49	45	60
Addlestone & Weybridge	38	16	9	13	68	54	57
Waterlooville	38	15	10	13	71	63	55
Canterbury City	38	15	7	16	61	64	52
Woodford Town	38	13	13	12	46	53	52
Tonbridge AFC	38	16	3	19	59	62	51
Andover	38	15	5	18	44	50	50
Dorchester Town	38	13	7	18	45	60	46
Cambridge City	38	11	11	16	59	71	44
Chatham Town	38	12	8	18	44	66	44
Ashford Town	38	10	9	19	54	69	69
Dunstable	38	8	10	20	35	56	64
Dover Athletic	38	7	7	24	39	78	28
Erith & Belvedere	38	6	8	24	36	65	26

1985-86

Premier Division

Welling United	38	29	6	3	95	31	93
Chelmsford City	38	20	10	8	68	41	70
Fisher Athletic	38	20	7	11	67	45	67
Alvechurch	38	19	9	10	71	56	66
Worcester City	38	19	9	10	64	50	66
Crawley Town	38	18	5	15	76	59	59
Shepshed Charterhouse	38	19	1	18	51	52	58
Aylesbury United	38	14	10	14	52	49	52
Folkestone	38	14	10	14	56	56	52
Bedworth United	38	14	8	16	44	49	50
Willenhall Town	38	12	13	13	51	44	49
Dudley Town	38	15	4	19	58	62	49
Corby Town	38	14	7	17	61	67	49
King's Lynn	38	12	10	16	39	42	46
Basingstoke Town	38	13	4	21	36	67	43
RS Southampton	38	11	9	18	44	61	42
Witney Town	38	11	6	21	44	74	39
Gosport Borough	38	10	8	20	42	66	38
Fareham Town	38	8	13	17	40	62	37
Gravesend & Northfleet	38	9	9	20	29	55	36

Midland Division

Bromsgrove Rovers	40	29	5	6	95	44	92
Redditch United	40	23	6	11	70	42	75
Merthyr Tydfil	40	21	10	9	60	40	73
VS Rugby	40	19	9	12	41	31	65
Stourbridge	40	15	14	11	62	49	59
Rusden Town	40	17	7	16	69	74	58
Bilston Town	40	15	12	13	60	48	57
Bridgnorth Town	40	13	18	9	56	45	57
Gloucester City	40	15	12	13	61	57	57
Grantham	40	16	7	17	46	59	55
Wellingborough Town	40	15	9	16	56	56	54
Sutton Coldfield Town	40	13	14	13	60	45	53
Hednesford Town	40	14	9	17	67	70	51
Forest Green Rovers	40	14	9	17	52	56	51
Mile Oak Rovers	40	14	8	18	56	73	50
Leicester United	40	13	10	17	41	48	49
Banbury United	40	13	8	19	38	55	47
Coventry Sporting	40	10	15	15	42	48	45
Moor Green	40	12	6	22	63	91	42
Leamington	40	10	6	24	40	77	36
Oldbury United	40	8	7	25	50	87	31

Southern Division

Cambridge City	40	23	11	6	87	41	80
Salisbury	40	24	8	8	84	51	80
Hastings Town	40	23	9	8	83	51	78
Dover Athletic	40	23	6	11	89	53	75
Corinthian	40	20	9	11	79	45	69
Tonbridge AFC	40	17	13	10	65	51	64
Dunstable	40	17	11	12	70	61	62
Ruislip	40	17	6	17	67	66	57
Erith & Belvedere	40	14	12	14	35	40	54
Waterlooville	40	16	6	18	52	58	54
Burnham & Hillingdon	40	16	6	18	44	59	54
Canterbury City	40	13	13	14	58	58	52
Trowbridge Town	40	13	13	14	57	63	52
Sheppey United	40	14	10	16	43	53	52
Thanet United	40	13	7	20	58	63	46
Woodford Town	40	12	10	18	49	62	46
Poole Town	40	12	7	21	55	63	43
Ashford Town	40	10	12	18	45	65	42
Chatham Town	40	8	15	17	53	70	39
Andover	40	10	8	22	52	92	38
Dorchester Town	40	5	8	27	35	94	23

1986-87

Premier Division

Fisher Athletic	42	25	11	6	72	29	86
Bromsgrove Rovers	42	24	11	7	82	41	83
Aylesbury United	42	24	11	7	72	40	83
Dartford	42	19	12	11	76	43	69
Chelmsford City	42	17	13	12	48	45	64
Cambridge City	42	14	20	8	68	52	62
Redditch United	42	16	14	12	59	54	62
Alvechurch	42	18	8	16	66	62	62
Corby Town	42	14	17	11	65	51	59
Worcester City	42	16	11	15	62	55	59
Shepshed Charterhouse	42	16	10	16	59	59	58
Bedworth United	42	15	12	15	55	51	57
Crawley Town	42	14	11	17	59	60	53
Fareham Town	42	11	17	14	58	49	50
Willenhall Town	42	13	11	18	48	57	50
Basingstoke Town	42	12	12	18	53	78	48
Witney Town	42	12	12	18	29	56	48
Gosport Borough	42	11	13	18	42	57	46
Salisbury	42	12	7	23	52	82	43
King's Lynn	42	9	13	20	48	72	40
Dudley Town	42	9	9	24	39	76	36
Folkestone	42	8	11	23	36	79	35

Midland Division

VS Rugby	38	25	5	8	81	43	80
Leicester United	38	26	1	11	89	49	79
Merthyr Tydfil	38	23	6	9	95	54	75
Moor Green	38	22	6	10	73	55	72
Halesowen Town	38	19	12	7	72	50	69
Hednesford Town	38	21	5	12	84	56	68
Gloucester City	38	19	5	14	77	59	62
Coventry Sporting	38	17	8	13	55	54	59
Forest Green Rovers	38	16	9	13	65	53	57
Stourbridge	38	16	7	15	56	56	55
Grantham	38	15	9	14	74	54	54
Banbury United	38	14	7	17	55	65	49
Buckingham Town	38	13	9	16	55	59	48
Bridgnorth Town	38	12	9	17	59	63	45
Wellingborough Town	38	13	6	19	55	76	45
Mile Oak Rovers	38	11	10	17	50	63	43
Sutton Coldfield Town	38	8	10	20	56	78	34
Bilston Town	38	8	7	23	37	76	31
Leamington	38	4	13	21	37	80	25
Rushden Town	38	1	10	27	42	124	13

Southern Division

Dorchester Town	38	23	8	7	83	42	77
Ashford Town	38	23	7	8	63	32	76
Woodford Town	38	22	6	10	72	44	72
Hastings Town	38	20	10	8	74	54	70
Dover Athletic	38	20	6	12	66	43	66
Gravesend & Northfleet	38	18	7	13	67	46	61
Tonbridge AFC	38	16	10	12	73	67	58
Erith & Belvedere	38	15	12	11	57	50	57
Chatham Town	38	16	9	13	53	46	57
Thanet United	38	14	14	10	56	50	56
Waterlooville	38	16	8	14	66	65	56
Trowbridge Town	38	15	9	14	77	65	54
Dunstable	38	13	9	16	60	57	48
Corinthian	38	11	12	15	56	65	45
Sheppey United	38	9	12	17	43	65	39
Andover	38	9	9	20	51	80	36
Burnham & Hillingdon	38	7	11	20	32	62	32
Poole Town	38	8	6	24	50	90	30
Ruislip	38	6	12	20	35	75	30
Canterbury City	38	8	5	25	46	82	29

1987-88

Premier Division

Aylesbury United	42	27	8	7	79	35	89
Dartford	42	27	8	7	79	39	89
Cambridge City	42	24	8	10	84	43	80
Bromsgrove Rovers	42	22	11	9	65	39	77
Worcester City	42	22	6	14	58	48	72
Crawley Town	42	17	14	11	73	63	65
Alvechurch	42	17	13	12	54	52	64
Leicester United	42	15	14	13	68	59	59
Fareham Town	42	16	11	15	51	59	59
Corby Town	42	16	8	18	61	64	56
Dorchester Town	42	14	14	14	51	57	56
Ashford Town	42	12	16	14	45	54	52
Shepshed Charterhouse	42	13	11	18	53	62	50
Bedworth United	42	12	14	16	49	64	50
Gosport Borough	42	10	17	15	39	49	47
Burton Albion	42	11	14	17	62	74	47
VS Rugby	42	10	16	16	52	57	46
Redditch United	42	10	13	19	55	63	43
Chelmsford City	42	11	10	21	60	75	43
Willenhall Town	42	9	12	21	39	76	39
Nuneaton Borough	42	8	13	21	58	77	37
Witney Town	42	8	11	23	45	71	35

Midland Division

Merthyr Tydfil	42	30	4	8	102	40	94
Moor Green	42	26	8	8	91	49	86
Grantham Town	42	27	4	11	97	53	85
Atherstone United	42	22	10	10	93	56	76
Sutton Coldfield Town	42	22	6	14	71	47	72
Halesowen Town	42	18	15	9	75	59	69
Gloucester City	42	18	14	10	86	62	68
Dudley Town	42	20	5	17	64	55	65
Forest Green Rovers	42	14	16	12	67	54	58
Banbury United	42	17	7	18	48	46	58
Bridgnorth Town	42	16	7	19	59	75	55
Buckingham Town	42	15	9	18	74	75	54
King's Lynn	42	16	6	20	53	63	54
Wellingborough Town	42	14	10	18	67	70	52
Rushden Town	42	14	9	19	69	85	51
Trowbridge Town	42	14	3	25	53	82	45
Bilston Town	42	12	8	22	52	87	44
Hednesford Town	42	11	10	21	50	81	43
Mile Oak Rovers	42	9	14	19	43	65	41
Coventry Sporting	42	11	8	23	46	83	41
Stourbridge	42	10	10	22	46	79	40
Paget Rangers	42	10	9	23	49	89	39

Southern Division

Dover Athletic	40	28	10	2	81	28	94
Waterlooville	40	27	10	3	88	33	91
Salisbury	40	24	11	5	71	33	83
Gravesend & Northfleet	40	20	12	8	60	32	72
Thanet United	40	17	13	10	60	38	64
Andover	40	17	13	10	64	58	64
Dunstable	40	17	12	11	78	56	63
Burnham	40	17	10	13	61	45	61
Bury Town	40	17	7	16	80	67	58
Erith & Belvedere	40	16	9	15	52	56	57
Sheppey United	40	14	10	16	58	52	52
Hastings Town	40	14	10	16	62	70	52
Tonbridge AFC	40	14	8	18	51	56	50
Poole Town	40	13	10	17	69	70	49
Baldock Town	40	12	12	16	44	53	48
Hounslow	40	11	8	21	41	76	41
Folkestone	40	9	11	20	47	76	38
Corinthian	40	9	10	21	49	67	37
Ruislip	40	5	13	22	33	80	28
Canterbury City	40	7	6	27	33	87	27
Chatham Town	40	7	5	28	39	88	26

1988-89

Premier Division

Merthyr Tydfil	42	26	7	9	104	58	85
Dartford	42	25	7	10	79	33	82
VS Rugby	42	24	7	11	64	43	79
Worcester City	42	20	13	9	72	49	73
Cambridge City	42	20	10	12	72	51	70
Dover Athletic	42	19	12	11	65	47	69
Gosport Borough	42	18	12	12	73	57	66
Burton Albion	42	18	10	14	79	68	64
Bath City	42	15	13	14	66	51	59
Bromsgrove Rovers	42	14	16	12	68	56	59
Wealdstone	42	16	10	16	60	53	59
Crawley Town	42	14	16	12	61	56	59
Dorchester Town	42	14	16	12	56	61	59
Alvechurch	42	16	8	18	56	59	56
Moor Green	42	14	13	15	58	70	55
Corby Town	42	14	11	17	55	59	53
Waterlooville	42	13	13	16	61	63	52
Ashford Town	42	13	13	16	59	76	52
Fareham Town	42	15	6	21	43	68	51
Leicester United	42	6	11	25	46	84	29
Redditch United	42	5	7	30	36	105	22
Bedworth United	42	4	7	31	36	102	19

Midland Division

Gloucester City	42	28	8	6	95	37	92
Atherstone United	42	26	9	7	85	38	87
Tamworth	42	26	9	7	85	45	87
Halesowen Town	42	25	10	7	85	42	85
Grantham Town	42	23	11	8	66	37	80
Nuneaton Borough	42	19	9	14	71	58	66
Rushden Town	42	19	8	15	71	50	65
Spalding United	42	17	13	12	72	64	64
Dudley Town	42	16	13	13	73	62	61
Sutton Coldfield Town	42	18	7	17	56	56	61
Willenhall Town	42	16	12	14	65	71	60
Forest Green Rovers	42	12	16	14	64	67	52
Bilston Town	42	15	7	20	63	71	52
Ashtree Highfield	42	12	15	15	57	62	51
Hednesford Town	42	12	15	15	49	57	51
Banbury United	42	10	14	18	53	74	44
Bridgnorth Town	42	12	7	23	59	77	43
Stourbridge	42	11	10	21	50	81	43
King's Lynn	42	7	13	22	31	67	34
Coventry Sporting	42	6	13	23	39	91	31
Wellingborough Town	42	5	15	22	39	72	30
Mile Oak Rovers	42	5	10	27	46	98	25

Southern Division

Chelmsford City	42	30	5	7	106	38	95
Gravesend & Northfleet	42	27	6	9	70	40	87
Poole Town	42	24	11	7	98	48	83
Bury Town	42	25	7	10	75	34	82
Burnham	42	22	13	7	78	47	79
Baldock Town	42	23	5	14	69	40	74
Hastings Town	42	21	11	10	75	48	74
Hounslow	42	21	6	15	75	60	69
Salisbury	42	20	5	17	79	58	65
Trowbridge Town	42	19	7	16	59	52	64
Folkestone	42	17	8	17	62	65	59
Corinthian	42	13	13	16	59	69	52
Canterbury City	42	14	8	20	52	60	50
Witney Town	42	13	11	18	61	71	50
Dunstable	42	11	14	17	42	57	47
Buckingham Town	42	12	10	20	56	79	46
Erith & Belvedere	42	11	10	21	48	63	43
Andover	42	11	9	22	56	90	42
Sheppey United	42	10	8	24	50	90	38
Thanet United	42	7	15	20	47	95	36
Tonbridge AFC	42	7	6	29	50	98	27
Ruislip	42	6	8	28	47	112	26

1989-90

Premier Division

Dover Athletic	42	32	6	4	87	27	102
Bath City	42	30	8	4	81	28	98
Dartford	42	26	9	7	80	35	87
Burton Albion	42	20	12	10	64	40	72
VS Rugby	42	19	12	11	51	35	69
Atherstone United	42	19	10	13	60	52	67
Gravesend & Northfleet	42	18	12	12	44	50	66
Cambridge City	42	17	11	14	76	56	62
Gloucester City	42	17	11	14	80	68	62
Bromsgrove Rovers	42	17	10	15	56	48	61
Moor Green	42	18	7	17	62	59	61
Wealdstone	42	16	9	17	55	54	57
Dorchester Town	42	16	7	19	52	67	55
Worcester City	42	15	10	17	62	63	54
Crawley Town	42	13	12	17	53	57	51
Waterlooville	42	13	10	19	63	81	49
Weymouth	42	11	13	18	50	70	46
Chelmsford City	42	11	10	21	52	72	43
Ashford Town	42	10	7	25	43	75	37
Corby Town	42	10	6	26	57	77	36
Alvechurch	42	7	5	30	46	95	26
Gosport Borough	42	6	5	31	28	93	23

Midland Division

Halesowen Town	42	28	8	6	100	49	92
Rushden Town	42	28	5	9	82	39	89
Nuneaton Borough	42	26	7	9	81	47	85
Tamworth	42	22	8	12	82	70	74
Barry Town	42	21	8	13	67	53	71
Spalding United	42	20	7	15	73	63	67
Sutton Coldfield Town	42	18	10	14	72	69	64
Stourbridge	42	17	12	13	73	61	63
Dudley Town	42	18	9	15	69	64	63
Stroud	42	16	13	13	75	62	61
Leicester United	42	17	5	20	66	77	56
Bridgnorth Town	42	13	14	15	68	73	53
King's Lynn	42	16	5	21	57	69	53
Grantham Town	42	14	10	18	57	63	52
Bedworth United	42	14	9	19	50	60	51
Hednesford Town	42	11	14	17	50	62	47
Bilston Town	42	11	14	17	40	54	47
Redditch United	42	11	13	18	57	64	46
Racing Club Warwick	42	11	11	20	45	66	44
Willenhall Town	42	9	9	24	37	66	36
Banbury United	42	9	9	24	46	83	34
Sandwell Borough	42	6	12	24	46	79	30

Southern Division

Bashley	42	25	7	10	80	47	82
Poole Town	42	23	8	11	85	60	77
Buckingham Town	42	22	10	10	67	46	76
Dunstable	42	20	14	8	56	38	74
Salisbury	42	21	9	12	72	50	72
Hythe Town	42	20	12	10	69	48	72
Trowbridge Town	42	20	9	13	79	64	69
Hastings Town	42	20	9	13	64	54	69
Bury Town	42	18	12	12	76	62	66
Baldock Town	42	18	11	13	69	52	65
Burnham	42	17	11	14	77	52	62
Fareham Town	42	14	14	14	49	53	56
Yate Town	42	16	6	20	53	52	54
Witney Town	42	16	6	20	54	56	54
Canterbury City	42	14	10	18	52	52	52
Margate	42	12	15	15	46	45	51
Folkestone	42	14	9	19	61	83	51
Andover	42	13	11	18	54	70	50
Hounslow	42	11	5	26	39	82	38
Erith & Belvedere	42	8	11	23	34	73	35
Corinthian	42	6	10	26	44	93	28
Sheppey United	42	6	7	29	35	83	25

1990-91

Premier Division

Farnborough Town	42	26	7	9	79	43	85
Gloucester City	42	23	14	5	86	49	83
Cambridge City	42	21	14	7	63	43	77
Dover Athletic	42	21	11	10	56	37	74
Bromsgrove Rovers	42	20	11	11	68	49	71
Worcester City	42	18	12	12	55	42	66
Burton Albion	42	15	15	12	59	48	60
Halesowen Town	42	17	9	16	73	67	60
VS Rugby	42	16	11	15	56	46	59
Bashley	42	15	12	15	56	52	57
Dorchester Town	42	15	12	15	47	54	57
Wealdstone	42	16	8	18	57	58	56
Dartford	42	15	9	18	61	64	54
Rushden Town	42	14	11	17	64	66	53
Atherstone United	42	14	10	18	55	58	52
Moor Green	42	15	6	21	64	75	51
Poole Town	42	12	13	17	56	69	49
Chelmsford City	42	11	15	16	37	68	48
Crawley Town	42	12	12	18	45	67	48
Waterlooville	42	11	13	18	51	70	46
Gravesend & Northfleet	42	9	7	26	46	91	34
Weymouth	42	4	12	26	50	88	24

Midland Division

Stourbridge	42	28	6	8	80	48	90
Corby Town	42	27	4	11	99	48	85
Hednesford Town	42	25	7	10	79	47	82
Tamworth	42	25	5	12	84	45	80
Nuneaton Borough	42	21	11	10	74	51	70
Barry Town	42	20	7	15	61	48	67
Newport AFC	42	19	6	17	54	46	63
King's Lynn	42	17	9	16	53	62	60
Grantham Town	42	17	7	18	62	56	56
Redditch United	42	16	10	16	66	75	58
Hinckley Town	42	16	9	17	72	68	57
Sutton Coldfield Town	42	15	11	16	56	65	56
Bedworth United	42	15	9	18	57	73	54
Bilston Town	42	14	9	19	69	79	51
Leicester United	42	14	10	18	65	77	51
Racing Club Warwick	42	12	13	17	56	65	49
Bridgnorth Town	42	13	9	20	62	74	48
Stroud	42	11	14	17	51	64	47
Dudley Town	42	11	13	18	48	73	46
Alvechurch	42	10	8	24	54	92	38
Willenhall Town	42	10	10	22	58	69	37
Spalding United	42	8	9	25	35	70	33

Southern Division

Buckingham Town	40	25	8	7	73	38	83
Trowbridge Town	40	22	12	6	67	31	78
Salisbury	40	22	11	7	63	39	77
Baldock Town	40	21	9	10	66	52	72
Ashford Town	40	22	5	13	82	52	71
Yate Town	40	21	8	11	76	48	71
Hastings Town	40	18	11	11	66	46	65
Hythe Town	40	17	9	14	55	44	59
Andover	40	16	6	18	69	76	54
Margate	40	14	11	15	52	55	53
Burnham	40	12	16	12	57	49	52
Bury Town	40	15	5	20	58	74	50
Sudbury Town	40	13	0	17	60	68	49
Newport IOW	40	13	9	18	56	62	48
Gosport Borough	40	12	11	17	47	58	47
Witney Town	40	12	11	17	57	75	47
Dunstable	40	9	15	16	48	63	42
Canterbury City	40	12	6	22	60	83	42
Erith & Belvedere	40	10	0	24	46	73	36
Fareham Town	40	9	9	22	46	74	36
Corinthian	40	5	12	23	34	78	27

1991-92

Premier Division

	P	W	D	L	F	A	Pts
Bromsgrove Rovers	42	27	9	6	78	34	90
Dover Athletic	42	23	15	4	66	30	84
VS Rugby	42	23	11	8	70	44	80
Bashley	42	22	8	12	70	44	74
Cambridge City	42	18	14	10	71	53	68
Dartford	42	17	15	10	62	45	66
Trowbridge Town	42	17	10	15	69	51	61
Halesowen Town	42	15	15	12	61	49	60
Moor Green	42	15	11	16	61	59	56
Burton Albion	42	15	10	17	59	61	55
Dorchester Town	42	14	13	15	66	73	55
Gloucester City	42	15	9	18	67	70	54
Atherstone United	42	15	8	19	54	66	53
Corby Town	42	13	12	17	66	81	51
Waterlooville	42	13	11	18	43	56	50
Worcester City	42	12	13	17	56	59	49
Crawley Town	42	12	12	18	62	67	48
Chelmsford City	42	12	12	18	49	56	48
Wealdstone	42	13	7	22	52	69	46
Poole Town	42	10	13	19	46	77	43
Fisher Athletic	42	9	11	22	53	89	38
Gravesend & Northfleet	42	8	9	25	39	87	33

Midland Division

	P	W	D	L	F	A	Pts
Solihull Borough	42	29	10	3	92	40	97
Hednesford Town	42	26	13	3	81	37	91
Sutton Coldfield Town	42	21	11	10	71	51	74
Barry Town	42	21	6	15	88	56	69
Bedworth United	42	16	15	11	67	63	63
Nuneaton Borough	42	17	11	14	68	53	62
Tamworth	42	16	12	14	66	52	60
Rushden Town	42	16	12	14	69	63	60
Stourbridge	42	17	8	17	85	62	59
Newport AFC	42	15	13	14	72	60	58
Yate Town	42	14	15	13	65	64	57
Bilston Town	42	15	10	17	56	67	55
Grantham Town	42	11	17	14	59	55	50
King's Lynn	42	13	11	18	61	68	50
Hinckley Town	42	14	8	20	61	87	50
Leicester United	42	12	13	17	56	63	49
Bridgnorth Town	42	12	12	18	61	74	48
Racing Club Warwick	42	11	14	17	45	61	47
Stroud	42	14	4	24	66	88	46
Redditch United	42	12	8	22	52	92	44
Alvechurch	42	11	10	21	54	88	43
Dudley Town	42	8	9	25	41	92	33

Southern Division

	P	W	D	L	F	A	Pts
Hastings Town	42	28	7	7	80	37	91
Weymouth	42	22	12	8	64	35	78
Havant Town	42	21	12	9	67	46	75
Braintree Town	42	21	8	13	77	58	71
Buckingham Town	42	19	15	8	57	26	69
Andover	42	18	10	14	73	68	64
Ashford Town	42	17	12	13	66	57	63
Sudbury Town	42	18	9	15	70	66	63
Sittingbourne	42	19	10	13	63	41	61
Burnham	42	15	14	13	57	55	59
Baldock Town	42	16	10	16	62	67	58
Salisbury	42	13	16	13	67	51	55
Hythe Town	42	15	10	17	61	62	55
Margate	42	13	16	13	49	56	55
Newport IOW	42	13	10	19	58	63	49
Dunstable	42	12	12	18	55	67	48
Bury Town	42	14	4	24	52	94	46
Witney Town	42	11	12	19	55	76	45
Fareham Town	42	12	8	22	45	71	44
Erith & Belvedere	42	11	10	21	44	67	43
Canterbury City	42	8	14	20	43	69	38
Gosport Borough	42	6	9	27	32	65	27

1992-93

Premier Division

	P	W	D	L	F	A	Pts
Dover Athletic	40	25	11	4	65	23	86
Cheltenham Town	40	21	10	9	76	40	73
Corby Town	40	20	12	8	68	43	72
Hednesford Town	40	21	7	12	72	52	70
Trowbridge Town	40	18	8	14	70	66	62
Crawley Town	40	16	12	12	68	59	60
Solihull Borough	40	17	9	14	68	59	60
Burton Albion	40	16	11	13	53	50	59
Bashley	40	18	8	14	60	60	59
Halesowen Town	40	15	11	14	67	54	56
Waterlooville	40	15	9	16	59	62	54
Chelmsford City	40	15	9	16	59	69	54
Gloucester City	40	14	11	15	66	68	53
Cambridge City	40	14	10	16	62	73	52
Atherstone United	40	13	14	13	56	60	50
Hastings Town	40	13	11	16	50	55	50
Worcester City	40	12	9	19	45	62	45
Dorchester Town	40	12	6	22	52	74	42
Moor Green	40	10	6	24	58	79	36
VS Rugby	40	10	6	24	40	63	36
Weymouth	40	5	10	25	39	82	23

Bashley had 3 points deducted

Midland Division

	P	W	D	L	F	A	Pts
Nuneaton Borough	42	29	5	8	102	45	92
Gresley Rovers	42	27	6	9	94	55	87
Rushden & Diamonds	42	25	10	7	85	41	85
Barri	42	26	5	11	82	49	83
Newport AFC	42	23	8	11	73	58	77
Bedworth United	42	22	8	12	72	55	74
Stourbridge	42	17	9	16	93	79	60
Sutton Coldfield Town	42	17	9	16	82	78	60
Redditch United	42	18	6	18	75	79	60
Tamworth	42	16	11	15	65	51	59
Weston-super-Mare	42	17	7	18	79	86	58
Leicester United	42	16	9	17	67	67	57
Grantham Town	42	16	9	17	60	73	57
Bilston Town	42	15	10	17	74	69	55
Evesham United	42	15	8	19	67	83	53
Bridgnorth Town	42	15	7	20	61	68	52
Dudley Town	42	14	8	20	60	75	50
Yate Town	42	15	5	22	63	81	50
Forest Green Rovers	42	12	6	24	61	97	42
Hinckley Athletic	42	9	11	22	56	89	37
King's Lynn	42	10	6	26	45	90	36
Racing Club Warwick	42	3	7	32	40	88	16

Southern Division

	P	W	D	L	F	A	Pts
Sittingbourne	42	26	12	4	102	43	90
Salisbury	42	27	7	8	87	50	88
Witney Town	42	25	9	8	77	37	84
Gravesend & Northfleet	42	25	4	13	99	63	79
Havant Town	42	23	6	13	78	55	75
Sudbury Town	42	20	11	11	89	54	71
Erith & Belvedere	42	22	5	15	73	66	71
Ashford Town	42	20	8	14	91	66	68
Braintree Town	42	20	6	16	95	65	66
Margate	42	19	7	16	65	58	64
Wealdstone	42	18	7	17	75	69	61
Buckingham Town	42	16	11	15	61	58	59
Baldock Town	42	15	9	18	59	63	54
Poole Town	42	15	7	20	61	69	52
Fareham Town	42	14	8	20	57	77	50
Burnham	42	14	8	20	53	77	50
Canterbury City	42	12	10	20	54	76	46
Newport IOW	42	9	16	17	44	56	43
Fisher Athletic	42	8	9	25	38	98	33
Andover	42	7	9	26	42	99	30
Dunstable	42	5	14	23	42	92	29
Bury Town	42	8	5	29	46	119	29

1993-94

Premier Division

Farnborough Town	42	25	7	10	74	44	82
Cheltenham Town	42	21	12	9	67	38	75
Halesowen Town	42	21	11	10	69	46	74
Atherstone United	42	22	7	13	57	43	73
Crawley Town	42	21	10	11	56	42	73
Chelmsford City	42	21	7	14	74	59	70
Trowbridge Town	42	16	17	9	52	41	65
Sittingbourne	42	17	13	12	65	48	64
Corby Town	42	17	8	17	52	56	59
Gloucester City	42	17	6	19	55	60	57
Burton Albion	42	15	11	10	57	49	56
Hastings Town	42	16	7	19	51	60	55
Hednesford Town	42	15	9	18	67	66	54
Gresley Rovers	42	14	11	17	61	72	53
Worcester City	42	14	9	19	61	70	51
Solihull Borough	42	13	11	18	52	57	50
Cambridge City	42	13	11	18	50	60	50
Dorchester Town	42	12	11	19	38	51	47
Moor Green	42	11	10	21	49	66	43
Waterlooville	42	11	10	21	47	69	43
Bashley	42	11	10	21	47	80	43
Nuneaton Borough	42	11	8	23	42	66	41

Midland Division

Rushden & Diamonds	42	29	11	2	109	37	98
VS Rugby	42	28	8	6	98	41	92
Weston-super-Mare	42	27	10	5	94	39	91
Newport AFC	42	26	9	7	84	37	87
Clevedon Town	42	24	10	8	75	46	82
Redditch United	42	19	11	12	79	62	68
Tamworth	42	19	7	16	82	68	64
Bilston Town	42	16	10	16	65	73	58
Stourbridge	42	17	6	19	71	75	57
Evesham United	42	16	8	18	50	60	56
Grantham Town	42	16	6	20	77	73	54
Bridgnorth Town	42	15	6	21	56	68	51
Racing Club Warwick	42	13	12	17	53	66	51
Dudley Town	42	13	10	19	64	61	49
Forest Green Rangers	42	12	12	18	61	84	48
Sutton Coldfield Town	42	12	8	22	53	75	44
Bedworth United	42	12	7	23	62	81	43
Hinckley Town	42	11	10	21	44	71	43
Leicester United	42	11	9	22	34	73	42
King's Lynn	42	9	11	22	47	72	38
Yate Town	42	10	6	26	48	86	36
Armitage	42	8	11	23	45	103	35

Southern Division

Gravesend & Northfleet	42	27	11	4	87	24	92
Sudbury Town	42	27	8	7	98	47	89
Witney Town	42	27	8	7	69	36	89
Salisbury City	42	26	10	6	90	39	88
Havant Town	42	27	4	11	101	41	85
Ashford Town	42	24	13	5	93	46	85
Baldock Town	42	26	7	9	76	40	85
Newport IOW	42	22	8	12	74	51	74
Margate	42	20	8	14	76	58	68
Weymouth	42	18	9	15	71	65	63
Tonbridge	42	19	5	18	59	62	62
Buckingham Town	42	14	14	14	43	42	56
Braintree Town	42	16	7	19	72	84	55
Fareham Town	42	12	12	18	54	75	48
Poole Town	42	13	6	23	54	86	45
Burnham	42	10	9	23	53	92	39
Fisher 93	42	9	10	23	52	81	37
Dunstable	42	9	7	26	50	91	34
Erith & Belvedere	42	9	5	28	40	72	32
Canterbury City	42	8	7	27	35	80	31
Wealdstone	42	6	7	29	45	95	25
Bury Town	42	3	5	34	36	121	14

1994-95

Premier Division

Hednesford Town	42	28	9	5	99	49	93
Cheltenham Town	42	25	11	6	87	39	86
Burton Albion	42	20	15	7	55	39	75
Gloucester City	42	22	8	12	76	48	74
Rushden & Diamonds	42	19	11	12	99	65	68
Dorchester Town	42	19	10	13	84	61	67
Leek Town	42	19	10	13	72	60	67
Gresley Rovers	42	17	12	13	70	63	63
Cambridge City	42	18	8	16	60	55	62
Worcester City	42	14	15	13	46	34	57
Crawley Town	42	15	10	17	64	71	55
Hastings Town	42	13	14	15	55	57	53
Halesowen Town	42	14	10	18	81	80	52
Gravesend & Northfleet	42	16	13	16	38	55	52
Chelmsford City	42	14	6	22	56	60	48
Atherstone United	42	12	12	18	51	67	48
VS Rugby	42	11	14	17	49	61	47
Sudbury Town	42	12	10	20	50	77	46
Solihull Borough	42	10	15	17	39	65	45
Sittingbourne	42	11	10	21	51	73	43
Trowbridge Town	42	9	13	20	43	69	40
Corby Town	42	4	10	28	36	113	21

Corby Town had 1 point deducted for fielding ineligible players

Midland Division

Newport AFC	42	29	8	5	106	39	95
Ilkeston Town	42	25	6	11	101	75	81
Tamworth	42	24	8	10	98	70	80
Moor Green	42	23	8	11	105	63	77
Bridgnorth Town	42	22	10	10	75	49	76
Buckingham Town	42	20	14	8	55	37	74
Nuneaton Borough	42	19	11	12	76	55	68
Rothwell Town	42	19	7	16	71	71	64
King's Lynn	42	18	8	16	76	64	62
Racing Club Warwick	42	17	11	14	68	63	62
Dudley Town	42	17	10	15	65	69	61
Bilston Town	42	17	8	17	73	64	59
Bedworth United	42	17	7	18	64	68	58
Evesham United	42	14	10	18	57	56	52
Hinckley Town	42	14	0	18	61	76	52
Stourbridge	42	15	7	20	59	77	52
Sutton Coldfield Town	42	12	10	20	62	72	46
Forest Green Rovers	42	11	13	18	56	76	46
Redditch United	42	8	14	20	47	64	38
Leicester United	42	10	8	24	51	99	38
Grantham Town	42	8	9	25	55	93	33
Armitage	42	2	5	35	35	116	11

Southern Division

Salisbury City	42	30	7	5	88	37	97
Baldock Town	42	28	10	4	92	44	94
Havant Town	42	25	10	7	81	34	85
Waterlooville	42	24	8	10	77	36	80
Ashford Town	42	21	12	9	106	72	75
Weston-super-Mare	42	18	13	11	82	54	67
Bashley	42	18	11	13	62	49	65
Weymouth	42	16	13	13	60	55	61
Newport IOW	42	17	10	15	67	67	61
Witney Town	42	14	14	14	57	57	56
Clevedon Town	42	14	13	15	73	64	55
Tonbridge Angels	42	14	12	16	74	87	54
Margate	42	15	7	20	60	72	52
Braintree Town	42	12	13	17	64	71	49
Wealdstone	42	13	8	21	76	94	47
Yate Town	42	11	13	18	57	75	46
Fisher 93	42	9	16	17	54	70	43
Bury Town	42	11	8	23	59	86	41
Erith & Belvedere	42	10	9	23	49	94	39
Poole Town	42	10	8	24	53	79	38
Fareham Town	42	10	8	24	46	91	38
Burnham	42	7	7	28	40	89	28

1995-96

Premier Division

	P	W	D	L	F	A	Pts
Rushden & Diamonds	42	29	7	6	99	41	94
Halesowen Town	42	27	11	4	70	36	92
Cheltenham Town	42	21	11	10	76	57	74
Gloucester City	42	21	8	13	65	47	71
Gresley Rovers	42	20	10	12	70	58	70
Worcester City	42	19	12	11	61	43	69
Merthyr Tydfil	42	19	6	17	67	59	63
Hastings Town	42	16	13	13	68	56	61
Crawley Town	42	15	13	14	57	56	58
Sudbury Town	42	15	10	17	69	71	55
Gravesend & Northfleet	42	15	10	17	60	62	55
Chelmsford City	42	13	16	13	46	53	55
Dorchester Town	42	15	8	19	62	57	53
Newport AFC	42	13	13	16	53	59	52
Salisbury City	42	14	10	18	57	69	52
Burton Albion	42	13	12	17	55	56	51
Atherstone United	42	12	12	18	58	75	48
Baldock Town	42	11	14	17	51	56	47
Cambridge City	42	12	10	20	56	68	46
Ilkeston Town	42	11	10	21	53	87	43
Stafford Rangers	42	11	4	27	58	90	37
VS Rugby	42	5	10	27	37	92	25

Midland Division

	P	W	D	L	F	A	Pts
Nuneaton Borough	42	30	5	7	82	35	95
King's Lynn	42	27	5	10	85	43	84
Bedworth United	42	24	10	8	76	42	81
Moor Green	42	22	8	12	81	47	74
Paget Rangers	42	21	9	12	70	45	72
Tamworth	42	22	3	17	97	64	69
Solihull Borough	42	19	9	14	77	64	66
Rothwell Town	42	17	14	11	79	62	65
Buckingham Town	42	18	9	15	74	62	63
Dudley Town	42	15	16	11	83	66	61
Stourbridge	42	17	8	17	60	63	59
Bilston Town	42	16	9	17	61	62	57
Sutton Coldfield Town	42	16	9	17	62	67	57
Grantham Town	42	17	5	20	71	83	56
Redditch United	42	14	11	17	57	77	53
Leicester United	42	13	13	16	58	72	52
Hinckley Town	42	14	7	21	62	83	49
Racing Club Warwick	42	10	13	19	67	90	43
Evesham United	42	11	6	25	59	94	39
Corby Town	42	9	7	26	52	95	34
Bury Town	42	8	8	26	57	95	32
Bridgnorth Town	42	7	6	29	53	112	27

Bedworth United 1 point deducted, King's Lynn had 2 points deducted

Southern Division

	P	W	D	L	F	A	Pts
Sittingbourne	42	28	4	10	102	44	88
Ashford Town	42	25	9	8	75	44	84
Waterlooville	42	24	8	10	87	44	80
Newport IOW	42	24	6	12	75	58	78
Braintree Town	42	24	8	10	93	70	77
Weymouth	42	24	4	14	75	55	76
Havant Town	42	23	11	8	73	42	74
Forest Green Rovers	42	22	8	12	85	55	74
Trowbridge Town	42	18	8	16	86	51	62
Yate Town	42	17	8	17	81	77	59
Margate	42	18	5	19	68	62	59
Witney Town	42	16	11	15	60	54	59
Weston-super-Mare	42	16	9	17	78	68	57
Cinderford Town	42	16	8	18	74	77	56
Fisher 93	42	14	13	15	58	59	55
Bashley	42	14	11	11	63	61	53
Clevedon Town	42	15	6	21	70	80	51
Tonbridge Angels	42	13	10	19	58	79	49
Fleet Town	42	14	5	23	58	79	47
Fareham Town	42	12	5	25	71	97	41
Erith & Belvedere	42	4	4	34	38	111	16
Poole Town	42	0	1	41	17	188	1

Braintree Town 3 points deducted, Havant Town had 6 points deducted

1996-97

Premier Division

	P	W	D	L	F	A	Pts
Gresley Rovers	42	25	10	7	75	40	85
Cheltenham Town	42	21	11	10	76	44	74
Gloucester City	42	21	10	11	81	56	73
Halesowen Town	42	21	10	11	77	54	73
King's Lynn	42	20	8	14	65	61	68
Burton Albion	42	18	12	12	70	53	66
Nuneaton Borough	42	19	9	14	61	52	66
Sittingbourne	42	19	7	16	76	65	64
Merthyr Tydfil	42	17	9	16	69	61	60
Worcester City	42	15	14	13	52	50	59
Atherstone United	42	15	13	14	46	47	58
Salisbury City	42	15	13	14	57	66	58
Sudbury Town	42	16	7	19	72	72	55
Gravesend & Northfleet	42	16	7	19	63	73	55
Dorchester Town	42	14	9	19	62	66	51
Hastings Town	42	12	15	15	49	60	51
Crawley Town	42	13	8	21	49	67	47
Cambridge City	42	11	13	18	57	65	46
Ashford Town	42	9	18	15	53	79	45
Baldock Town	42	11	8	23	52	90	41
Newport AFC	42	9	13	20	40	60	40
Chelmsford City	42	6	14	22	49	70	32

Midland Division

	P	W	D	L	F	A	Pts
Tamworth	40	30	7	3	90	28	97
Rothwell Town	40	20	11	9	82	54	71
Ilkeston Town	40	19	13	8	76	50	70
Grantham Town	40	22	4	14	65	46	70
Bedworth United	40	18	11	11	77	41	65
Solihull Borough	40	19	8	13	84	62	65
Bilston Town	40	18	10	12	74	57	64
Moor Green	40	18	7	15	88	68	61
Stafford Rangers	40	17	9	14	68	62	60
Raunds Town	40	16	11	13	61	66	59
Racing Club Warwick	40	16	10	14	70	72	58
Shepshed Dynamo	40	14	12	14	64	65	54
Redditch United	40	15	8	17	56	59	53
Paget Rangers	40	13	9	18	42	55	48
Dudley Town	40	12	10	18	70	89	46
Hinckley Town	40	11	11	18	39	63	44
Stourbridge	40	10	9	21	61	81	39
Evesham United	40	9	12	19	55	77	39
VS Rugby	40	9	9	22	49	81	36
Corby Town	40	8	8	24	49	88	32
Sutton Coldfield Town	40	7	9	24	29	85	30

Leicester United FC closed down and their record was expunged from the League table.

Southern Division

	P	W	D	L	F	A	Pts
Forest Green Rovers	42	27	10	5	87	40	91
St Leonards Stamcroft	42	26	9	7	95	48	87
Havant Town	42	23	10	9	81	49	79
Weston-super-Mare	42	21	13	8	82	43	76
Margate	42	21	9	12	70	47	72
Witney Town	42	20	11	11	71	42	71
Weymouth	42	20	10	12	82	51	70
Tonbridge Angels	42	17	15	10	56	44	66
Newport IOW	42	15	15	12	73	58	60
Fisher Athletic (London)	42	18	6	18	77	77	60
Clevedon Town	42	17	9	16	75	76	60
Fareham Town	42	14	12	16	53	70	54
Bashley	42	15	8	19	73	84	53
Dartford	42	14	10	18	59	64	52
Waterlooville	42	14	9	19	58	67	51
Cirencester Town	42	12	12	18	50	60	48
Cinderford Town	42	13	7	22	64	76	46
Trowbridge Town	42	11	11	20	50	61	44
Yate Town	42	12	8	22	55	87	44
Fleet Town	42	12	6	24	47	91	42
Erith & Belvedere	42	9	10	23	60	95	37
Buckingham Town	42	2	8	32	27	107	14

1997-98

Premier Division

Team	P	W	D	L	F	A	Pts
Forest Green Rovers	42	27	8	7	93	55	89
Merthyr Tydfil	42	24	12	6	80	42	84
Burton Albion	42	21	8	13	64	43	71
Dorchester Town	42	19	13	10	63	38	70
Halesowen Town	42	18	15	9	70	38	69
Bath City	42	19	12	11	72	51	69
Worcester City	42	19	12	11	54	44	69
King's Lynn	42	18	11	13	64	65	65
Atherstone United	42	17	12	13	55	49	63
Crawley Town	42	17	8	17	63	60	59
Gloucester City	42	16	11	15	57	57	59
Nuneaton Borough	42	17	6	19	68	61	57
Cambridge City	42	16	8	18	62	70	56
Hastings Town	42	14	12	16	67	70	54
Tamworth	42	14	11	17	68	65	53
Rothwell Town	42	11	16	15	55	73	49
Gresley Rovers	42	14	6	22	59	77	48
Salisbury City	42	12	12	18	53	72	48
Bromsgrove Rovers	42	13	6	23	67	85	45
Sittingbourne	42	12	8	22	47	66	44
Ashford Town	42	8	5	29	34	85	29
St Leonards Stamcroft	42	5	10	27	48	97	25

1998-99

Premier Division

Team	P	W	D	L	F	A	Pts
Nuneaton Borough	42	27	9	6	91	33	90
Boston United	42	17	16	9	69	51	67
Ilkeston Town	42	18	13	11	72	59	67
Bath City	42	18	11	13	70	44	65
Hastings Town	42	18	11	13	57	49	65
Gloucester City	42	18	11	13	57	52	65
Worcester City	42	18	9	15	58	54	63
Halesowen Town	42	17	11	14	72	60	62
Tamworth	42	19	5	18	62	67	62
King's Lynn	42	17	10	15	53	46	61
Crawley Town	42	17	10	15	57	58	61
Salisbury City	42	16	12	14	56	61	60
Burton Albion	42	17	7	18	58	52	58
Weymouth	42	14	14	14	56	55	56
Merthyr Tydfil	42	15	8	19	52	62	53
Atherstone United	42	12	14	16	47	52	50
Grantham Town	42	14	8	20	51	58	50
Dorchester Town	42	11	15	16	49	63	48
Rothwell Town	42	13	9	20	47	67	48
Cambridge City	42	11	12	19	47	68	45
Gresley Rovers	42	12	8	22	49	73	44
Bromsgrove Rovers	42	8	7	27	38	84	31

Hastings Town resigned from the League

Midland Division (1997-98)

Team	P	W	D	L	F	A	Pts
Grantham Town	40	30	4	6	87	39	94
Ilkeston Town	40	29	6	5	123	39	93
Solihull Borough	40	22	9	9	81	48	75
Raunds Town	40	20	8	12	73	44	68
Wisbech Town	40	20	7	13	79	57	67
Moor Green	40	20	7	13	72	55	67
Bilston Town	40	20	5	15	69	57	65
Blakenall	40	17	13	10	66	55	64
Stafford Rangers	40	18	6	16	57	56	60
Redditch United	40	16	11	13	59	41	59
Stourbridge	40	16	9	15	57	55	57
Hinckley United	40	15	11	14	59	56	56
Brackley Town	40	15	7	18	45	57	52
Bedworth United	40	15	5	20	50	73	50
Racing Club Warwick	40	11	9	20	49	56	42
Shepshed Dynamo	40	9	14	17	55	74	41
Sutton Coldfield Town	40	9	12	19	42	68	39
Paget Rangers	40	9	12	19	40	75	39
VS Rugby	40	8	12	20	53	93	36
Evesham United	40	7	9	24	47	94	30
Corby Town	40	2	8	30	41	112	14

Midland Division (1998-99)

Team	P	W	D	L	F	A	Pts
Clevedon Town	42	28	8	6	83	35	92
Newport AFC	42	26	7	9	92	51	85
Redditch United	42	22	12	8	81	45	75
Hinckley United	42	20	12	10	58	40	72
Stafford Rangers	42	21	8	13	92	60	71
Bilston Town	42	20	11	11	79	69	71
Solihull Borough	42	19	12	11	76	53	69
Moor Green	42	20	7	15	71	61	67
Blakenall	42	17	14	11	65	54	65
Shepshed Dynamo	42	17	12	13	62	54	63
Sutton Coldfield Town	42	17	8	17	46	57	59
Stourbridge	42	16	10	16	60	55	58
Evesham United	42	16	9	17	63	63	57
Wisbech Town	42	16	9	17	59	66	57
Weston-super-Mare	42	15	10	17	59	56	55
Bedworth United	42	15	9	18	63	52	54
Cinderford Town	42	13	8	21	61	74	47
Stamford AFC	42	13	7	22	60	75	46
Paget Rangers	42	11	12	19	49	58	45
VS Rugby	42	12	9	21	53	74	45
Racing Club Warwick	42	5	8	29	38	93	23
Bloxwich Town	42	1	2	39	26	151	5

Southern Division (1997-98)

Team	P	W	D	L	F	A	Pts
Weymouth	42	32	2	8	107	48	98
Chelmsford City	42	29	8	5	86	39	95
Bashley	42	29	4	9	101	59	91
Newport IOW	42	25	9	8	72	34	84
Fisher Athletic (London)	42	25	5	12	87	50	80
Margate	42	23	8	11	71	42	77
Newport AFC	42	21	6	15	83	65	69
Witney Town	42	20	9	13	74	58	69
Clevedon Town	42	20	7	15	57	55	67
Waterlooville	42	17	7	18	69	64	58
Dartford	42	17	7	18	60	60	58
Havant Town	42	13	14	16	65	70	53
Fleet Town	42	16	5	21	63	83	53
Tonbridge Angels	42	14	10	18	49	55	52
Trowbridge Town	42	14	6	22	55	69	48
Erith & Belvedere	42	11	13	18	47	68	46
Fareham Town	42	12	9	21	75	87	45
Cirencester Town	42	12	7	23	63	88	43
Weston-super-Mare	42	12	5	25	49	86	41
Baldock Town	42	10	5	27	53	81	35
Cinderford Town	42	6	5	31	40	112	23
Yate Town	42	5	7	30	44	97	22

Southern Division (1998-99)

Team	P	W	D	L	F	A	Pts
Havant & Waterlooville	42	29	7	6	86	32	94
Margate	42	27	8	7	84	33	89
Folkestone Invicta	42	26	8	8	92	47	86
Newport IOW	42	23	7	12	68	40	76
Chelmsford City	42	20	12	10	91	51	72
Raunds Town	42	19	13	10	87	50	70
Ashford Town	42	17	12	13	59	54	63
Baldock Town	42	17	9	16	60	59	60
Fisher Athletic (London)	42	16	11	15	58	54	59
Bashley	42	17	7	18	74	77	58
Witney Town	42	15	12	15	56	48	57
Cirencester Town	42	16	8	18	61	66	56
Sittingbourne	42	11	18	12	53	56	54
Dartford	42	14	10	18	48	53	52
Erith & Belvedere	42	15	7	20	48	64	52
Tonbridge Angels	42	12	15	15	48	59	51
St Leonards	42	14	8	20	57	72	50
Fleet Town	42	11	11	19	54	72	47
Corby Town	42	10	10	22	48	73	40
Yate Town	42	10	7	25	37	79	37
Andover	42	6	10	26	50	115	28
Brackley Town	42	6	8	28	41	105	26

1999-2000

Premier Division

	P	W	D	L	F	A	Pts
Boston United	42	27	11	4	102	39	92
Burton Albion	42	23	9	10	73	43	78
Margate	42	23	8	11	64	43	77
Bath City	42	19	15	8	70	49	72
King's Lynn	42	19	14	9	59	43	71
Tamworth	42	20	10	12	80	51	70
Newport County	42	16	18	8	67	50	66
Clevedon Town	42	18	9	15	52	52	63
Ilkeston Town	42	16	12	14	77	69	60
Weymouth	42	14	16	12	60	51	58
Halesowen Town	42	14	14	14	52	54	56
Crawley Town	42	15	8	19	68	82	53
Havant & Waterlooville	42	13	13	16	63	68	52
Cambridge City	42	14	10	18	52	66	52
Worcester City	42	13	11	18	60	66	50
Salisbury City	42	14	8	20	70	84	50
Merthyr Tydfil	42	13	9	20	51	63	48
Dorchester Town	42	10	17	15	56	65	47
Grantham Town	42	14	5	23	63	76	47
Gloucester City	42	8	14	20	40	82	38
Rothwell Town	42	5	14	23	48	85	29
Atherstone United	42	5	13	24	30	76	28

Eastern Division

	P	W	D	L	F	A	Pts
Fisher Athletic (London)	42	31	5	6	107	42	98
Folkestone Invicta	42	30	7	5	101	39	97
Newport IOW	42	25	7	10	74	40	82
Chelmsford City	42	24	8	10	74	38	80
Hastings Town	42	22	9	11	76	56	75
Ashford Town	42	21	9	12	70	49	72
Tonbridge Angels	42	20	10	12	82	60	70
Dartford	42	17	6	19	52	58	57
Burnham	42	15	9	18	55	64	54
Baldock Town	42	14	10	18	57	69	52
Erith & Belvedere	42	14	9	19	62	68	51
Witney Town	42	13	11	18	48	60	50
VS Rugby	42	13	11	18	58	79	50
Wisbech Town	42	14	7	21	58	66	49
Spalding United	42	14	6	22	52	71	48
Sittingbourne	42	13	7	22	48	75	46
Stamford	42	9	18	15	50	62	45
St Leonards	42	11	12	19	67	81	45
Raunds Town	42	11	12	19	44	63	45
Bashley	42	12	7	23	56	95	43
Corby Town	42	11	12	19	56	62	42
Fleet Town	42	8	8	26	54	104	32

Corby Town had 3 points deducted for fielding an ineligible player
Raunds Town gave notice to withdraw and take the place of the 2nd relegated Club. They then unsuccessfully sought re-election

Western Division

	P	W	D	L	F	A	Pts
Stafford Rangers	42	29	6	7	107	47	93
Moor Green	42	26	12	4	85	33	90
Hinckley United	42	25	12	5	89	47	87
Tiverton Town	42	26	7	9	91	44	85
Solihull Borough	42	20	11	11	85	66	71
Blakenall	42	19	12	11	70	46	69
Cirencester Town	42	20	8	14	72	64	68
Bilston Town	42	16	18	8	66	52	66
Cinderford Town	42	17	11	14	62	64	62
Redditch United	42	17	10	15	73	65	61
Gresley Rovers	42	14	15	13	54	49	57
Weston-super-Mare	42	16	9	17	55	55	57
Sutton Coldfield Town	42	13	17	12	49	52	56
Evesham Town	42	13	12	17	69	61	51
Bedworth Town	42	13	10	19	52	71	49
Rocester	42	12	12	18	63	78	48
Bromsgrove Rovers	42	13	7	22	59	72	46
Shepshed Dynamo	42	12	7	23	46	66	43
Paget Rangers	42	11	4	27	44	82	37
Racing Club Warwick	42	7	14	21	41	82	35
Stourbridge	42	10	3	29	45	101	33
Yate Town	42	3	3	36	28	108	12

2000-2001

Premier Division

	P	W	D	L	F	A	Pts
Margate	42	28	7	7	75	27	91
Burton Albion	42	25	13	4	76	36	88
King's Lynn	42	18	11	13	67	58	65
Welling United	42	17	13	12	59	55	64
Weymouth	42	17	12	13	69	51	63
Havant & Waterlooville	42	18	9	15	65	53	63
Stafford Rangers	42	18	9	15	70	59	63
Worcester City	42	18	8	16	52	53	62
Moor Green	42	18	8	16	49	53	62
Newport County	42	17	10	15	70	61	61
Crawley Town	42	17	10	15	61	54	61
Tamworth	42	17	8	17	58	55	59
Salisbury City	42	17	8	17	64	69	59
Ilkeston Town	42	16	11	15	51	61	59
Bath City	42	15	13	14	67	68	55
Cambridge City	42	13	11	18	56	59	50
Folkestone Invicta	42	14	6	22	49	74	48
Merthyr Tydfil	42	11	13	18	49	62	46
Clevedon Town	42	11	7	24	61	74	40
Fisher Athletic (London)	42	12	6	24	51	85	39
Dorchester Town	42	10	8	24	40	70	38
Halesowen Town	42	8	13	21	47	69	37

Bath City and Fisher Athletic (London) both had 3 points deducted

Eastern Division

	P	W	D	L	F	A	Pts
Newport IOW	42	28	10	4	91	30	94
Chelmsford City	42	27	9	6	102	45	90
Grantham Town	42	25	11	6	100	47	86
Histon	42	23	11	8	84	53	80
Baldock Town	42	23	10	9	81	44	79
Hastings Town	42	22	10	10	72	50	76
Stamford	42	20	11	11	69	59	71
Tonbridge Angels	42	18	11	13	79	58	65
Langney Sports	42	19	8	15	75	55	65
Rothwell Town	42	20	5	17	86	74	62
Corby Town	42	14	10	18	64	92	52
Ashford Town	42	15	4	23	53	83	49
Banbury United	42	12	11	19	57	54	47
Witney Town	42	12	11	19	55	71	47
Bashley	42	10	14	18	57	71	44
Dartford	42	11	11	20	49	67	44
Burnham	42	10	14	18	39	65	43
Wisbech Town	42	10	9	23	45	89	39
St Leonards	42	9	10	23	55	87	37
Erith & Belvedere	42	10	7	25	49	92	37
Sittingbourne	42	8	9	25	41	79	33
Spalding United	42	7	12	23	35	73	33

Burnham had 1 point deducted, Rothwell Town had 3 points deducted

Western Division

	P	W	D	L	F	A	Pts
Hinckley United	42	30	8	4	102	38	98
Tiverton Town	42	28	7	7	97	36	91
Bilston Town	42	27	9	6	88	48	90
Evesham United	42	27	5	10	86	46	86
Mangotsfield United	42	25	9	8	91	45	84
Solihull Borough	42	22	12	8	73	43	78
Redditch United	42	17	13	12	76	69	64
Weston-super-Mare	42	17	10	15	68	58	61
Atherstone United	42	16	11	15	64	58	59
Rochester	42	18	5	19	57	77	59
Cirencester Town	42	14	15	13	65	74	57
Rugby United	42	13	10	19	51	68	49
Gloucester City	42	12	11	19	76	86	47
Blakenall	42	13	10	19	54	64	46
Shepshed Dynamo	42	12	9	21	56	73	45
Bedworth United	42	12	9	21	38	60	45
Racing Club Warwick	42	13	6	23	46	77	45
Gresley Rovers	42	11	8	23	46	65	41
Cinderford Town	42	11	8	23	56	84	41
Sutton Coldfield Town	42	7	14	21	45	66	35
Paget Rovers	42	9	4	29	38	93	31
Bromsgrove Rovers	42	7	9	26	47	92	30

Blakenall had 3 points deducted

2001-2002

Premier Division

Kettering Town	42	27	6	9	80	41	87
Tamworth	42	24	13	5	81	41	85
Havant & Waterlooville	42	22	9	11	74	50	75
Crawley Town	42	21	10	11	67	48	73
Newport County	42	19	9	14	61	48	66
Tiverton Town	42	17	10	15	70	63	61
Moor Green	42	18	7	17	64	62	61
Worcester City	42	16	12	14	65	54	60
Stafford Rangers	42	17	9	16	70	62	60
Ilkeston Town	42	14	16	12	58	61	58
Weymouth United	42	15	11	16	59	67	56
Hinckley Town	42	14	13	15	64	62	55
Folkestone Invicta	42	14	12	16	51	61	54
Cambridge City	42	12	16	14	60	70	52
Welling United	42	13	12	17	69	66	51
Hednesford Town	42	15	6	21	59	70	51
Bath City	42	13	11	18	56	65	50
Chelmsford City	42	13	11	18	63	75	50
Newport IOW	42	12	12	18	38	61	48
King's Lynn	42	11	13	18	44	57	46
Merthyr Tydfil	42	12	8	22	53	71	44
Salisbury City	42	6	8	28	36	87	26

Eastern Division

Hastings Town	42	29	8	5	85	38	95
Grantham Town	42	29	6	7	99	43	93
Dorchester Town	42	26	10	6	81	36	88
Histon	42	23	8	11	83	49	77
Stamford	42	24	4	14	76	61	76
Fisher Athletic (London)	42	20	10	12	83	56	70
Eastbourne Borough	42	21	6	15	63	46	69
Dartford	42	18	5	19	62	66	59
Erith & Belvedere	42	18	3	21	75	79	57
Bashley	42	15	11	16	71	63	56
Burnham	42	15	10	17	52	54	55
Rugby United	42	16	6	20	55	67	54
Rothwell Town	42	14	8	20	46	66	50
Ashford Town	42	14	6	22	58	78	48
Banbury United	42	13	9	20	53	66	47
Chatham Town	42	13	8	21	56	87	47
Sittingbourne	42	14	4	24	46	69	46
Spalding	42	13	6	23	72	84	45
Tonbridge Angels	42	13	6	23	65	80	45
St Leonards	42	14	3	25	52	88	45
Corby Town	42	10	13	19	54	82	43
Wisbech Town	42	11	8	23	56	84	41

Western Division

Halesowen Town	40	27	9	4	85	24	90
Chippenham Town	40	26	9	5	81	28	87
Weston-super-Mare	40	22	10	8	70	38	76
Solihull Borough	40	20	11	9	75	42	71
Gresley Rovers	40	19	9	12	59	50	66
Sutton Coldfield Town	40	17	11	12	53	46	62
Mangotsfield United	40	17	10	13	74	54	61
Stourport Swifts	40	18	6	16	59	59	60
Atherstone United	40	16	8	16	61	59	56
Clevedon Town	40	15	11	14	57	58	56
Bedworth United	40	16	7	17	59	63	55
Evesham United	40	16	7	17	54	70	55
Cirencester Town	40	17	3	20	64	69	54
Gloucester City	40	14	10	16	48	63	52
Cinderford Town	40	14	9	17	54	67	51
Shepshed Dynamo	40	10	10	20	64	84	40
Bilston Town	40	11	7	22	50	72	40
Redditch United	40	11	6	23	47	77	39
Swindon Supermarine	40	11	4	25	52	76	37
Racing Club Warwick	40	8	11	21	38	63	35
Rocester	40	5	12	23	33	75	27

2002-2003

Premier Division

Tamworth	42	26	10	6	73	32	88
Stafford Rangers	42	21	12	9	76	40	75
Dover Athletic	42	19	14	9	42	35	71
Tiverton Town	42	19	12	11	60	43	69
Chippenham Town	42	17	17	8	59	37	68
Worcester City	42	18	13	11	60	39	67
Crawley Town	42	17	13	12	64	51	64
Havant & Waterlooville	42	15	15	12	67	64	60
Chelmsford City	42	15	12	15	65	63	57
Newport County	42	15	11	16	53	52	56
Hednesford Town	42	14	13	15	59	60	55
Moor Green	42	13	14	15	49	58	53
Hinckley Town	42	12	16	14	61	64	52
Bath City	42	13	13	16	50	61	52
Welling United	42	13	12	17	55	58	51
Grantham Town	42	14	9	19	59	65	51
Weymouth	42	12	15	15	44	62	51
Cambridge City	42	13	10	19	54	56	49
Halesowen Town	42	12	13	17	52	63	49
Hastings United	42	10	13	19	44	57	43
Ilkeston Town	42	10	10	22	54	92	40
Folkestone Invicta	42	7	7	28	57	105	28

Eastern Division

Dorchester Town	42	28	9	5	114	40	93
Eastbourne Borough	42	29	6	7	92	33	93
Stamford	42	27	6	9	80	39	87
Salisbury City	42	27	8	7	81	42	86
Bashley	42	23	12	7	90	44	81
King's Lynn	42	24	7	11	98	62	79
Rothwell Town	42	22	10	10	77	52	76
Banbury United	42	21	11	10	75	50	74
Tonbridge Angels	42	20	11	11	71	55	71
Histon	42	20	7	15	99	62	67
Ashford Town	42	18	9	15	63	57	63
Sittingbourne	42	15	8	19	57	69	53
Burnham	42	15	7	20	62	79	52
Fisher Athletic	42	15	5	22	57	80	50
Chatham Town	42	14	5	23	54	84	47
Newport IOW	42	12	6	24	53	87	42
Dartford	42	11	8	23	48	78	41
Erith & Belvedere	42	11	6	25	65	96	39
Corby Town	42	9	11	22	49	84	38
Fleet Town	42	8	8	26	34	80	32
Spalding United	42	4	6	32	40	108	18
St. Leonards	42	4	4	34	38	116	16

Western Division

Merthyr Tydfil	42	28	8	6	78	32	92
Weston-super-Mare	42	26	7	9	77	42	85
Bromsgrove Rovers	42	23	7	12	73	41	76
Solihull Borough	42	21	13	8	77	48	76
Gloucester City	42	22	9	11	87	58	75
Mangotsfield United	42	21	10	11	106	53	73
Redditch United	42	22	6	14	76	42	72
Rugby United	42	20	9	13	58	43	69
Gresley Rovers	42	19	10	13	63	54	67
Taunton Town	42	20	7	15	76	78	67
Sutton Coldfield Town	42	18	10	14	63	53	64
Evesham United	42	19	6	17	76	72	63
Clevedon Town	42	14	13	15	54	60	55
Cirencester Town	42	15	7	20	62	82	52
Cinderford Town	42	13	12	17	50	67	51
Shepshed Dynamo	42	12	6	24	48	76	42
Stourport Swifts	42	10	11	21	48	66	41
Bedworth United	42	11	7	24	46	74	40
Swindon Supermarine	42	11	5	26	52	85	38
Atherstone United	42	9	10	23	45	78	37
Rocester	42	9	10	23	34	74	37
Racing Club Warwick	42	3	9	30	33	104	18

2003-2004

Premier Division

Crawley Town	42	25	9	8	77	43	84
Weymouth	42	20	12	10	76	47	72
Stafford Rangers	42	19	11	12	55	43	68
Nuneaton Borough	42	17	15	10	65	49	66
Worcester City	42	18	9	15	71	50	63
Hinckley United	42	15	14	13	55	46	59
Newport County	42	15	14	13	52	50	59
Cambridge City	42	14	15	13	54	53	57
Welling United	42	16	8	18	56	58	56
Weston-super-Mare	42	14	13	15	52	52	55
Eastbourne Borough	42	14	13	15	48	56	55
Havant & Waterlooville	42	15	10	17	59	70	55
Moor Green	42	14	12	16	42	54	54
Merthyr Tydfil	42	13	14	15	60	66	53
Tiverton Town	42	12	15	15	63	64	51
Bath City	42	13	12	17	49	57	51
Dorchester Town	42	14	9	19	56	69	51
Chelmsford City	42	11	16	15	46	53	49
Dover Athletic	42	12	13	17	50	59	49
Hednesford Town	42	12	12	18	56	69	48
Chippenham Town	42	10	17	15	51	63	47
Grantham Town	42	10	15	17	45	67	45

Eastern Division

King's Lynn	42	28	7	7	90	35	91
Histon	42	26	10	6	96	41	88
Tonbridge Angels	42	27	7	8	82	46	88
* Eastleigh	42	27	4	11	88	40	82
Folkestone Invicta	42	20	15	7	91	45	75
Salisbury City	42	21	11	10	73	45	74
Stamford	42	20	11	11	63	45	71
Banbury United	42	19	10	13	65	57	67
Burgess Hill Town	42	19	7	16	67	54	64
Sittingbourne	42	18	8	16	61	55	62
Bashley	42	18	7	17	66	58	61
Ashford Town	42	15	9	18	51	53	54
Chatham Town	42	13	10	19	49	67	49
Fisher Athletic	42	13	10	19	61	81	49
Corby Town	42	12	9	21	44	75	45
Dartford	42	13	6	23	48	81	45
* Burnham	42	12	11	19	52	76	44
Hastings United	42	12	7	23	60	91	43
Newport IOW	42	11	7	24	42	69	40
Rothwell Town	42	9	11	22	30	47	38
Erith & Belvedere	42	7	10	25	45	84	31
Fleet Town	42	5	7	30	35	114	22

* Eastleigh and Burnham both had 3 points deducted.

Western Division

Redditch United	40	25	9	6	75	30	84
Gloucester City	40	24	7	9	77	46	79
Cirencester Town	40	24	4	12	73	40	76
Halesowen Town	40	20	13	7	64	40	73
Rugby United	40	21	8	11	57	40	71
Team Bath	40	21	6	13	62	41	69
Solihull Borough	40	19	9	12	50	31	66
Sutton Coldfield	40	16	15	9	52	38	63
Bromsgrove Rovers	40	16	11	13	60	48	59
Ilkeston Town	40	16	10	14	58	59	58
Clevedon Town	40	16	5	19	55	59	53
Gresley Rovers	40	15	7	18	52	60	52
Mangotsfield United	40	14	8	18	70	70	50
Evesham United	40	15	5	20	56	57	50
Taunton Town	40	14	8	18	50	55	50
Yate Town	40	11	9	20	51	79	42
Swindon Supermarine	40	10	9	21	41	69	39
Stourport Swifts	40	9	11	20	43	62	38
Bedworth United	40	8	12	20	39	61	36
Cinderford Town	40	7	9	24	50	94	30
Shepshed Dynamo	40	5	13	22	31	87	28

2004-2005

Premier Division

Histon	42	24	6	12	93	57	78
Chippenham Town	42	22	9	11	81	55	75
Merthyr Tydfil	42	19	14	9	62	47	71
Hednesford Town	42	20	10	12	68	40	70
Bedford Town	42	19	12	11	70	52	69
Bath City	42	19	12	11	57	43	69
Cirencester Town	42	19	11	12	63	52	68
Tiverton Town	42	18	13	11	70	55	67
Halesowen Town	42	19	9	14	64	52	66
Aylesbury United	42	20	3	19	67	66	63
King's Lynn	42	19	4	19	78	69	61
Chesham United	42	18	5	19	84	82	59
Grantham Town	42	17	7	18	57	55	58
Team Bath	42	14	12	16	54	68	54
Gloucester City	42	12	17	13	63	61	53
Rugby United	42	13	12	17	48	60	51
Banbury United	42	13	9	20	56	69	48
Hitchin Town	42	13	9	20	55	77	48
Hemel Hempstead Town	42	11	10	21	60	88	43
Dunstable Town	42	11	6	25	56	98	39
Stamford	42	6	18	18	40	60	36
Solihull Borough	42	10	4	28	45	85	34

Eastern Division

Fisher Athletic	42	30	6	6	96	41	96
East Thurrock United	42	25	12	5	92	38	87
Maldon Town	42	27	6	9	92	51	87
Uxbridge	42	26	7	9	87	37	85
Wivenhoe Town	42	21	11	10	74	49	74
Barking & East Ham United	42	20	10	12	63	37	70
Boreham Wood	42	19	9	14	80	61	66
Barton Rovers	42	20	4	18	76	72	64
Waltham Forest	42	16	9	17	68	61	57
Leighton Town	42	13	15	14	57	59	54
Chatham Town	42	15	9	18	53	63	54
Wingate & Finchley	42	15	8	19	60	75	53
Arlesey Town	42	14	10	18	53	67	52
Beaconsfield SYCOB	42	12	12	18	54	65	48
Harlow Town	42	13	8	21	53	65	47
Dartford	42	11	13	18	58	75	46
Aveley	42	12	9	21	57	69	45
Berkhamsted Town	42	15	7	20	66	101	45
Sittingbourne	42	10	12	20	53	70	42
Great Wakering Rovers	42	9	11	22	45	78	38
Erith & Belvedere	42	11	7	24	56	92	37
Tilbury	42	6	9	27	41	108	27

Berkhamsted Town had 7 points deducted.
Erith & Belvedere had 3 points deducted.

Western Division

Mangotsfield United	42	24	11	7	89	49	83
Yate Town	42	24	9	9	83	40	81
Evesham United	42	23	10	9	66	31	79
Clevedon Town	42	24	6	12	82	49	78
Bromsgrove Rovers	42	19	15	8	60	42	72
Ashford Town (Middlesex)	42	17	13	12	63	46	64
Brackley Town	42	18	10	14	69	53	64
Paulton Rovers	42	18	7	17	62	61	61
Burnham	42	17	7	18	64	64	58
Rothwell Town	42	16	10	16	57	57	58
Thame United	42	17	6	19	58	69	57
Corby Town	42	14	12	16	52	52	54
Marlow	42	13	14	15	58	67	53
Stourport Swifts	42	15	7	20	62	63	52
Bedworth United	42	15	7	20	51	60	52
Cinderford Town	42	13	12	17	50	64	51
Taunton Town	42	14	8	20	66	75	50
Sutton Coldfield	42	16	11	15	54	61	48
Swindon Supermarine	42	12	12	18	43	60	48
Bracknell Town	42	10	13	19	53	75	43
Oxford City	42	11	8	23	49	71	41
Egham Town	42	6	4	32	25	97	22

Sutton Coldfield had 11 points deducted.

FOOTBALL CONFERENCE

1979-80

Altrincham	38	24	8	6	79	35	56
Weymouth	38	22	10	6	73	37	54
Worcester City	38	19	11	8	53	36	49
Boston United	38	16	13	9	52	43	45
Gravesend & Northfleet	38	17	10	11	49	44	44
Maidstone United	38	16	11	11	54	37	43
Kettering Town	38	15	13	10	55	50	43
Northwich Victoria	38	16	10	12	50	38	42
Bangor City	38	14	14	10	41	46	42
Nuneaton Borough	38	13	13	12	58	44	39
Scarborough	38	12	15	11	47	38	39
Yeovil Town	38	13	10	15	46	49	36
Telford United	38	13	8	17	52	60	34
Barrow	38	14	6	18	47	55	34
Wealdstone	38	9	15	14	42	54	33
Bath City	38	10	12	16	43	69	32
Barnet	38	10	10	18	32	48	30
AP Leamington	38	7	11	20	32	63	25
Stafford Rangers	38	6	10	22	41	57	22
Redditch United	38	5	8	25	26	69	18

1980-81

Altrincham	38	23	8	7	72	41	54
Kettering Town	38	21	9	8	66	37	51
Scarborough	38	17	13	8	49	29	47
Northwich Victoria	38	17	11	10	53	40	45
Weymouth	38	19	6	13	54	40	44
Bath City	38	16	10	12	51	32	42
Maidstone United	38	16	9	13	64	53	41
Boston United	38	16	9	13	63	58	41
Barrow	38	15	8	15	50	49	38
Frickley Athletic	38	15	8	15	61	62	38
Stafford Rangers	38	11	15	12	56	56	37
Worcester City	38	14	7	17	47	54	35
Telford United	38	13	9	16	47	59	35
Yeovil Town	38	14	6	18	60	64	34
Gravesend & Northfleet	38	13	8	17	48	55	34
AP Leamington	38	10	11	17	47	66	31
Barnet	38	12	7	19	39	64	31
Nuneaton Borough	38	10	9	19	49	65	29
Wealdstone	38	9	11	18	37	56	29
Bangor City	38	6	12	20	35	68	24

1981-82

Runcorn	42	28	9	5	75	37	93
Enfield	42	26	8	8	90	46	86
Telford United	42	23	8	11	70	51	77
Worcester City	42	21	8	13	70	60	71
Dagenham	42	19	12	11	69	51	69
Northwich Victoria	42	20	9	13	56	46	69
Scarborough	42	19	11	12	65	52	68
Barrow	42	18	11	13	59	50	65
Weymouth	42	18	9	15	56	47	63
Boston United	42	17	11	14	61	57	62
Altrincham	42	14	13	15	66	56	55
Bath City	42	15	10	17	50	57	55
Yeovil Town	42	14	11	17	56	68	53
Stafford Rangers	42	12	16	14	48	47	52
Frickley Athletic	42	14	10	18	47	60	52
Maidstone United	42	11	15	16	55	59	48
Trowbridge Town	42	12	11	19	38	54	47
Barnet	42	9	14	19	36	52	41
Kettering Town	42	9	13	20	64	76	40
Gravesend & Northfleet	42	10	10	22	51	69	40
Dartford	42	10	9	23	47	69	39
AP Leamington	42	4	10	28	40	105	22

1982-83

Enfield	42	25	9	8	95	48	84
Maidstone United	42	25	8	9	83	34	83
Wealdstone	42	22	13	7	80	41	79
Runcorn	42	22	8	12	73	53	74
Boston United	42	20	12	10	77	57	72
Telford United	42	20	11	11	69	48	71
Weymouth	42	20	10	12	63	48	70
Northwich Victoria	42	18	10	14	68	63	64
Scarborough	42	17	12	13	71	58	63
Bath City	42	17	9	16	58	55	60
Nuneaton Borough	42	15	13	14	57	60	58
Altrincham	42	15	10	17	62	56	55
Bangor City	42	14	13	15	71	77	55
Dagenham	42	12	15	15	60	65	51
Barnet	42	16	3	23	55	78	51
Frickley Athletic	42	12	13	17	66	77	49
Worcester City	42	12	10	20	58	87	46
Trowbridge Town	42	12	7	23	56	88	43
Kettering Town	42	11	7	24	69	99	40
Yeovil Town	42	11	7	24	63	99	40
Barrow	42	8	12	22	46	74	36
Stafford Rangers	42	5	14	23	40	75	29

1983-84

Maidstone United	42	23	13	6	71	34	70
Nuneaton Borough	42	24	11	7	70	40	69
Altrincham	42	23	9	10	64	39	65
Wealdstone	42	21	14	7	75	36	62
Runcorn	42	20	13	9	61	45	62
Bath City	42	17	12	13	60	48	53
Northwich Victoria	42	16	14	12	54	47	51
Worcester City	42	15	13	14	64	55	49
Barnet	42	16	10	16	55	58	49
Kidderminster Harriers	42	14	14	14	54	61	49
Telford United	42	17	11	14	50	58	49
Frickley Athletic	42	17	10	15	68	56	48
Scarborough	42	14	16	12	52	55	48
Enfield	42	14	9	19	61	58	43
Weymouth	42	13	8	21	54	65	42
Gateshead	42	12	13	17	59	73	42
Boston United	42	13	12	17	66	80	41
Dagenham	42	14	8	20	57	69	40
Kettering Town	42	12	9	21	53	67	37
Yeovil Town	42	12	8	22	55	77	35
Bangor City	42	10	6	26	54	82	29
Trowbridge Town	42	5	7	30	33	87	19

2 points awarded for a Home win, 3 points awarded for an Away win, 1 point awarded for any Draw

1984-85

Wealdstone	42	20	10	12	64	54	62
Nuneaton Borough	42	19	14	9	85	53	58
Dartford	42	17	13	12	57	48	57
Bath City	42	21	9	12	52	49	57
Altrincham	42	21	6	15	63	47	56
Scarborough	42	17	13	12	69	62	54
Enfield	42	17	13	12	84	61	53
Kidderminster Harriers	42	17	8	17	79	77	51
Northwich Victoria	42	16	11	15	50	46	50
Telford United	42	15	14	13	59	54	49
Frickley Athletic	42	18	7	17	65	71	49
Kettering Town	42	15	12	15	68	59	48
Maidstone United	42	15	13	14	58	51	48
Runcorn	42	13	15	14	48	47	48
Barnet	42	15	11	16	59	52	47
Weymouth	42	15	13	14	70	66	45
Boston United	42	15	10	17	69	69	45
Barrow	42	11	16	15	47	57	43
Dagenham	42	13	10	19	47	67	41
Worcester City	42	12	9	21	55	84	38
Gateshead	42	9	12	21	51	82	33
Yeovil Town	42	6	11	25	44	87	25

2 points awarded for a Home win, 3 points awarded for an Away win, 1 point awarded for any Draw.   Gateshead had 1 point deducted

1985-86

Team	P	W	D	L	F	A	Pts
Enfield	42	27	10	5	94	47	76
Frickley Athletic	42	25	10	7	78	50	69
Kidderminster Harriers	42	24	7	11	99	62	67
Altrincham	42	22	11	9	70	49	63
Weymouth	42	19	15	8	75	60	61
Runcorn	42	19	14	9	70	44	60
Stafford Rangers	42	19	13	10	61	54	60
Telford United	42	18	10	14	68	66	51
Kettering Town	42	15	15	12	55	53	49
Wealdstone	42	16	9	17	57	56	47
Cheltenham Town	42	16	11	15	69	69	46
Bath City	42	13	11	18	53	54	45
Boston United	42	16	7	19	66	76	44
Barnet	42	13	11	18	56	60	41
Scarborough	42	13	11	18	54	66	40
Northwich Victoria	42	10	12	20	42	54	37
Maidstone United	42	9	16	17	57	66	36
Nuneaton Borough	42	13	5	24	58	73	36
Dagenham	42	10	12	20	48	66	36
Wycombe Wanderers	42	10	13	19	55	84	36
Dartford	42	8	9	25	51	82	26
Barrow	42	7	8	27	41	86	24

2 points awarded for a Home win; 3 points awarded for an Away win;
1 point awarded for any Draw

1986-87

Team	P	W	D	L	F	A	Pts
Scarborough	42	27	10	5	64	33	91
Barnet	42	25	10	7	86	39	85
Maidstone United	42	21	10	11	71	48	73
Enfield	42	21	7	14	66	47	70
Altrincham	42	18	15	9	66	53	69
Boston United	42	21	6	15	82	74	69
Sutton United	42	19	11	12	81	51	68
Runcorn	42	18	13	11	71	58	67
Telford United	42	18	10	14	69	59	64
Bath City	42	17	12	13	63	62	63
Cheltenham Town	42	16	13	13	64	50	61
Kidderminster Harriers	42	17	4	21	77	81	55
Stafford Rangers	42	14	11	17	58	60	53
Weymouth	42	13	12	17	68	77	51
Dagenham	42	14	7	21	56	72	49
Kettering Town	42	12	11	19	54	66	47
Northwich Victoria	42	10	14	18	53	69	44
Nuneaton Borough	42	10	14	18	48	73	44
Wealdstone	42	11	10	21	50	70	43
Welling United	42	10	10	22	61	84	40
Frickley Athletic	42	7	11	24	47	82	32
Gateshead	42	6	13	23	48	95	31

1987-88

Team	P	W	D	L	F	A	Pts
Lincoln City	42	24	10	8	86	48	82
Barnet	42	23	11	8	93	45	80
Kettering Town	42	22	9	11	68	48	75
Runcorn	42	21	11	10	68	47	74
Telford United	42	20	10	12	65	50	70
Stafford Rangers	42	20	9	13	79	58	69
Kidderminster Harriers	42	18	15	9	75	66	69
Sutton United	42	16	18	8	77	54	66
Maidstone United	42	18	9	15	79	64	63
Weymouth	42	18	9	15	53	43	63
Macclesfield Town	42	18	9	15	64	62	63
Enfield	42	15	10	17	68	78	55
Cheltenham Town	42	11	20	11	64	67	53
Altrincham	42	14	10	18	59	59	52
Fisher Athletic	42	13	13	16	58	61	52
Boston United	42	14	7	21	60	75	49
Northwich Victoria	42	10	17	15	46	57	47
Wycombe Wanderers	42	11	13	18	50	76	46
Welling United	42	11	9	22	50	72	42
Bath City	42	9	10	23	48	76	37
Wealdstone	42	5	17	20	39	76	32
Dagenham	42	5	6	31	37	104	21

1988-89

Team	P	W	D	L	F	A	Pts
Maidstone United	40	25	9	6	92	46	84
Kettering Town	40	23	7	10	56	39	76
Boston United	40	22	8	10	61	51	74
Wycombe Wanderers	40	20	11	9	68	52	71
Kidderminster Harriers	40	21	6	13	68	57	69
Runcorn	40	19	8	13	77	53	65
Macclesfield Town	40	17	10	13	63	57	61
Barnet	40	18	7	15	64	69	61
Yeovil Town	40	15	11	14	68	67	56
Northwich Victoria	40	14	11	15	64	65	53
Welling United	40	14	11	15	45	46	53
Sutton United	40	12	15	13	64	54	51
Enfield	40	14	8	18	62	67	50
Altrincham	40	13	10	17	51	61	49
Cheltenham Town	40	12	12	16	55	58	48
Telford United	40	13	9	18	37	43	48
Chorley	40	13	6	21	57	71	45
Fisher Athletic	40	10	11	19	55	65	41
Stafford Rangers	40	11	7	22	49	74	40
Aylesbury United	40	9	9	22	43	71	36
Weymouth	40	7	10	23	37	70	31
Newport County	29	4	7	18	31	62	19

Newport County expelled from League – their record was deleted.

1989-90

Team	P	W	D	L	F	A	Pts
Darlington	42	26	9	7	76	25	87
Barnet	42	26	7	9	81	41	85
Runcorn	42	19	13	10	79	62	70
Macclesfield Town	42	17	15	10	56	41	66
Kettering Town	42	18	12	12	66	53	66
Welling United	42	18	10	14	62	50	64
Yeovil Town	42	17	12	13	62	54	63
Sutton United	42	19	6	17	68	64	63
Merthyr Tydfil	42	16	14	12	67	63	62
Wycombe Wanderers	42	17	10	15	64	56	61
Cheltenham Town	42	16	11	15	58	60	59
Telford United	42	15	13	14	56	63	58
Kidderminster Harriers	42	15	9	18	64	67	54
Barrow	42	12	16	14	51	67	52
Northwich Victoria	42	15	5	22	51	67	50
Altrincham	42	12	13	17	49	48	49
Stafford Rangers	42	12	12	18	50	62	48
Boston United	42	13	8	21	48	67	47
Fisher Athletic	42	13	7	22	55	78	46
Chorley	42	13	6	23	42	67	45
Farnborough Town	42	10	12	20	60	73	42
Enfield	42	10	6	26	52	89	36

1990-91

Team	P	W	D	L	F	A	Pts
Barnet	42	26	9	7	103	52	87
Colchester United	42	25	10	7	68	35	85
Altrincham	42	23	13	6	87	46	82
Kettering Town	42	23	11	8	67	45	80
Wycombe Wanderers	42	21	11	10	75	46	74
Telford United	42	20	7	15	62	52	67
Macclesfield Town	42	17	12	13	63	52	63
Runcorn	42	16	10	16	69	67	58
Merthyr Tydfil	42	16	9	17	62	61	57
Barrow	42	15	12	15	59	65	57
Welling United	42	13	15	14	55	55	54
Northwich Victoria	42	13	13	16	65	75	52
Kidderminster Harrier	42	14	10	18	56	67	52
Yeovil Town	42	13	11	18	58	58	50
Stafford Rangers	42	12	14	16	48	51	50
Cheltenham Town	42	12	12	18	54	72	48
Gateshead	42	14	6	22	52	92	48
Boston United	42	12	11	19	55	69	47
Slough Town	42	13	6	23	51	80	45
Bath City	42	10	12	20	55	61	42
Sutton United	42	10	9	23	62	82	39
Fisher Athletic	42	5	15	22	38	79	30

1991-92

Team	P	W	D	L	F	A	Pts
Colchester United	42	28	10	4	98	40	94
Wycombe Wanderers	42	30	4	8	84	35	94
Kettering Town	42	20	13	9	72	50	73
Merthyr Tydfil	42	18	14	10	59	56	68
Farnborough Town	42	18	13	12	68	53	66
Telford United	42	19	7	16	62	66	64
Redbridge Forest	42	18	9	15	69	56	63
Boston United	42	18	9	15	71	66	63
Bath City	42	16	12	14	54	51	60
Witton Albion	42	16	10	16	63	60	58
Northwich Victoria	42	16	6	20	63	58	54
Welling United	42	14	12	16	69	79	54
Macclesfield Town	42	13	13	16	50	50	52
Gateshead	42	12	13	18	49	57	48
Yeovil Town	42	11	14	17	40	49	47
Runcorn	42	11	13	18	50	63	46
Stafford Rangers	42	10	16	16	41	59	46
Altrincham	42	11	12	19	61	82	45
Kidderminster Harriers	42	12	9	21	56	77	45
Slough Town	42	13	6	23	56	82	45
Cheltenham Town	42	10	13	19	56	83	43
Barrow	42	8	14	20	52	72	38

1992-93

Team	P	W	D	L	F	A	Pts
Wycombe Wanderers	42	24	11	7	84	37	83
Bromsgrove Rovers	42	18	14	10	67	49	68
Dagenham & Redbridge	42	19	11	12	75	47	67
Yeovil Town	42	18	12	12	59	49	66
Slough Town	42	18	11	13	60	55	65
Stafford Rangers	42	18	10	14	55	47	64
Bath City	42	15	14	13	53	46	59
Woking	42	17	8	17	58	62	59
Kidderminster Harriers	42	14	16	12	60	60	58
Altrincham	42	15	13	14	49	52	58
Northwich Victoria	42	16	8	18	68	55	56
Stalybridge Celtic	42	13	17	12	48	55	56
Kettering Town	42	14	13	15	61	63	55
Gateshead	42	14	10	18	53	56	52
Telford United	42	14	10	18	55	60	52
Merthyr Tydfil	42	14	10	18	51	79	52
Witton Albion	42	11	17	14	62	65	50
Macclesfield	42	12	13	17	40	50	49
Runcorn	42	13	10	19	58	76	49
Welling United	42	12	12	18	57	72	48
Farnborough Town	42	12	11	19	68	87	47
Boston United	42	9	13	20	50	69	40

Dagenham & Redbridge had 1 point deducted

1993-94

Team	P	W	D	L	F	A	Pts
Kidderminster Harriers	42	22	9	11	63	35	75
Kettering Town	42	18	15	8	46	24	72
Woking	42	18	13	11	58	58	67
Southport	42	18	12	12	57	51	66
Runcorn	42	14	19	9	63	57	61
Dagenham & Redbridge	42	15	14	13	62	54	59
Macclesfield Town	42	16	11	15	48	49	59
Dover Athletic	42	17	7	18	48	49	58
Stafford Rangers	42	14	15	13	56	52	57
Altrincham	42	16	9	17	41	42	57
Gateshead	42	15	12	15	45	53	57
Bath City	42	13	17	12	47	38	56
Halifax Town	42	13	16	13	55	49	55
Stalybridge Celtic	42	14	12	16	54	55	54
Northwich Victoria	42	11	19	12	44	45	52
Welling United	42	13	12	17	47	49	51
Telford United	42	13	12	17	41	49	51
Bromsgrove Rovers	42	12	15	15	54	66	51
Yeovil Town	42	14	9	19	49	62	51
Merthyr Tydfil	42	12	15	15	60	61	49
Slough Town	42	11	14	17	44	58	47
Witton Albion	42	7	13	22	37	63	44

Merthyr Tydfil had 2 points deducted

1994-95

Team	P	W	D	L	F	A	Pts
Macclesfield Town	42	24	8	10	70	40	80
Woking	42	21	12	9	76	54	75
Southport	42	21	9	12	68	50	72
Altrincham Town	42	20	8	14	77	60	68
Stevenage Borough	42	20	7	15	68	49	67
Kettering Town	42	19	10	13	73	56	67
Gateshead	42	19	10	13	61	53	67
Halifax Town	42	17	12	13	68	54	63
Runcorn	42	16	10	16	59	71	58
Northwich Victoria	42	14	15	13	77	66	57
Kidderminster Harriers	42	16	9	17	63	61	57
Bath City	42	15	12	15	55	56	57
Bromsgrove Rovers	42	14	3	15	66	69	55
Farnborough Town	42	15	10	17	45	64	55
Dagenham & Redbridge	42	13	13	16	56	69	52
Dover Athletic	42	11	16	15	48	55	49
Welling United	42	13	10	19	57	74	49
Stalybridge Celtic	42	11	14	17	52	72	47
Telford United	42	10	16	16	53	62	46
Merthyr Tydfil	42	11	11	20	53	63	44
Stafford Rangers	42	9	11	22	53	79	38
Yeovil Town	42	8	14	20	50	71	37

Yeovil Town had 1 point deducted for fielding an ineligible player

1995-96

Team	P	W	D	L	F	A	Pts
Stevenage Borough	42	27	10	5	101	44	91
Woking	42	25	8	9	83	54	83
Hednesford Town	42	23	7	12	71	46	76
Macclesfield Town	42	22	9	11	66	49	75
Gateshead	42	18	13	11	58	46	67
Southport	42	18	12	12	77	64	66
Kidderminster Harriers	42	18	10	14	78	66	64
Northwich Victoria	42	16	12	14	72	64	60
Morecambe	42	17	8	17	78	72	59
Farnborough Town	42	15	14	13	63	58	59
Bromsgrove Rovers	42	15	14	13	59	57	59
Altrincham	42	15	13	14	64	58	58
Telford United	42	15	10	17	51	56	55
Stalybridge Celtic	42	16	7	19	59	68	55
Halifax Town	42	13	13	16	49	63	52
Kettering Town	42	13	9	20	68	84	48
Slough Town	42	13	8	21	63	76	47
Bath City	42	13	7	22	45	66	46
Welling United	42	10	15	17	42	53	45
Dover Athletic	42	11	7	24	51	74	40
Runcorn	42	9	8	25	48	87	35
Dagenham & Redbridge	42	7	12	23	43	73	33

1996-97

Team	P	W	D	L	F	A	Pts
Macclesfield Town	42	27	9	6	80	30	90
Kidderminster Harriers	42	26	7	9	84	42	85
Stevenage Borough	42	24	10	8	87	53	82
Morecambe	42	19	9	14	69	56	66
Woking	42	18	10	14	71	63	64
Northwich Victoria	42	17	12	13	61	54	63
Farnborough Town	42	16	13	13	58	53	61
Hednesford Town	42	16	12	14	52	50	60
Telford United	42	16	10	16	46	56	58
Gateshead	42	15	11	16	59	63	56
Southport	42	15	10	17	51	61	55
Rushden & Diamonds	42	14	11	17	61	63	53
Stalybridge Celtic	42	14	10	18	53	58	52
Kettering Town	42	14	9	19	53	62	51
Hayes	42	12	14	16	54	55	50
Slough Town	42	12	14	16	62	65	50
Dover Athletic	42	12	14	16	57	68	50
Welling United	42	13	9	20	50	60	48
Halifax Town	42	12	12	18	55	74	48
Bath City	42	12	11	19	53	80	47
Bromsgrove Rovers	42	12	5	25	41	67	41
Altrincham	42	9	12	21	49	73	39

1997-98

Team							
Halifax Town	42	25	12	5	74	43	87
Cheltenham Town	42	23	9	10	63	43	78
Woking	42	22	8	12	72	46	74
Rushden & Diamonds	42	23	5	14	79	57	74
Morecambe	42	21	10	11	77	64	73
Hereford United	42	18	13	11	56	49	67
Hednesford Town	42	18	12	12	59	50	66
Slough Town	42	18	10	14	58	49	64
Northwich Victoria	42	15	15	12	63	59	60
Welling United	42	17	9	16	64	62	60
Yeovil Town	42	17	8	17	73	63	59
Hayes	42	16	10	16	62	52	58
Dover Athletic	42	15	10	17	60	70	55
Kettering Town	42	13	13	16	53	60	52
Stevenage Borough	42	13	12	17	59	63	51
Southport	42	13	11	18	56	58	50
Kidderminster Harriers	42	11	14	17	56	63	49
Farnborough Town	42	12	8	22	56	70	44
Leek Town	42	10	14	18	52	67	44
Telford United	42	10	12	20	53	76	42
Gateshead	42	8	11	23	51	87	35
Stalybridge Celtic	42	7	8	27	48	93	29

1998-99

Team							
Cheltenham Town	42	22	14	6	71	36	80
Kettering Town	42	22	10	10	58	37	76
Hayes	42	22	8	12	63	50	74
Rushden & Diamonds	42	20	12	10	71	42	72
Yeovil Town	42	20	11	11	68	54	71
Stevenage Borough	42	17	17	8	62	45	68
Northwich Victoria	42	19	9	14	60	51	66
Kingstonian	42	17	13	12	50	49	64
Woking	42	18	9	15	51	45	62
Hednesford Town	42	15	16	11	49	44	61
Dover Athletic	42	15	13	14	54	48	58
Forest Green Rovers	42	15	13	14	55	50	58
Hereford United	42	15	10	17	49	46	55
Morecambe	42	15	8	19	60	76	53
Kidderminster Harriers	42	14	9	19	56	52	51
Doncaster Rovers	42	12	12	18	51	55	48
Telford United	42	10	16	16	44	60	46
Southport	42	10	15	17	47	59	45
Barrow	42	11	10	21	40	63	43
Welling United	42	9	14	19	44	65	41
Leek Town	42	8	8	26	48	76	32
Farnborough United	42	7	11	24	41	89	32

1999-2000

Team							
Kidderminster Harriers	42	26	7	9	75	40	85
Rushden & Diamonds	42	21	13	8	71	42	76
Morecambe	42	18	16	8	70	48	70
Scarborough	42	19	12	11	60	35	69
Kingstonian	42	20	7	15	58	44	67
Dover Athletic	42	18	12	12	65	56	66
Yeovil Town	42	18	10	14	60	63	64
Hereford United	42	15	14	13	61	52	59
Southport	42	15	13	14	55	56	58
Stevenage Borough	42	16	9	17	60	54	57
Hayes	42	16	8	18	57	58	56
Doncaster Rovers	42	15	9	18	46	48	54
Kettering Town	42	12	16	14	44	50	52
Woking	42	13	13	16	45	53	52
Nuneaton Borough	42	12	15	15	49	53	51
Telford United	42	14	9	19	56	66	51
Hednesford Town	42	15	6	21	45	68	51
Northwich Victoria	42	13	12	17	53	78	51
Forest Green Rovers	42	13	8	21	54	63	47
Welling United	42	13	8	21	54	66	47
Altrincham	42	9	19	14	51	60	46
Sutton United	42	8	10	24	39	75	34

2000-2001

Team							
Rushden & Diamonds	42	25	11	6	78	36	86
Yeovil Town	42	24	8	10	73	50	80
Dagenham & Redbridge	42	23	8	11	71	54	77
Southport	42	20	9	13	58	46	69
Leigh RMI	42	19	11	12	63	57	68
Telford United	42	19	8	15	51	51	65
Stevenage Borough	42	15	18	9	71	61	63
Chester City	42	16	14	12	49	43	62
Doncaster Rovers	42	15	13	14	47	43	58
Scarborough	42	14	16	12	56	54	58
Hereford United	42	14	15	13	60	46	57
Boston United	42	13	17	12	74	63	56
Nuneaton Borough	42	13	15	14	60	60	54
Woking	42	13	15	14	52	57	54
Dover Athletic	42	14	11	17	54	56	53
Forest Green Rovers	42	11	15	16	43	54	48
Northwich Victoria	42	11	13	18	49	67	46
Hayes	42	12	10	20	44	71	46
Morecambe	42	11	12	19	64	66	45
Kettering Town	42	11	10	21	46	62	43
Kingstonian	42	8	10	24	47	73	34
Hednesford Town	42	5	13	24	46	86	28

2001-2002

Team							
Boston United	42	25	9	8	84	42	84
Dagenham & Redbridge	42	24	12	6	70	47	84
Yeovil Town	42	19	13	10	66	53	70
Doncaster Rovers	42	18	13	11	68	46	67
Barnet	42	19	10	13	64	48	67
Morecambe	42	17	11	14	63	67	62
Farnborough Town	42	18	7	17	66	54	61
Margate	42	14	16	12	59	53	58
Telford United	42	14	15	13	63	58	57
Nuneaton Borough	42	16	9	17	57	57	57
Stevenage Borough	42	15	10	17	57	60	55
Scarborough	42	14	14	14	55	63	55
Northwich Victoria	42	16	7	19	57	70	55
Chester City	42	15	9	18	54	51	54
Southport	42	13	14	15	53	49	53
Leigh RMI	42	15	8	19	56	58	53
Hereford United	42	14	10	18	50	53	52
Forest Green Rovers	42	12	15	15	54	76	51
Woking	42	13	9	20	59	70	48
Hayes	42	13	5	24	53	80	44
Stalybridge Celtic	42	11	10	21	40	69	43
Dover Athletic	42	11	6	25	41	65	39

2002-2003

Team							
Yeovil Town	42	28	11	3	100	37	95
Morecambe	42	23	9	10	86	42	78
Doncaster Rovers	42	22	12	8	73	47	78
Chester City	42	21	12	9	59	31	75
Dagenham & Redbridge	42	21	9	12	71	59	72
Hereford United	42	19	7	16	64	51	64
Scarborough	42	18	10	14	63	54	64
Halifax Town	42	18	10	14	50	51	64
Forest Green Rovers	42	17	8	17	61	62	59
Margate	42	15	11	16	60	66	56
Barnet	42	13	14	15	65	68	53
Stevenage Borough	42	14	10	18	61	55	52
Farnborough Town	42	13	12	17	57	56	51
Northwich Victoria	42	13	12	17	66	72	51
Telford United	42	14	7	21	54	69	49
Burton Albion	42	13	10	19	52	77	49
Gravesend & Northfleet	42	12	12	18	62	73	48
Leigh RMI	42	14	6	22	44	71	48
Woking	42	11	14	17	52	81	47
Nuneaton Borough	42	13	7	22	51	78	46
Southport	42	11	12	19	54	69	45
Kettering Town	42	8	7	27	37	73	31

2003-2004

Chester City	42	27	11	4	85	34	92
Hereford United	42	28	7	7	103	44	91
Shrewsbury Town	42	20	14	8	67	42	74
Barnet	42	19	14	9	60	46	71
Aldershot Town	42	20	10	12	80	67	70
Exeter City	42	19	12	11	71	57	69
Morecambe	42	20	7	15	66	66	67
Stevenage Borough	42	18	9	15	58	52	63
Woking	42	15	16	11	65	52	61
Accrington Stanley	42	15	13	14	68	61	58
Gravesend & Northfleet	42	14	15	13	69	66	57
Telford United	42	15	10	17	49	51	55
Dagenham & Redbridge	42	15	9	18	59	64	54
* Burton Albion	42	15	7	20	57	59	51
Scarborough	42	12	15	15	51	54	51
Margate	42	14	9	19	56	64	51
Tamworth	42	13	10	19	49	68	49
Forest Green Rovers	42	12	12	18	58	80	48
Halifax Town	42	12	8	22	43	65	44
Farnborough Town	42	10	9	23	53	74	39
Leigh RMI	42	7	8	27	46	97	29
Northwich Victoria	42	4	11	27	30	80	23

* Burton Albion had 1 point deducted.

2004-2005

Conference National

Barnet	42	26	8	8	90	44	86
Hereford United	42	21	11	10	68	41	74
Carlisle United	42	20	13	9	74	37	73
Aldershot Town	42	21	10	11	68	52	73
Stevenage Borough	42	22	6	14	65	52	72
Exeter City	42	20	11	11	71	50	71
Morecambe	42	19	14	9	69	50	71
Woking	42	18	14	10	58	45	68
Halifax Town	42	19	9	14	74	56	66
Accrington Stanley	42	18	11	13	72	58	65
Dagenham & Redbridge	42	19	8	15	68	60	65
Crawley Town	42	16	9	17	50	50	57
Scarborough	42	14	14	14	60	46	56
Gravesend & Northfleet	42	13	11	18	58	64	50
Tamworth	42	14	11	17	53	63	50
Burton Albion	42	13	11	18	50	66	50
York City	42	11	10	21	39	66	43
Canvey Island	42	9	15	18	53	65	42
Northwich Victoria	42	14	10	18	58	72	42
Forest Green Rovers	42	6	15	21	41	81	33
Farnborough Town	42	6	11	25	35	89	29
Leigh RMI	42	4	6	32	31	98	18

Northwich Victoria had 10 points deducted.
Tamworth had 3 points deducted.

Conference North

Southport	42	25	9	8	83	45	84
Nuneaton Borough	42	25	6	11	68	45	81
Droylsden	42	24	7	11	82	52	79
Kettering Town	42	21	7	14	56	50	70
Altrincham	42	19	12	11	66	46	69
Harrogate Town	42	19	11	12	62	49	68
Worcester City	42	16	12	14	59	53	60
Stafford Rangers	42	14	17	11	52	44	59
Redditch United	42	18	8	16	65	59	59
Hucknall Town	42	15	14	13	59	57	59
Gainsborough Trinity	42	16	9	17	55	55	57
Hinckley United	42	15	11	16	55	62	56
Lancaster City	42	14	12	16	51	59	54
Alfreton Town	42	15	8	19	53	55	53
Vauxhall Motors	42	14	11	17	48	57	53
Barrow	42	14	10	18	50	64	52
Worksop Town	42	16	12	14	59	59	50
Moor Green	42	13	10	19	55	64	49
Stalybridge Celtic	42	12	12	18	52	70	48
Runcorn FC Halton	42	10	12	20	44	63	42
Ashton United	42	8	9	25	46	79	33
Bradford Park Avenue	42	5	9	28	37	70	24

Worksop Town had 10 points deducted.
Redditch United had 3 points deducted.

Conference South

Grays Athletic	42	30	8	4	118	31	98
Cambridge City	42	23	6	13	60	44	75
Thurrock	42	21	6	15	61	56	69
Lewes	42	18	11	13	73	64	65
Eastbourne Borough	42	18	10	14	65	47	64
Basingstoke Town	42	19	6	17	57	52	63
Weymouth	42	17	11	14	62	59	62
Dorchester Town	42	17	11	14	77	81	62
Bognor Regis Town	42	17	9	16	70	65	60
Bishop's Stortford	42	17	8	17	70	66	59
Weston-super-Mare	42	15	13	14	55	60	58
Hayes	42	15	11	16	55	57	56
Havant & Waterlooville	42	16	7	19	64	69	55
St. Albans City	42	16	6	20	64	76	54
Sutton United	42	14	11	17	60	71	53
Welling United	42	15	7	20	64	68	52
Hornchurch	42	17	10	15	71	63	51
Newport County	42	13	11	18	56	61	50
Carshalton Athletic	42	13	9	20	44	72	48
Maidenhead United	42	12	10	20	54	81	46
Margate	42	12	8	22	54	75	34
Redbridge	42	11	3	28	50	86	33

Horchurch and Margate had 10 points deducted.
Redbridge had 3 points deducted.

ISTHMIAN LEAGUE

1905-06

London Caledonians	10	7	1	2	25	8	15
Clapton	10	6	1	3	11	13	13
Casuals	10	3	4	3	14	14	10
Civil Service	10	4	1	5	16	20	9
Ealing Association	10	3	2	5	15	19	8
Ilford	10	1	3	6	5	12	5

1906-07

Ilford	10	8	2	0	26	9	18
London Caledonians	10	6	0	4	19	14	12
Clapton	10	4	3	3	18	11	11
Civil Service	10	3	1	6	11	19	7
Ealing Association	10	3	1	6	12	22	7
Casuals	10	2	1	7	15	26	5

1907-08

London Caledonians	10	5	2	3	20	15	12
Clapton	10	4	3	3	24	14	11
Ilford	10	5	1	4	28	22	11
Oxford City	10	5	1	4	20	20	11
Dulwich Hamlet	10	3	2	5	15	18	8
West Norwood	10	3	1	6	13	31	7

1908-09

Bromley	18	11	1	6	42	29	23
Leytonstone	18	9	4	5	43	31	22
Ilford	18	9	4	5	37	36	22
Dulwich Hamlet	18	9	2	7	39	30	20
Clapton	18	8	4	6	34	32	20
Oxford City	18	6	4	8	29	32	16
Nunhead	18	7	2	9	31	35	16
Shepherd's Bush	18	6	3	9	26	44	15
London Caledonians	18	4	6	8	25	34	14
West Norwood	18	5	2	11	40	43	12

1909-10

Bromley	18	11	4	3	32	10	26
Clapton	18	10	4	4	56	19	24
Nunhead	18	10	4	4	49	26	24
Ilford	18	10	3	5	31	17	23
Dulwich Hamlet	18	8	4	6	26	26	20
Leytonstone	18	7	3	8	44	46	17
Oxford City	18	5	4	9	28	45	14
London Caledonians	18	5	3	10	19	40	13
West Norwood	18	5	2	11	28	54	12
Shepherd's Bush	18	2	3	13	23	55	7

1910-11

Clapton	18	11	4	3	39	19	26
Leytonstone	18	12	1	5	47	30	25
Dulwich Hamlet	18	8	5	5	28	22	21
Oxford City	18	7	4	7	32	43	18
Ilford	18	8	1	9	41	32	17
Shepherd's Bush	18	7	3	8	31	27	17
Bromley	18	8	4	6	32	27	16
Nunhead	18	5	4	9	32	36	14
West Norwood	18	4	5	9	24	43	13
London Caledonians	18	3	3	12	18	45	9
Bromley had 4 points deducted

1911-12

London Caledonians	20	11	7	2	39	25	29
Ilford	20	11	3	6	37	24	25
Nunhead	20	10	5	5	36	30	25
Dulwich Hamlet	20	8	5	7	33	23	21
West Norwood	20	9	3	8	38	38	21
Clapton	20	7	5	8	37	37	19
Woking	20	7	5	8	38	41	19
Shepherd's Bush	20	5	6	9	39	49	16
Leytonstone	20	5	6	9	28	38	16
Oxford City	20	5	5	10	33	36	15
Tunbridge Wells	20	5	4	11	23	40	14

1912-13

London Caledonians	20	14	5	1	38	12	33
Leytonstone	20	12	3	5	45	20	27
Nunhead	20	12	3	5	36	23	27
Clapton	20	7	7	6	23	20	21
Dulwich Hamlet	20	8	4	8	34	28	20
Woking	20	7	5	8	33	40	19
Oxford City	20	6	6	8	23	39	18
Ilford	20	6	5	9	27	37	17
Shepherd's Bush	20	5	5	10	26	38	15
Tunbridge Wells	20	5	4	11	22	36	14
West Norwood	20	3	3	14	23	37	9

1913-14

London Caledonians	20	12	6	2	55	23	30
Nunhead	20	11	6	3	49	27	28
Ilford	20	11	4	5	52	35	26
Dulwich Hamlet	20	10	4	6	34	22	24
New Crusaders	20	10	3	7	40	30	23
Oxford City	20	10	0	10	42	42	20
Leytonstone	20	8	4	8	29	32	20
Clapton	20	8	3	9	29	27	19
Shepherd's Bush	20	7	2	11	24	46	16
West Norwood	20	4	3	13	27	47	11
Woking	20	1	1	18	11	61	3

1919

Leytonstone	8	5	1	2	21	7	11
Ilford	8	4	2	2	22	16	10
Dulwich Hamlet	8	3	2	3	19	17	8
Nunhead	8	3	2	3	18	19	8
Clapton	8	0	3	5	14	35	3

1919-20

Dulwich Hamlet	22	15	3	4	58	16	33
Nunhead	22	14	5	3	48	26	33
Tufnell Park	22	12	4	6	45	32	28
Ilford	22	13	1	8	63	42	27
Oxford City	22	12	3	7	63	51	27
London Caledonians	22	10	3	9	32	30	23
Leytonstone	22	8	3	11	50	43	19
Clapton	22	8	3	11	38	44	19
Civil Service	22	7	4	11	35	40	18
Woking	22	6	3	13	36	42	15
West Norwood	22	5	4	13	19	53	14
Casuals	22	3	2	17	20	88	8

1920-21

Ilford	22	16	4	2	70	24	36
London Caledonians	22	13	5	4	45	17	31
Tufnell Park	22	14	3	5	43	24	31
Nunhead	22	12	5	5	53	33	29
Dulwich Hamlet	22	11	6	5	60	30	28
Oxford City	22	12	3	7	56	38	27
Leytonstone	22	8	6	8	36	29	22
Clapton	22	7	7	8	33	52	21
Civil Service	22	3	7	12	28	45	13
Woking	22	3	5	14	16	43	11
Casuals	22	3	3	16	31	87	9
West Norwood	22	2	2	18	18	67	6

1921-22

Ilford	26	17	4	5	66	34	38
Dulwich Hamlet	26	14	8	4	65	24	36
London Caledonians	26	16	4	6	41	21	36
Nunhead	26	12	5	9	65	41	29
Clapton	26	13	3	10	51	46	29
Tufnell Park	26	10	7	9	44	39	27
Oxford City	26	18	2	12	48	47	26
Wycombe Wanderers	26	18	2	12	61	64	26
Civil Service	26	9	8	9	60	48	26
Woking	26	10	6	10	39	49	26
Leytonstone	26	9	6	11	41	48	24
West Norwood	26	8	5	13	43	57	21
Wimbledon	26	7	4	15	52	56	18
Casuals	26	0	2	24	25	107	2

1922-23

Clapton	26	15	7	4	51	33	37
Nunhead	26	15	5	6	52	32	35
London Caledonians	26	13	7	6	43	26	33
Ilford	26	11	7	8	57	38	29
Casuals	26	12	5	9	68	51	29
Civil Service	26	9	10	7	39	36	28
Wycombe Wanderers	26	11	4	11	61	61	26
Dulwich Hamlet	26	9	7	10	60	44	25
Leytonstone	26	9	7	10	45	56	25
Tufnell Park	26	9	5	12	41	45	23
Wimbledon	26	10	2	14	49	50	22
Woking	26	7	6	13	42	67	20
Oxford City	26	6	5	15	45	68	17
West Norwood	26	5	5	16	25	71	15

1923-24

St Albans City	26	17	5	4	72	38	39
Dulwich Hamlet	26	15	6	5	49	28	36
Clapton	26	14	5	7	73	50	33
Wycombe Wanderers	26	14	5	7	88	65	33
London Caledonians	26	14	3	9	53	49	31
Civil Service	26	12	5	9	52	47	29
Casuals	26	13	1	12	65	54	27
Ilford	26	9	6	11	56	59	24
Nunhead	26	8	8	10	41	46	24
Wimbledon	26	8	4	14	43	62	20
Tufnell Park	26	8	2	16	38	53	18
Woking	26	5	8	13	31	62	18
Oxford City	26	7	2	17	53	74	16
Leytonstone	26	6	4	16	41	68	16

1924-25

London Caledonians	26	18	5	3	76	36	41
Clapton	26	19	1	6	64	34	39
St Albans City	26	16	2	8	69	39	34
Tufnell Park	26	11	4	11	47	41	26
Ilford	26	11	4	11	46	42	26
Leytonstone	26	12	2	12	55	63	26
The Casuals	26	12	1	13	55	58	25
Wycombe Wanderers	26	11	2	13	58	61	24
Civil Service	26	10	4	12	52	64	24
Nunhead	26	9	5	12	45	43	23
Wimbledon	26	10	2	14	50	54	22
Dulwich Hamlet	26	8	5	13	42	57	21
Oxford City	26	9	2	15	38	71	20
Woking	26	5	3	18	33	67	13

1925-26

Dulwich Hamlet	26	20	1	5	80	49	41
London Caledonians	26	18	1	7	81	44	37
Clapton	26	14	4	8	64	50	32
Wycombe Wanderers	26	14	3	9	97	83	31
St Albans City	26	12	6	8	76	54	30
Nunhead	26	13	4	9	49	43	30
Ilford	26	13	2	11	81	70	28
Leytonstone	26	12	1	13	75	63	25
Woking	26	8	6	12	56	73	22
Tufnell Park	26	8	5	13	36	53	21
The Casuals	26	8	4	14	48	61	20
Wimbledon	26	9	1	16	61	77	19
Oxford City	26	8	1	17	48	76	17
Civil Service	26	5	1	20	43	99	11

1926-27

St Albans City	26	20	1	5	96	34	41
Ilford	26	18	0	9	76	57	34
Wimbledon	26	15	3	8	72	45	33
Nunhead	26	11	8	7	51	33	30
Woking	26	12	6	8	68	60	30
London Caledonians	26	11	7	8	58	47	29
Clapton	26	11	4	11	58	60	26
Leytonstone	26	11	1	14	54	78	23
Dulwich Hamlet	26	9	4	13	60	58	22
Wycombe Wanderers	26	10	2	14	59	86	22
Tufnell Park	26	8	4	14	45	55	20
Oxford City	26	7	5	14	46	72	19
The Casuals	26	8	3	15	37	78	19
Civil Service	26	6	4	16	48	65	16

1927-28

St Albans City	26	15	5	6	86	50	35
London Caledonians	26	12	9	5	63	38	33
Ilford	26	14	4	8	72	54	32
Woking	26	13	5	8	72	56	31
Nunhead	26	13	2	11	57	54	28
Wimbledon	26	12	3	11	57	48	27
Leytonstone	26	13	1	12	53	56	27
Clapton	26	8	10	8	52	47	26
Dulwich Hamlet	26	8	9	9	56	49	25
The Casuals	26	8	8	10	54	58	24
Wycombe Wanderers	26	9	5	12	60	69	23
Oxford City	26	7	7	12	36	57	21
Civil Service	26	8	4	14	38	76	20
Tufnell Park	26	4	4	18	38	82	12

1928-29

Nunhead	26	15	6	5	47	35	36
London Caledonians	26	15	4	7	65	33	34
Dulwich Hamlet	26	14	6	6	65	34	34
Wimbledon	26	9	10	7	66	54	28
Ilford	26	12	3	11	67	52	27
Clapton	26	11	5	10	60	55	27
Tufnell Park	26	11	5	10	58	55	27
St Albans City	26	12	3	11	63	69	27
Leytonstone	26	11	3	12	56	79	25
Wycombe Wanderers	26	10	3	13	58	60	23
Oxford City	26	10	3	13	61	71	23
The Casuals	26	8	5	13	49	60	21
Woking	26	8	3	15	39	65	19
Civil Service	26	4	5	17	39	71	13

1929-30

Nunhead	26	19	3	4	69	36	41
Dulwich Hamlet	26	15	6	5	74	39	36
Kingstonian	26	15	4	7	57	37	34
Ilford	26	16	1	9	84	60	33
Woking	26	11	5	10	66	65	27
Wimbledon	26	11	2	13	64	66	24
Wycombe Wanderers	26	10	4	12	49	52	24
The Casuals	26	8	7	11	50	51	23
Oxford City	26	10	3	13	45	60	23
St Albans City	26	9	4	13	54	77	22
Clapton	26	8	4	14	47	57	20
London Caledonians	26	8	3	15	49	69	19
Leytonstone	26	8	3	15	48	68	19
Tufnell Park	26	6	7	13	35	54	19

1930-31

Wimbledon	26	18	6	2	69	37	42
Dulwich Hamlet	26	12	9	5	51	39	33
Wycombe Wanderers	26	12	6	8	67	45	30
The Casuals	26	12	6	8	71	56	30
St Albans City	26	11	7	8	67	66	29
Ilford	26	10	6	10	70	62	26
Oxford City	26	10	5	11	43	48	25
London Caledonians	26	8	8	10	43	53	24
Kingstonian	26	10	4	12	49	64	24
Tufnell Park	26	9	5	12	45	61	23
Nunhead	26	9	4	13	49	54	22
Woking	26	9	4	13	56	63	22
Clapton	26	7	4	15	62	75	18
Leytonstone	26	6	4	16	46	65	16

1931-32

Wimbledon	26	17	2	7	60	35	36
Ilford	26	13	9	4	71	45	35
Dulwich Hamlet	26	15	3	8	69	43	33
Wycombe Wanderers	26	14	5	7	72	50	33
Oxford City	26	15	2	9	63	49	32
Kingstonian	26	13	3	10	71	50	29
Tufnell Park	26	9	7	10	50	48	25
Nunhead	26	9	7	10	54	61	25
The Casuals	26	10	4	12	59	65	24
Clapton	26	9	5	12	50	57	23
Leytonstone	26	9	3	14	36	61	21
St Albans City	26	8	4	14	57	78	20
Woking	26	6	5	15	44	64	17
London Caledonians	26	2	7	17	24	74	11

1932-33

Dulwich Hamlet	26	15	6	5	71	45	36
Leytonstone	26	16	4	6	66	43	36
Kingstonian	26	15	2	9	77	49	32
Ilford	26	14	0	12	60	58	28
The Casuals	26	12	2	12	48	36	26
Tufnell Park	26	11	3	12	51	51	25
St Albans City	26	12	1	13	57	63	25
Clapton	26	10	5	11	51	65	25
Oxford City	26	9	6	11	49	54	24
Woking	26	10	4	12	53	61	24
Wycombe Wanderers	26	10	4	12	47	56	24
Nunhead	26	8	6	12	42	50	22
Wimbledon	26	8	5	13	55	67	21
London Caledonians	26	5	6	15	35	64	16

1933-34

Kingstonian	26	15	7	4	80	42	37
Dulwich Hamlet	26	15	5	6	68	36	35
Wimbledon	26	13	7	6	62	35	33
Tufnell Park	26	14	5	7	55	50	33
Ilford	26	15	2	9	60	56	32
The Casuals	26	13	5	8	47	32	31
Leytonstone	26	13	3	10	55	48	29
Nunhead	26	10	5	11	48	44	25
London Caledonians	26	7	8	11	29	51	22
Wycombe Wanderers	26	9	2	15	57	60	20
St Albans City	26	8	4	14	44	75	20
Oxford City	26	7	4	15	45	57	18
Clapton	26	5	6	15	35	62	16
Woking	26	6	1	19	43	81	13

1934-35

Wimbledon	26	14	7	5	63	30	35
Oxford City	26	14	4	8	69	50	32
Leytonstone	26	15	2	9	49	36	32
Dulwich Hamlet	26	11	7	8	66	45	29
Tufnell Park	26	11	7	8	53	44	29
Kingstonian	26	11	6	9	44	40	28
Nunhead	26	10	7	9	35	34	27
London Caledonians	26	9	7	10	40	41	25
St Albans City	26	9	6	11	61	80	24
Ilford	26	9	6	11	40	56	24
Clapton	26	7	7	12	46	48	21
Woking	26	9	3	14	44	68	21
Wycombe Wanderers	26	7	6	13	51	69	20
The Casuals	26	6	5	15	37	57	17

1935-36

Wimbledon	26	19	2	5	82	29	40
The Casuals	26	14	5	7	60	45	33
Ilford	26	13	3	10	67	47	29
Dulwich Hamlet	26	10	8	8	64	47	28
Nunhead	26	11	6	9	51	40	28
Wycombe Wanderers	26	13	2	11	60	68	28
Clapton	26	11	5	10	42	46	27
Oxford City	26	11	4	11	60	58	26
St Albans City	26	11	2	13	59	64	24
Woking	26	9	4	13	43	62	22
Tufnell Park	26	9	3	14	42	61	21
London Caledonians	26	9	3	14	35	52	21
Kingstonian	26	9	2	15	43	56	20
Leytonstone	26	7	3	16	34	67	17

1936-37

Kingstonian	26	18	3	5	63	43	39
Nunhead	26	17	3	6	77	32	37
Leytonstone	26	16	4	6	71	42	36
Ilford	26	14	5	7	86	39	33
Dulwich Hamlet	26	12	6	8	64	48	30
Wycombe Wanderers	26	10	5	11	55	52	25
Wimbledon	26	9	7	10	52	53	25
Clapton	26	10	5	11	42	51	25
The Casuals	26	10	3	13	46	58	23
Woking	26	9	4	13	53	69	22
Oxford City	26	8	5	13	56	89	21
St Albans City	26	7	5	14	44	62	19
Tufnell Park	26	4	7	15	43	74	15
London Caledonians	26	5	4	17	26	66	14

1937-38

Leytonstone	26	17	6	3	72	34	40
Ilford	26	17	3	6	70	39	37
Tufnell Park	26	15	2	9	62	47	32
Nunhead	26	14	3	9	52	44	31
Wycombe Wanderers	26	12	5	9	69	55	29
Dulwich Hamlet	26	13	3	10	57	46	29
Kingstonian	26	12	4	10	51	48	28
Clapton	26	9	6	11	49	53	24
Wimbledon	26	10	3	13	62	49	23
London Caledonians	26	9	4	13	44	55	22
Oxford City	26	7	7	12	35	71	21
The Casuals	26	8	3	15	51	74	19
Woking	26	7	2	17	41	72	16
St Albans City	26	4	5	17	31	60	13

1938-39

Leytonstone	26	18	4	4	68	32	40
Ilford	26	17	4	5	68	32	38
Kingstonian	26	17	3	6	62	39	37
Dulwich Hamlet	26	15	5	6	60	32	35
Wimbledon	26	14	3	9	88	56	31
Nunhead	26	11	6	9	54	44	28
The Casuals	26	11	6	9	54	51	28
Clapton	26	12	2	12	69	61	26
Wycombe Wanderers	26	10	6	10	62	62	26
St Albans City	26	8	5	13	44	50	21
Woking	26	9	2	15	35	56	20
Oxford City	26	4	4	18	44	84	12
Tufnell Park	26	4	4	18	33	87	12
London Caledonians	26	3	4	19	26	81	10

1945-46

Walthamstow Avenue	26	21	0	5	100	31	42
Oxford City	26	17	6	3	91	40	40
Romford	26	15	3	8	83	59	33
Dulwich Hamlet	26	14	2	10	63	59	30
Tufnell Park	26	12	4	10	70	55	28
Woking	26	10	7	9	56	54	27
Ilford	26	12	2	12	56	71	26
Leytonstone	26	11	3	12	61	75	25
Wycombe Wanderers	26	9	3	14	80	88	21
Wimbledon	26	7	6	13	52	72	20
Corinthian Casuals	26	8	4	14	58	83	20
Clapton	26	8	3	15	51	62	19
St Albans City	26	6	6	14	48	85	18
Kingstonian	26	6	3	17	48	86	15

1946-47

Leytonstone	26	19	2	5	92	36	40
Dulwich Hamlet	26	17	3	6	78	46	37
Romford	26	13	8	5	76	52	34
Walthamstow Avenue	26	13	4	9	64	37	30
Oxford City	26	12	6	8	70	51	30
Kingstonian	26	12	4	10	54	57	28
Wycombe Wanderers	26	9	8	9	62	62	26
Wimbledon	26	10	5	11	68	64	25
Ilford	26	7	7	12	66	78	21
Tufnell Park	26	8	5	13	45	69	21
Woking	26	7	7	12	34	62	21
Clapton	26	6	8	12	41	59	20
St Albans City	26	7	5	14	47	79	19
Corinthian Casuals	26	4	4	18	36	80	12

1947-48

Leytonstone	26	19	1	6	87	38	39
Kingstonian	26	16	6	4	74	39	38
Walthamstow Avenue	26	17	3	6	61	37	37
Dulwich Hamlet	26	17	2	7	71	39	36
Wimbledon	26	13	6	7	66	40	32
Romford	26	14	1	11	53	47	29
Oxford City	26	10	5	11	50	68	25
Woking	26	10	3	13	63	55	23
Ilford	26	7	8	11	51	59	22
St Albans City	26	9	2	15	43	56	20
Wycombe Wanderers	26	7	5	14	51	65	19
Tufnell Park	26	7	4	15	38	83	18
Clapton	26	5	4	17	35	69	14
Corinthian Casuals	26	5	2	19	33	81	12

1948-49

Dulwich Hamlet	26	15	6	5	60	31	36
Walthamstow Avenue	26	16	4	6	65	38	36
Wimbledon	26	15	4	7	64	41	34
Ilford	26	14	3	9	56	36	31
Oxford City	26	13	5	8	48	34	31
Leytonstone	26	12	6	8	49	41	30
Woking	26	14	1	11	64	59	29
Romford	26	11	3	12	47	54	25
Kingstonian	26	10	4	12	43	47	24
Corinthian Casuals	26	11	2	13	47	59	24
Wycombe Wanderers	26	11	2	13	49	61	24
St Albans City	26	6	6	14	40	60	16
Clapton	26	5	5	16	32	61	15
Tufnell Park	26	1	5	20	28	70	7

St Albans City had 2 points deducted

1949-50

Leytonstone	26	17	5	4	77	31	39
Wimbledon	26	18	2	6	72	51	38
Kingstonian	26	16	3	7	59	39	35
Walthamstow Avenue	26	14	6	6	73	42	34
Dulwich Hamlet	26	14	3	9	60	47	31
St Albans City	26	12	3	11	59	45	27
Woking	26	10	6	10	60	71	26
Wycombe Wanderers	26	9	7	10	51	52	25
Romford	26	10	4	12	45	49	24
Ilford	26	10	4	12	46	53	24
Clapton	26	8	6	12	51	59	22
Oxford City	26	6	6	14	35	54	18
Corinthian Casuals	26	4	5	17	41	69	13
Tufnell Park	26	3	2	21	24	91	8

1950-51

Leytonstone	26	20	3	3	72	26	43
Walthamstow Avenue	26	15	4	7	57	37	34
Romford	26	15	3	8	58	49	33
Wimbledon	26	13	5	8	58	39	31
Dulwich Hamlet	26	14	2	10	54	43	30
Woking	26	11	6	9	65	55	28
Ilford	26	12	4	10	44	45	28
Corinthian Casuals	26	13	0	13	62	60	26
St Albans City	26	11	4	11	32	36	26
Kingstonian	26	9	4	13	46	54	22
Wycombe Wanderers	26	8	3	15	46	64	19
Oxford City	26	7	4	15	47	65	18
Clapton	26	6	5	15	29	50	17
Tufnell Park Edmonton	26	4	1	21	24	73	9

1951-52

Leytonstone	26	13	9	4	63	36	35
Wimbledon	26	16	3	7	65	44	35
Walthamstow Avenue	26	15	4	7	71	43	34
Romford	26	14	4	8	64	42	32
Kingstonian	26	11	7	8	62	48	29
Wycombe Wanderers	26	12	5	9	64	59	29
Woking	26	11	5	10	60	71	27
Dulwich Hamlet	26	11	4	11	60	53	26
Corinthian Casuals	26	11	4	11	55	66	26
St Albans City	26	9	7	10	48	53	25
Ilford	26	8	5	13	32	47	21
Clapton	26	9	2	15	50	59	20
Oxford City	26	6	3	17	50	72	15
Tufnell Park Edmonton	26	2	6	18	25	73	10

1952-53

Walthamstow Avenue	28	19	6	3	53	25	44
Bromley	28	17	4	7	71	35	38
Leytonstone	28	14	6	8	60	38	34
Wimbledon	28	14	5	9	68	37	33
Kingstonian	28	13	6	9	62	50	32
Dulwich Hamlet	28	15	2	11	62	52	32
Romford	28	12	8	8	62	52	32
Wycombe Wanderers	28	14	2	12	54	62	30
St Albans City	28	11	6	11	43	57	28
Barking	28	9	7	12	42	51	25
Ilford	28	10	4	14	59	57	24
Woking	28	10	4	14	57	72	24
Corinthian Casuals	28	7	9	12	45	56	23
Oxford City	28	5	2	21	37	87	12
Clapton	28	2	5	21	27	71	9

1953-54

Bromley	28	18	3	7	76	45	39
Walthamstow Avenue	28	13	7	8	55	30	33
Wycombe Wanderers	28	15	3	10	65	44	33
Ilford	28	11	10	7	48	44	32
Corinthian Casuals	28	12	7	9	59	44	31
Woking	28	13	4	11	54	58	30
Leytonstone	28	12	5	11	58	48	29
St Albans City	28	11	6	11	54	55	28
Dulwich Hamlet	28	11	6	11	55	57	28
Romford	28	11	5	12	57	54	27
Clapton	28	11	5	12	42	56	27
Barking	28	11	2	15	59	84	24
Kingstonian	28	8	7	13	59	71	23
Wimbledon	28	7	8	13	43	59	22
Oxford City	28	4	6	18	49	84	14

1954-55

Walthamstow Avenue	28	21	1	6	80	38	43
St Albans City	28	18	3	7	61	41	39
Bromley	28	18	2	8	66	34	38
Wycombe Wanderers	28	16	3	9	68	43	35
Ilford	28	13	5	10	64	46	31
Barking	28	15	1	12	55	51	31
Woking	28	12	3	13	75	79	27
Kingstonian	28	10	7	11	47	57	27
Leytonstone	28	10	4	14	35	51	24
Oxford City	28	10	3	15	43	74	23
Clapton	28	9	4	15	41	50	22
Wimbledon	28	10	2	16	48	62	22
Corinthian Casuals	28	9	3	16	50	65	21
Dulwich Hamlet	28	7	5	16	48	60	19
Romford	28	4	10	14	43	73	18

1955-56

Wycombe Wanderers	28	19	5	4	82	36	43
Bromley	28	12	7	9	54	43	31
Leytonstone	28	12	7	9	50	44	31
Woking	28	14	3	11	62	60	31
Barking	28	12	7	9	41	45	31
Kingstonian	28	12	6	10	67	64	30
Walthamstow Avenue	28	13	3	12	61	45	29
Ilford	28	10	8	10	44	52	28
Oxford City	28	10	7	11	48	55	27
Clapton	28	9	8	11	45	48	26
Wimbledon	28	12	2	14	51	62	26
Corinthian Casuals	28	9	7	12	56	56	25
Dulwich Hamlet	28	9	6	13	55	67	24
Romford	28	9	6	13	42	55	24
St Albans City	28	2	10	16	36	62	14

1956-57

Wycombe Wanderers	30	18	6	6	86	53	42
Woking	30	20	1	9	104	47	41
Bromley	30	16	5	9	78	60	37
Oxford City	30	16	3	11	65	57	35
Ilford	30	12	8	10	59	65	32
Tooting & Mitcham United	30	10	11	9	53	48	31
Kingstonian	30	11	9	10	72	77	31
Walthamstow Avenue	30	11	8	11	48	46	30
Dulwich Hamlet	30	13	3	14	65	54	29
St Albans City	30	13	3	14	62	71	29
Leytonstone	30	11	6	13	50	50	28
Clapton	30	9	9	12	48	59	27
Wimbledon	30	10	5	15	47	66	25
Romford	30	10	5	15	53	81	25
Barking	30	7	6	17	48	72	20
Corinthian Casuals	30	7	4	19	46	78	18

1957-58

Tooting & Mitcham United	30	20	6	4	79	33	46
Wycombe Wanderers	30	19	4	7	78	42	42
Walthamstow Avenue	30	17	5	8	63	35	39
Bromley	30	13	9	8	66	51	35
Oxford City	30	13	6	11	59	48	32
Leytonstone	30	13	6	11	49	48	32
Wimbledon	30	15	2	13	64	66	32
Corinthian Casuals	30	12	8	10	62	68	32
Woking	30	12	7	11	70	58	31
Barking	30	10	6	14	49	61	26
St Albans City	30	11	3	16	56	76	25
Clapton	30	8	9	13	42	65	25
Kingstonian	30	7	8	15	45	66	22
Dulwich Hamlet	30	7	7	16	49	64	21
Ilford	30	8	4	18	46	70	20
Romford	30	6	8	16	45	71	20

1958-59

Wimbledon	30	22	3	5	91	38	47
Dulwich Hamlet	30	18	5	7	68	44	41
Wycombe Wanderers	30	18	4	8	93	50	40
Oxford City	30	17	4	9	87	58	38
Walthamstow Avenue	30	16	5	9	59	40	37
Tooting & Mitcham United	30	15	4	11	84	55	34
Barking	30	14	2	14	59	53	30
Woking	30	12	6	12	66	66	30
Bromley	30	11	7	12	56	55	29
Clapton	30	10	6	14	55	67	26
Ilford	30	10	6	14	46	67	26
Kingstonian	30	9	4	17	54	72	22
St Albans City	30	8	6	16	53	89	22
Leytonstone	30	7	6	17	40	87	20
Romford	30	7	5	18	54	76	19
Corinthian Casuals	30	7	5	18	44	92	19

1959-60

Tooting & Mitcham United	30	17	8	5	75	43	42
Wycombe Wanderers	30	19	3	8	84	46	41
Wimbledon	30	18	3	9	66	36	39
Kingstonian	30	18	3	9	76	51	39
Corinthian Casuals	30	18	1	11	69	61	37
Bromley	30	15	6	9	75	46	36
Dulwich Hamlet	30	14	6	10	65	47	34
Walthamstow Avenue	30	11	11	8	48	38	33
Oxford City	30	10	10	10	57	57	30
Leytonstone	30	10	8	12	43	46	28
Woking	30	10	6	14	54	61	26
St Albans City	30	10	6	14	50	65	26
Maidstone United	30	10	5	15	53	60	25
Barking	30	7	4	19	30	75	18
Ilford	30	5	6	19	34	86	16
Clapton	30	3	4	23	32	92	10

1960-61

Bromley	30	20	6	4	89	42	46
Walthamstow Avenue	30	20	5	5	87	38	45
Wimbledon	30	18	6	6	72	43	42
Dulwich Hamlet	30	17	4	9	71	59	35
Maidstone United	30	14	8	8	63	39	36
Leytonstone	30	15	6	9	46	34	36
Tooting & Mitcham United	30	14	3	13	69	51	31
Wycombe Wanderers	30	12	5	13	63	61	29
St Albans City	30	12	4	14	45	72	28
Oxford City	30	10	7	13	59	59	27
Corinthian Casuals	30	9	9	12	49	59	27
Kingstonian	30	10	6	14	55	61	26
Woking	30	10	6	14	58	71	26
Ilford	30	5	8	17	30	69	18
Barking	30	3	8	19	30	76	14
Clapton	30	3	5	22	25	77	11

1961-62

Wimbledon	30	19	6	5	68	24	44
Leytonstone	30	17	7	6	61	44	41
Walthamstow Avenue	30	14	8	8	51	31	36
Kingstonian	30	15	5	10	65	48	35
Tooting & Mitcham United	30	12	10	8	62	47	34
Oxford City	30	12	9	9	56	49	33
Wycombe Wanderers	30	12	7	11	57	51	31
Corinthian Casuals	30	12	7	11	45	51	31
St Albans City	30	10	9	11	55	55	29
Woking	30	9	9	12	51	60	27
Dulwich Hamlet	30	11	4	15	55	66	26
Barking	30	9	8	13	40	64	26
Ilford	30	7	10	13	50	59	24
Bromley	30	10	4	16	49	69	24
Clapton	30	6	8	16	45	67	20
Maidstone United	30	6	7	17	34	59	19

1962-63

Wimbledon	30	19	8	3	84	33	46
Kingstonian	30	18	8	4	79	37	44
Tooting & Mitcham United	30	17	8	5	65	37	42
Ilford	30	19	3	8	70	44	41
Walthamstow Avenue	30	14	7	9	51	44	35
Maidstone United	30	13	8	9	56	45	34
Bromley	30	12	10	8	57	51	34
Leytonstone	30	12	7	11	48	50	31
Wycombe Wanderers	30	10	10	10	56	61	30
St Albans City	30	11	5	14	54	49	27
Barking	30	8	10	12	39	50	26
Oxford City	30	8	9	13	55	64	25
Woking	30	8	6	16	42	66	22
Clapton	30	7	4	19	30	71	18
Dulwich Hamlet	30	4	5	21	30	71	13
Corinthian Casuals	30	4	4	22	28	71	12

1963-64

Wimbledon	38	27	6	5	87	44	60
Hendon	38	25	4	9	124	38	54
Kingstonian	38	24	4	10	100	62	52
Sutton United	38	23	5	10	99	64	51
Enfield	38	20	10	8	96	56	50
Oxford City	38	20	8	10	90	55	48
Tooting & Mitcham United	38	19	8	11	78	51	46
St Albans City	38	14	12	12	62	63	40
Ilford	38	16	8	14	75	79	40
Maidstone United	38	15	8	15	65	71	38
Walthamstow Avenue	38	15	6	17	70	66	36
Leytonstone	38	14	8	16	66	71	36
Wycombe Wanderers	38	13	6	19	74	80	32
Hitchin Town	38	14	4	20	67	100	32
Bromley	38	11	8	19	64	75	30
Barking	38	10	9	19	46	69	29
Woking	38	10	9	19	48	88	29
Corinthian Casuals	38	10	4	24	52	92	24
Dulwich Hamlet	38	6	12	20	47	97	24
Clapton	38	2	5	31	31	120	9

1964-65

Hendon	38	28	7	3	123	49	63
Enfield	38	29	5	4	98	35	63
Kingstonian	38	24	8	6	86	44	56
Leytonstone	38	24	5	9	115	62	53
Oxford City	38	20	7	11	76	51	47
St Albans City	38	18	9	11	63	43	45
Sutton United	38	17	11	10	74	57	45
Wealdstone	38	19	6	13	93	68	44
Bromley	38	14	11	13	71	80	39
Tooting & Mitcham United	38	15	7	16	71	66	37
Hitchin Town	38	13	9	16	61	66	35
Walthamstow Avenue	38	15	5	18	63	82	35
Wycombe Wanderers	38	13	7	18	70	85	33
Corinthian Casuals	38	13	7	18	56	77	33
Barking	38	10	8	20	58	80	28
Ilford	38	8	8	22	43	89	24
Maidstone United	38	8	6	24	49	86	22
Dulwich Hamlet	38	8	5	25	45	79	21
Clapton	38	8	3	27	43	91	19
Woking	38	7	4	27	45	113	18

Hendon beat Enfield in a play-off to decide the Championship

1965-66

Leytonstone	38	27	7	4	98	33	63
Hendon	38	27	5	6	111	55	59
Enfield	38	24	8	6	104	54	56
Wycombe Wanderers	38	25	6	7	100	65	56
Kingstonian	38	24	5	9	94	55	53
Wealdstone	38	20	6	12	90	64	46
Maidstone United	38	19	6	13	74	61	44
St Albans City	38	19	5	14	57	56	43
Sutton United	38	17	7	14	83	72	41
Tooting & Mitcham United	38	16	7	15	65	58	39
Corinthian Casuals	38	17	5	16	74	67	39
Woking	38	12	10	16	60	83	34
Walthamstow Avenue	38	12	9	17	81	75	33
Oxford City	38	10	9	19	49	72	29
Barking	38	10	7	21	51	72	27
Bromley	38	10	5	23	69	101	25
Ilford	38	7	10	21	50	84	24
Hitchin Town	38	6	8	24	57	118	20
Clapton	38	5	6	27	46	103	16
Dulwich Hamlet	38	5	5	28	30	95	15

1966-67

Sutton United	38	26	7	5	89	33	59
Walthamstow Avenue	38	22	12	4	89	47	56
Wycombe Wanderers	38	23	8	7	92	54	54
Enfield	38	25	2	11	87	33	52
Hendon	38	20	9	9	64	37	49
Tooting & Mitcham United	38	19	10	9	76	60	48
Leytonstone	38	19	9	10	67	38	47
St Albans City	38	16	12	10	59	45	44
Kingstonian	38	18	8	12	60	49	44
Oxford City	38	15	9	14	74	61	39
Woking	38	13	10	15	65	71	36
Wealdstone	38	13	8	17	72	73	34
Barking	38	11	12	15	56	61	34
Bromley	38	12	7	19	50	67	31
Clapton	38	10	8	20	49	92	28
Ilford	38	8	10	20	43	77	26
Corinthian Casuals	38	9	7	22	45	68	25
Maidstone United	38	6	10	22	43	90	22
Hitchin Town	38	8	6	24	39	89	22
Dulwich Hamlet	38	3	4	31	33	107	10

1967-68

Enfield	38	28	8	2	85	22	64
Sutton United	38	22	11	5	89	27	55
Hendon	38	23	6	9	90	36	52
Leytonstone	38	21	10	7	78	41	52
St Albans City	38	20	8	10	78	41	48
Walthamstow Avenue	38	19	9	10	81	64	47
Wealdstone	38	19	8	11	80	45	46
Tooting & Mitcham United	38	19	5	14	57	45	43
Barking	38	17	8	13	75	57	42
Oxford City	38	17	4	17	59	58	38
Kingstonian	38	14	10	14	56	61	38
Hitchin Town	38	14	9	15	61	73	37
Bromley	38	12	10	16	58	80	34
Wycombe Wanderers	38	13	5	20	73	85	31
Dulwich Hamlet	38	10	7	21	39	66	27
Clapton	38	10	7	21	51	88	27
Woking	38	8	8	22	50	90	24
Corinthian Casuals	38	7	10	21	40	80	24
Ilford	38	7	7	24	41	77	21
Maidstone United	38	3	4	31	26	131	10

1968-69

Enfield	38	27	7	4	103	28	61
Hitchin Town	38	23	10	5	67	41	56
Sutton United	38	22	9	7	83	29	53
Wycombe Wanderers	38	23	6	9	70	37	52
Wealdstone	38	20	11	7	73	48	51
Hendon	38	22	5	11	69	47	49
St Albans City	38	17	13	8	75	44	47
Barking	38	20	7	11	69	46	47
Oxford City	38	18	8	12	76	64	44
Tooting & Mitcham United	38	16	10	12	68	55	42
Leytonstone	38	18	4	16	71	53	40
Kingstonian	38	15	8	15	62	56	38
Walthamstow Avenue	38	10	10	18	47	71	30
Maidstone United	38	10	8	20	47	75	28
Clapton	38	10	7	21	52	76	27
Woking	38	8	7	23	45	77	23
Bromley	38	8	7	23	52	95	23
Dulwich Hamlet	38	6	9	23	31	77	21
Ilford	38	6	8	24	33	77	20
Corinthian Casuals	38	2	4	32	23	120	8

1969-70

Enfield	38	27	8	3	91	26	62
Wycombe Wanderers	38	25	11	2	85	24	61
Sutton United	38	24	9	5	75	35	57
Barking	38	21	9	8	93	47	51
Hendon	38	19	12	7	77	44	50
St Albans City	38	21	8	9	69	40	50
Hitchin Town	38	19	10	9	71	40	48
Tooting & Mitcham United	38	19	5	14	88	62	43
Leytonstone	38	17	7	14	57	41	41
Wealdstone	38	15	10	13	53	48	40
Oxford City	38	15	7	16	61	78	37
Kingstonian	38	13	9	16	55	57	35
Ilford	38	8	15	15	42	73	31
Dulwich Hamlet	38	8	12	18	46	66	28
Woking	38	10	7	21	46	69	27
Walthamstow Avenue	38	11	5	22	52	81	27
Clapton	38	9	7	22	45	87	25
Maidstone United	38	7	8	23	48	84	22
Corinthian Casuals	38	6	3	29	30	99	15
Bromley	38	3	4	31	28	111	10

1970-71

Wycombe Wanderers	38	28	6	4	93	32	62
Sutton United	38	29	3	6	76	35	61
St Albans City	38	23	10	5	87	26	56
Enfield	38	24	7	7	67	24	55
Ilford	38	21	7	10	74	51	49
Hendon	38	18	11	9	81	37	47
Barking	38	20	4	14	89	59	44
Leytonstone	38	17	10	11	68	50	44
Woking	38	18	6	14	57	50	42
Walthamstow Avenue	38	14	11	13	63	52	39
Oxford City	38	13	10	15	51	48	36
Hitchin Town	38	12	9	17	46	60	33
Wealdstone	38	12	8	18	45	64	32
Tooting & Mitcham United	38	11	9	18	44	66	31
Kingstonian	38	11	8	19	53	71	30
Bromley	38	10	6	22	34	77	26
Dulwich Hamlet	38	7	10	21	30	66	24
Maidstone United	38	7	6	25	42	84	20
Clapton	38	5	7	26	33	101	17
Corinthian Casuals	38	2	8	28	23	103	12

1971-72

Wycombe Wanderers	40	31	3	6	102	20	65
Enfield	40	26	8	6	90	41	60
Walton & Hersham	40	24	8	8	69	25	56
Hendon	40	23	10	7	79	35	56
Bishop's Stortford	40	24	5	11	61	37	53
Sutton United	40	21	10	9	77	43	52
St Albans City	40	23	4	13	74	47	50
Ilford	40	17	11	12	62	52	45
Barking	40	20	4	16	65	61	44
Hitchin Town	40	17	10	13	68	66	44
Bromley	40	16	10	14	67	64	42
Hayes	40	14	12	14	50	48	40
Oxford City	40	13	9	18	67	74	35
Woking	40	11	10	19	52	58	32
Kingstonian	40	10	12	18	49	59	32
Walthamstow Avenue	40	12	8	20	58	71	32
Leytonstone	40	11	8	21	48	68	30
Tooting & Mitcham United	40	6	9	25	38	93	21
Clapton	40	7	7	26	45	118	21
Dulwich Hamlet	40	4	12	24	35	81	20
Corinthian Casuals	40	3	4	33	21	116	10

Second Division

Dagenham	30	22	4	4	68	23	70
Slough Town	30	18	6	6	46	23	60
Hertford Town	30	17	5	8	46	29	56
Chesham Town	30	16	6	8	61	43	54
Aveley	30	16	5	9	50	28	53
Tilbury	30	14	5	11	47	36	47
Maidenhead United	30	12	11	7	36	30	47
Horsham	30	12	9	9	47	35	45
Harwich & Parkeston	30	11	9	10	46	41	42
Staines Town	30	10	8	12	34	41	38
Carshalton Athletic	30	8	8	14	34	51	32
Hampton	30	6	10	14	33	51	28
Harlow Town	30	6	9	15	33	48	27
Finchley	30	6	7	17	29	52	25
Southall	30	3	10	17	17	52	19
Wokingham Town	30	3	8	19	30	74	17

1972-73

Hendon	42	34	6	2	88	18	74
Walton & Hersham	42	25	11	6	60	25	61
Leatherhead	42	23	10	9	76	32	56
Wycombe Wanderers	42	25	6	11	66	32	56
Walthamstow Avenue	42	20	12	10	66	48	52
Tooting & Mitcham United	42	20	11	11	73	39	51
Sutton United	42	21	9	12	69	48	51
Kingstonian	42	20	10	12	60	49	50
Enfield	42	20	8	14	90	54	48
Bishop's Stortford	42	18	12	12	58	51	48
Hayes	42	19	8	15	69	42	46
Dulwich Hamlet	42	18	9	15	59	52	45
Ilford	42	18	9	15	61	59	45
Leytonstone	42	17	11	14	55	54	45
Woking	42	18	8	16	61	56	44
Hitchin Town	42	15	9	18	52	64	39
Barking	42	8	7	27	45	88	23
St Albans City	42	5	12	25	34	76	22
Oxford City	42	6	7	29	30	101	19
Bromley	42	4	10	28	31	70	18
Clapton	42	3	11	28	31	100	17
Corinthian Casuals	42	3	8	31	30	106	14

1973-74

First Division

Wycombe Wanderers	42	27	9	6	96	34	90
Hendon	42	25	13	4	63	20	88
Bishop's Stortford	42	26	9	7	78	26	87
Dulwich Hamlet	42	22	11	9	71	38	77
Leatherhead	42	23	6	13	81	44	75
Walton & Hersham	42	20	12	10	68	50	72
Woking	42	22	6	14	63	55	72
Leytonstone	42	20	9	13	63	44	69
Ilford	42	20	8	14	60	44	68
Hayes	42	17	14	11	65	43	65
Oxford City	42	15	16	11	45	47	61
Sutton United	42	13	16	13	51	52	55
Hitchin Town	42	15	10	17	68	73	55
Barking	42	14	12	16	57	58	54
Kingstonian	42	12	15	15	47	46	51
Tooting & Mitcham United	42	14	9	19	57	62	51
Enfield	42	13	11	18	50	57	50
Walthamstow Avenue	42	11	13	18	46	62	46
Bromley	42	7	9	26	37	81	30
Clapton	42	8	3	31	36	128	27
St Albans City	42	4	7	31	30	92	19
Corinthian Casuals	42	3	4	35	31	107	13

1974-75

First Division

Wycombe Wanderers	42	28	11	3	93	30	95
Enfield	42	29	8	5	78	26	95
Dagenham	42	28	5	9	95	44	89
Tooting & Mitcham United	42	25	9	8	78	46	84
Dulwich Hamlet	42	24	10	8	75	38	82
Leatherhead	42	23	10	9	83	42	79
Ilford	42	23	10	9	98	51	79
Oxford City	42	17	9	16	63	56	60
Slough Town	42	17	6	19	68	52	57
Sutton United	42	17	6	19	68	63	57
Bishop's Stortford	42	17	6	19	56	64	57
Hitchin Town	42	15	10	17	57	71	55
Hendon	42	15	7	20	59	74	52
Walthamstow Avenue	42	13	9	20	56	62	48
Woking	42	12	10	20	53	73	46
Hayes	42	10	14	18	52	66	44
Barking	42	12	8	22	57	81	44
Leytonstone	42	12	7	23	42	61	43
Kingstonian	42	13	4	25	48	73	43
Clapton	42	12	4	26	46	96	40
Walton & Hersham	42	9	4	29	37	108	31
Bromley	42	6	3	33	25	110	21

Second Division

Staines Town	34	23	2	9	65	23	71
Southall	34	20	3	11	55	41	63
Tilbury	34	19	5	10	64	36	60
Harwich & Parkeston	34	18	4	12	52	44	58
Chesham United	34	17	6	11	59	39	57
St Albans City	34	15	11	8	42	37	56
Harlow Town	34	16	6	12	53	47	54
Horsham	34	16	5	13	59	49	53
Maidenhead United	34	13	7	14	38	40	46
Hampton	34	12	7	15	44	42	43
Croydon	34	11	10	13	48	55	43
Hertford Town	34	10	7	17	35	52	37
Boreham Wood	34	7	15	12	41	49	36
Wokingham Town	34	10	6	18	32	43	36
Finchley	34	9	9	16	36	53	36
Carshalton Athletic	34	9	9	16	38	58	36
Aveley	34	9	7	18	34	63	34
Corinthian Casuals	34	8	9	17	35	59	33

Tilbury had 2 points deducted

1975-76

First Division

	P	W	D	L	F	A	Pts
Enfield	42	26	9	7	83	38	87
Wycombe Wanderers	42	24	10	8	71	41	82
Dagenham	42	25	6	11	89	55	81
Ilford	42	22	10	10	58	39	76
Dulwich Hamlet	42	22	5	15	67	41	71
Hendon	42	20	11	11	60	41	71
Tooting & Mitcham United	42	19	11	12	73	49	68
Leatherhead	42	19	10	13	63	53	67
Staines Town	42	19	9	14	46	37	66
Slough Town	42	17	12	13	58	45	63
Sutton United	42	17	11	14	71	60	62
Bishop's Stortford	42	15	12	15	51	47	57
Walthamstow Avenue	42	14	11	17	47	60	53
Woking	42	14	9	19	58	62	51
Barking	42	15	6	21	57	70	51
Hitchin Town	42	13	11	18	45	57	50
Hayes	42	10	19	13	44	48	49
Kingstonian	42	13	8	21	53	87	47
Southall & Ealing Borough	42	11	9	22	56	69	42
Leytonstone	42	10	10	22	41	63	40
Oxford City	42	9	8	25	29	65	35
Clapton	42	3	3	36	19	112	12

Second Division

	P	W	D	L	F	A	Pts
Tilbury	42	32	6	4	97	30	102
Croydon	42	28	14	0	81	27	98
Carshalton Athletic	42	28	6	8	75	37	90
Chesham United	42	21	12	9	91	51	75
Harwich & Parkeston	42	21	11	10	78	56	74
Hampton	42	21	9	12	72	52	72
St Albans City	42	18	12	12	59	48	66
Boreham Wood	42	17	12	13	68	50	63
Harrow Borough	42	15	12	15	71	74	57
Hornchurch	42	15	11	16	61	61	56
Horsham	42	14	13	15	60	55	55
Wembley	42	14	13	15	51	54	55
Wokingham Town	42	13	16	13	45	52	55
Walton & Hersham	42	14	12	16	61	56	54
Finchley	42	14	11	17	52	53	53
Bromley	42	11	11	20	64	86	44
Aveley	42	11	9	22	34	51	42
Harlow Town	42	11	9	22	50	73	42
Maidenhead United	42	6	17	19	32	65	35
Ware	42	7	12	23	50	95	33
Hertford Town	42	5	9	28	32	87	24
Corinthian Casuals	42	4	7	31	42	113	19

1976-77

First Division

	P	W	D	L	F	A	Pts
Enfield	42	24	12	6	63	34	84
Wycombe Wanderers	42	25	8	9	71	34	83
Dagenham	42	23	10	9	80	39	79
Hendon	42	19	10	13	60	48	67
Tilbury	42	18	13	11	57	49	67
Tooting & Mitcham	42	18	10	14	85	72	64
Walthamstow Avenue	42	19	7	16	61	55	64
Slough Town	42	18	9	15	51	46	63
Hitchin Town	42	19	6	17	60	66	63
Leatherhead	42	18	7	17	61	47	61
Staines Town	42	16	13	13	52	48	61
Leytonstone	42	16	11	15	59	57	59
Barking	42	16	9	17	63	61	57
Southall & Ealing Borough	42	15	8	19	52	64	53
Croydon	42	13	10	19	38	52	49
Sutton United	42	14	7	21	40	55	49
Kingstonian	42	13	7	22	45	60	46
Hayes	42	12	10	20	49	69	46
Woking	42	11	12	19	47	61	45
Bishop's Stortford	42	11	11	20	51	71	44
Dulwich Hamlet	42	11	8	23	52	68	41
Ilford	42	10	8	24	32	73	38

Second Division

	P	W	D	L	F	A	Pts
Boreham Wood	42	35	4	5	80	26	103
Carshalton Athletic	42	25	12	5	80	33	87
Harwich & Parkeston	42	23	8	11	93	61	77
Wembley	42	23	8	11	82	58	77
Harrow Borough	42	21	12	9	78	44	75
Horsham	42	23	5	14	67	56	74
Bromley	42	20	10	12	71	46	70
Oxford City	42	20	8	14	73	55	68
Hampton	42	20	8	14	62	45	68
Wokingham Town	42	16	14	12	60	44	62
Hornchurch	42	18	7	17	62	53	61
Chesham United	42	17	10	15	63	66	61
St Albans City	42	16	12	14	59	53	60
Walton & Hersham	42	17	9	16	57	56	60
Aveley	42	14	8	20	49	62	50
Corinthian Casuals	42	13	6	23	52	75	45
Harlow Town	42	11	8	23	39	77	41
Hertford Town	42	9	9	24	45	80	36
Maidenhead United	42	8	8	26	36	73	32
Clapton	42	7	9	28	43	87	30
Finchley	42	5	13	24	36	82	28
Ware	42	5	8	29	43	98	23

1977-78

Premier Division

	P	W	D	L	F	A	Pts
Enfield	42	35	5	2	96	27	110
Dagenham	42	24	7	11	78	55	79
Wycombe Wanderers	42	22	9	11	66	41	75
Tooting & Mitcham United	42	22	8	12	64	49	74
Hitchin Town	42	20	9	13	69	53	69
Sutton United	42	18	12	12	66	57	66
Leatherhead	42	18	11	13	62	48	65
Croydon	42	18	10	14	61	52	64
Walthamstow Avenue	42	17	12	13	64	61	63
Barking	42	17	7	18	76	66	58
Carshalton Athletic	42	15	11	16	60	62	56
Hayes	42	15	11	16	46	53	56
Hendon	42	16	7	19	57	55	55
Woking	42	14	11	17	62	62	53
Boreham Wood	42	15	8	19	48	65	53
Slough Town	42	14	8	20	52	69	0
Staines Town	42	12	13	17	46	60	49
Tilbury	42	11	12	19	57	68	45
Kingstonian	42	8	13	21	43	65	37
Leytonstone	42	7	15	20	44	71	36
Southall & Ealing Borough	42	6	15	21	43	74	33
Bishop's Stortford	42	7	8	27	36	83	29

First Division

	P	W	D	L	F	A	Pts
Dulwich Hamlet	42	28	9	5	91	25	93
Oxford City	42	26	5	11	85	44	83
Bromley	42	23	13	6	74	41	82
Walton & Hersham	42	22	11	9	69	41	77
Ilford	42	21	14	7	57	47	77
St Albans City	42	22	10	10	83	46	76
Wokingham Town	42	19	12	11	69	48	69
Harlow Town	42	19	8	15	63	49	65
Harrow Borough	42	17	10	15	59	54	61
Maidenhead United	42	16	13	13	55	54	61
Hertford Town	42	15	14	13	57	51	59
Chesham United	42	14	13	15	69	70	55
Hampton	42	13	13	16	49	53	52
Harwich & Parkeston	42	12	13	17	68	79	49
Wembley	42	15	3	24	56	82	48
Horsham	42	12	10	20	41	57	46
Finchley	42	11	13	18	41	68	46
Aveley	42	13	7	22	47	75	46
Ware	42	8	13	21	61	95	37
Clapton	42	10	6	26	46	78	36
Hornchurch	42	8	10	24	47	81	34
Corinthian Casuals	42	3	10	29	40	88	19

Second Division

	P	W	D	L	F	A	Pts
Epsom & Ewell	32	21	5	6	65	34	68
Metropolitan Police	32	19	6	7	53	30	63
Farnborough Town	32	19	4	9	68	40	61
Molesey	32	17	8	7	47	27	59
Egham Town	32	15	9	8	52	34	54
Tring Town	32	14	11	7	62	32	53
Letchworth Garden City	32	14	11	7	67	48	53
Lewes	32	13	7	12	52	51	46
Rainham Town	32	13	6	13	42	50	45
Worthing	32	11	9	12	40	45	42
Eastbourne United	32	10	8	14	40	50	38
Cheshunt	32	9	6	17	43	60	33
Feltham	32	7	9	16	30	49	30
Camberley Town	32	6	11	15	32	49	29
Hemel Hempstead	32	6	9	17	33	50	27
Epping Town	32	7	6	19	37	64	27
Willesden	32	7	3	22	38	88	24

Second Division

	P	W	D	L	F	A	Pts
Farnborough Town	34	26	3	5	77	34	81
Camberley Town	34	21	8	5	71	32	71
Molesey	34	19	11	4	55	33	68
Lewes	34	19	6	9	66	50	63
Feltham	34	16	7	11	47	36	55
Letchworth Garden City	34	14	10	10	56	48	52
Eastbourne United	34	16	4	14	47	45	52
Hemel Hempstead	34	13	11	10	46	37	50
Epping Town	34	14	7	13	49	44	49
Rainham Town	34	13	10	11	42	41	49
Cheshunt	34	11	8	15	43	49	41
Hungerford Town	34	11	8	15	48	58	41
Worthing	34	9	8	17	40	50	35
Hornchurch	34	9	8	17	39	62	35
Egham Town	34	7	12	15	48	54	33
Tring Town	34	6	8	20	33	56	26
Willesden	34	6	8	20	41	77	26
Corinthian Casuals	34	4	7	23	23	65	19

1978-79

Premier Division

	P	W	D	L	F	A	Pts
Barking	42	28	9	5	92	50	93
Dagenham	42	25	6	11	83	63	81
Enfield	42	22	11	9	69	37	77
Dulwich Hamlet	42	21	13	8	69	39	76
Slough Town	42	20	12	10	61	44	72
Wycombe Wanderers	42	20	9	13	59	44	69
Woking	42	18	14	10	79	59	68
Croydon	42	19	9	14	61	51	66
Hendon	42	16	14	12	55	48	62
Leatherhead	42	17	9	16	57	45	60
Sutton United	42	17	9	16	62	51	60
Tooting & Mitcham United	42	15	14	13	52	52	59
Walthamstow Avenue	42	15	6	21	61	69	51
Tilbury	42	13	1	18	60	76	50
Boreham Wood	42	13	10	19	50	67	49
Hitchin Town	42	12	11	19	59	71	47
Carshalton Athletic	42	10	16	16	49	69	46
Hayes	42	9	18	15	45	58	45
Oxford City	42	12	7	23	50	80	43
Staines Town	42	6	16	20	40	64	34
Leytonstone	42	8	7	27	36	75	31
Kingstonian	42	3	15	24	35	72	24

1979-80

Premier Division

	P	W	D	L	F	A	Pts
Enfield	42	25	9	8	74	32	84
Walthamstow Avenue	42	24	9	9	87	48	81
Dulwich Hamlet	42	21	16	5	66	37	79
Sutton United	42	20	13	9	67	40	73
Dagenham	42	20	13	9	82	56	73
Tooting & Mitcham United	42	21	6	15	62	59	69
Barking	42	19	10	13	72	51	67
Harrow Borough	42	17	15	10	64	51	66
Woking	42	17	13	12	78	59	64
Wycombe Wanderers	42	17	13	12	72	53	64
Harlow Town	42	14	12	16	55	61	54
Hitchin Town	42	13	15	14	55	69	54
Hendon	42	12	13	17	50	57	49
Slough Town	42	13	10	19	54	71	49
Boreham Wood	42	13	10	19	50	69	49
Staines Town	42	14	6	22	46	67	48
Hayes	42	12	9	21	48	68	45
Leatherhead	42	11	11	20	51	60	44
Carshalton Athletic	42	12	7	23	48	78	43
Croydon	42	10	10	22	51	59	40
Oxford City	42	10	9	23	49	87	39
Tilbury	42	7	11	24	41	90	30

Tilbury had 2 points deducted

First Division

	P	W	D	L	F	A	Pts
Harlow Town	42	31	7	4	93	32	100
Harrow Borough	42	26	8	8	85	49	86
Maidenhead United	42	25	6	11	72	50	81
Bishop's Stortford	42	22	11	9	68	40	77
Horsham	42	23	7	12	63	47	76
Hertford Town	42	21	11	10	62	41	74
Harwich & Parkeston	42	22	5	15	90	57	71
Bromley	42	18	12	12	76	50	66
Hampton	42	17	11	14	59	47	62
Epsom & Ewell	42	18	7	17	69	41	61
Wembley	42	15	14	13	57	57	59
Aveley	42	17	6	19	57	67	57
Wokingham Town	42	17	8	17	64	68	56
Clapton	42	15	8	19	67	80	53
Metropolitan Police	42	12	13	17	58	55	49
Walton & Hersham	42	12	9	21	47	71	45
Ilford	42	13	5	24	48	80	44
Ware	42	11	10	21	46	69	43
Chesham United	42	11	9	22	46	66	42
Finchley	42	7	15	20	43	75	36
St Albans City	42	7	7	28	43	90	28
Southall & Ealing Borough	42	5	5	32	41	114	20

Wokingham Town had 3 points deducted

First Division

	P	W	D	L	F	A	Pts
Leytonstone & Ilford	42	31	6	5	83	35	99
Bromley	42	24	10	8	93	44	82
Maidenhead United	42	24	8	10	81	46	80
Bishop's Stortford	42	24	8	10	74	47	80
Kingstonian	42	22	8	12	59	44	74
Chesham United	42	18	13	11	68	56	67
St Albans City	42	17	13	12	65	47	64
Farnborough Town	42	19	7	16	70	57	64
Epsom & Ewell	42	18	7	17	62	57	61
Camberley Town	42	16	10	16	43	38	58
Walton & Hersham	42	15	12	15	61	50	57
Wembley	42	16	8	18	46	52	56
Wokingham Town	42	14	11	17	45	49	53
Hertford Town	42	13	11	18	71	74	50
Aveley	42	12	13	17	45	55	49
Hampton	42	14	7	21	57	74	49
Finchley	42	13	9	20	44	59	48
Metropolitan Police	42	13	8	21	46	67	47
Ware	42	11	12	19	45	61	45
Clapton	42	14	3	25	48	77	45
Harwich & Parkeston	42	11	6	25	51	84	38
Horsham	42	6	4	32	29	113	22

Harwich & Parkeston had 1 point deducted

Second Division

Billericay Town	36	31	3	2	100	18	96
Lewes	36	24	7	5	82	33	79
Hungerford Town	36	21	8	7	78	36	71
Eastbourne United	36	21	6	9	77	45	69
Letchworth Garden City	36	21	6	9	63	32	69
Hornchurch	36	21	6	9	66	39	69
Molesey	36	15	9	12	67	60	54
Barton Rovers	36	15	7	14	49	49	52
Worthing	36	14	9	13	58	54	51
Cheshunt	36	13	7	16	47	52	46
Rainham Town	36	12	7	17	54	65	43
Egham Town	36	11	9	16	47	53	42
Southall & Ealing Borough	36	11	6	19	43	69	39
Feltham	36	8	11	17	23	49	35
Tring Town	36	7	13	16	38	55	34
Epping Town	36	10	4	22	44	69	34
Willesden	36	9	6	21	32	83	33
Hemel Hempstead	36	4	9	23	33	72	21
Corinthian Casuals	36	6	3	27	24	92	21

Second Division

Feltham	38	24	10	4	65	30	82
Hornchurch	38	25	6	7	74	35	81
Hungerford Town	38	23	10	5	84	29	79
Barton Rovers	38	19	11	8	61	25	68
Worthing	38	19	11	8	74	43	68
Cheshunt	38	19	11	8	57	33	68
Letchworth Garden City	38	18	7	13	49	40	61
Southall	38	14	11	13	48	52	53
Dorking Town	38	13	12	13	47	45	51
Horsham	38	16	3	19	47	47	51
Hemel Hempstead	38	14	7	17	47	54	49
Egham Town	38	13	9	16	45	62	48
Harwich & Parkeston	38	12	11	15	57	58	47
Rainham Town	38	11	13	14	44	45	46
Epping Town	38	12	7	19	37	50	43
Eastbourne United	38	11	10	17	59	75	43
Willesden	38	11	8	19	57	68	41
Tring Town	38	11	6	21	40	71	39
Molesey	38	4	9	25	31	83	21
Corinthian Casuals	38	1	8	29	17	95	11

1980-81

Premier Division

Slough Town	42	23	13	6	73	34	82
Enfield	42	23	11	8	81	43	80
Wycombe Wanderers	42	22	9	11	76	49	75
Leytonstone & Ilford	42	19	12	11	78	57	69
Sutton United	42	19	12	11	82	65	69
Hendon	42	18	10	14	66	58	64
Dagenham	42	17	11	14	79	66	62
Hayes	42	18	8	16	45	50	62
Harrow Borough	42	16	11	15	57	52	59
Bromley	42	16	9	17	63	69	57
Staines Town	42	15	9	18	60	61	54
Tooting & Mitcham United	42	15	8	19	49	53	53
Hitchin Town	42	14	10	18	64	62	52
Croydon	42	12	15	15	51	51	51
Dulwich Hamlet	42	13	12	17	62	67	51
Leatherhead	42	12	14	16	36	50	50
Carshalton Athletic	42	14	8	20	57	82	50
Barking	42	13	12	17	58	72	49
Harlow Town	42	11	15	16	53	66	48
Walthamstow Avenue	42	13	7	22	50	81	46
Boreham Wood	42	10	13	19	46	69	43
Woking	42	11	7	24	40	69	37

Barking had 1 point deducted
Woking had 3 points deducted

1981-82

Premier Division

Leytonstone & Ilford	42	26	5	11	91	52	83
Sutton United	42	22	9	11	72	49	75
Wycombe Wanderers	42	21	10	11	63	48	73
Staines Town	42	21	9	12	58	45	72
Walthamstow Avenue	42	21	7	14	81	62	70
Harrow Borough	42	18	13	11	77	55	67
Tooting & Mitcham United	42	19	10	13	58	47	67
Slough Town	42	17	13	12	64	54	64
Leatherhead	42	16	12	14	57	52	60
Hayes	42	16	10	16	58	52	58
Croydon	42	16	9	17	59	57	57
Barking	42	14	14	14	53	51	56
Hendon	42	13	13	16	56	65	52
Dulwich Hamlet	42	14	10	18	47	59	52
Bishop's Stortford	42	15	5	22	50	70	50
Carshalton Athletic	42	14	8	20	58	86	50
Billericay Town	42	11	16	15	41	50	49
Hitchin Town	42	12	11	19	56	77	47
Bromley	42	13	7	22	63	79	46
Woking	42	11	13	18	57	75	46
Harlow Town	42	10	11	21	50	73	41
Boreham Wood	42	8	13	21	47	58	37

First Division

Bishop's Stortford	42	30	6	6	84	28	96
Billericay Town	42	29	6	7	67	34	93
Epsom & Ewell	42	24	12	6	80	36	84
Farnborough Town	42	23	11	8	75	39	80
St Albans City	42	24	5	13	85	61	77
Kingstonian	42	20	9	13	63	52	66
Oxford City	42	18	9	15	71	48	63
Wokingham Town	42	16	15	11	70	56	63
Metropolitan Police	42	18	7	17	61	58	61
Chesham United	42	17	7	18	64	64	58
Lewes	42	17	7	18	72	83	58
Maidenhead United	42	16	7	19	58	62	55
Walton & Hersham	42	12	15	15	46	53	51
Hertford Town	42	13	11	18	46	65	50
Hampton	42	12	13	17	46	53	49
Aveley	42	13	9	20	54	55	48
Wembley	42	13	8	21	47	61	47
Clapton	42	12	8	22	53	86	44
Ware	42	9	13	20	50	69	40
Tilbury	42	10	8	24	42	84	35
Camberley Town	42	8	7	27	42	88	31
Finchley	42	6	11	25	36	77	29

Kingstonian and Tilbury both had 3 points deducted

First Division

Wokingham Town	40	29	5	6	86	30	92
Bognor Regis Town	40	23	10	7	65	34	79
Metropolitan Police	40	22	11	7	75	48	77
Oxford City	40	21	11	8	82	47	74
Feltham	40	20	8	12	65	49	68
Lewes	40	19	7	14	73	66	64
Hertford Town	40	16	10	14	62	54	58
Wembley	40	14	15	11	69	55	57
Farnborough Town	40	15	11	14	71	57	56
Epsom & Ewell	40	16	8	16	52	44	56
Kingstonian	40	16	7	17	57	56	55
Hampton	40	15	9	16	52	52	54
Hornchurch	40	13	15	12	42	50	54
Aveley	40	14	10	16	46	58	54
St Albans City	40	14	9	17	55	55	51
Maidenhead United	40	11	10	19	49	70	43
Tilbury	40	9	15	16	49	66	42
Walton & Hersham	40	10	11	19	43	65	41
Chesham United	40	9	9	22	41	71	36
Clapton	40	9	7	24	44	75	34
Ware	40	5	2	33	29	105	17

Second Division

Worthing	40	29	6	5	95	25	93
Cheshunt	40	25	7	8	79	33	82
Hungerford Town	40	22	10	8	89	42	74
Barton Rovers	40	22	8	10	65	32	74
Windsor & Eton	40	22	6	12	69	49	72
Corinthian Casuals	40	19	12	9	67	50	69
Harwich & Parkeston	40	19	12	9	64	47	69
Letchworth Garden City	40	15	11	14	67	55	56
Dorking Town	40	13	17	10	52	44	56
Hemel Hempstead	40	15	9	16	54	49	54
Basildon United	40	16	5	19	64	51	53
Finchley	40	14	9	17	57	68	51
Southall	40	12	14	14	36	42	50
Epping Town	40	12	11	17	48	62	47
Molesey	40	13	7	20	61	73	46
Egham Town	40	11	9	20	56	64	42
Rainham Town	40	11	9	20	53	83	42
Tring Town	40	9	13	18	49	78	40
Eastbourne United	40	9	12	19	51	73	39
Horsham	40	10	9	21	42	79	39
Camberley Town	40	3	2	35	21	140	11

Hungerford Town had 2 points deducted

Second Division

Clapton	42	30	4	8	96	46	94
Windsor & Eton	42	27	7	8	98	43	88
Barton Rovers	42	26	6	10	86	48	84
Leyton Wingate	42	25	8	9	111	41	83
Basildon United	42	23	13	6	92	42	82
Uxbridge	42	22	12	8	80	42	78
Hungerford Town	42	22	10	10	82	39	76
Corinthian Casuals	42	23	6	13	95	48	75
Egham Town	42	21	8	13	77	67	71
Tring Town	42	20	10	12	86	59	70
Letchworth Garden City	42	18	13	11	68	53	66
Southall	42	18	7	17	81	80	61
Molesey	42	17	9	16	73	56	60
Dorking Town	42	15	9	18	56	75	54
Hemel Hempstead	42	12	14	16	53	59	50
Rainham Town	42	14	4	24	57	94	46
Eastbourne United	42	10	6	26	54	104	36
Epping Town	42	6	8	28	29	89	26
Ware	42	6	6	30	34	97	24
Finchley	42	4	12	26	28	92	24
Horsham	42	5	7	30	32	106	22
Harwich & Parkeston	42	5	7	30	42	130	22

Letchworth Garden City had 1 point deducted

1982-83

Premier Division

Wycombe Wanderers	42	26	7	9	79	47	85
Leytonstone & Ilford	42	24	9	9	71	39	81
Harrow Borough	42	24	7	11	91	58	79
Hayes	42	23	9	10	63	41	78
Sutton United	42	20	8	14	96	71	68
Dulwich Hamlet	42	18	14	10	59	52	68
Slough Town	42	18	13	11	73	36	67
Bognor Regis Town	42	19	8	15	53	48	65
Tooting & Mitcham United	42	18	9	15	65	62	63
Billericay Town	42	17	10	15	54	51	61
Croydon	42	17	9	16	68	58	60
Hendon	42	18	6	18	68	61	60
Bishop's Stortford	42	17	9	16	61	58	60
Barking	42	14	14	14	47	55	56
Bromley	42	14	12	16	51	50	54
Carshalton Athletic	42	15	9	18	58	60	54
Wokingham Town	42	13	9	20	37	51	48
Walthamstow Avenue	42	12	11	19	48	64	47
Staines Town	42	12	11	19	62	79	47
Hitchin Town	42	11	9	22	49	77	42
Woking	42	6	6	30	30	79	24
Leatherhead	42	4	5	33	35	121	17

First Division

Worthing	40	25	6	9	76	39	81
Harlow Town	40	21	11	8	84	55	74
Farnborough Town	40	20	13	7	69	39	73
Hertford Town	40	20	11	9	70	61	71
Oxford City	40	19	13	8	70	49	70
Boreham Wood	40	21	6	13	62	42	69
Metropolitan Police	40	19	9	12	77	57	66
Walton & Hersham	40	17	6	17	65	59	57
Hampton	40	15	10	15	62	60	55
Wembley	40	14	10	16	62	61	52
Aveley	40	15	7	18	52	62	52
Kingstonian	40	13	12	15	53	53	51
Tilbury	40	12	10	18	41	47	46
Feltham	40	11	12	17	45	54	45
Chesham United	40	13	6	21	43	70	45
Epsom & Ewell	40	10	14	16	44	49	44
Lewes	40	12	8	20	47	71	44
Cheshunt	40	10	13	17	41	49	43
Hornchurch	40	11	8	21	45	74	41
Maidenhead United	40	10	10	20	57	87	40
St Albans City	40	10	9	21	52	79	37

St Albans City had 2 points deducted

1983-84

Premier Division

Harrow Borough	42	25	13	4	73	42	88
Worthing	42	20	11	11	89	72	71
Slough Town	42	20	9	13	73	56	69
Sutton United	42	18	12	12	67	45	66
Hayes	42	17	13	12	56	41	64
Hitchin Town	42	16	15	11	58	57	63
Wycombe Wanderers	42	16	14	12	63	52	62
Wokingham Town	42	18	10	14	78	55	61
Hendon	42	17	10	15	62	51	61
Dulwich Hamlet	42	16	11	15	61	64	59
Bishop's Stortford	42	15	13	14	56	57	58
Harlow Town	42	15	11	16	64	70	56
Bognor Regis Town	42	14	13	15	62	69	55
Staines Town	42	15	9	18	63	72	54
Billericay Town	42	15	8	19	53	73	53
Barking	42	13	13	16	60	64	52
Croydon	42	14	10	18	52	58	52
Walthamstow Avenue	42	13	10	19	53	67	49
Leytonstone & Ilford	42	13	9	20	54	67	48
Carshalton Athletic	42	11	10	21	59	72	43
Tooting & Mitcham United	42	10	13	19	50	63	43
Bromley	42	7	11	24	33	72	32

Wokingham Town had 3 points deducted

First Division

Windsor & Eton	42	26	7	9	89	44	85
Epsom & Ewell	42	23	9	10	73	51	78
Wembley	42	21	11	10	65	32	74
Maidenhead United	42	22	8	12	67	42	74
Boreham Wood	42	22	7	13	74	43	73
Farnborough Town	42	18	12	12	78	60	66
Hampton	42	18	12	12	65	49	66
Metropolitan Police	42	20	5	17	79	64	65
Chesham United	42	18	8	16	64	57	62
Tilbury	42	17	10	15	54	64	61
Leatherhead	42	15	10	17	67	56	55
Aveley	42	15	10	17	49	53	55
Woking	42	16	7	19	66	73	55
Hertford Town	42	15	9	18	56	73	54
Oxford City	42	14	9	19	57	56	51
Lewes	42	13	12	17	49	65	51
Walton & Hersham	42	13	10	19	52	70	49
Hornchurch	42	13	10	19	43	65	49
Kingstonian	42	13	9	20	47	67	48
Clapton	42	12	11	19	49	67	47
Cheshunt	42	12	8	22	45	64	44
Feltham	42	7	4	31	31	106	25

Second Division

Basildon United	42	30	7	5	88	27	97
St Albans City	42	29	9	5	100	46	96
Leyton Wingate	42	29	4	9	97	41	91
Tring Town	42	23	11	8	89	44	80
Corinthian Casuals	42	23	11	8	75	47	80
Hungerford Town	42	21	12	9	94	47	75
Uxbridge	42	18	15	9	61	36	69
Grays Athletic	42	20	9	13	72	57	69
Dorking	42	21	5	16	66	54	68
Southall	42	20	8	14	79	60	65
Egham Town	42	16	15	11	59	49	63
Epping Town	42	15	16	11	61	50	61
Molesey	42	13	14	15	59	68	53
Barton Rovers	42	15	8	19	54	64	53
Letchworth Garden City	42	15	7	20	48	66	52
Newbury Town	42	14	5	23	60	82	47
Hemel Hempstead	42	12	9	21	63	69	45
Rainham Town	42	7	5	30	38	114	26
Finchley	42	5	9	28	28	78	24
Eastbourne United	42	7	3	32	36	98	24
Ware	42	6	6	30	48	114	24
Horsham	42	7	4	31	40	104	23

Southall had 2 points deducted
Horsham had 3 points deducted

1984-85

Premier Division

Sutton United	42	23	15	4	115	55	84
Worthing	42	24	8	10	89	59	80
Wycombe Wanderers	42	24	6	12	68	46	78
Wokingham Town	42	20	13	9	74	54	73
Windsor & Eton	42	19	10	13	65	55	67
Bognor Regis Town	42	20	6	16	67	58	66
Dulwich Hamlet	42	16	17	9	82	57	65
Harrow Borough	42	18	8	16	70	56	62
Hayes	42	17	8	17	60	56	59
Tooting & Mitcham United	42	16	11	15	64	66	59
Walthamstow Avenue	42	15	11	16	64	65	56
Croydon	42	15	12	15	62	63	54
Epsom & Ewell	42	13	14	15	65	62	53
Slough Town	42	13	12	17	69	74	51
Carshalton Athletic	42	14	8	20	55	68	50
Bishop's Stortford	42	12	12	18	48	67	48
Hendon	42	9	19	14	62	65	46
Billericay Town	42	11	14	17	53	74	46
Barking	42	13	7	22	43	75	46
Hitchin Town	42	10	15	17	55	70	45
Leytonstone & Ilford	42	11	10	21	37	72	43
Harlow Town	42	5	12	25	45	95	27

Billericay Town had 1 point deducted
Croydon had 3 points deducted

First Division

Farnborough Town	42	26	8	8	101	45	86
Kingstonian	42	23	10	9	67	39	79
Leatherhead	42	23	10	9	109	61	76
Chesham United	42	22	8	12	78	46	74
Wembley	42	20	10	12	59	40	70
St Albans City	42	19	10	13	79	60	67
Tilbury	42	18	13	11	86	68	67
Bromley	42	18	9	15	71	64	63
Hampton	42	17	11	14	75	62	62
Staines Town	42	16	11	15	59	53	59
Maidenhead United	42	17	8	17	65	64	59
Walton & Hersham	42	16	8	18	60	69	55
Aveley	42	16	7	19	62	78	55
Oxford City	42	14	12	16	62	53	54
Lewes	42	15	9	18	70	72	54
Basildon United	42	15	8	19	55	61	53
Boreham Wood	42	15	7	20	72	83	52
Hornchurch	42	15	6	21	55	74	51
Woking	42	15	6	21	60	91	51
Metropolitan Police	42	10	12	20	65	92	42
Clapton	42	5	11	26	50	124	26
Hertford Town	42	5	10	27	36	97	25

Walton & Hersham had 1 point deducted
Leatherhead had 3 points deducted

Second Division North

Leyton Wingate	38	24	9	5	98	50	81
Finchley	38	24	8	6	66	31	79
Heybridge Swifts	38	22	9	7	71	33	75
Stevenage Borough	38	23	6	9	79	49	75
Saffron Walden Town	38	22	8	8	73	31	74
Tring Town	38	19	11	8	76	41	68
Chalfont St Peter	38	17	10	11	72	41	61
Flackwell Heath	38	16	11	11	54	40	59
Berkhamsted Town	38	15	12	11	50	42	57
Letchworth Garden City	38	17	6	15	66	69	57
Royston Town	38	13	9	16	47	77	48
Cheshunt	38	14	5	19	52	57	47
Marlow	38	13	6	19	64	81	45
Hemel Hempstead	38	11	7	20	49	65	40
Barton Rovers	38	9	8	21	40	62	35
Wolverton Town	38	9	8	21	38	77	35
Kingsbury Town	38	9	7	22	53	72	34
Harefield United	38	7	9	22	51	81	30
Haringey Borough	38	6	12	20	38	79	30
Ware	38	7	5	26	40	100	26

Finchley had 1 point deducted
The record of Epping Town was expunged

Second Division South

Grays Athletic	36	24	9	3	84	25	81
Uxbridge	36	22	10	4	81	20	76
Molesey	36	20	5	11	62	42	65
Hungerford Town	36	18	9	9	71	49	63
Whyteleafe	36	17	10	9	66	34	61
Egham Town	36	17	7	12	54	42	58
Southall	36	18	3	15	54	57	57
Bracknell Town	36	15	7	14	54	48	52
Banstead Athletic	36	14	8	14	63	70	50
Horsham	36	13	10	13	44	39	49
Ruislip Manor	36	13	10	13	48	49	49
Dorking	36	12	11	13	45	50	47
Rainham Town	36	12	8	16	58	61	44
Feltham	36	10	13	13	44	58	43
Camberley Town	36	10	12	14	44	54	42
Eastbourne United	36	10	9	17	66	72	39
Petersfield Town	36	9	5	22	41	80	32
Newbury Town	36	8	7	21	35	69	16
Chertsey Town	36	2	3	31	23	118	6

Chertsey Town had 3 points deducted
Newbury Town had 15 points deducted

1985-86

Premier Division

Sutton United	42	29	8	5	109	39	95
Yeovil Town	42	28	7	7	92	48	91
Farnborough Town	42	23	8	11	90	50	77
Croydon	42	23	7	12	70	50	76
Harrow Borough	42	21	8	13	76	66	71
Slough Town	42	18	8	16	66	68	62
Bishop's Stortford	42	17	10	15	55	61	61
Kingstonian	42	15	15	12	57	56	60
Dulwich Hamlet	42	17	9	16	64	79	60
Wokingham Town	42	16	10	16	67	64	58
Windsor & Eton	42	17	7	18	58	75	58
Tooting & Mitcham United	42	14	11	17	65	76	53
Walthamstow Avenue	42	12	14	16	69	70	50
Worthing	42	13	10	19	72	82	49
Bognor Regis Town	42	15	6	21	63	70	48
Hayes	42	10	17	15	36	42	47
Hitchin Town	42	11	14	17	53	69	47
Barking	42	11	13	18	45	55	46
Hendon	42	10	13	19	59	77	43
Carshalton Athletic	42	9	13	20	56	79	40
Billericay Town	42	9	12	21	59	78	39
Epsom & Ewell	42	8	12	22	63	90	36

Bognor Regis Town had 3 points deducted

First Division

St Albans City	42	23	11	8	92	61	80
Bromley	42	24	8	10	68	41	80
Wembley	42	22	12	8	59	30	78
Oxford City	42	22	11	9	75	51	77
Hampton	42	21	11	10	63	45	74
Leyton Wingate	42	21	10	11	77	56	73
Uxbridge	42	20	8	14	64	49	68
Staines Town	42	18	10	14	69	66	64
Boreham Wood	42	15	16	11	62	54	61
Walton & Hersham	42	16	10	16	68	71	58
Lewes	42	16	8	18	61	75	56
Leytonstone & Ilford	42	13	15	14	57	67	54
Finchley	42	12	17	13	61	59	53
Grays Athletic	42	13	11	18	69	75	50
Leatherhead	42	14	8	20	62	68	50
Tilbury	42	13	11	18	60	66	50
Maidenhead United	42	13	7	22	61	67	46
Basildon United	42	12	9	21	52	72	45
Hornchurch	42	11	11	20	44	59	44
Chesham United	42	12	6	24	51	87	42
Harlow Town	42	8	14	20	53	70	38
Aveley	42	8	6	28	59	98	30

Second Division North

Stevenage Borough	38	26	6	6	71	24	84
Kingsbury Town	38	25	8	5	84	35	83
Heybridge Swifts	38	20	8	10	65	46	68
Cheshunt	38	18	10	10	60	40	64
Hertford Town	38	17	7	14	60	50	58
Chalfont St Peter	38	15	11	12	53	50	56
Tring Town	38	14	13	11	58	46	55
Royston Town	38	13	13	12	59	57	52
Saffron Walden Town	38	13	12	13	61	65	51
Berkhamsted Town	38	14	8	16	45	52	50
Haringey Borough	38	14	7	17	49	51	49
Letchworth Garden City	38	13	8	17	46	52	47
Rainham Town	38	14	4	20	54	91	46
Hemel Hempstead	38	12	9	17	50	66	45
Ware	38	11	11	16	56	61	44
Vauxhall Motors	38	11	10	17	58	62	43
Barton Rovers	38	12	7	19	50	60	43
Harefield United	38	9	12	17	56	72	39
Clapton	38	10	7	21	51	90	37
Wolverton Town	38	8	11	19	42	58	35

Second Division South

Southwick	38	25	8	5	86	34	83
Bracknell Town	38	24	9	5	80	23	81
Woking	38	23	9	6	94	45	78
Newbury Town	38	22	7	9	86	53	73
Whyteleafe	38	21	10	7	61	41	73
Molesey	38	21	8	9	59	39	71
Metropolitan Police	38	20	6	12	72	48	66
Southall	38	19	7	12	76	58	64
Dorking	38	18	10	10	70	57	64
Feltham	38	16	7	15	65	60	55
Banstead Athletic	38	15	8	15	60	66	53
Petersfield United	38	12	9	17	61	71	45
Hungerford Town	38	11	6	21	57	78	39
Flackwell Heath	38	11	6	21	46	72	39
Eastbourne United	38	9	8	21	51	81	35
Camberley Town	38	9	7	22	53	64	34
Egham Town	38	7	8	23	41	83	29
Horsham	38	6	10	22	33	74	28
Ruislip Manor	38	5	12	21	44	87	27
Marlow	38	6	5	27	47	108	23

1986-87

Premier Division

Wycombe Wanderers	42	32	5	5	103	32	101
Yeovil Town	42	28	8	6	71	27	92
Slough Town	42	23	8	11	70	44	77
Hendon	42	22	7	13	67	53	73
Bognor Regis Town	42	20	10	12	85	61	70
Harrow Borough	42	20	10	12	68	44	70
Croydon	42	18	10	14	51	48	64
Barking	42	16	14	12	76	56	62
Farnborough Town	42	17	11	14	66	72	62
Bishop's Stortford	42	15	15	12	62	57	60
Bromley	42	16	11	15	63	72	59
Kingstonian	42	16	9	17	58	50	57
Windsor & Eton	42	13	15	14	47	52	54
St Albans City	42	14	9	19	61	70	51
Carshalton Athletic	42	13	9	20	55	68	48
Wokingham Town	42	14	6	22	47	61	48
Hayes	42	12	12	18	45	68	48
Dulwich Hamlet	42	12	10	20	62	71	46
Tooting & Mitcham United	42	12	9	21	51	53	45
Hitchin Town	42	13	5	24	56	69	44
Worthing	42	8	9	25	58	107	33
Walthamstow Avenue	42	4	6	32	36	113	18

First Division

Leytonstone & Ilford	42	30	5	7	78	29	95
Leyton Wingate	42	23	13	6	68	31	82
Bracknell Town	42	24	9	9	92	48	81
Southwick	42	23	7	12	80	66	76
Wembley	42	21	9	12	61	47	72
Grays Athletic	42	19	10	13	76	64	67
Kingsbury Town	42	20	7	15	69	67	67
Boreham Wood	42	20	6	16	59	52	66
Uxbridge	42	18	9	15	60	59	63
Leatherhead	42	17	11	14	45	48	62
Hampton	42	18	5	19	57	55	59
Basildon United	42	16	10	16	58	60	58
Billericay Town	42	14	12	16	57	52	54
Staines Town	42	13	13	16	40	51	52
Lewes	42	15	6	21	55	65	51
Stevenage Borough	42	12	11	19	61	67	47
Oxford City	42	11	10	21	64	72	43
Walton & Hersham	42	11	10	21	53	74	43
Tilbury	42	12	7	23	46	70	43
Epsom & Ewell	42	12	7	23	44	68	43
Maidenhead United	42	11	4	27	44	76	37
Finchley	42	6	11	25	44	90	29

Second Division North

Chesham United	42	28	6	8	81	48	90
Wolverton Town	42	23	14	5	74	32	83
Haringey Borough	42	22	13	7	86	40	79
Heybridge Swifts	42	21	11	10	54	34	74
Aveley	42	19	13	10	68	50	70
Letchworth Garden City	42	19	11	12	77	62	68
Barton Rovers	42	18	11	13	49	39	65
Tring Town	42	19	7	16	69	49	64
Collier Row	42	19	5	18	67	65	62
Ware	42	17	8	17	51	50	59
Saffron Walden Town	42	14	14	14	56	54	56
Wivenhoe Town	42	15	11	16	61	61	56
Vauxhall Motors	42	15	10	17	61	57	55
Hornchurch	42	13	16	13	60	60	55
Hertford Town	42	14	13	15	52	53	55
Berkhamsted Town	42	12	16	14	62	64	52
Harlow Town	42	13	11	18	45	55	50
Rainham Town	42	12	11	19	53	70	47
Clapton	42	10	11	21	45	63	41
Hemel Hempstead	42	9	12	21	48	77	39
Royston Town	42	4	12	26	37	109	24
Cheshunt	42	5	6	31	43	114	21

Second Division South

Woking	40	27	7	6	110	32	88
Marlow	40	28	4	8	78	36	88
Dorking	40	24	12	4	78	30	84
Feltham	40	25	3	12	79	34	78
Ruislip Manor	40	22	10	8	85	47	76
Chertsey Town	40	18	11	11	56	44	65
Metropolitan Police	40	16	13	11	70	61	61
Chalfont St Peter	40	17	10	13	60	55	61
Hungerford Town	40	14	14	12	55	48	56
Harefield United	40	14	14	12	53	47	56
Eastbourne United	40	15	10	15	72	59	55
Whyteleafe	40	12	15	13	52	63	51
Horsham	40	14	8	18	54	61	50
Egham Town	40	14	6	20	45	77	48
Camberley Town	40	13	3	24	62	89	42
Flackwell Heath	40	9	11	20	34	63	38
Banstead Athletic	40	7	15	18	44	61	36
Petersfield United	40	9	8	23	45	84	34
Molesey	40	7	12	21	37	89	33
Newbury Town	40	6	14	20	51	83	32
Southall	40	6	6	28	28	85	24

Second Division North

Wivenhoe Town	42	26	10	6	105	42	88
Collier Row	42	22	13	7	71	39	79
Tilbury	42	18	15	9	61	40	69
Berkhamsted Town	42	19	12	11	71	53	69
Harlow Town	42	17	16	9	67	36	67
Ware	42	17	15	10	63	58	66
Witham Town	42	17	14	11	69	47	65
Vauxhall Motors	42	16	17	9	56	42	65
Heybridge Swifts	42	17	13	12	56	50	64
Tring Town	42	18	6	18	69	67	60
Letchworth Garden City	42	18	5	19	59	64	59
Finchley	42	16	10	16	67	54	58
Clapton	42	14	15	13	50	62	57
Hornchurch	42	13	15	14	56	65	54
Barton Rovers	42	13	10	19	43	60	49
Rainham Town	42	12	12	18	63	66	48
Royston Town	42	13	8	21	49	70	47
Saffron Walden Town	42	13	7	22	34	67	46
Hemel Hempstead	42	11	12	19	38	71	45
Haringey Borough	42	11	8	23	54	78	41
Aveley	42	8	13	21	42	65	37
Hertford Town	42	8	4	30	45	92	28

Second Division South

Chalfont St Peter	42	26	9	7	81	35	87
Metropolitan Police	42	23	17	2	80	32	86
Dorking	42	25	11	6	86	39	86
Feltham	42	21	12	9	74	41	75
Epsom & Ewell	42	21	11	10	71	49	74
Chertsey Town	42	22	7	13	63	47	73
Whyteleafe	42	20	11	11	84	55	71
Hungerford Town	42	21	7	14	66	54	70
Ruislip Manor	42	21	5	16	74	57	68
Yeading	42	19	10	13	83	56	67
Maidenhead United	42	18	12	12	69	54	66
Eastbourne United	42	18	10	14	67	57	64
Harefield Town	42	18	6	18	59	60	60
Egham Town	42	12	12	18	45	55	48
Horsham	42	12	10	20	45	66	46
Southall	42	13	7	22	45	72	46
Molesey	42	11	11	20	42	63	44
Newbury Town	42	8	13	21	40	81	37
Camberley Town	42	9	9	24	51	94	36
Flackwell Heath	42	6	8	28	42	96	26
Banstead Athletic	42	6	7	29	34	81	25
Petersfield United	42	6	7	29	45	102	25

1987-88

Premier Division

Yeovil Town	42	24	9	9	66	34	81
Bromley	42	23	7	12	68	40	76
Slough Town	42	21	9	12	67	41	72
Leytonstone & Ilford	42	20	11	11	59	43	71
Wokingham Town	42	21	7	14	62	52	70
Hayes	42	20	9	13	62	48	69
Windsor & Eton	42	16	17	9	59	43	65
Farnborough Town	42	17	11	14	63	60	62
Carshalton Athletic	42	16	13	13	49	41	61
Hendon	42	16	12	14	62	58	60
Tooting & Mitcham United	42	15	14	13	57	59	59
Harrow Borough	42	15	11	16	53	58	56
Bishop's Stortford	42	15	10	17	55	58	55
Kingstonian	42	14	12	16	47	53	54
St Albans City	42	15	6	21	60	69	51
Bognor Regis Town	42	14	9	19	41	57	51
Leyton Wingate	42	14	8	20	58	64	50
Croydon	42	11	13	18	40	52	46
Barking	42	11	12	19	44	57	45
Dulwich Hamlet	42	10	11	21	46	64	41
Hitchin Town	42	10	8	24	46	79	38
Basingstoke Town	42	6	17	19	37	71	35

First Division

Marlow	42	32	5	5	100	44	101
Grays Athletic	42	30	10	2	74	25	100
Woking	42	25	7	10	91	52	82
Boreham Wood	42	21	9	12	65	45	72
Staines Town	42	19	11	12	71	48	68
Wembley	42	18	11	13	54	46	65
Basildon United	42	18	9	15	65	58	63
Walton & Hersham	42	15	16	11	53	44	61
Hampton	42	17	10	15	59	54	61
Leatherhead	42	16	11	15	64	53	59
Southwick	42	13	12	17	59	63	51
Oxford City	42	13	12	17	70	77	51
Worthing	42	14	8	20	67	73	50
Kingsbury Town	42	11	17	14	62	69	50
Walthamstow Avenue	42	13	11	18	53	63	50
Lewes	42	12	13	17	83	77	49
Uxbridge	42	11	16	15	41	47	49
Chesham United	42	12	10	20	69	77	46
Bracknell Town	42	12	9	21	54	80	45
Billericay Town	42	11	11	20	58	88	44
Stevenage Borough	42	11	9	22	36	64	42
Wolverton Town	42	3	3	36	23	124	12

1988-89

Premier Division

Leytonstone & Ilford	42	26	11	5	76	36	89
Farnborough Town	42	24	9	9	85	61	81
Slough Town	42	24	6	12	72	42	78
Carshalton Athletic	42	19	15	8	59	36	72
Grays Athletic	42	19	13	10	62	47	70
Kingstonian	42	19	11	12	54	37	68
Bishop's Stortford	42	20	6	16	70	56	66
Hayes	42	18	12	12	6	47	66
Bognor Regis Town	42	17	11	14	38	49	62
Barking	42	16	13	13	49	45	61
Wokingham Town	42	15	11	16	60	54	56
Hendon	42	13	17	12	51	68	56
Windsor & Eton	42	14	13	15	52	50	55
Bromley	42	13	15	14	61	48	54
Leyton Wingate	42	13	15	14	55	56	54
Dulwich Hamlet	42	12	12	18	58	57	48
St Albans City	42	12	9	21	51	59	45
Dagenham	42	11	12	19	53	68	45
Harrow Borough	42	9	13	20	53	75	40
Marlow	42	9	11	22	48	83	38
Tooting & Mitcham United	42	10	6	26	41	81	36
Croydon	42	4	9	29	27	81	21

First Division

Staines Town	40	26	9	5	79	29	87
Basingstoke Town	40	25	8	7	85	36	83
Woking	40	24	10	6	72	30	82
Hitchin Town	40	21	11	8	60	32	74
Wivenhoe Town	40	22	6	12	62	44	72
Lewes	40	21	8	11	72	54	71
Walton & Hersham	40	21	7	12	56	36	70
Kingsbury Town	40	20	7	13	65	41	67
Uxbridge	40	19	7	14	60	54	64
Wembley	40	18	6	16	45	58	60
Boreham Wood	40	16	9	15	57	52	57
Leatherhead	40	14	8	18	56	58	50
Metropolitan Police	40	13	9	18	52	68	48
Chesham United	40	12	9	19	54	67	45
Southwick	40	9	15	16	44	58	42
Chalfont St Peter	40	11	9	20	56	82	42
Hampton	40	7	14	19	37	62	35
Worthing	40	8	10	22	49	80	32
Collier Row	40	8	7	25	37	82	31
Bracknell Town	40	8	6	26	38	70	30
Basildon Town	40	6	7	27	34	77	25

Worthing had 2 points deducted.

Second Division North

Harlow Town	42	27	9	6	83	38	90
Purfleet	42	22	12	8	60	42	78
Tring Town	42	22	10	10	65	44	76
Stevenage Borough	42	20	13	9	84	55	73
Heybridge Swifts	42	21	9	12	64	43	72
Billericay Town	42	19	11	12	65	52	68
Clapton	42	18	11	13	65	56	65
Barton Rovers	42	18	11	13	58	50	65
Aveley	42	18	10	14	54	52	64
Hertford Town	42	16	13	13	62	49	59
Ware	42	17	8	17	60	65	59
Hemel Hempstead	42	16	10	16	55	58	58
Witham Town	42	16	7	19	69	67	55
Vauxhall Motors	42	15	9	18	53	57	54
Berkhamsted Town	42	14	10	18	57	70	52
Hornchurch	42	11	16	15	59	61	49
Tilbury	42	13	10	19	53	60	49
Royston Town	42	12	7	23	46	72	43
Rainham Town	42	9	15	18	49	62	42
Saffron Walden Town	42	8	16	18	54	72	40
Letchworth Garden City	42	4	18	20	34	71	30
Wolverton Town	42	5	7	30	42	95	13

Hertford Town 2 points deducted, Wolverton Town 9 points deducted.

Second Division South

Dorking	40	32	4	4	109	35	100
Whyteleafe	40	25	9	6	86	41	84
Finchley	40	21	9	10	70	45	72
Molesey	40	19	13	8	58	42	70
Harefield United	40	19	7	14	56	45	64
Hungerford Town	40	17	13	10	55	45	64
Ruislip Manor	40	16	9	15	56	43	57
Feltham	40	16	9	15	58	53	57
Epsom & Ewell	40	16	8	16	55	55	56
Egham Town	40	16	7	17	54	58	55
Eastbourne United	40	15	9	16	68	61	54
Chertsey Town	40	13	14	13	55	58	53
Flackwell Heath	40	13	11	16	51	49	50
Camberley Town	40	15	5	20	51	71	50
Yeading	40	13	9	18	47	63	46
Banstead Athletic	40	12	8	20	50	65	44
Maidenhead United	40	10	13	17	44	61	43
Southall	40	11	10	19	41	73	43
Newbury Town	40	11	8	21	47	65	41
Horsham	40	7	14	19	36	68	35
Petersfield United	40	5	7	28	36	87	22

Yeading had 2 points deducted.

1989-90

Premier Division

Slough Town	42	27	11	4	85	38	92
Wokingham Town	42	26	11	5	67	34	89
Aylesbury United	42	25	9	8	86	30	84
Kingstonian	42	24	9	9	87	51	81
Grays Athletic	42	19	13	10	59	44	70
Dagenham	42	17	15	10	54	43	66
Leyton Wingate	42	20	6	16	54	48	66
Basingstoke Town	42	18	9	15	65	55	63
Bishop's Stortford	42	19	6	17	60	59	63
Carshalton Athletic	42	19	5	18	63	59	59
Redbridge Forest	42	16	11	15	65	62	59
Hendon	42	15	10	17	54	63	55
Windsor & Eton	42	13	15	14	51	47	54
Hayes	42	14	11	17	61	59	53
St Albans City	42	13	10	19	49	59	49
Staines Town	42	14	6	22	53	69	48
Marlow	42	11	13	18	42	59	46
Harrow Borough	42	11	10	21	51	79	43
Bognor Regis Town	42	9	14	19	37	67	41
Barking	42	7	11	24	53	86	32
Bromley	42	7	11	24	32	69	32
Dulwich Hamlet	42	6	8	28	32	80	26

Carshalton Athletic had 3 points deducted.

First Division

Wivenhoe Town	42	31	7	4	94	36	100
Woking	42	30	8	4	102	29	98
Southwick	42	23	15	4	68	30	84
Hitchin Town	42	22	13	7	60	30	79
Walton & Hersham	42	20	10	12	68	50	70
Dorking	42	19	12	11	66	41	69
Boreham Wood	42	17	13	12	60	59	64
Harlow Town	42	16	13	13	60	53	61
Metropolitan Police	42	16	11	15	54	59	59
Chesham United	42	15	12	15	46	49	57
Chalfont St Peter	42	14	13	15	50	59	55
Tooting & Mitcham United	42	14	13	15	51	52	55
Worthing	42	15	8	19	56	63	53
Whyteleafe	42	11	16	15	50	65	49
Lewes	42	12	11	19	55	65	47
Wembley	42	11	10	21	57	68	43
Croydon	42	9	16	17	43	57	43
Uxbridge	42	11	10	21	52	75	43
Hampton	42	8	13	21	28	51	37
Leatherhead	42	7	10	25	34	77	31
Purfleet	42	7	8	27	33	78	29
Kingsbury Town	42	8	10	24	45	78	25

Kingsbury Town had 9 points deducted

Second Division North

Heybridge Swifts	42	26	9	7	79	29	87
Aveley	42	23	16	3	68	24	85
Hertford Town	42	24	11	7	92	51	83
Stevenage Borough	42	21	16	5	70	31	79
Barton Rovers	42	22	6	14	60	45	72
Tilbury	42	20	9	13	68	54	69
Basildon United	42	13	20	9	50	44	59
Collier Row	42	15	13	14	43	45	58
Royston Town	42	15	11	16	63	72	56
Saffron Walden Town	42	15	11	16	60	73	56
Vauxhall Motors	42	14	13	15	55	54	55
Clapton	42	13	16	13	50	46	54
Ware	42	14	11	17	53	59	53
Hemel Hempstead	42	12	15	15	58	70	51
Billericay Town	42	13	11	18	49	58	50
Hornchurch	42	12	12	18	49	64	48
Berkhamsted Town	42	9	16	17	44	68	43
Finchley	42	11	10	21	50	75	43
Tring Town	42	10	9	23	48	70	39
Witham Town	42	8	14	20	44	56	38
Rainham Town	42	9	11	22	48	75	38
Letchworth Garden City	42	7	12	23	30	68	33

Clapton had 1 point deducted

Second Division South

Yeading	40	29	4	7	86	37	91
Molesey	40	24	11	5	76	30	83
Abingdon Town	40	22	9	9	64	39	75
Ruislip Manor	40	20	12	8	60	32	72
Maidenhead United	40	20	12	8	66	39	72
Southall	40	22	5	13	56	33	71
Newbury Town	40	21	7	12	50	36	70
Flackwell Heath	40	16	11	13	69	65	59
Hungerford Town	40	14	16	10	54	51	58
Egham Town	40	12	14	14	39	38	50
Banstead Athletic	40	14	8	18	46	47	50
Harefield United	40	13	9	18	44	46	48
Chertsey Town	40	13	9	18	53	58	48
Epsom & Ewell	40	13	9	18	49	54	48
Malden Vale	40	13	7	20	36	67	46
Eastbourne United	40	11	10	19	47	65	43
Camberley Town	40	11	9	20	44	66	42
Feltham	40	11	7	22	47	80	40
Bracknell Town	40	10	9	21	40	57	39
Petersfield United	40	10	8	22	48	93	38
Horsham	40	4	8	28	29	70	20

Second Division North

Stevenage Borough	42	34	5	3	122	29	107
Vauxhall Motors	42	24	10	8	82	50	82
Billericay Town	42	22	8	12	70	41	74
Ware	42	22	8	12	78	51	74
Berkhamsted Town	42	19	11	12	60	51	68
Witham Town	42	19	10	13	70	59	67
Purfleet	42	17	14	11	68	57	65
Rainham Town	42	19	7	16	57	46	64
Hemel Hempstead	42	16	14	12	62	56	62
Barton Rovers	42	17	10	15	61	58	61
Saffron Walden Town	42	16	13	13	72	77	61
Collier Row	42	16	11	15	63	63	59
Kingsbury Town	42	17	8	17	64	72	59
Edgware Town	42	17	7	18	73	65	58
Hertford Town	42	16	10	16	69	70	58
Royston Town	42	14	15	13	78	62	57
Tilbury	42	14	6	22	70	79	48
Basildon United	42	11	10	21	61	90	43
Hornchurch	42	10	9	23	53	87	39
Clapton	42	9	10	23	54	93	34
Finchley	42	6	7	29	50	112	24
Tring Town	42	1	9	32	30	99	12

Finchley had 1 point deducted
Clapton had 3 points deducted

1990-91

Premier Division

Redbridge Forest	42	29	6	7	74	43	93
Enfield	42	26	11	5	83	30	89
Aylesbury United	42	24	11	7	90	47	83
Woking	42	24	10	8	84	39	82
Kingstonian	42	21	12	9	86	57	75
Grays Athletic	42	20	8	14	66	53	68
Marlow	42	18	13	11	72	49	67
Hayes	42	20	5	17	60	57	65
Carshalton Athletic	42	19	7	16	80	67	64
Wivenhoe Town	42	16	11	15	69	66	59
Wokingham Town	42	15	13	14	58	54	58
Windsor & Eton	42	15	10	17	48	63	55
Bishop's Stortford	42	14	12	16	54	49	54
Dagenham	42	13	11	18	62	68	50
Hendon	42	12	10	20	48	62	46
St Albans City	42	11	12	19	60	74	45
Bognor Regis Town	42	12	8	22	44	71	44
Basingstoke Town	42	12	7	23	57	95	43
Staines Town	42	10	10	22	46	79	39
Harrow Borough	42	10	8	24	57	84	38
Barking	42	8	10	24	41	85	34
Leyton Wingate	42	7	7	28	44	91	28

Staines Town had 1 point deducted

First Division

Chesham United	42	27	8	7	102	37	89
Bromley	42	22	14	6	62	37	80
Yeading	42	23	8	11	75	45	77
Aveley	42	21	9	12	76	43	72
Hitchin Town	42	21	9	12	78	50	72
Tooting & Mitcham United	42	20	12	10	71	48	72
Walton & Hersham	42	21	8	13	73	48	71
Molesey	42	22	5	15	65	46	71
Whyteleafe	42	21	6	15	62	53	69
Dorking	42	20	5	17	78	67	65
Chalfont St Peter	42	19	5	18	56	63	62
Dulwich Hamlet	42	16	11	15	67	54	59
Harlow Town	42	17	8	17	73	64	59
Boreham Wood	42	15	8	19	46	53	53
Wembley	42	13	12	17	62	59	51
Uxbridge	42	15	5	22	45	61	50
Croydon	42	15	5	22	44	85	50
Heybridge Swifts	42	13	10	19	46	59	49
Southwick	42	13	8	21	49	75	47
Lewes	42	10	8	24	49	82	38
Metropolitan Police	42	9	6	27	55	76	33
Worthing	42	2	4	36	28	157	10

Second Division South

Abingdon Town	42	29	7	6	95	28	94
Maidenhead United	42	28	8	6	85	33	92
Egham Town	42	27	6	9	100	46	87
Malden Vale	42	26	5	11	72	44	83
Ruislip Manor	42	25	5	12	93	44	80
Southall	42	23	10	9	84	43	79
Harefield United	42	23	10	9	81	56	79
Newbury Town	42	23	8	11	71	45	77
Hungerford Town	42	16	13	13	84	69	61
Leatherhead	42	17	9	16	82	55	60
Banstead Athletic	42	15	13	14	58	62	58
Hampton	42	14	15	13	62	43	57
Epsom & Ewell	42	15	12	15	49	50	57
Chertsey Town	42	15	9	18	76	72	54
Horsham	42	14	7	21	58	67	49
Flackwell Heath	42	11	11	20	56	78	44
Bracknell Town	42	11	7	24	60	97	40
Feltham	42	10	8	24	45	80	38
Cove	42	10	7	25	56	94	37
Eastbourne United	42	10	7	25	53	109	37
Petersfield United	42	6	3	33	35	119	21
Camberley Town	42	1	6	35	27	143	9

1991-92

Premier Division

Woking	42	30	7	5	96	25	97
Enfield	42	24	7	11	59	45	79
Sutton United	42	19	13	10	88	51	70
Chesham United	42	20	10	12	67	48	70
Wokingham Town	42	19	10	13	73	58	67
Marlow	42	20	7	15	56	50	67
Aylesbury United	42	16	17	9	69	46	65
Carshalton Athletic	42	18	8	16	64	67	62
Dagenham	42	15	16	11	70	59	61
Kingstonian	42	17	8	17	71	65	59
Windsor & Eton	42	15	11	16	56	56	56
Bromley	42	14	12	16	51	57	54
St Albans City	42	14	11	17	66	70	53
Basingstoke Town	42	14	11	17	56	65	53
Grays Athletic	42	14	11	17	53	68	53
Wivenhoe Town	42	16	4	22	56	81	52
Hendon	42	13	9	20	59	73	48
Harrow Borough	42	11	13	18	58	78	46
Hayes	42	10	14	18	52	63	44
Staines Town	42	11	10	21	43	73	43
Bognor Regis Town	42	9	11	22	51	89	38
Bishop's Stortford	42	7	12	23	41	68	33

First Division

Stevenage Borough	40	30	6	4	95	37	96
Yeading	40	24	10	6	83	34	82
Dulwich Hamlet	40	22	9	9	71	40	75
Boreham Wood	40	22	7	11	65	40	73
Wembley	40	21	6	13	54	43	69
Abingdon Town	40	19	8	13	60	47	65
Tooting & Mitcham United	40	16	13	11	57	45	61
Hitchin Town	40	17	10	13	55	45	61
Walton & Hersham	40	15	13	12	62	50	58
Molesey	40	16	9	15	55	61	57
Dorking	40	16	7	17	68	65	55
Barking	40	14	11	15	51	54	53
Chalfont St Peter	40	15	6	19	62	70	51
Leyton Wingate	40	13	11	16	53	56	50
Uxbridge	40	13	8	19	47	62	47
Maidenhead United	40	13	7	20	52	61	46
Harlow Town	40	11	9	20	50	70	42
Croydon	40	11	6	23	44	68	39
Heybridge Swifts	40	8	9	23	33	71	33
Whyteleafe	40	7	10	23	42	78	31
Aveley	40	8	3	29	33	95	27

Second Division

Purfleet	42	27	8	7	97	48	89
Lewes	42	23	14	5	74	36	83
Billericay Town	42	24	8	10	75	44	80
Leatherhead	42	23	6	13	68	40	75
Ruislip Manor	42	20	9	13	74	51	69
Egham Town	42	19	12	11	81	62	69
Metropolitan Police	42	20	9	13	76	58	69
Saffron Walden Town	42	19	11	12	86	67	68
Hemel Hempstead	42	18	10	14	63	50	64
Hungerford Town	42	18	7	17	53	58	61
Barton Rovers	42	17	8	17	61	64	59
Worthing	42	17	8	17	67	72	59
Witham Town	42	16	11	15	56	61	59
Banstead Athletic	42	16	10	16	69	58	58
Malden Vale	42	15	12	15	63	48	57
Rainham Town	42	14	13	15	53	48	55
Ware	42	14	9	19	58	62	51
Berkhamsted Town	42	13	11	18	56	57	50
Harefield United	42	11	7	24	47	66	40
Southall	42	8	7	27	39	93	31
Southwick	42	6	2	34	29	115	20
Newbury Town	42	4	8	30	30	117	20

Third Division

Edgware Town	40	30	3	7	106	44	93
Chertsey Town	40	29	4	7	115	44	91
Tilbury	40	26	9	5	84	40	87
Hampton	40	26	5	9	93	35	83
Horsham	40	23	8	9	92	51	77
Cove	40	21	9	10	74	49	72
Flackwell Heath	40	19	12	9	78	50	69
Thame United	40	19	7	14	73	46	64
Epsom & Ewell	40	17	11	12	55	50	62
Collier Row	40	17	9	14	67	59	60
Royston Town	40	17	7	16	59	58	58
Kingsbury Town	40	12	10	18	54	61	46
Hertford Town	40	12	10	18	55	73	46
Petersfield United	40	12	9	19	45	67	45
Camberley Town	40	11	8	21	52	69	41
Feltham & Hounslow	40	11	2	22	53	78	40
Bracknell Town	40	10	7	23	48	90	37
Hornchurch	40	8	7	25	40	87	31
Tring Town	40	9	4	27	35	94	31
Clapton	40	9	3	28	47	92	30
Eastbourne United	40	5	5	30	34	121	20

1992-93

Premier Division

Chesham United	42	30	8	4	104	34	98
St Albans City	42	28	9	5	103	50	93
Enfield	42	25	6	11	94	48	81
Carshalton Athletic	42	22	10	10	96	56	76
Sutton United	42	18	14	10	74	57	68
Grays Athletic	42	18	11	13	61	64	65
Stevenage Borough	42	8	16	62	60	62
Harrow Borough	42	16	14	12	59	60	62
Hayes	42	16	13	13	64	59	61
Aylesbury United	42	18	6	18	70	77	60
Hendon	42	12	18	12	52	54	54
Basingstoke Town	42	12	17	13	49	45	53
Kingstonian	42	14	10	18	59	58	52
Dulwich Hamlet	42	12	14	16	52	66	50
Marlow	42	12	11	19	72	73	47
Wokingham Town	42	11	13	18	62	81	46
Bromley	42	11	13	18	51	72	46
Wivenhoe Town	42	13	7	22	41	75	46
Yeading	42	11	12	19	58	66	45
Staines Town	42	10	13	19	59	77	43
Windsor & Eton	42	8	7	27	40	90	31
Bognor Regis Town	42	5	10	27	46	106	25

First Division

Hitchin Town	40	25	7	8	67	29	82
Molesey	40	23	11	6	81	38	80
Dorking	40	23	9	8	73	40	78
Purfleet	40	19	12	9	67	42	69
Bishop's Stortford	40	19	10	11	63	42	67
Abingdon Town	40	17	13	10	65	47	64
Tooting & Mitcham United	40	17	12	11	68	46	63
Billericay Town	40	18	6	16	67	61	60
Wembley	40	14	15	11	44	34	57
Walton & Hersham	40	14	12	14	58	54	54
Boreham Wood	40	12	14	14	44	43	50
Maidenhead United	40	10	18	12	45	50	48
Leyton	40	11	14	15	56	61	47
Whyteleafe	40	12	10	18	63	71	46
Uxbridge	40	11	13	16	50	59	46
Heybridge Swifts	40	11	9	20	47	65	42
Croydon	40	11	9	20	54	82	42
Chalfont St Peter	40	7	17	16	48	70	38
Barking	40	10	8	22	42	80	38
Lewes	40	9	10	21	34	80	37
Aveley	40	9	7	24	45	87	34

Second Division

Worthing	42	28	7	7	105	50	91
Ruislip Manor	42	25	12	5	78	33	87
Berkhamsted Town	42	24	8	10	77	55	80
Hemel Hempstead	42	22	12	8	84	52	78
Metropolitan Police	42	22	6	14	84	51	72
Malden Vale	42	20	9	13	78	54	69
Chertsey Town	42	20	7	15	84	60	67
Saffron Walden Town	42	19	10	13	63	49	67
Newbury Town	42	14	18	10	53	51	60
Hampton	42	16	11	15	59	59	59
Edgware Town	42	16	10	16	84	75	58
Egham Town	42	16	9	17	60	71	57
Banstead Athletic	42	14	13	15	67	52	55
Leatherhead	42	14	11	17	66	61	53
Ware	42	12	11	19	68	76	47
Witham Town	42	10	16	16	54	65	46
Tilbury	42	12	8	22	55	101	44
Barton Rovers	42	9	14	19	40	66	41
Hungerford Town	42	11	8	23	37	93	41
Rainham Town	42	9	10	23	56	80	37
Harefield United	42	10	7	25	37	72	37
Southall	42	7	7	28	43	106	28

Third Division

Aldershot Town	38	28	8	2	90	35	92
Thame United	38	21	11	6	84	38	74
Collier Row	38	21	11	6	68	30	74
Leighton Town	38	21	10	7	89	47	73
Cove	38	21	8	9	69	42	71
Northwood	38	19	11	8	84	68	68
Royston Town	38	17	8	13	59	42	59
East Thurrock United	38	17	7	14	69	58	58
Kingsbury Town	38	15	9	14	62	59	54
Hertford Town	38	14	10	14	61	64	52
Flackwell Heath	38	15	6	17	82	76	51
Tring Town	38	12	11	15	59	63	47
Hornchurch	38	11	13	14	53	52	46
Horsham	38	12	7	19	63	72	43
Epsom & Ewell	38	10	11	17	52	67	41
Bracknell Town	38	7	13	18	52	94	34
Clapton	38	8	7	23	46	74	31
Camberley Town	38	8	7	23	37	72	31
Petersfield United	38	6	12	20	36	90	30
Feltham & Hounslow	38	5	4	29	47	119	19

Second Division

Newbury Town	42	32	7	3	115	36	103
Chertsey Town	42	33	3	6	121	48	102
Aldershot Town	42	30	7	5	78	27	97
Barton Rovers	42	25	8	9	68	37	83
Witham Town	42	21	10	11	68	51	73
Malden Vale	42	20	10	12	70	49	70
Thame United	42	19	12	11	87	51	69
Metropolitan Police	42	20	9	13	75	54	69
Banstead Athletic	42	19	9	14	56	53	66
Aveley	42	19	5	18	60	66	62
Edgware Town	42	16	10	16	88	75	58
Saffron Walden Town	42	17	7	18	61	62	58
Hemel Hempstead	42	14	11	17	47	43	53
Egham Town	42	14	8	20	48	65	50
Ware	42	14	7	21	48	76	49
Hungerford Town	42	13	7	22	56	66	46
Tilbury	42	13	3	26	59	81	42
Hampton	42	12	5	25	42	70	41
Leatherhead	42	10	6	26	46	92	36
Lewes	42	8	11	24	38	85	34
Collier Row	42	7	8	27	37	88	29
Rainham Town	42	4	2	36	24	116	14

Third Division

Bracknell Town	40	25	8	7	78	29	83
Cheshunt	40	23	12	5	62	34	81
Oxford City	40	24	6	10	94	55	78
Harlow Town	40	22	11	7	61	36	77
Southall	40	17	12	11	66	53	63
Camberley Town	40	18	7	15	56	50	61
Hertford Town	40	18	6	16	67	65	60
Royston Town	40	15	11	14	44	41	56
Northwood	40	15	11	14	78	77	56
Epsom & Ewell	40	15	9	16	63	62	54
Harefield United	40	12	15	13	45	55	51
Cove	40	15	6	19	59	74	51
Kingsbury Town	40	12	14	14	57	54	50
Feltham & Hounslow	40	14	7	19	60	63	49
Leighton Town	40	12	11	17	51	64	47
East Thurrock Town	40	10	15	15	65	64	45
Clapton	40	12	9	19	51	65	45
Hornchurch	40	12	8	20	42	60	44
Tring Town	40	10	11	19	48	64	41
Flackwell Heath	40	9	11	20	44	83	38
Horsham	40	6	8	26	43	86	26

1993-94

Premier Division

Stevenage Borough	42	31	4	7	88	39	97
Enfield	42	28	8	6	80	28	92
Marlow	42	25	7	10	90	67	82
Chesham United	42	24	8	10	73	45	80
Sutton United	42	23	10	9	77	31	79
Carshalton Athletic	42	22	7	13	81	53	73
St Albans City	42	21	10	11	81	54	73
Hitchin Town	42	21	7	14	81	56	70
Harrow Borough	42	18	11	13	54	56	65
Kingstonian	42	18	9	15	101	64	63
Hendon	42	18	9	15	61	51	63
Aylesbury United	42	17	7	18	64	67	58
Hayes	42	15	8	19	63	72	53
Grays Athletic	42	15	5	22	56	69	50
Bromley	42	14	7	21	56	69	49
Dulwich Hamlet	42	13	8	21	52	74	47
Yeading	42	11	13	18	58	66	46
Molesey	42	11	11	20	44	62	44
Wokingham Town	42	11	6	25	38	67	39
Dorking	42	9	4	29	58	104	31
Basingstoke Town	42	5	12	25	38	86	27
Wivenhoe Town	42	5	3	34	38	152	18

First Division

Bishop's Stortford	42	24	13	5	83	31	85
Purfleet	42	22	12	8	70	44	78
Walton & Hersham	42	22	11	9	81	53	77
Tooting & Mitcham United	42	21	12	9	66	37	75
Heybridge Swifts	42	20	11	11	72	45	71
Billericay Town	42	20	11	11	70	51	71
Abingdon Town	42	20	10	12	61	50	70
Worthing	42	19	11	12	79	46	68
Leyton	42	20	8	14	88	66	68
Boreham Wood	42	17	15	10	69	50	66
Staines Town	42	18	9	15	85	56	63
Bognor Regis Town	42	15	14	13	57	48	59
Wembley	42	16	10	16	66	52	58
Barking	42	15	11	16	63	69	56
Uxbridge	42	15	8	19	57	58	53
Whyteleafe	42	15	6	21	71	90	51
Maidenhead United	42	12	13	17	52	48	49
Berkhamsted Town	42	12	9	21	65	77	45
Ruislip Manor	42	10	8	24	42	79	38
Chalfont St Peter	42	7	10	25	40	79	31
Windsor & Eton	42	8	7	27	47	94	31
Croydon	42	3	3	36	37	198	12

1994-95

Premier Division

Enfield	42	26	9	5	106	43	93
Slough Town	42	22	13	7	82	56	79
Hayes	42	20	14	8	66	47	74
Aylesbury United	42	21	6	15	86	59	69
Hitchin Town	42	18	12	12	68	59	66
Bromley	42	18	11	13	76	67	65
St Albans City	42	17	13	12	96	81	64
Molesey	42	18	8	16	65	61	62
Yeading	42	14	15	13	60	59	57
Harrow Borough	42	17	6	19	64	67	57
Dulwich Hamlet	42	16	9	17	70	82	57
Carshalton Athletic	42	16	9	17	69	84	57
Kingstonian	42	16	8	18	62	57	56
Walton & Hersham	42	14	11	17	75	73	53
Sutton United	42	13	12	17	74	69	51
Purfleet	42	13	12	17	76	90	51
Hendon	42	12	14	16	57	65	50
Grays Athletic	42	11	16	15	57	61	49
Bishop's Stortford	42	12	11	19	53	76	47
Chesham United	42	12	9	21	60	87	45
Marlow	42	10	9	23	52	84	39
Wokingham Town	42	6	9	27	39	86	27

First Division

Boreham Wood	42	31	5	6	90	38	98
Worthing	42	21	13	8	93	49	76
Chertsey Town	42	21	11	10	109	57	74
Aldershot Town	42	23	5	14	80	53	74
Billericay Town	42	20	9	13	68	52	69
Staines Town	42	17	12	13	83	65	63
Basingstoke Town	42	17	10	15	81	71	61
Tooting & Mitcham United	42	15	14	13	58	48	59
Wembley	42	16	11	15	70	61	59
Abingdon Town	42	16	11	15	67	69	59
Whyteleafe	42	17	7	18	70	78	58
Maidenhead United	42	15	12	15	73	76	57
Uxbridge	42	15	11	16	54	62	56
Leyton	42	15	10	17	67	66	55
Barking	42	16	7	19	74	77	55
Heybridge Swifts	42	16	6	20	73	78	54
Ruislip Manor	42	14	11	17	70	75	53
Bognor Regis Town	42	13	14	15	57	63	53
Berkhamsted Town	42	14	10	18	54	70	52
Newbury Town	42	12	15	15	58	71	51
Wivenhoe Town	42	8	7	27	47	94	31
Dorking	42	3	3	36	40	163	12

Second Division

Thame United	42	30	3	9	97	49	93
Barton Rovers	42	25	7	10	93	51	82
Oxford City	42	24	8	10	86	47	80
Bracknell Town	42	23	9	10	86	47	78
Metropolitan Police	42	19	12	11	81	65	69
Hampton	42	20	9	13	79	74	69
Croydon	42	20	5	17	85	65	65
Banstead Athletic	42	18	10	14	73	59	64
Saffron Walden Town	42	17	13	12	64	59	64
Chalfont St Peter	42	17	12	13	67	54	63
Witham Town	42	18	9	15	75	64	63
Leatherhead	42	16	12	14	71	75	60
Edgware Town	42	16	10	16	70	66	58
Tilbury	42	15	9	18	62	82	54
Cheshunt	42	13	13	16	66	81	52
Ware	42	14	7	21	61	81	49
Egham Town	42	11	14	17	60	65	47
Hemel Hempstead	42	10	11	21	45	76	41
Hungerford Town	42	11	7	24	55	81	40
Windsor & Eton	42	10	8	24	58	84	38
Aveley	42	9	5	28	48	95	32
Malden Vale	42	5	9	28	46	108	24

Third Division

Collier Row	40	30	5	5	86	23	95
Canvey Island	40	28	4	8	88	42	88
Bedford Town	40	22	11	7	90	50	77
Northwood	40	22	8	10	80	47	74
Horsham	40	22	6	12	84	61	72
Southall	40	21	8	11	87	59	71
Leighton Town	40	20	8	12	66	43	68
Camberley Town	40	19	8	13	59	39	65
Kingsbury Town	40	18	11	1	72	54	65
Hornchurch	40	17	8	15	64	63	59
Clapton	40	14	11	15	69	61	53
Tring Town	40	13	12	15	68	69	51
East Thurrock United	40	14	8	18	60	79	50
Epsom & Ewell	40	13	10	17	58	62	49
Harlow Town	40	13	8	19	53	83	47
Harefield United	40	12	8	20	51	79	44
Hertford Town	40	11	10	19	56	78	43
Feltham & Hounslow	40	13	4	23	64	87	43
Flackwell Heath	40	8	4	28	50	99	28
Lewes	40	6	5	29	34	104	23
Cove	40	3	5	32	37	94	14

1995-96

Premier Division

Hayes	42	24	14	4	76	32	86
Enfield	42	26	8	8	78	35	86
Boreham Wood	42	24	1	7	69	29	83
Yeovil Town	42	23	11	8	83	51	80
Dulwich Hamlet	42	23	11	8	85	59	80
Carshalton Athletic	42	22	8	12	68	49	74
St Albans City	42	20	12	10	70	41	72
Kingstonian	42	20	11	11	62	38	71
Harrow Borough	42	19	10	13	70	56	67
Sutton United	42	17	14	11	71	56	65
Aylesbury United	42	17	12	13	71	58	63
Bishop's Stortford	42	16	9	17	61	62	57
Yeading	42	11	14	17	48	60	47
Hendon	42	12	10	20	52	65	46
Chertsey Town	42	13	6	23	45	71	45
Purfleet	42	12	8	22	48	67	44
Grays Athletic	42	11	11	20	43	63	44
Hitchin Town	42	10	10	22	41	74	40
Bromley	42	10	7	25	52	91	37
Molesey	42	9	9	24	46	81	36
Walton & Hersham	42	9	7	26	42	79	34
Worthing	42	4	7	31	42	106	19

First Division

Oxford City	42	28	7	7	98	60	91
Heybridge Swifts	42	27	7	8	97	43	88
Staines Town	42	23	11	8	82	59	80
Leyton Pennant	42	22	7	13	77	57	73
Aldershot Town	42	21	9	12	81	46	72
Billericay Town	42	19	9	14	58	58	66
Bognor Regis Town	42	18	11	13	71	53	65
Marlow	42	19	5	18	72	75	62
Basingstoke Town	42	16	13	13	70	60	61
Uxbridge	42	16	12	14	46	49	60
Wokingham Town	42	16	10	16	62	65	58
Chesham United	42	15	12	15	51	44	57
Thame United	42	14	13	15	64	73	55
Maidenhead United	42	12	14	16	50	63	50
Whyteleafe	42	12	13	17	71	81	49
Abingdon Town	42	13	9	20	63	80	48
Barton Rovers	42	12	10	20	69	87	46
Berkhamsted Town	42	11	11	20	52	68	44
Tooting & Mitcham United	42	11	10	21	45	64	43
Ruislip Manor	42	11	9	22	55	77	42
Wembley	42	11	8	23	49	66	41
Barking	42	4	12	26	35	90	24

Second Division

Canvey Island	40	25	12	3	91	36	87
Croydon	40	25	6	9	78	42	81
Hampton	40	23	10	7	74	44	79
Banstead Athletic	40	21	11	8	72	36	74
Collier Row	40	21	11	8	73	41	74
Wivenhoe Town	40	21	8	11	82	57	71
Metropolitan Police	40	18	10	12	57	45	64
Bedford Town	40	18	10	12	69	59	64
Bracknell Town	40	18	8	14	69	50	62
Edgware Town	40	16	9	15	72	67	57
Tilbury	40	12	11	17	52	62	47
Ware	40	13	8	19	55	80	47
Chalfont St Peter	40	11	13	16	58	63	46
Leatherhead	40	12	10	18	71	77	46
Saffron Walden Town	40	11	12	17	56	58	45
Cheshunt	40	10	12	18	56	90	42
Hemel Hempstead	40	10	10	20	46	62	40
Egham Town	40	12	3	25	42	74	39
Witham Town	40	8	10	22	35	68	34
Hungerford Town	40	9	7	24	44	79	34
Dorking	40	8	5	27	44	104	29

Third Division

Horsham	40	29	5	6	95	40	92
Leighton Town	40	28	5	7	95	34	89
Windsor & Eton	40	27	6	7	117	46	87
Wealdstone	40	23	8	9	104	39	77
Harlow Town	40	22	10	8	85	62	76
Northwood	40	20	9	11	76	56	69
Epsom & Ewell	40	18	14	8	95	57	68
Kingsbury Town	40	15	16	9	61	48	61
East Thurrock United	40	17	8	15	61	50	59
Aveley	40	16	10	14	62	53	58
Wingate & Finchley	40	16	7	17	74	70	55
Lewes	40	14	7	19	56	72	49
Flackwell Heath	40	14	5	21	60	84	47
Hornchurch	40	11	8	21	55	77	41
Harefield United	40	11	7	22	49	89	40
Tring Town	40	10	8	22	40	78	38
Camberley Town	40	9	9	22	45	81	36
Hertford Town	40	10	5	25	72	103	35
Cove	40	8	10	22	37	89	34
Clapton	40	9	6	25	48	89	33
Southall	40	9	5	26	34	104	32

Second Division

Collier Row & Romford	42	28	12	2	93	33	96
Leatherhead	42	30	5	7	116	45	95
Wembley	42	23	11	8	92	45	80
Barking	42	22	13	7	69	40	79
Horsham	42	22	11	9	78	48	77
Edgware Town	42	20	14	8	74	50	74
Bedford Town	42	21	8	13	77	43	71
Banstead Athletic	42	21	5	16	75	52	68
Windsor & Eton	42	17	13	12	65	62	64
Leighton Town	42	17	12	13	64	52	63
Bracknell Town	42	17	9	16	78	71	60
Wivenhoe Town	42	17	9	16	69	62	60
Chalfont St Peter	42	14	13	15	53	61	55
Hungerford Town	42	14	13	15	68	77	55
Metropolitan Police	42	14	7	21	72	75	49
Tilbury	42	14	7	21	68	77	49
Witham Town	42	11	10	21	39	67	43
Egham Town	42	10	9	23	47	86	39
Cheshunt	42	9	3	30	37	101	30
Ware	42	7	8	27	44	80	29
Dorking	42	7	6	29	40	100	27
Hemel Hempstead	42	5	6	31	34	125	21

Third Division

Wealdstone	32	24	3	5	72	24	75
Braintree Town	32	23	5	4	99	29	74
Northwood	32	18	10	4	60	31	64
Harlow Town	32	19	4	9	60	41	61
Aveley	32	17	6	9	64	39	57
East Thurrock United	32	16	6	10	58	51	54
Camberley Town	32	15	6	11	55	44	51
Wingate & Finchley	32	11	7	14	52	63	40
Hornchurch	32	11	6	15	35	51	39
Clapton	32	11	6	15	31	49	39
Lewes	32	10	8	14	45	53	38
Kingsbury Town	32	11	4	17	41	54	37
Hertford Town	32	10	6	16	55	65	36
Epsom & Ewell	32	8	5	19	62	78	29
Flackwell Heath	32	8	5	19	36	71	29
Tring Town	32	7	3	22	33	74	24
Southall	32	6	4	22	28	69	22

1996-97

Premier Division

Yeovil Town	42	31	8	3	83	34	101
Enfield	42	28	11	3	91	29	98
Sutton United	42	18	13	11	87	70	67
Dagenham & Redbridge	42	18	11	13	57	43	65
Yeading	42	17	14	11	58	47	65
St Albans City	42	18	11	13	65	55	65
Aylesbury United	42	18	11	13	64	54	65
Purfleet	42	17	11	14	67	63	62
Heybridge Swifts	42	16	14	12	62	62	62
Boreham Wood	42	15	13	14	56	52	58
Kingstonian	42	16	8	18	79	79	56
Dulwich Hamlet	42	14	13	15	57	57	55
Carshalton Athletic	42	14	11	17	51	56	53
Hitchin Town	42	15	7	20	67	73	52
Oxford City	42	14	10	18	67	83	52
Hendon	42	13	12	17	53	59	51
Harrow Borough	42	12	14	16	58	62	50
Bromley	42	13	9	20	67	72	48
Bishop's Stortford	42	10	13	19	43	64	43
Staines Town	42	10	8	24	46	71	38
Grays Athletic	42	8	9	25	43	78	33
Chertsey Town	42	8	7	27	40	98	31

First Division

Chesham United	42	27	6	9	80	46	87
Basingstoke Town	42	22	13	7	81	38	79
Walton & Hersham	42	21	13	8	67	41	76
Hampton	42	21	12	9	62	39	75
Billericay Town	42	21	12	9	69	49	75
Bognor Regis Town	42	21	9	12	63	44	72
Aldershot Town	42	19	14	9	67	45	71
Uxbridge	42	15	17	10	65	48	62
Whyteleafe	42	18	7	17	71	68	61
Molesey	42	17	9	16	50	53	60
Abingdon Town	42	15	11	16	44	42	56
Leyton Pennant	42	14	12	16	71	72	54
Maidenhead United	42	15	10	17	57	57	52
Wokingham Town	42	14	10	18	41	45	52
Thame United	42	13	10	19	57	69	49
Worthing	42	11	11	20	58	77	44
Barton Rovers	42	11	11	20	61	58	44
Croydon	42	11	10	21	40	57	43
Berkhamsted Town	42	11	9	22	47	66	42
Canvey Island	42	9	14	19	52	71	41
Marlow	42	11	6	25	41	84	39
Tooting & Mitcham United	42	8	8	26	40	85	32

Maidenhead United had 3 points deducted

1997-98

Premier Division

Kingstonian	42	25	12	5	84	35	87
Boreham Wood	42	23	11	8	81	42	80
Sutton United	42	22	12	8	83	56	78
Dagenham & Redbridge	42	21	10	11	73	50	73
Hendon	42	21	10	11	69	50	73
Heybridge Swifts	42	18	11	13	74	62	65
Enfield	42	18	8	16	66	58	62
Basingstoke Town	42	17	11	14	56	60	62
Walton & Hersham	42	18	6	18	50	70	60
Purfleet	42	15	13	14	57	58	58
St Albans City	42	17	7	18	54	59	58
Harrow Borough	42	15	10	17	60	67	55
Gravesend & Northfleet	42	15	8	19	65	67	53
Chesham United	42	14	10	18	71	70	52
Bromley	42	13	13	16	53	53	52
Dulwich Hamlet	42	13	11	18	56	67	50
Carshalton Athletic	42	13	9	20	54	77	48
Aylesbury United	42	13	8	21	55	70	47
Bishop's Stortford	42	14	5	23	53	69	47
Yeading	42	12	11	19	49	65	47
Hitchin Town	42	8	15	19	45	62	39
Oxford City	42	7	9	26	35	76	30

First Division

Aldershot Town	42	28	8	6	89	36	92
Billericay Town	42	25	6	11	78	44	81
Hampton	42	22	15	5	75	47	81
Maidenhead United	42	25	5	12	76	37	80
Uxbridge	42	23	6	13	66	59	75
Grays Athletic	42	21	10	11	79	49	73
Romford	42	21	8	13	92	59	71
Bognor Regis Town	42	20	9	13	77	45	69
Leatherhead	42	18	11	13	70	51	65
Leyton Pennant	42	17	11	14	66	58	62
Chertsey Town	42	16	13	13	83	70	61
Worthing	42	17	6	19	64	71	57
Berkhamsted Town	42	15	8	19	59	69	53
Staines Town	42	13	10	19	54	74	49
Croydon	42	13	10	19	47	64	49
Barton Rovers	42	11	13	18	53	72	46
Wembley	42	10	15	17	38	61	45
Molesey	42	10	11	21	47	65	41
Whyteleafe	42	10	10	22	48	83	40
Wokingham Town	42	7	10	25	41	74	31
Abingdon Town	42	9	4	29	47	101	31
Thame United	42	7	9	25	33	96	30

Second Division

Canvey Island	42	30	8	4	116	41	98
Braintree Town	42	29	11	2	117	45	98
Wealdstone	42	24	11	7	81	46	83
Bedford Town	42	22	12	8	55	25	78
Metropolitan Police	42	21	8	13	80	65	71
Wivenhoe Town	42	18	12	12	84	66	66
Edgware Town	42	18	10	14	81	65	64
Chalfont St Peter	42	17	13	12	63	60	64
Northwood	42	17	11	14	65	69	62
Windsor & Eton	42	17	7	18	75	72	58
Tooting & Mitcham United	42	16	9	17	58	56	57
Barking	42	15	12	15	62	75	57
Banstead Athletic	42	15	9	18	60	63	54
Marlow	42	16	5	21	64	78	53
Horsham	42	13	9	20	67	75	48
Bracknell Town	42	13	8	21	68	93	47
Leighton Town	42	13	6	23	45	78	45
Hungerford Town	42	11	11	20	66	77	44
Witham Town	42	9	13	20	55	68	40
Tilbury	42	9	12	21	57	88	39
Egham Town	42	9	5	28	47	101	32
Cheshunt	42	4	10	28	31	90	32

Third Division

Hemel Hempstead	38	27	6	5	86	28	87
Hertford Town	38	26	5	7	77	31	83
Harlow Town	38	24	11	3	81	43	83
Camberley Town	38	24	7	7	93	43	79
Ford United	38	23	9	6	90	34	78
East Thurrock United	38	23	7	8	70	40	76
Epsom & Ewell	38	17	6	15	69	57	57
Ware	38	17	6	15	69	57	57
Aveley	38	16	7	15	65	57	55
Corinthian Casuals	38	16	6	16	59	57	54
Hornchurch	38	12	9	17	55	68	45
Clapton	38	13	6	19	46	61	45
Flackwell Heath	38	12	9	17	50	76	45
Croydon Athletic	38	12	7	19	58	63	43
Tring Town	38	12	7	19	51	69	43
Southall	38	10	6	22	41	85	46
Dorking	38	9	6	23	49	94	33
Wingate & Finchley	38	7	8	23	46	80	29
Lewes	38	7	5	26	34	88	26
Kingsbury Town	38	5	3	30	35	93	18

1998-99

Premier Division

Sutton United	42	27	7	8	89	39	88
Aylesbury United	42	23	8	11	67	38	77
Dagenham & Redbridge	42	20	13	9	71	44	73
Purfleet	42	22	7	13	71	54	73
Enfield	42	21	9	12	73	49	72
St Albans City	42	17	17	8	71	52	68
Aldershot Town	42	16	14	12	83	48	62
Basingstoke Town	42	17	10	15	63	53	61
Harrow Borough	42	17	9	16	72	66	60
Gravesend & Northfleet	42	18	6	18	54	53	60
Slough Town	42	16	11	15	60	53	59
Billericay Town	42	15	13	14	54	56	58
Hendon	42	16	9	17	70	71	57
Boreham Wood	42	14	15	13	59	63	57
Chesham United	42	15	9	18	58	79	54
Dulwich Hamlet	42	14	8	20	53	63	50
Heybridge Swifts	42	13	9	20	51	85	48
Walton & Hersham	42	12	7	23	50	77	43
Hampton	42	10	12	20	41	71	42
Carshalton Athletic	42	10	10	22	47	82	40
Bishops Stortford	42	9	10	23	49	90	37
Bromley	42	8	11	23	50	72	35

First Division

Canvey Island	42	28	6	8	76	41	90
Hitchin Town	42	25	10	7	75	38	85
Wealdstone	42	26	6	10	75	48	84
Braintree Town	42	20	10	12	75	48	70
Bognor Regis Town	42	20	8	14	63	44	68
Grays Athletic	42	19	11	12	56	42	68
Oxford City	42	16	14	12	58	51	62
Croydon	42	16	13	13	53	53	61
Chertsey Town	42	14	16	12	57	57	58
Romford	42	14	15	13	58	63	57
Maidenhead United	42	13	15	14	50	46	54
Worthing	42	13	13	16	47	61	52
Leyton Pennant	42	13	12	17	62	70	51
Uxbridge	42	13	11	18	54	51	50
Barton Rovers	42	11	15	16	43	49	48
Yeading	42	12	10	20	51	55	46
Leatherhead	42	12	9	21	48	59	45
Whyteleafe	42	13	6	23	51	72	45
Staines Town	42	10	15	17	33	57	45
Molesey	42	8	20	14	35	52	44
Wembley	42	10	10	22	36	71	40
Berkhamsted Town	42	10	7	25	53	81	37

Second Division

Bedford Town	42	29	7	6	89	31	94
Harlow Town	42	27	8	7	100	47	89
Thame United	42	26	8	8	89	50	86
Hemel Hempstead	42	21	12	9	90	50	75
Windsor & Eton	42	22	6	14	87	55	72
Banstead Athletic	42	21	8	13	83	62	71
Northwood	42	20	7	15	67	68	67
Tooting & Mitcham United	42	19	9	14	63	62	66
Chalfont St Peter	42	16	12	14	70	71	60
Metropolitan Police	42	17	8	17	61	58	59
Leighton Town	42	16	10	16	60	64	58
Horsham	42	17	6	19	74	67	57
Marlow	42	16	9	17	72	68	57
Edgware Town	42	14	10	18	65	68	52
Witham Town	42	12	15	15	64	64	51
Hungerford Town	42	13	12	17	59	61	51
Wivenhoe Town	42	14	8	20	71	83	50
Wokingham Town	42	14	4	24	44	79	46
Barking	42	10	11	21	50	75	41
Hertford Town	42	11	2	29	44	96	35
Bracknell Town	42	7	10	25	48	92	31
Abingdon Town	42	6	6	30	48	124	24

Third Division

Ford United	38	27	5	6	110	42	86
Wingate & Finchley	38	25	5	8	79	38	80
Cheshunt	38	23	10	5	70	41	79
Lewes	38	25	3	10	86	45	78
Epsom & Ewell	38	19	5	14	61	51	62
Ware	38	19	4	15	79	60	61
Tilbury	38	17	8	13	74	52	59
Croydon Athletic	38	16	10	12	82	59	58
East Thurrock United	38	15	13	10	74	56	58
Egham Town	38	16	8	14	65	58	56
Corinthian Casuals	38	16	7	15	70	71	55
Southall	38	14	9	15	68	66	51
Camberley Town	38	14	8	16	66	77	50
Aveley	38	12	7	19	50	67	43
Flackwell Heath	38	11	9	18	59	70	42
Hornchurch	38	10	9	19	48	73	39
Clapton	38	11	6	21	48	89	39
Dorking	38	8	7	23	52	98	31
Kingsbury Town	38	6	3	29	40	98	21
Tring Town	38	5	6	27	38	108	21

1999-2000

Premier Division

Dagenham & Redbridge	42	32	5	5	97	35	101
Aldershot Town	42	24	5	13	71	51	77
Chesham United	42	20	10	12	64	50	70
Purfleet	42	18	15	9	70	48	69
Canvey Island	42	21	6	15	70	53	69
St Albans City	42	19	10	13	75	55	67
Billericay Town	42	18	12	12	62	62	66
Hendon	42	18	8	16	61	64	62
Slough Town	42	17	9	16	61	59	60
Dulwich Hamlet	42	17	5	20	62	68	56
Gravesend & Northfleet	42	15	10	17	66	67	55
Farnborough Town	42	14	11	17	52	55	53
Hampton & Richmond Borough	42	13	13	16	49	57	52
Enfield	42	13	11	18	64	68	50
Heybridge Swifts	42	13	11	18	57	65	50
Hitchin Town	42	13	11	18	59	72	50
Carshalton Athletic	42	12	12	18	55	65	48
Basingstoke Town	42	13	9	20	56	71	48
Harrow Borough	42	14	6	22	54	70	48
Aylesbury United	42	13	9	20	64	81	48
Boreham Wood	42	11	10	21	44	71	43
Walton & Hersham	42	11	8	23	44	70	41

First Division

Croydon	42	25	9	8	85	47	84
Grays Athletic	42	21	12	9	80	44	75
Maidenhead United	42	20	15	7	72	45	75
Thame United	42	20	13	9	61	38	73
Worthing	42	19	12	11	80	60	69
Staines Town	42	19	12	11	63	52	69
Whyteleafe	42	20	9	13	66	49	69
Bedford Town	42	17	12	13	59	52	63
Bromley	42	17	9	16	63	65	60
Uxbridge	42	15	13	14	60	44	58
Bishop's Stortford	42	16	10	16	57	62	58
Barton Rovers	42	16	8	18	64	83	56
Oxford City	42	17	4	21	57	55	55
Braintree Town	42	15	10	17	65	74	55
Yeading	42	12	18	12	53	54	54
Wealdstone	42	13	12	17	51	58	51
Bognor Regis Town	42	12	13	17	47	53	49
Harlow Town	42	11	13	18	62	76	46
Romford	42	12	9	21	51	70	45
Leatherhead	42	9	13	20	47	70	40
Chertsey Town	42	9	5	28	50	84	32
Leyton Pennant	42	7	9	26	34	85	30

Second Division

Hemel Hempstead	42	31	8	3	98	27	101
Northwood	42	29	9	4	109	40	96
Ford United	42	28	8	6	108	41	92
Berkhamsted Town	42	22	8	12	75	52	74
Windsor & Eton	42	20	13	9	73	53	73
Wivenhoe Town	42	20	9	13	61	47	69
Barking	42	18	13	11	70	51	67
Marlow	42	20	4	18	86	66	64
Metropolitan Police	42	18	7	17	75	71	61
Banstead Athletic	42	16	11	15	55	56	59
Tooting & Mitcham United	42	16	7	19	72	74	55
Wokingham Town	42	15	9	18	58	80	54
Wembley	42	14	11	17	47	53	53
Edgware Town	42	13	11	18	72	71	50
Hungerford Town	42	13	10	19	61	78	49
Cheshunt	42	12	12	18	53	61	48
Horsham	42	13	8	21	66	81	47
Leighton Town	42	13	8	21	65	84	47
Molesey	42	10	12	20	54	69	42
Wingate & Finchley	42	11	7	24	54	97	40
Witham Town	42	7	9	26	39	110	30
Chalfont St Peter	42	2	8	32	39	124	14

Third Division

East Thurrock United	40	26	7	7	89	42	85
Great Wakering Rovers	40	25	7	8	81	41	82
Tilbury	40	21	12	7	67	39	75
Hornchurch	40	19	12	9	72	57	69
Croydon Athletic	40	19	11	10	85	52	68
Epsom & Ewell	40	18	12	10	67	46	66
Lewes	40	18	10	12	73	51	64
Bracknell Town	40	15	16	9	81	64	61
Aveley	40	17	10	13	73	64	61
Corinthian Casuals	40	16	10	14	59	51	58
Flackwell Heath	40	17	6	17	74	76	57
Ware	40	16	8	16	74	62	56
Egham Town	40	14	13	13	48	43	55
Hertford Town	40	15	10	15	63	60	55
Abingdon Town	40	10	12	18	48	64	42
Kingsbury Town	40	11	8	21	55	86	41
Camberley Town	40	11	7	22	44	79	40
Tring Town	40	10	9	21	37	64	39
Dorking	40	9	10	21	53	69	37
Clapton	40	9	7	24	50	93	34
Southall	40	3	5	32	33	123	14

2000-2001

Premier Division

Farnborough Town	42	31	6	5	86	27	99
Canvey Island	42	27	8	7	79	41	89
Basingstoke Town	42	22	13	7	73	40	79
Aldershot Town	41	21	11	9	73	39	74
Chesham United	42	22	6	14	78	52	72
Gravesend & Northfleet	42	22	5	15	62	45	71
Heybridge Swifts	42	18	13	11	74	60	67
Billericay Town	41	18	13	10	62	54	67
Hampton & Richmond Borough	42	18	12	12	73	60	66
Hitchin Town	42	18	5	19	72	69	59
Purfleet	42	14	13	15	55	55	55
Hendon	42	16	6	18	62	62	54
Sutton United	41	14	11	16	74	70	53
St Albans City	42	15	5	22	50	69	50
Grays Athletic	42	14	8	20	49	68	50
Maidenhead United	42	15	2	25	47	63	47
Croydon	42	12	10	20	55	77	46
Enfield	42	12	9	21	48	74	45
Harrow Borough	41	10	11	20	61	90	41
Slough Town	42	10	9	23	40	62	39
Carshalton Athletic	42	10	6	26	40	85	36
Dulwich Hamlet	42	4	10	28	33	84	22

First Division

Boreham Wood	42	26	7	9	82	49	85
Bedford Town	42	22	16	4	81	40	82
Braintree Town	42	25	6	11	112	60	81
Bishop's Stortford	42	24	6	12	103	76	78
Thame United	42	22	8	12	86	54	74
Ford United	42	19	12	11	70	58	69
Uxbridge	42	21	5	16	73	55	68
Northwood	42	20	8	14	89	81	68
Whyteleafe	42	20	6	16	62	69	66
Oxford City	42	16	13	13	64	49	61
Harlow Town	42	15	16	11	70	66	61
Worthing	42	16	9	17	69	69	57
Staines Town	42	16	8	18	60	66	56
Aylesbury United	42	17	4	21	65	55	55
Yeading	42	15	9	18	72	74	54
Bognor Regis Town	42	13	11	18	71	71	50
Walton & Hersham	42	14	8	20	59	80	50
Bromley	42	14	6	22	63	86	48
Wealdstone	42	12	9	21	54	73	45
Leatherhead	42	12	4	26	37	87	40
Romford	42	9	4	29	53	113	31
Barton Rovers	42	2	9	31	30	94	15

Second Division

Tooting & Mitcham United	42	26	11	5	92	35	89
Windsor	42	24	10	8	70	40	82
Barking	42	23	13	6	82	54	82
Berkhamsted Town	42	24	8	10	99	49	80
Wivenhoe Town	42	23	11	8	78	52	80
Hemel Hempstead	42	22	10	10	74	44	76
Horsham	42	19	9	14	84	61	66
Chertsey Town	42	18	9	15	59	59	63
Great Wakering Rovers	42	16	13	13	69	59	61
Tilbury	42	18	6	18	61	67	60
Banstead Athletic	42	17	8	17	69	58	59
East Thurrock United	42	16	11	15	72	64	59
Metropolitan Police	42	18	4	20	64	77	58
Marlow	42	15	11	16	62	61	56
Molesey	42	14	9	19	53	61	51
Wembley	42	12	10	20	39	63	46
Hungerford Town	42	11	9	22	40	73	42
Leyton Pennant	42	10	11	21	47	74	41
Cheshunt	42	11	6	25	48	77	39
Edgware Town	42	9	9	24	41	77	36
Leighton Town	42	8	10	24	44	87	34
Wokingham Town	42	3	12	27	39	94	20

Wokingham Town had 1 point deducted

Third Division

Arlesey Town	42	34	6	2	138	37	108
Lewes	41	25	11	5	104	34	86
Ashford Town	42	26	7	9	102	49	85
Flackwell Heath	42	24	10	8	93	51	82
Corinthian Casuals	42	24	10	8	83	50	82
Aveley	42	24	3	15	85	61	75
Epsom & Ewell	42	23	4	15	76	52	73
Witham Town	42	21	9	12	76	57	72
Bracknell Town	41	19	10	12	90	70	67
Croydon Athletic	41	15	12	14	78	63	57
Ware	42	17	6	19	75	76	57
Tring Town	42	16	9	17	60	71	57
Egham Town	42	15	11	16	60	60	56
Hornchurch	42	14	13	15	73	60	55
Wingate & Finchley	42	15	7	20	75	75	52
Kingsbury Town	42	11	8	23	74	100	41
Abingdon Town	42	12	7	23	53	102	40
Dorking	42	10	9	23	59	99	39
Hertford Town	41	9	8	24	57	97	35
Camberley Town	42	8	8	26	53	107	32
Clapton	42	5	9	28	48	121	24
Chalfont St Peter	42	4	1	37	30	150	13

Abingdon Town had 3 points deducted

2001-2002

Premier Division

Gravesend & Northfleet	42	31	6	5	90	33	99
Canvey Island	42	30	5	7	107	41	95
Aldershot Town	42	22	7	13	76	51	73
Braintree Town	42	23	4	15	66	61	73
Purfleet	42	19	15	8	67	44	72
Grays Athletic	42	20	10	12	65	55	70
Chesham United	42	19	10	13	69	53	67
Hendon Town	42	19	5	18	66	54	62
Billericay Town	42	16	13	13	59	60	61
St Albans City	42	16	9	17	71	60	57
Hitchin Town	42	15	10	17	73	81	55
Sutton Albion	42	13	15	14	62	62	54
Heybridge Swifts	42	15	9	18	68	85	54
Kingstonian	42	13	13	16	50	56	52
Boreham Wood	42	15	6	21	49	62	51
Maidenhead United	42	15	5	22	51	63	50
Bedford Town	42	12	12	18	64	69	48
Basingstoke Town	42	11	15	16	50	68	48
Enfield	42	11	9	22	48	77	42
Hampton & Richmond Borough	42	9	13	20	51	71	40
Harrow Borough	42	8	10	24	50	89	34
Croydon	42	7	5	30	36	93	26

First Division

Ford United	42	27	7	8	92	56	88
Bishop's Stortford	42	26	9	7	104	51	87
Aylesbury United	42	23	10	9	96	64	79
Bognor Regis Town	42	20	13	9	74	55	73
Northwood	42	19	11	12	92	64	68
Carshalton Athletic	42	17	16	9	64	53	67
Harlow Town	42	19	9	14	77	65	66
Slough Town	42	17	11	14	68	51	62
Uxbridge	42	18	6	18	68	65	60
Oxford City	42	17	9	16	59	66	60
Thame United	42	15	14	13	75	61	59
Tooting & Mitcham United	42	16	11	15	70	70	59
Walton & Hersham	42	16	10	16	75	70	58
Yeading	42	16	10	16	84	90	58
Worthing	42	15	8	19	69	65	53
Staines Town	42	12	11	19	45	60	47
Dulwich Hamlet	42	11	13	18	64	76	46
Wealdstone	42	11	12	19	60	82	45
Bromley	42	10	11	21	44	74	41
Whyteleafe	42	10	11	21	46	86	41
Barking & East Ham United	42	8	7	27	61	123	31
Windsor & Eton	42	7	5	30	53	93	26

Second Division

Lewes	42	29	9	4	108	31	96
Horsham	42	27	9	6	104	44	90
Berkhamstead Town	42	23	10	9	82	51	79
Arlesey Town	42	23	6	13	89	55	75
Banstead Athletic	42	22	8	12	83	54	74
Leyton Pennant	42	22	8	12	84	60	74
Great Wakering Rovers	42	21	8	13	64	37	71
East Thurrock United	42	21	8	13	67	59	71
Marlow	42	18	13	11	73	63	67
Hemel Hempstead Town	42	18	10	14	82	66	64
Leatherhead	42	17	6	19	72	62	57
Ashford Town	42	15	11	16	58	71	56
Metropolitan Police	42	16	7	19	84	84	55
Barton Rovers	42	15	9	18	54	60	54
Hungerford Town	42	14	9	19	56	75	51
Tilbury	42	15	6	21	55	74	51
Chertsey Town	42	10	14	18	79	112	44
Wembley	42	9	10	23	51	82	37
Molesey	42	10	6	26	40	93	36
Cheshunt	42	7	13	22	51	84	34
Wivenhoe Town	42	8	9	25	55	111	33
Romford	42	4	7	31	42	105	19

Third Division

Croydon Athletic	42	30	5	7	138	41	95
Hornchurch	42	25	11	6	96	46	86
Aveley	42	26	6	10	109	55	84
Bracknell Town	42	25	8	9	96	54	83
Epsom & Ewell	42	20	15	7	79	51	75
Egham Town	42	21	11	10	72	59	74
Wingate & Finchley	42	20	9	13	80	60	69
Dorking	42	18	14	10	77	66	68
Tring Town	42	19	11	12	64	62	68
Corinthian-Casuals	42	18	13	11	69	44	67
Hertford Town	42	20	7	15	88	74	67
Witham Town	42	15	10	17	66	72	55
Ware	42	14	10	18	74	76	52
Chalfont St Peter	42	15	4	23	69	92	49
Wokingham Town	42	14	6	22	79	105	48
Abingdon Town	42	13	7	22	61	75	46
Leighton Town	42	8	12	22	56	95	36
Kingsbury Town	42	8	11	23	58	91	35
Edgware Town	42	9	7	26	65	101	34
Flackwell Heath	42	9	8	25	53	99	32
Clapton	42	9	4	29	45	118	31
Camberley Town	42	7	9	26	37	95	30

2002-2003

Premier Division

Aldershot Town	46	33	6	7	81	36	105
Canvey Island	46	28	8	10	112	56	92
Hendon	46	22	13	11	70	56	79
St. Albans City	46	23	8	15	73	65	77
Basingstoke Town	46	23	7	16	80	60	76
Sutton United	46	22	9	15	77	62	75
Hayes	46	20	13	13	67	54	73
Purfleet	46	19	15	12	68	48	72
Bedford Town	46	21	9	16	66	58	72
Maidenhead United	46	16	17	13	75	63	65
Kingstonian	46	16	17	13	71	64	65
Billericay Town	46	17	11	18	46	44	62
Bishop's Stortford	46	16	11	19	74	72	59
Hitchin Town	46	15	13	18	69	67	58
Ford United	46	15	12	19	78	84	57
Braintree Town	46	14	12	20	59	71	54
Aylesbury United	46	13	15	18	62	75	54
Harrow Borough	46	15	9	22	54	75	54
Grays Athletic	46	14	11	21	53	59	53
Heybridge Swifts	46	13	14	19	52	80	53
Chesham United	46	14	10	22	56	81	52
Boreham Wood	46	11	15	20	50	58	48
Enfield	46	9	11	26	47	101	38
Hampton & Richmond Borough	46	3	14	29	35	86	23

Division One (North)

Northwood	46	28	7	11	109	56	91
Hornchurch	46	25	15	6	85	48	90
Hemel Hempstead Town	46	26	7	13	70	55	85
Slough Town	46	22	14	10	86	59	80
Uxbridge	46	23	10	13	62	41	79
Aveley	46	21	14	11	66	48	77
Berkhamsted Town	46	21	13	12	92	68	76
Thame United	46	20	12	14	84	51	72
Wealdstone	46	21	9	16	85	69	72
Harlow Town	46	20	12	14	66	53	72
Marlow	46	19	10	17	74	63	67
Barking & East Ham United	46	19	9	18	73	76	66
Yeading	46	18	11	17	77	69	65
Great Wakering Rovers	46	17	14	15	64	70	65
Oxford City	46	17	13	16	55	51	64
Arlesey Town	46	17	12	17	69	71	63
East Thurrock United	46	17	10	19	75	79	61
Wingate & Finchley	46	15	11	20	70	74	56
Barton Rovers	46	15	7	24	53	65	52
Tilbury	46	14	7	25	55	96	49
Wivenhoe Town	46	9	11	26	56	94	38
Leyton Pennant	46	9	7	30	38	81	34
Wembley	46	7	11	28	57	111	32
Hertford Town	46	6	6	34	46	119	24

Division One (South)

Carshalton Athletic	46	28	8	10	73	44	92
Bognor Regis Town	46	26	10	10	92	34	88
Lewes	46	24	16	6	106	50	88
Dulwich Hamlet	46	23	12	11	73	49	81
Whyteleafe	46	21	13	12	74	51	76
Bromley	46	21	13	12	70	53	76
Walton & Hersham	46	20	13	13	87	63	73
Horsham	46	21	9	16	80	58	72
Epsom & Ewell	46	19	12	15	67	66	69
Egham Town	46	19	10	17	62	71	67
Tooting & Mitcham United	46	18	9	19	83	78	63
Worthing	46	17	12	17	78	75	63
Windsor & Eton	46	18	9	19	66	65	63
Leatherhead	46	16	13	17	71	66	61
Staines Town	46	14	16	16	57	63	58
Banstead Athletic	46	14	15	17	58	59	57
Ashford Town (Middlesex)	46	14	11	21	47	70	53
Croydon	46	15	8	23	56	87	53
Croydon Athletic	46	13	13	20	52	66	52
Bracknell Town	46	12	16	18	57	74	52
Corinthian Casuals	46	12	14	20	50	68	50
Molesey	46	13	9	24	52	79	48
Metropolitan Police	46	12	10	24	50	76	46
Chertsey Town	46	3	7	36	43	139	16

Division Two

Cheshunt	30	25	3	2	91	29	78
Leyton	30	21	5	4	77	22	68
Flackwell Heath	30	17	3	10	52	44	54
Abingdon Town	30	14	11	5	65	42	53
Hungerford Town	30	12	12	6	49	36	48
Leighton Town	30	14	3	13	61	43	45
Witham Town	30	12	8	10	40	43	44
Ware	30	12	5	13	47	53	41
Clapton	30	12	5	13	40	47	41
Tring Town	30	11	5	14	49	58	38
Kingsbury Town	30	9	11	10	38	48	38
Edgware Town	30	10	3	17	49	65	33
Wokingham Town	30	7	7	16	34	81	28
Dorking	30	6	6	18	49	63	24
Chalfont St. Peter	30	6	5	19	34	63	23
Camberley Town	30	4	4	22	23	61	16

2003-2004

Premier Division

Canvey Island	46	32	8	6	106	42	104
Sutton United	46	25	10	11	94	56	85
Thurrock	46	24	11	11	87	45	83
Hendon	46	25	8	13	68	47	83
* Hornchurch	46	24	11	11	63	35	82
Grays Athletic	46	22	15	9	82	39	81
Carshalton Athletic	46	24	9	13	66	55	81
Hayes	46	21	11	14	56	46	74
Kettering Town	46	20	11	15	63	63	71
Bognor Regis Town	46	20	10	16	69	67	70
Bishop's Stortford	46	20	9	17	78	61	69
Maidenhead United	46	18	9	19	60	68	63
Ford United	46	16	14	16	69	63	62
Basingstoke Town	46	17	9	20	58	64	60
Bedford Town	46	14	13	19	62	63	55
Heybridge Swifts	46	14	11	21	57	78	53
Harrow Borough	46	12	14	20	47	63	50
Kingstonian	46	12	13	21	40	56	49
St. Albans City	46	12	12	22	55	83	48
Hitchin Town	46	13	8	25	55	89	47
Northwood	46	12	9	25	65	95	45
Billericay Town	46	11	11	24	51	66	44
Braintree Town	46	11	6	29	41	88	39
Aylesbury United	46	5	14	27	41	101	29

* Hornchurch had 1 point deducted

Division One (North)

Yeading	46	32	7	7	112	54	103
Leyton	46	29	9	8	90	53	96
Cheshunt	46	27	10	9	119	54	91
Chesham United	46	24	9	13	104	60	81
Dunstable Town	46	23	9	14	86	61	78
Hemel Hempstead Town	46	22	12	12	75	72	78
Wealdstone	46	23	7	16	81	51	76
Arlesey Town	46	23	7	16	95	70	76
Boreham Wood	46	20	13	13	82	59	73
Harlow Town	46	20	10	16	75	51	70
Wingate & Finchley	46	19	13	14	68	63	70
East Thurrock United	46	19	11	16	62	54	68
Uxbridge	46	15	14	17	59	57	59
Aveley	46	15	14	17	67	71	59
Thame United	46	16	9	21	72	83	57
* Waltham Forest	46	15	13	18	62	60	55
Wivenhoe Town	46	15	10	21	79	104	55
Barton Rovers	46	16	6	24	52	80	54
Oxford City	46	14	11	21	55	65	53
Berkhamstead Town	46	12	10	24	66	88	46
Great Wakering Rovers	46	10	13	23	47	97	43
Tilbury	46	10	9	27	56	100	39
Barking & East Ham United	46	8	7	31	37	100	31
Enfield	46	5	7	34	44	138	22

* Waltham Forest had 3 points deducted.

2004-2005
Premier Division

Yeading	42	25	11	6	74	48	86
Billericay Town	42	23	11	8	78	40	80
Eastleigh	42	22	13	7	84	49	79
Braintree Town	42	19	17	6	67	33	74
Leyton	42	21	8	13	71	57	71
Hampton & Richmond	42	21	8	13	64	53	71
Heybridge Swifts	42	18	9	15	76	65	63
Chelmsford City	42	17	11	14	63	58	62
Staines Town	42	17	9	16	59	53	60
Worthing	42	16	11	15	50	45	59
Hendon	42	17	7	18	48	60	58
Salisbury City	42	16	9	17	60	64	57
Slough Town	42	15	10	17	61	66	55
Folkestone Invicta	42	14	10	18	51	53	52
Windsor & Eton	42	12	14	16	48	62	50
Harrow Borough	42	13	10	19	41	54	49
Northwood	42	14	7	21	49	66	49
Wealdstone	42	13	8	21	60	73	47
Cheshunt	42	12	11	19	58	71	47
Tonbridge Angels	42	11	10	21	47	73	43
Dover Athletic	42	10	9	23	50	66	39
Kingstonian	42	7	5	30	43	93	26

Division One (South)

Lewes	46	29	7	10	113	61	94
Worthing	46	26	14	6	87	46	92
Windsor & Eton	46	26	13	7	75	39	91
Slough Town	46	28	6	12	103	63	90
Hampton & Richmond Borough	46	26	11	9	82	45	89
Staines Town	46	26	9	11	85	52	87
Dulwich Hamlet	46	23	15	8	77	57	84
Bromley	46	22	10	14	80	58	76
Walton & Hersham	46	20	14	12	76	55	74
Croydon Athletic	46	20	10	16	70	54	70
Tooting & Mitcham United	46	20	9	17	82	68	69
Ashford Town (Middlesex)	46	18	13	15	69	62	67
Leatherhead	46	19	9	18	83	88	66
Bracknell Town	46	19	6	21	81	87	63
Horsham	46	16	11	19	71	69	59
Marlow	46	16	11	19	50	64	59
Whyteleafe	46	17	4	25	66	93	55
Banstead Athletic	46	15	8	23	56	73	53
Molesey	46	12	6	28	45	84	42
Metropolitan Police	46	9	14	23	58	84	41
Croydon	46	10	10	26	57	88	40
Egham Town	46	8	8	30	55	92	32
Corinthian Casuals	46	6	6	34	48	110	24
Epsom & Ewell	46	5	8	33	40	117	23

Division One

AFC Wimbledon	42	29	10	3	91	33	97
Walton & Hersham	42	28	4	10	80	34	88
Horsham	42	24	6	12	90	61	78
Bromley	42	22	9	11	69	44	75
Metropolitan Police	42	22	8	12	72	51	74
Cray Wanderers	42	19	16	7	95	54	73
Leatherhead	42	20	13	9	73	55	73
Tooting & Mitcham United	42	18	15	9	92	60	69
Whyteleafe	42	20	6	16	60	59	66
Burgess Hill Town	42	19	6	17	73	62	63
Hastings United	42	15	11	16	55	57	56
Croydon Athletic	42	13	16	13	66	65	55
Corinthian-Casuals	42	15	9	18	56	64	54
Bashley	42	13	13	16	68	74	52
Dulwich Hamlet	42	10	14	18	61	64	44
Molesey	42	12	8	22	46	70	44
Banstead Athletic	42	10	10	22	50	64	40
Newport IOW	42	10	10	22	50	88	40
Fleet Town	42	11	5	26	47	86	38
Ashford Town	42	8	12	22	47	85	36
Dorking	42	8	11	23	43	89	35
Croydon	42	5	10	27	37	91	25

Division Two

Leighton Town	42	28	7	7	111	36	91
Dorking	42	27	8	7	87	47	89
Hertford Town	42	24	9	9	74	35	81
Chertsey Town	42	22	9	11	75	53	75
Flackwell Heath	42	22	5	15	71	53	71
Witham Town	42	20	10	12	75	54	70
Kingsbury Town	42	14	11	17	60	64	53
Ware	42	14	10	18	67	60	52
Abingdon Town	42	15	6	21	83	81	51
Camberley Town	42	15	6	21	51	71	51
Wembley	42	13	9	20	46	67	48
Wokingham Town	42	12	7	23	55	94	43
Edgware Town	42	12	6	24	62	88	42
Chalfont St. Peter	42	12	6	24	57	89	42
Clapton	42	8	5	29	47	129	29

Division Two

Ilford	30	22	3	5	62	23	69
Enfield	30	21	3	6	64	33	66
Brook House	30	20	4	6	65	25	64
Hertford Town	30	17	7	6	65	40	58
Witham Town	30	16	3	11	67	53	51
Chertsey Town	30	15	6	9	55	48	51
Abingdon Town	30	13	9	8	65	42	48
Edgware Town	30	12	3	15	40	41	39
Flackwell Heath	30	11	5	14	50	55	38
Ware	30	9	10	11	41	55	37
Chalfont St Peter	30	9	7	14	41	52	34
Camberley Town	30	9	5	16	36	44	32
Wembley	30	8	5	17	41	55	29
Epsom & Ewell	30	8	4	18	41	64	28
Kingsbury Town	30	5	4	21	35	76	19
Clapton	30	3	6	21	20	82	15

NORTHERN PREMIER LEAGUE

1968-69

Macclesfield Town	38	27	6	5	82	38	60
Wigan Athletic	38	18	12	8	59	41	48
Morecambe	38	16	14	8	64	37	46
Gainsborough Trinity	38	19	8	11	64	43	46
South Shields	38	19	8	11	78	56	46
Bangor City	38	18	9	11	102	64	45
Hyde United	38	16	10	12	71	65	42
Goole Town	38	15	10	13	80	78	40
Altrincham	38	14	10	14	69	52	38
Fleetwood	38	16	6	16	58	58	38
Gateshead	38	14	9	15	42	48	37
South Liverpool	38	12	13	13	56	66	37
Northwich Victoria	38	16	5	17	59	82	37
Boston United	38	14	8	16	59	65	36
Runcorn	38	12	11	15	59	63	35
Netherfield	38	12	4	22	51	69	28
Scarborough	38	9	10	19	49	68	28
Ashington	38	10	8	20	48	74	28
Chorley	38	8	9	21	46	75	25
Worksop Town	38	6	8	24	34	88	20

1969-70

Macclesfield Town	38	22	8	8	72	41	52
Wigan Athletic	38	20	12	6	56	32	52
Boston United	38	21	8	9	65	33	50
Scarborough	38	20	10	8	74	39	50
South Shields	38	19	7	12	66	43	45
Gainsborough Trinity	38	16	11	11	64	49	43
Stafford Rangers	38	16	7	15	59	52	39
Bangor City	38	15	9	14	68	63	39
Northwich Victoria	38	15	8	15	60	66	38
Netherfield	38	14	9	15	56	54	37
Hyde United	38	15	7	16	59	59	37
Altincham	38	14	8	16	62	65	36
Fleetwood	38	13	10	15	53	60	36
Runcorn	38	11	13	14	57	72	35
Morecambe	38	10	13	15	41	51	33
South Liverpool	38	11	11	16	44	55	33
Great Harwood	38	10	9	19	63	92	29
Matlock Town	38	8	12	18	52	67	28
Goole Town	38	10	6	22	50	71	26
Gateshead	38	5	12	21	37	94	22

1970-71

Wigan Athletic	42	27	13	2	91	32	67
Stafford Rangers	42	27	7	8	87	51	61
Scarborough	42	23	12	7	83	40	58
Boston United	42	22	12	8	69	31	56
Macclesfield Town	42	23	10	9	84	45	56
Northwich Victoria	42	22	5	15	71	55	49
Bangor City	42	19	10	13	72	61	48
Altrincham	42	19	10	13	80	76	48
South Liverpool	42	15	15	12	67	57	45
Chorley	42	14	14	14	58	61	42
Gainsborough Trinity	42	15	11	16	65	63	41
Morecambe	42	14	11	17	67	79	39
South Shields	42	12	14	16	67	66	38
Bradford Park Avenue	42	15	8	19	54	73	38
Lancaster City	42	12	12	18	53	76	36
Netherfield	42	13	9	20	59	57	35
Matlock Town	42	10	13	19	58	80	33
Fleetwood	42	10	11	21	56	90	31
Great Harwood	42	8	13	21	66	98	29
Runcorn	42	10	5	27	58	84	25
Kirkby Town	42	6	13	23	57	93	25
Goole Town	42	10	4	28	44	98	24

1971-72

Stafford Rangers	46	30	11	5	91	32	71
Boston United	46	28	13	5	87	37	69
Wigan Athletic	46	27	10	9	70	43	64
Scarborough	46	21	15	10	75	46	57
Northwich Victoria	46	20	14	12	65	59	54
Macclesfield Town	46	18	15	13	61	50	51
Gainsborough Trinity	46	21	9	16	93	79	51
South Shields	46	18	14	14	75	57	50
Bangor City	46	20	8	18	93	74	48
Altrincham	46	18	11	17	72	58	47
Skelmersdale United	46	19	9	18	61	58	47
Matlock Town	46	20	7	19	67	75	47
Chorley	46	17	12	17	66	59	46
Lancaster City	46	15	14	17	84	84	44
Great Harwood	46	15	14	17	60	74	44
Ellesmere Port Town	46	17	9	20	67	71	43
Morecambe	46	15	10	21	51	64	40
Bradford Park Avenue	46	13	13	20	54	71	39
Netherfield	46	16	5	25	51	73	37
Fleetwood	46	11	15	20	43	67	37
South Liverpool	46	12	12	22	61	73	36
Runcorn	46	8	14	24	48	80	30
Goole Town	46	9	10	27	51	97	28
Kirkby Town	46	6	12	28	38	104	24

1972-73

Boston United	46	27	16	3	88	34	70
Scarborough	46	26	9	11	72	39	61
Wigan Athletic	46	23	14	9	69	38	60
Altrincham	46	22	16	8	75	55	60
Bradford Park Avenue	46	19	17	10	63	50	55
Stafford Rangers	46	20	11	15	63	46	51
Gainsborough Trinity	46	18	13	15	70	50	49
Northwich Victoria	46	17	15	14	74	62	49
Netherfield	46	20	9	17	68	65	49
Macclesfield Town	46	16	16	14	58	47	48
Ellesmere Port Town	46	18	11	17	52	56	47
Skelmersdale United	46	15	16	15	58	59	46
Bangor City	46	16	13	17	70	60	45
Mossley	46	17	11	18	70	73	45
Morecambe	46	17	11	18	62	70	45
Great Harwood	46	14	15	17	63	74	43
South Liverpool	46	12	19	15	47	57	43
Runcorn	46	15	12	19	75	78	42
Goole Town	46	13	13	20	64	73	39
South Shields	46	17	4	25	64	81	38
Matlock Town	46	11	11	24	42	80	33
Lancaster City	46	10	11	25	53	78	31
Barrow	46	12	6	28	52	101	30
Fleetwood	46	5	15	26	31	77	25

1973-74

Boston United	46	27	11	8	69	32	65
Wigan Athletic	46	28	8	10	96	39	64
Altrincham	46	26	11	9	77	34	63
Stafford Rangers	46	27	9	10	101	45	63
Scarborough	46	22	14	10	62	43	58
South Shields	46	25	6	15	87	48	56
Runcorn	46	21	14	11	72	47	56
Macclesfield Town	46	18	15	13	48	47	51
Bangor City	46	19	11	16	65	56	49
Gainsborough Trinity	46	18	11	17	77	64	47
South Liverpool	46	16	15	15	55	47	47
Skelmersdale United	46	16	13	17	50	59	45
Goole Town	46	14	15	17	60	69	43
Fleetwood	46	14	15	17	48	68	43
Mossley	46	15	11	20	53	65	41
Northwich Victoria	46	14	13	19	68	75	41
Morecambe	46	13	13	20	62	84	39
Buxton	46	14	10	22	45	71	38
Matlock Town	46	11	14	21	50	79	36
Great Harwood	46	10	14	22	52	74	34
Bradford Park Avenue	46	9	15	22	42	84	33
Barrow	46	13	7	26	46	94	33
Lancaster City	46	10	12	24	52	67	32
Netherfield	46	11	5	30	42	88	27

1974-75

Team	P	W	D	L	F	A	Pts
Wigan Athletic	46	33	6	7	94	38	72
Runcorn	46	30	8	8	102	42	68
Altrincham	46	26	12	8	87	43	64
Stafford Rangers	46	25	13	8	81	39	63
Scarborough	46	24	12	10	73	45	60
Mossley	46	23	11	12	78	52	57
Gateshead United	46	22	12	12	74	48	56
Goole Town	46	19	12	15	75	71	50
Northwich Victoria	46	18	12	16	83	71	48
Great Harwood	46	17	14	15	69	66	48
Matlock Town	46	19	8	19	87	79	46
Boston United	46	16	14	16	64	63	46
Morecambe	46	14	15	17	71	87	43
Worksop Town	46	14	14	18	69	66	42
South Liverpool	46	14	14	18	59	71	42
Buxton	46	11	17	18	50	77	39
Macclesfield Town	46	11	14	21	46	62	36
Lancaster City	46	13	10	23	53	76	36
Bangor City	46	13	9	24	56	67	35
Gainsborough Trinity	46	10	15	21	46	79	35
Skelmersdale United	46	13	7	26	63	93	33
Barrow	46	9	15	22	45	72	33
Netherfield	46	12	8	26	42	91	32
Fleetwood	46	5	10	31	26	97	20

1975-76

Team	P	W	D	L	F	A	Pts
Runcorn	46	29	10	7	95	42	68
Stafford Rangers	46	26	15	5	81	41	67
Scarborough	46	26	10	10	84	43	62
Matlock Town	46	26	9	11	96	63	61
Boston United	46	27	6	13	95	58	60
Wigan Athletic	46	21	15	10	81	42	57
Altrincham	46	20	14	12	77	57	54
Bangor City	46	21	12	13	80	70	54
Mossley	46	21	11	14	70	58	53
Goole Town	46	20	13	13	58	49	53
Northwich Victoria	46	17	17	12	79	59	51
Lancaster City	46	18	9	19	61	70	45
Worksop Town	46	17	10	19	63	56	44
Gainsborough Trinity	46	13	17	16	58	69	43
Macclesfield Town	46	15	12	19	50	64	42
Gateshead United	46	17	7	22	64	63	41
Buxton	46	11	13	22	37	62	35
Skelmersdale United	46	12	10	24	45	74	34
Netherfield	46	11	11	24	55	76	33
Morecambe	46	11	11	24	47	67	33
Great Harwood	46	13	7	26	58	86	33
South Liverpool	46	12	9	25	45	78	33
Barrow	46	12	9	25	47	84	33
Fleetwood	46	3	9	34	36	131	15

1976-77

Team	P	W	D	L	F	A	Pts
Boston United	44	27	11	6	82	35	65
Northwich Victoria	44	27	11	6	85	43	65
Matlock Town	44	26	11	7	108	57	63
Bangor City	44	22	11	11	87	52	55
Scarborough	44	21	12	11	77	66	54
Goole Town	44	23	6	15	64	50	52
Lancaster City	44	21	9	14	71	58	51
Gateshead United	44	18	12	14	80	64	48
Mossley	44	17	14	13	74	59	48
Altrincham	44	19	9	16	60	53	47
Stafford Rangers	44	16	14	14	60	55	46
Runcorn	44	15	14	15	57	49	44
Worksop Town	44	16	12	16	50	58	44
Wigan Athletic	44	14	15	15	62	54	43
Morecambe	44	13	11	20	59	75	37
Gainsborough Trinity	44	13	10	21	58	74	36
Great Harwood	44	11	14	19	63	84	36
Buxton	44	11	13	20	48	63	35
Macclesfield Town	44	8	15	21	41	68	31
Frickley Athletic	44	11	8	25	53	93	30
Barrow	44	11	6	27	56	87	28
South Liverpool	44	10	8	26	51	104	28
Netherfield	44	9	8	27	47	92	26

1977-78

Team	P	W	D	L	F	A	Pts
Boston United	46	31	9	6	85	35	71
Wigan Athletic	46	25	15	6	83	45	65
Bangor City	46	26	10	10	92	50	62
Scarborough	46	26	10	10	80	39	62
Altrincham	46	22	15	9	84	49	59
Northwich Victoria	46	22	14	10	83	55	50
Stafford Rangers	46	22	13	11	71	41	57
Runcorn	46	19	18	9	70	44	56
Mossley	46	22	11	13	85	73	55
Matlock Town	46	21	12	13	79	60	54
Lancaster City	46	15	14	17	66	82	44
Frickley Athletic	46	15	12	19	77	81	42
Barrow	46	14	12	20	50	61	40
Goole Town	46	15	9	22	60	68	39
Great Harwood	46	13	13	20	66	83	39
Gainsborough Trinity	46	14	10	22	61	74	38
Gateshead	46	16	5	25	65	74	37
Netherfield	46	11	13	22	50	80	35
Workington	46	13	8	25	48	80	34
Worksop Town	46	12	10	24	46	84	34
Morecambe	46	11	11	24	67	92	33
Macclesfield Town	46	12	9	25	60	92	33
Buxton	46	13	6	27	60	95	32
South Liverpool	46	9	7	30	53	111	25

1978-79

Team	P	W	D	L	F	A	Pts
Mossley	44	32	5	7	117	48	69
Altrincham	44	25	11	8	93	39	61
Matlock Town	44	24	8	12	100	59	56
Scarborough	44	19	14	11	61	44	52
Southport	44	19	14	11	62	49	52
Boston United	44	17	18	9	40	33	52
Runcorn	44	21	9	14	79	54	51
Stafford Rangers	44	18	14	12	67	41	50
Goole Town	44	17	15	12	56	61	49
Northwich Victoria	44	18	11	15	64	52	47
Lancaster City	44	17	12	15	62	54	46
Bangor City	44	15	14	15	65	66	44
Worksop Town	44	13	14	17	55	67	40
Workington	44	16	7	21	62	74	39
Netherfield	44	13	11	20	39	69	37
Barrow	44	14	9	21	47	78	37
Gainsborough Trinity	44	12	12	20	52	67	36
Morecambe	44	11	13	20	55	65	35
Frickley Athletic	44	13	9	22	58	70	35
South Liverpool	44	12	10	22	48	85	34
Gateshead	44	11	11	22	42	63	33
Buxton	44	11	9	24	50	84	31
Macclesfield Town	44	8	10	26	40	92	26

1979-80

Team	P	W	D	L	F	A	Pts
Mossley	42	28	9	5	96	41	65
Witton Albion	42	28	8	6	89	30	64
Frickley Athletic	42	24	13	5	93	48	61
Burton Albion	42	25	6	11	83	42	56
Matlock Town	42	18	17	7	87	53	53
Buxton	42	21	9	12	61	48	51
Worksop Town	42	20	10	12	65	52	50
Macclesfield Town	42	18	11	13	67	53	47
Grantham	42	18	8	16	71	65	44
Marine	42	16	10	16	65	57	42
Goole Town	42	14	13	15	61	63	41
Lancaster City	42	13	13	16	74	77	39
Oswestry Town	42	12	14	16	44	60	38
Gainsborough Trinity	42	14	8	20	64	75	36
Runcorn	42	11	11	20	46	63	33
Gateshead	42	11	11	20	50	77	33
Morecambe	42	10	12	20	40	59	32
Netherfield	42	7	15	20	37	66	29
Southport	42	8	13	21	30	75	29
South Liverpool	42	7	14	21	51	84	28
Workington	42	8	12	22	50	85	28
Tamworth	42	8	9	25	26	77	25

1980-81

Team	P	W	D	L	F	A	Pts
Runcorn	42	32	7	3	99	22	71
Mossley	42	24	7	11	95	55	55
Marine	42	22	10	10	60	41	54
Buxton	42	21	7	14	64	50	49
Gainsborough Trinity	42	17	13	12	50	57	47
Burton Albion	42	19	8	15	63	54	46
Witton Albion	42	19	8	15	70	62	46
Goole Town	42	14	16	12	56	50	44
South Liverpool	42	19	6	17	59	64	44
Workington	42	15	13	14	57	48	43
Gateshead	42	12	18	12	65	61	42
Worksop Town	42	15	11	16	66	61	41
Macclesfield Town	42	13	13	16	52	69	39
Grantham	42	14	9	19	57	74	37
Matlock Town	42	12	12	18	57	80	36
Lancaster City	42	13	9	20	48	70	35
Netherfield	42	11	12	19	73	81	34
Oswestry Town	42	13	8	21	54	67	34
King's Lynn	42	8	18	16	46	65	34
Southport	42	11	11	26	42	68	33
Morecambe	42	11	8	23	42	74	30
Tamworth	42	9	12	21	38	76	30

1981-82

Team	P	W	D	L	F	A	Pts
Bangor City	42	27	8	7	108	60	62
Mossley	42	24	11	7	76	43	59
Witton Albion	42	22	10	10	75	44	54
Gateshead	42	19	14	9	65	49	52
King's Lynn	42	19	12	11	61	36	50
Grantham	42	18	13	11	65	53	49
Burton Albion	42	19	9	14	71	62	47
Southport	42	16	14	12	63	55	46
Marine	42	17	12	13	64	57	46
Macclesfield Town	42	17	9	16	67	58	43
Workington	42	18	7	17	62	60	43
Worksop Town	42	15	13	14	52	60	43
South Liverpool	42	13	13	16	55	57	39
Goole Town	42	13	13	16	56	60	39
Oswestry Town	42	14	11	17	55	59	39
Buxton	42	14	11	17	48	56	39
Lancaster City	42	13	12	17	47	50	38
Gainsborough Trinity	42	10	13	19	60	69	33
Tamworth	42	10	9	23	31	56	29
Morecambe	42	9	11	22	43	86	29
Matlock Town	42	7	12	23	38	72	26
Netherfield	42	5	9	28	31	91	19

1982-83

Team	P	W	D	L	F	A	Pts
Gateshead	42	32	4	6	114	43	100
Mossley	42	25	9	8	77	42	84
Burton Albion	42	24	9	9	81	53	81
Chorley	42	23	11	8	77	49	80
Macclesfield Town	42	24	8	10	71	49	80
Marine	42	17	17	8	81	57	68
Workington	42	19	10	13	71	55	67
Hyde United	42	18	12	12	91	63	66
King's Lynn	42	17	13	12	62	44	64
Matlock Town	42	18	10	14	70	65	64
Witton Albion	42	17	12	13	82	52	63
Buxton	42	17	9	16	60	62	60
Morecambe	42	16	11	15	75	66	59
Grantham	42	15	13	14	49	50	58
Southport	42	11	14	17	58	65	47
Goole Town	42	13	7	22	52	66	46
Gainsborough Trinity	42	11	9	22	60	71	42
Oswestry Town	42	10	8	24	56	99	38
South Liverpool	42	7	15	20	57	91	36
Tamworth	42	7	8	27	44	97	29
Worksop Town	42	5	10	27	50	98	25
Netherfield	42	2	9	31	28	129	15

1983-84

Team	P	W	D	L	F	A	Pts
Barrow	42	29	10	3	92	38	97
Matlock Town	42	23	8	11	72	48	77
South Liverpool	42	22	11	9	55	44	77
Grantham	42	20	8	14	64	51	68
Burton Albion	42	17	13	12	61	47	64
Macclesfield Town	42	18	10	14	65	55	64
Rhyl	42	19	6	17	64	55	63
Horwich	42	18	9	15	64	59	63
Gainsborough Trinity	42	17	11	14	82	66	62
Stafford Rangers	42	15	17	10	65	52	62
Hyde United	42	17	8	17	61	63	59
Marine	42	16	10	16	63	68	58
Witton Albion	42	14	14	14	64	57	56
Chorley	42	14	11	17	68	65	53
Workington	42	14	9	19	53	57	51
Southport	42	14	8	20	57	74	50
Worksop Town	42	13	8	21	57	74	47
Goole Town	42	12	10	20	59	80	46
Morecambe	42	11	12	19	59	75	45
Oswestry Town	42	11	8	23	66	97	41
Buxton	42	11	6	25	52	91	39
Mossley	42	9	9	24	47	74	33

Mossley had 3 points deducted

1984-85

Team	P	W	D	L	F	A	Pts
Stafford Rangers	42	26	8	8	81	40	86
Macclesfield Town	42	23	13	6	67	39	82
Witton Albion	42	22	8	12	57	39	74
Hyde United	42	21	8	13	68	52	71
Marine	42	18	15	9	59	34	69
Burton Albion	42	18	15	9	70	49	69
Worksop Town	42	19	10	13	68	56	67
Workington	42	18	9	15	59	53	53
Horwich	42	16	14	12	67	60	52
Bangor City	42	17	9	16	70	61	60
Gainsborough Trinity	42	14	14	14	72	73	56
Southport	42	15	9	18	65	66	54
Matlock Town	42	14	9	19	56	66	51
Oswestry Town	42	14	9	19	59	75	51
Mossley	42	14	9	19	45	65	51
Goole Town	42	13	11	18	60	65	50
Rhyl	42	11	14	17	52	63	47
Morecambe	42	11	14	17	51	67	47
Chorley	42	12	10	20	47	63	46
South Liverpool	42	9	15	18	43	71	42
Grantham	42	8	13	21	41	69	36
Buxton	42	8	6	28	38	79	30

Grantham had 1 point deducted

1985-86

Team	P	W	D	L	F	A	Pts
Gateshead	42	24	10	8	85	51	82
Marine	42	23	11	8	63	35	80
Morecambe	42	17	17	8	59	39	68
Gainsborough Trinity	42	18	14	10	66	52	68
Burton Albion	42	18	12	12	64	47	66
Southport	42	17	11	14	70	66	62
Worksop Town	42	17	10	15	55	48	61
Workington	42	14	18	10	54	46	59
Macclesfield Town	42	17	8	17	67	65	59
Hyde United	42	14	15	13	63	62	57
Witton Albion	42	15	13	14	56	59	57
Mossley	42	13	16	13	56	60	55
Bangor City	42	13	15	14	51	51	54
Rhyl	42	14	10	18	65	71	52
South Liverpool	42	11	17	14	43	44	50
Horwich	42	15	6	21	53	69	50
Caernarfon Town	42	11	17	14	51	63	50
Oswestry Town	42	12	13	17	51	60	49
Buxton	42	11	12	19	55	76	45
Chorley	42	9	15	18	56	64	42
Matlock Town	42	9	15	18	59	75	42
Goole Town	42	7	11	24	37	78	31

Workington, Witton Albion, Horwich and Goole Town all had 1 point deducted.

1986-87

Macclesfield Town	42	26	10	6	80	47	88
Bangor City	42	25	12	5	74	35	87
Caernarfon Town	42	20	16	6	67	40	76
Marine	42	21	10	11	70	43	73
South Liverpool	42	21	10	11	58	40	73
Morecambe	42	20	12	10	68	49	72
Matlock Town	42	20	10	12	81	67	70
Southport	42	19	11	12	67	49	68
Chorley	42	16	12	14	58	59	60
Mossley	42	15	12	15	57	52	57
Hyde United	42	15	10	17	81	70	55
Burton Albion	42	16	6	20	56	68	54
Buxton	42	13	14	15	71	68	53
Witton Albion	42	15	8	19	68	79	53
Barrow	42	15	7	20	42	57	52
Goole Town	42	13	12	17	58	62	51
Oswestry Town	42	14	8	20	55	83	50
Rhyl	42	10	15	17	56	74	45
Worksop Town	42	9	13	20	56	74	40
Gainsborough Trinity	42	9	10	23	53	77	37
Workington	42	5	14	23	38	70	28
Horwich RMI	42	3	12	27	36	85	20

Workington and Horwich RMI both had 1 point deducted.

1987-88

Premier Division

Chorley	42	26	10	6	78	35	88
Hyde United	42	25	10	7	91	52	85
Caernarfon Town	42	22	10	10	56	34	76
Morecambe	42	19	15	8	61	41	72
Barrow	42	21	8	13	70	41	71
Worksop Town	42	20	11	11	74	55	71
Bangor City	42	20	10	12	71	55	70
Rhyl	42	18	13	11	70	42	67
Marine	42	19	10	13	67	45	67
Frickley Athletic	42	18	11	13	61	55	65
Witton Albion	42	16	12	14	61	47	60
Goole Town	42	17	9	16	71	61	60
Horwich	42	17	9	16	46	42	60
Southport	42	15	12	15	43	48	57
South Liverpool	42	10	19	13	56	64	49
Buxton	42	11	14	17	72	76	47
Mossley	42	11	11	20	54	75	44
Gateshead	42	11	7	24	52	71	40
Matlock Town	42	10	8	24	58	89	38
Gainsborough Trinity	42	8	10	24	38	81	34
Oswestry Town	42	6	10	26	44	101	28
Workington	42	6	3	33	28	113	21

First Division

Fleetwood Town	36	22	7	7	85	45	73
Stalybridge Celtic	36	22	6	8	72	42	72
Leek Town	36	20	10	6	63	38	70
Accrington Stanley	36	21	6	9	71	39	69
Farsley Celtic	36	18	9	9	64	48	60
Droylsden	36	16	10	10	63	48	58
Eastwood Hanley	36	14	12	10	50	37	54
Winsford United	36	15	6	15	59	47	51
Congleton Town	36	12	16	8	43	39	51
Harrogate Town	36	13	9	14	51	50	48
Alfreton Town	36	13	8	15	53	54	47
Radcliffe Borough	36	11	13	12	66	62	46
Irlam Town	36	12	10	14	39	45	46
Penrith	36	11	11	14	46	51	44
Sutton Town	36	11	5	20	51	96	38
Lancaster City	36	10	6	20	45	72	36
Eastwood Town	36	8	10	18	45	65	34
Curzon Ashton	36	8	4	24	43	73	28
Netherfield	36	4	4	28	35	93	16

Congleton Town had 1 point deducted
Farsley Celtic had 3 points deducted

1988-89

Premier Division

Barrow	42	26	9	7	89	35	87
Hyde United	42	24	8	10	77	44	80
Witton Albion	42	22	13	7	67	39	79
Bangor City	42	22	10	10	77	48	76
Marine	42	23	7	12	69	48	76
Goole Town	42	22	7	13	75	60	73
Fleetwood Town	42	19	16	7	53	44	73
Rhyl	42	18	10	14	75	65	64
Frickley Athletic	42	17	10	15	64	53	61
Mossley	42	17	9	16	56	58	60
South Liverpool	42	15	13	14	65	57	58
Caernarfon Town	42	15	10	17	49	53	55
Matlock Town	42	16	5	21	65	73	53
Southport	42	13	12	17	66	52	51
Buxton	42	12	14	16	61	63	50
Morecambe	42	13	9	20	55	60	47
Gainsborough Trinity	42	12	11	19	56	73	47
Shepshed Charterhouse	42	14	8	20	19	80	44
Stalybridge Celtic	42	9	13	20	16	81	40
Horwich	42	7	14	21	12	70	35
Gateshead	42	7	13	22	36	70	34
Worksop Town	42	6	5	31	42	103	23

Morecambe had 1 point deducted
Shepshed Charterhouse had 6 points deducted

First Division

Colne Dynamo	42	30	11	1	102	21	98
Bishop Auckland	42	28	5	9	78	28	89
Leek Town	42	25	11	6	74	41	85
Droylsden	42	25	9	8	84	48	84
Whitley Bay	42	23	6	13	77	49	75
Accrington Stanley	42	21	10	11	81	60	73
Lancaster City	42	21	8	13	76	54	71
Harrogate Town	42	19	7	16	68	61	64
Newtown	42	15	12	15	65	59	57
Congleton Town	42	15	11	16	62	66	56
Workington	42	17	3	22	59	74	54
Eastwood Town	42	14	10	13	55	61	52
Curzon Ashton	42	13	11	18	74	72	50
Farsley Celtic	42	12	13	17	52	73	49
Irlam Town	42	11	14	17	53	63	47
Penrith	42	14	5	23	61	91	47
Radcliffe Borough	42	12	10	20	62	86	46
Eastwood Hanley	42	11	12	10	46	67	45
Winsford United	42	13	6	23	58	93	35
Alfreton Town	42	8	11	23	44	92	35
Netherfield	42	8	9	25	57	90	32
Sutton Town	42	7	6	29	70	109	23

Leek Town and Netherfield both had 1 point deducted
Colne Dynamo had 3 points deducted
Sutton Town had 4 points deducted

1989-90

Premier Division

Colne Dynamoes	42	32	6	4	86	40	102
Gateshead	42	22	10	10	78	58	76
Witton Albion	42	22	7	13	67	39	73
Hyde United	42	21	8	13	73	50	71
South Liverpool	42	20	9	13	89	79	69
Matlock Town	42	18	12	12	61	42	66
Southport	42	17	14	11	54	48	65
Fleetwood Town	42	17	12	13	73	66	63
Marine	42	16	14	12	59	55	62
Bangor City	42	15	15	12	64	58	60
Bishop Auckland	42	17	8	17	72	64	59
Frickley Athletic	42	16	8	18	56	61	56
Horwich	42	15	13	14	66	69	55
Morecambe	42	15	9	18	58	70	54
Gainsborough Trinity	42	16	8	18	59	55	53
Buxton	42	15	8	19	59	72	53
Stalybridge Celtic	42	12	9	21	48	61	45
Mossley	42	11	10	21	61	82	43
Goole Town	42	12	5	25	54	77	41
Shepshed	42	11	7	24	55	82	40
Caernarfon Town	42	10	8	24	56	86	38
Rhyl	42	7	10	25	43	77	30

Rhyl had 1 point deducted
Horwich and Gainsborough Trinity both had 3 points deducted

First Division

Leek Town	42	26	8	8	70	31	86
Droylsden	42	27	6	9	81	46	80
Accrington Stanley	42	22	10	10	80	53	76
Whitley Bay	42	21	11	10	93	59	74
Emley	42	20	9	13	70	42	69
Congleton Town	42	20	12	10	65	53	69
Winsford United	42	18	10	14	65	53	64
Curzon Ashton	42	17	11	14	66	60	62
Harrogate Town	42	17	9	16	68	62	60
Lancaster City	42	15	14	13	73	54	59
Eastwood Town	42	16	11	15	61	64	59
Farsley Celtic	42	17	6	19	71	75	57
Rossendale United	42	15	9	18	73	69	54
Newtown	42	14	12	16	49	62	54
Irlam Town	42	14	11	17	61	66	53
Workington	42	14	8	20	56	64	50
Radcliffe Borough	42	14	7	21	47	63	49
Alfreton Town	42	13	8	21	59	85	47
Worksop Town	42	13	5	24	56	95	44
Netherfield	42	11	6	25	56	89	39
Eastwood Hanley	42	10	6	26	45	76	36
Penrith	42	9	9	24	44	88	36

Congleton Town 3 points deducted. Droylsden 7 points deducted.

1990-91

Premier Division

Witton Albion	40	28	9	3	81	31	93
Stalybridge Celtic	40	22	11	7	44	26	77
Morecambe	40	19	16	5	72	44	73
Fleetwood Town	40	20	9	11	69	44	69
Southport	40	18	14	8	66	48	68
Marine	40	18	11	11	56	39	65
Bishop Auckland	40	17	10	13	62	56	61
Buxton	40	17	11	12	66	61	59
Leek Town	40	15	11	14	48	44	56
Frickley Athletic	40	16	6	18	64	62	54
Hyde United	40	14	11	15	73	63	53
Goole Town	40	14	10	16	68	74	52
Droylsden	40	12	11	17	67	70	47
Chorley	40	12	10	18	55	55	46
Mossley	40	13	10	17	55	68	45
Horwich	40	13	6	21	62	81	45
Matlock Town	40	12	7	21	52	70	43
Bangor City	40	9	12	19	52	70	39
South Liverpool	40	10	9	21	58	92	39
Gainsborough Trinity	40	9	11	20	57	84	38
Shepshed Charterhouse	40	6	7	27	38	83	25

First Division

Whitley Bay	42	25	10	7	95	38	85
Emley	42	24	12	6	78	37	84
Worksop Town	42	25	7	10	85	56	82
Accrington Stanley	42	21	13	8	83	57	76
Rhyl	42	21	7	14	62	63	70
Eastwood Town	42	17	11	14	70	60	62
Warrington Town	42	17	10	15	68	52	61
Lancaster City	42	19	8	15	58	56	61
Bridlington Town	42	15	15	12	72	52	60
Curzon Ashton	42	14	14	14	49	57	56
Congleton Town	42	14	12	16	57	71	54
Netherfield	42	14	11	17	67	66	53
Newtown	42	13	12	17	68	75	51
Caernarfon Town	42	13	10	19	51	64	49
Rossendale United	42	12	13	17	66	67	48
Radcliffe Borough	42	12	12	18	50	69	48
Irlam Town	42	12	11	19	55	76	47
Winsford United	42	11	13	18	51	66	46
Harrogate Town	42	11	13	18	55	73	46
Workington	42	11	11	20	54	67	41
Farsley Celtic	42	11	9	22	49	78	39
Alfreton Town	42	7	12	23	41	84	33

1991-92

Premier Division

Stalybridge Celtic	42	26	14	2	84	33	92
Marine	42	23	9	10	64	32	78
Morecambe	42	21	13	8	70	44	76
Leek Town	42	21	10	11	62	49	73
Buxton	42	21	9	12	65	47	72
Emley	42	18	11	13	69	47	65
Southport	42	16	17	9	57	48	65
Accrington Stanley	42	17	12	13	78	62	63
Hyde United	42	17	9	16	69	67	60
Fleetwood United	42	17	8	17	67	64	59
Bishop Auckland	42	16	9	17	48	58	57
Goole Town	42	15	9	18	60	72	54
Horwich	42	13	14	15	44	52	53
Frickley Athletic	42	12	16	14	61	57	52
Droylsden	42	12	14	16	62	72	50
Mossley	42	15	4	23	51	73	49
Whitley Bay	42	13	9	20	53	79	48
Gainsborough Trinity	42	11	13	18	48	63	46
Matlock Town	42	12	9	21	59	87	45
Bangor City	42	11	10	21	46	57	43
Chorley	42	11	9	22	61	82	42
Shepshed Albion	42	6	8	28	46	79	26

First Division

Colwyn Bay	42	30	4	8	99	49	94
Winsford United	42	29	6	7	96	41	93
Worksop Town	42	25	5	12	101	54	80
Guiseley	42	22	12	8	93	56	78
Caernarfon Town	42	23	9	10	78	47	78
Bridlington Town	42	22	9	11	86	46	75
Warrington Town	42	20	8	14	79	64	68
Knowsley United	42	18	10	14	69	52	64
Netherfield	42	18	7	17	54	61	61
Harrogate Town	42	14	16	12	73	69	58
Curzon Ashton	42	15	9	18	71	83	54
Farsley Celtic	42	15	9	18	79	101	53
Radcliffe Borough	42	15	9	18	67	72	51
Newtown	42	15	6	21	60	95	51
Eastwood Town	42	13	11	18	59	70	50
Lancaster City	42	10	19	13	55	62	49
Congleton Town	42	14	5	23	59	81	47
Rhyl	42	11	10	21	59	69	43
Rossendale United	42	9	11	22	61	90	38
Alfreton Town	42	12	2	28	63	98	38
Irlam Town	42	9	7	26	45	95	33
Workington	42	7	8	27	45	99	28

Farsley Celtic 1 point deducted. Radcliffe Borough 3 points deducted.

1992-93

Premier Division

Southport	42	29	9	4	103	31	96
Winsford United	42	27	9	6	91	43	90
Morecambe	42	25	11	6	93	51	86
Marine	42	26	8	8	83	47	86
Leek Town	42	21	11	10	86	51	74
Accrington Stanley	42	20	13	9	79	45	73
Frickley Athletic	42	21	6	15	62	52	69
Barrow	42	18	11	13	71	55	65
Hyde United	42	17	13	12	87	71	64
Bishop Auckland	42	17	11	14	63	52	62
Gainsborough Trinity	42	17	8	17	63	66	59
Colwyn Bay	42	16	6	20	80	79	54
Horwich	42	14	10	18	72	79	52
Buxton	42	13	10	19	60	75	49
Matlock Town	42	13	11	18	56	79	47
Emley	42	13	6	23	62	91	45
Whitley Bay	42	11	8	23	57	96	41
Chorley	42	10	10	22	52	93	40
Fleetwood Town	42	10	7	25	50	77	37
Droylsden	42	10	7	25	47	84	37
Mossley	42	7	8	27	53	95	29
Goole Town	42	6	9	27	47	105	27

Matlock Town had 3 points deducted

First Division

Bridlington Town	40	25	11	4	84	35	86
Knowsley United	40	23	7	10	86	48	76
Ashton United	40	22	8	10	81	54	74
Guiseley	40	20	10	10	90	64	70
Warrington Town	40	19	10	11	85	57	67
Gretna	40	17	12	11	64	47	63
Curzon Ashton	40	16	15	9	69	63	63
Great Harwood Town	40	17	9	14	66	57	60
Alfreton Town	40	15	9	16	80	80	54
Harrogate Town	40	14	12	14	77	81	54
Worksop Town	40	15	9	16	66	70	54
Radcliffe Borough	40	13	14	13	66	69	53
Workington	40	13	13	14	51	61	52
Eastwood Town	40	3	11	16	49	52	50
Netherfield	40	11	14	15	68	63	47
Caernarfon Town	40	13	8	19	66	74	47
Farsley Celtic	40	12	8	20	64	77	44
Lancaster City	40	10	12	18	49	76	42
Shepshed Albion	40	9	12	19	46	66	39
Congleton Town	40	10	7	23	58	95	37
Rossendale United	40	5	5	30	50	126	20

1993-94

Premier Division

Marine	42	27	9	6	106	62	90
Leek Town	42	27	8	7	79	50	89
Boston United	42	23	9	10	90	43	78
Bishop Auckland	42	23	9	10	73	58	78
Frickley Athletic	42	21	12	9	90	51	75
Colwyn Bay	42	18	14	10	74	51	68
Morecambe	42	20	7	15	90	56	67
Barrow	42	18	10	14	59	51	64
Hyde United	42	17	10	15	80	71	61
Chorley	42	17	10	15	70	67	61
Whitley Bay	42	17	9	16	61	72	60
Gainsborough Trinity	42	15	11	16	64	66	56
Emley	42	12	16	14	63	71	52
Matlock Town	42	13	12	17	71	76	51
Buxton	42	13	10	19	67	73	49
Accrington Stanley	42	14	7	21	63	85	49
Droylsden	42	11	14	17	57	82	47
Knowsley United	42	11	11	20	52	66	44
Winsford United	42	9	11	22	50	74	38
Horwich RMI	42	9	11	22	50	75	35
Bridlington Town	42	7	10	25	41	91	28
Fleetwood Town	42	7	7	28	55	114	28

Horwich RMI 1 point deducted. Bridlington Town 3 points deducted

First Division

Guiseley	40	29	6	5	87	37	93
Spennymoor United	40	25	6	9	95	50	81
Ashton United	40	24	7	9	85	41	79
Lancaster City	40	20	10	10	74	46	70
Netherfield	40	20	6	14	68	60	66
Alfreton Town	40	18	10	12	83	70	64
Warrington Town	40	17	11	12	52	48	62
Goole Town	40	16	11	13	72	58	59
Great Harwood Town	40	15	14	11	56	60	59
Gretna	40	16	7	17	64	65	55
Workington	40	14	10	16	70	74	52
Worksop Town	40	14	9	17	79	87	51
Bamber Bridge	40	13	11	16	62	59	50
Curzon Ashton	40	13	8	19	62	71	47
Congleton Town	40	12	9	19	53	68	45
Radcliffe Borough	40	10	14	16	62	75	44
Mossley	40	10	12	18	44	68	39
Caernarfon Town	40	9	11	20	54	88	38
Farsley Celtic	40	6	16	18	42	77	34
Harrogate Town	40	8	9	23	40	86	33
Eastwood Town	40	7	11	22	47	63	32

Mossley had 3 points deducted

1994-95

Premier Division

Marine	42	29	11	2	83	27	98
Morecambe	42	28	10	4	99	34	94
Guiseley	42	28	9	5	96	50	93
Hyde United	42	22	10	10	89	59	76
Boston United	42	20	11	11	80	43	71
Spennymoor United	42	20	11	11	66	52	71
Buxton	42	18	9	15	65	62	63
Gainsborough Trinity	42	16	13	13	69	61	61
Bishop Auckland	42	16	12	14	68	55	57
Witton Albion	42	14	14	14	54	56	56
Barrow	42	17	5	20	68	71	56
Colwyn Bay	42	16	8	18	71	80	56
Emley	42	14	13	15	62	68	55
Matlock Town	42	15	5	22	62	72	50
Accrington Stanley	42	12	13	17	55	77	49
Knowsley United	42	11	14	17	64	83	47
Winsford United	42	10	11	21	56	75	41
Chorley	42	11	7	24	64	87	40
Frickley Athletic	42	10	10	22	53	79	40
Droylsden	42	10	8	24	56	93	38
Whitley Bay	42	8	8	26	46	97	32
Horwich RMI	42	9	4	29	49	94	31

Bishop Auckland had 3 points deducted

First Division

Blyth Spartans	42	26	9	7	95	55	87
Bamber Bridge	42	25	10	7	101	51	85
Warrington Town	42	25	9	8	74	40	84
Alfreton Town	42	25	7	10	94	49	82
Lancaster City	42	23	10	9	81	44	79
Worksop Town	42	19	14	9	95	68	71
Radcliffe Borough	42	18	10	14	76	70	64
Ashton United	42	18	8	16	80	70	62
Netherfield	42	17	7	118	54	56	58
Eastwood Town	42	14	13	15	67	61	55
Gretna	42	14	13	15	64	66	55
Atherton Laburnum Rovers	42	14	8	20	60	67	50
Harrogate Town	42	14	8	20	57	78	50
Caernarfon Town	42	13	10	19	59	62	49
Curzon Ashton	42	10	16	16	64	80	46
Great Harwood Town	42	11	13	18	66	87	46
Congleton Town	42	11	13	18	52	75	46
Fleetwood	42	12	11	19	51	74	44
Farsley Celtic	42	12	7	23	66	100	43
Workington	42	12	6	24	61	91	42
Goole Town	42	11	7	24	46	81	40
Mossley	42	11	5	26	52	90	37

Mossley had 1 point deducted. Fleetwood had 3 points deducted

1995-96

Premier Division

Bamber Bridge	42	20	16	6	81	49	76
Boston United	42	23	6	13	86	59	75
Hyde United	42	21	11	10	86	51	74
Barrow	42	20	13	9	69	42	73
Gainsborough Trinity	42	20	13	9	60	41	73
Blyth Spartans	42	17	13	12	75	61	64
Accrington Stanley	42	17	14	11	62	54	62
Emley	42	17	10	15	57	53	61
Spennymoor United	42	14	18	10	67	61	60
Guiseley	42	15	14	13	62	57	59
Bishop Auckland	42	16	11	15	60	55	59
Marine	42	15	14	13	59	54	59
Witton Albion	42	17	8	17	60	62	59
Chorley	42	14	9	19	67	74	48
Knowsley United	42	14	6	22	61	89	48
Winsford United	42	10	16	16	56	79	46
Leek Town	42	10	15	17	52	55	45
Colwyn Bay	42	8	21	13	43	57	45
Frickley Athletic	42	11	14	17	63	87	44
Buxton	42	9	11	22	43	72	38
Droylsden	42	10	8	24	58	100	38
Matlock Town	42	8	11	23	71	86	35

Accrington Stanley, Chorley & Frickley Town all had 3 points deducted

First Division

Lancaster City	40	24	11	5	79	38	83
Alfreton Town	40	23	9	8	79	47	78
Lincoln United	40	22	7	11	80	56	73
Curzon Ashton	40	20	7	13	73	53	67
Farsley Celtic	40	19	9	12	66	61	66
Radcliffe Borough	40	17	13	10	70	48	64
Eastwood Town	40	18	9	13	60	47	63
Whitley Bay	40	18	8	14	72	62	62
Ashton United	40	19	7	14	73	65	60
Atherton Laburnum Rovers	40	15	12	13	60	61	57
Worksop Town	40	16	8	16	84	90	56
Gretna	40	13	13	14	75	65	52
Warrington Town	40	13	10	17	75	72	49
Leigh	40	14	7	19	53	59	49
Netherfield	40	13	10	17	64	73	49
Workington	40	11	12	17	50	62	45
Bradford Park Avenue	40	9	14	17	57	72	41
Congleton Town	40	11	11	18	36	59	41
Great Harwood Town	40	9	7	24	44	78	33
Fleetwood	40	7	10	23	41	81	31
Harrogate Town	40	7	10	23	54	96	31

Great Harwood Town had 1 point deducted, Congleton Town had 3 points deducted and Ashton United had 4 points deducted

1996-97

Premier Division

Leek Town	44	28	9	7	71	35	93
Bishop Auckland	44	23	14	7	88	43	83
Hyde United	44	22	16	6	93	46	82
Emley	44	23	12	9	89	54	81
Barrow	44	23	11	10	71	45	80
Boston United	44	22	13	9	74	47	79
Blyth Spartans	44	22	11	11	74	49	77
Marine	44	20	15	9	53	37	75
Guiseley	44	20	11	13	63	54	71
Gainsborough Trinity	44	18	12	14	65	46	66
Accrington Stanley	44	18	12	14	77	70	66
Runcorn	44	15	15	14	63	62	60
Chorley	44	16	9	19	69	66	57
Winsford United	44	13	14	17	50	56	53
Knowsley United	44	12	14	18	58	79	49
Colwyn Bay	44	11	13	20	60	76	46
Lancaster City	44	12	9	23	48	75	45
Frickley Athletic	44	12	8	24	62	91	44
Spennymoor United	44	10	10	24	52	68	40
Bamber Bridge	44	11	7	26	59	99	40
Alfreton Town	44	8	13	23	45	83	37
Witton Albion	44	5	14	25	41	91	39
Buxton	44	5	12	27	33	86	27

Knowsley United had 1 point deducted

First Division

Radcliffe Borough	42	26	7	9	77	33	85
Leigh	42	24	11	7	65	33	83
Lincoln United	42	25	8	9	78	47	83
Farsley Celtic	42	23	8	11	75	48	77
Worksop Town	42	20	12	10	68	38	69
Stocksbridge Park Steels	42	19	11	12	66	54	68
Bradford Park Avenue	42	20	8	14	58	50	68
Ashton United	42	17	14	11	73	52	65
Great Harwood Town	42	16	12	14	56	46	60
Droylsden	42	15	14	13	69	67	59
Matlock Town	42	16	10	16	61	69	58
Whitley Bay	42	14	12	16	47	54	54
Flixton	42	15	7	20	57	72	52
Netherfield	42	12	14	16	54	56	50
Eastwood Town	42	12	14	16	42	50	50
Gretna	42	10	18	14	55	68	48
Harrogate Town	42	13	8	21	55	76	47
Congleton Town	42	12	9	21	47	64	45
Workington	42	10	12	20	45	63	42
Curzon Ashton	42	8	10	24	48	79	34
Warrington Town	42	5	18	19	42	79	33
Atherton Laburnum Rovers	42	7	9	26	45	85	30

Worksop Town had 3 points deducted

1997-98

Premier Division

Barrow	42	25	8	9	61	29	83
Boston United	42	22	12	8	55	40	78
Leigh RMI	42	21	13	8	63	41	76
Runcorn	42	22	9	11	80	50	75
Gainsborough Trinity	42	22	9	11	60	39	75
Emley	42	22	8	12	81	61	74
Winsford United	42	19	12	11	54	43	69
Altrincham	42	18	11	13	76	44	65
Guiseley	42	16	16	10	61	53	64
Bishop Auckland	42	17	12	13	78	60	63
Marine	42	15	11	16	56	59	56
Hyde United	42	13	16	13	60	55	55
Colwyn Bay	42	15	9	18	53	57	54
Spennymoor United	42	14	11	17	58	72	52
Chorley	42	14	7	21	51	70	49
Frickley Athletic	42	12	12	18	45	62	48
Lancaster City	42	13	8	21	55	74	47
Blyth Spartans	42	12	13	17	52	63	39
Bamber Bridge	42	9	12	21	51	74	39
Accrington Stanley	42	8	14	20	49	68	38
Radcliffe Borough	42	6	12	24	39	70	30
Alfreton Town	42	3	13	26	32	86	22

Spennymoor United had 1 point deducted
Blyth Spartans had 10 points deducted

First Division

Whitby Town	42	30	8	4	99	48	98
Worksop Town	42	28	7	7	93	44	91
Ashton Town	42	26	9	7	93	43	87
Droylsden	42	24	8	10	70	49	80
Lincoln United	42	20	11	11	76	62	71
Farsley Celtic	42	20	10	12	72	66	70
Witton Albion	42	19	9	14	77	55	66
Eastwood Town	42	18	12	12	68	51	66
Bradford Park Avenue	42	18	11	13	62	46	65
Belper Town	42	18	7	17	68	66	61
Stocksbridge Park Steels	42	17	9	16	68	63	60
Trafford	42	16	6	20	59	61	54
Whitley Bay	42	14	12	16	60	63	54
Matlock Town	42	14	11	17	68	65	53
Gretna	42	13	9	20	58	64	48
Netherfield	42	12	11	19	55	75	47
Flixton	42	10	12	20	45	73	42
Congleton Town	42	11	8	23	65	101	41
Harrogate Town	42	8	14	20	57	80	38
Great Harwood Town	42	8	12	22	42	88	36
Workington	42	8	7	27	38	84	31
Buxton	42	7	3	32	41	87	24

1998-99

Premier Division

Altrincham	42	23	11	8	67	33	80
Worksop Town	42	22	10	10	66	48	76
Guiseley	42	21	9	12	64	47	72
Bamber Bridge	42	18	15	9	63	48	69
Gateshead	42	18	11	13	69	58	65
Gainsborough Trinity	42	19	8	15	65	59	65
Whitby Town	42	17	13	12	77	62	64
Leigh	42	16	15	11	63	54	63
Hyde United	42	16	11	15	61	48	59
Stalybridge Celtic	42	16	11	15	71	63	59
Winsford United	42	14	15	13	56	52	57
Runcorn	42	12	19	11	46	49	55
Emley	42	12	17	13	47	49	53
Blyth Spartans	42	14	9	19	56	64	51
Colwyn Bay	42	12	13	17	60	71	49
Frickley Athletic	42	11	15	16	55	71	48
Marine	42	10	17	15	61	69	47
Spennymoor United	42	12	11	19	52	71	47
Lancaster City	42	11	13	18	50	62	46
Bishop Auckland	42	10	15	17	49	67	45
Chorley	42	8	15	19	45	68	39
Accrington Stanley	42	9	9	24	47	77	36

First Division

Droylsden	42	26	8	8	97	55	86
Hucknall Town	42	26	11	5	80	38	86
Ashton United	42	22	12	8	79	46	78
Lincoln United	42	20	12	10	94	65	72
Eastwood Town	42	20	8	14	65	69	68
Radcliffe Borough	42	19	8	15	78	62	65
Burscough	42	19	8	15	67	61	65
Witton Albion	42	18	9	15	70	63	63
Bradford Park Avenue	42	17	11	14	64	55	62
Stocksbridge Park Steels	42	16	13	13	64	60	61
Harrogate Town	42	17	7	18	75	77	58
Gretna	42	16	10	16	73	80	58
Belper Town	42	15	11	16	58	57	56
Trafford	42	14	11	17	50	58	53
Netherfield Kendal	42	13	10	19	51	64	49
Flixton	42	12	12	18	50	64	48
Matlock Town	42	14	6	22	53	72	48
Farsley Celtic	42	11	13	18	56	73	46
Whitley Bay	42	10	9	23	53	77	39
Congleton Town	42	8	15	19	65	91	39
Great Harwood Town	42	10	8	24	51	73	38
Alfreton Town	42	9	8	25	53	86	35

Hucknall Town had 3 points deducted

1999-2000

Premier Division

Leigh	44	28	8	8	91	45	92
Hyde United	44	24	13	7	77	44	85
Gateshead	44	23	13	8	79	41	82
Marine	44	21	16	7	78	46	79
Emley	44	20	12	12	54	41	72
Lancaster City	44	20	11	13	65	55	71
Stalybridge Celtic	44	18	12	14	64	54	66
Bishop Auckland	44	18	11	15	63	61	65
Runcorn	44	18	10	16	64	55	64
Worksop Town	44	19	6	19	78	65	63
Gainsborough Trinity	44	16	15	13	59	49	63
Whitby Town	44	15	13	16	66	66	58
Barrow	44	14	15	15	65	59	57
Blyth Spartans	44	15	9	20	62	67	54
Droylsden	44	14	12	18	53	60	54
Frickley Athletic	44	15	9	20	64	85	54
Bamber Bridge	44	14	11	19	70	67	53
Hucknall Town	44	14	11	19	55	61	53
Leek Town	44	14	10	20	58	79	52
Colwyn Bay	44	12	12	20	46	85	48
Spennymoor United	44	10	13	21	41	71	42
Guiseley	44	8	17	19	52	72	41
Winsford United	44	3	7	34	40	116	16

Spennymoor United had 1 point deducted

First Division

Accrington Stanley	42	25	9	8	96	43	84
Burscough	42	22	18	2	81	35	84
Witton Albion	42	23	15	4	88	46	84
Bradford Park Avenue	42	23	9	10	77	48	78
Radcliffe Borough	42	22	12	8	71	48	78
Farsley Celtic	42	19	11	12	66	52	68
Matlock Town	42	17	16	9	72	55	67
Ossett Town	42	17	8	17	77	55	59
Stocksbridge Park Steels	42	16	8	18	55	70	56
Eastwood Town	42	15	11	16	64	65	55
Harrogate Town	42	14	12	16	65	67	54
Congleton Town	42	14	12	16	63	73	54
Chorley	42	13	15	14	53	64	54
Ashton United	42	12	16	14	65	67	52
Workington	42	13	13	16	49	55	52
Lincoln United	42	13	12	17	52	80	51
Belper Town	42	13	11	18	59	72	50
Trafford	42	11	12	19	55	63	45
Gretna	42	11	7	24	48	78	40
Netherfield Kendal	42	8	9	25	46	82	33
Flixton	42	7	9	26	47	85	30
Whitley Bay	42	7	9	26	41	87	30

Eastwood Town had 1 point deducted

2000-2001

Premier Division

Stalybridge Celtic	44	31	9	4	96	32	102
Emley	44	31	8	5	86	42	101
Bishop Auckland	44	26	7	11	89	53	85
Lancaster City	44	24	9	11	84	60	81
Worksop Town	44	20	13	11	102	60	73
Barrow	44	21	9	14	83	53	72
Altrincham	44	20	10	14	80	59	70
Gainsborough Trinity	44	17	14	13	59	56	65
Accrington Stanley	44	18	10	16	72	65	64
Hucknall Town	44	17	12	15	57	63	63
Gateshead	44	16	12	16	67	61	60
Bamber Bridge	44	17	8	19	63	65	59
Runcorn	44	15	10	19	56	71	55
Blyth Spartans	44	15	9	20	61	64	54
Burscough	44	14	10	20	59	68	52
Hyde United	44	13	12	19	72	79	51
Whitby Town	44	13	11	20	60	76	50
Marine	44	12	13	19	62	78	49
Colwyn Bay	44	12	10	22	68	102	46
Frickley Athletic	44	10	15	19	50	79	45
Droylsden	44	13	6	25	50	80	45
Leek Town	44	12	8	24	45	70	44
Spennymoor United	44	4	5	35	32	108	17

First Division

Bradford Park Avenue	42	28	5	9	83	40	89
Vauxhall Motors	42	23	10	9	95	50	79
Ashton United	42	23	9	10	91	49	78
Stocksbridge Park Steels	42	19	13	10	80	60	70
Trafford	42	20	9	13	70	62	68
Belper Town	42	18	11	13	71	62	65
Witton Albion	42	15	16	11	51	50	61
Ossett Town	42	16	12	14	66	58	60
Radcliffe Borough	42	17	8	17	72	71	59
Chorley	42	15	14	13	71	70	59
Harrogate Town	42	15	10	17	60	70	55
Matlock Town	42	14	10	18	70	74	52
North Ferriby United	42	14	10	18	64	73	52
Workington	42	13	12	17	53	60	51
Lincoln United	42	13	12	17	60	75	51
Gretna	42	12	12	18	72	82	48
Guiseley	42	11	15	16	37	50	48
Kendal Town	42	12	12	18	60	69	47
Farsley Celtic	42	12	11	19	53	71	47
Eastwood Town	42	12	8	21	40	63	47
Winsford United	42	13	11	18	61	70	44
Congleton Town	42	6	8	28	43	94	30

Trafford and Kendal Town both had 1 point deducted
Winsford United had 6 points deducted

2001-2002

Premier Division

Burton Albion	44	31	11	2	106	30	104
Vauxhall Motors	44	27	8	9	86	55	89
Lancaster City	44	23	9	12	80	57	78
Worksop Town	44	23	9	12	74	51	78
Emley	44	22	9	13	69	55	75
Accrington Stanley	44	21	9	14	89	64	72
Runcorn FC Halton	44	21	8	15	76	53	71
Barrow	44	19	10	15	75	59	67
Altrincham	44	19	9	16	66	58	66
Bradford Park Avenue	44	18	5	21	77	76	59
Droylsden	44	17	8	19	65	78	59
Blyth Spartans	44	14	16	14	59	62	58
Frickley Athletic	44	16	11	17	63	69	58
Gateshead	44	14	14	16	58	71	56
Whitby Town	44	15	8	21	61	76	53
Hucknall Town	44	14	9	21	50	68	51
Marine	44	11	17	16	62	71	50
Burscough	44	15	5	24	69	86	50
Gainsborough Trinity	44	13	10	21	61	76	49
Colwyn Bay	44	12	11	21	49	82	47
Bishop Auckland	44	12	8	24	46	68	44
Hyde United	44	10	10	24	61	87	40
Bamber Bridge	44	7	10	27	38	88	30

First Division

Harrogate Town	42	25	11	6	80	35	86
Ossett Town	42	21	13	8	73	44	76
Ashton United	42	21	12	9	90	63	75
Spennymoor United	42	22	6	14	75	73	72
Radcliffe Borough	42	20	8	14	73	51	68
Leek Town	42	20	8	14	67	51	68
Gretna	42	19	7	16	66	66	63
Eastwood Town	42	17	11	14	61	59	62
Rossendale United	42	17	10	15	69	58	61
Witton Albion	42	17	10	15	72	68	61
Guiseley	42	18	7	17	60	67	61
North Ferriby United	42	14	16	12	71	60	58
Chorley	42	16	9	17	59	57	57
Matlock Town	42	15	9	18	49	48	54
Trafford	42	14	9	19	64	80	51
Workington	42	12	12	18	51	57	48
Farsley Celtic	42	12	11	19	64	78	47
Belper Town	42	12	11	19	49	66	47
Lincoln United	42	11	14	17	62	80	47
Stocksbridge Park Steels	42	12	9	21	55	76	45
Kendal Town	42	9	9	24	52	76	36
Ossett Albion	42	8	8	26	43	92	32

2002-2003

Premier Division

Accrington Stanley	44	30	10	4	97	44	100
Barrow	44	24	12	8	84	52	84
Vauxhall Motors	44	22	10	12	81	46	76
Stalybridge Celtic	44	21	13	10	77	51	76
Worksop Town	44	21	9	14	82	67	72
Harrogate Town	44	21	8	15	75	63	71
Bradford Park Avenue	44	20	10	14	73	70	70
Hucknall Town	44	17	15	12	72	62	66
Droylsden	44	18	10	16	62	52	64
Whitby Town	44	17	12	15	80	69	63
Marine	44	17	10	17	63	60	61
Wakefield & Emley	44	14	18	12	46	49	60
Runcorn FC Halton	44	15	15	14	69	74	60
Altrincham	44	17	9	18	58	63	60
Gainsborough Trinity	44	16	11	17	67	66	59
Ashton United	44	15	13	16	71	79	58
Lancaster City	44	16	9	19	71	75	57
Burscough	44	14	9	21	44	51	51
Blyth Spartans	44	14	9	21	67	87	51
Frickley Athletic	44	13	8	23	45	78	47
Gateshead	44	10	11	23	60	81	41
Colwyn Bay	44	5	9	30	52	99	24
Hyde United	44	5	8	31	40	98	23

Division One

Alfreton Town	42	26	9	7	106	59	87
Spennymoor United	42	27	6	9	81	42	87
Radcliffe Borough	42	25	10	7	90	46	85
North Ferriby United	42	23	9	10	78	45	78
Chorley	42	21	10	11	80	51	73
Belper Town	42	20	13	9	53	42	73
Witton Albion	42	19	15	8	67	50	72
Matlock Town	42	20	10	12	67	48	70
Leek Town	42	20	9	13	63	46	69
Workington	42	19	10	13	73	60	67
Farsley Celtic	42	17	11	14	66	67	62
Kendal Town	42	18	7	17	68	58	61
Bamber Bridge	42	15	9	18	55	59	54
Guiseley	42	14	11	17	68	63	53
Bishop Auckland	42	13	10	19	58	83	49
Lincoln United	42	12	9	21	67	77	45
Stocksbridge PS	42	11	9	22	54	81	42
Rossendale United	42	12	5	25	58	88	41
Kidsgrove Athletic	42	9	11	22	49	71	38
Ossett Town	42	8	9	25	39	80	33
Eastwood Town	42	5	8	29	33	92	23
Trafford	42	5	6	31	34	99	21

2003-2004

Premier Division

Hucknall Town	44	29	8	7	83	38	95
Droylsden	44	26	8	10	96	64	86
Barrow	44	22	14	8	82	52	80
Alfreton Town	44	23	9	12	73	43	78
Harrogate Town	44	24	5	15	79	63	77
Southport	44	20	10	14	71	52	70
Worksop Town	44	19	13	12	69	50	70
Lancaster City	44	20	9	15	62	49	69
Vauxhall Motors	44	19	10	15	78	75	67
Gainsborough Trinity	44	17	13	14	70	52	64
Stalybridge Celtic	44	18	10	16	72	66	64
Altrincham	44	16	15	13	66	51	63
Runcorn FC Halton	44	16	13	15	67	63	61
Ashton United	44	17	8	19	59	79	59
Whitby Town	44	14	11	19	55	70	53
Marine	44	13	12	19	62	74	51
Bradford Park Avenue	44	12	14	18	48	62	50
Spennymoor United	44	14	6	24	55	93	48
Burscough	44	10	15	19	47	67	45
Radcliffe Borough	44	12	6	26	74	99	42
Blyth Spartans	44	10	10	24	54	74	40
Frickley Athletic	44	11	7	26	51	83	40
Wakefield & Emley	44	8	6	30	45	99	30

Division One

Hyde United	42	24	8	10	79	49	80
Matlock Town	42	23	7	12	78	51	76
Farsley Celtic	42	20	14	8	78	56	74
Lincoln United	42	20	11	11	73	53	71
Witton Albion	42	17	12	13	61	56	63
Gateshead	42	21	4	17	65	68	63
Workington	42	17	11	14	70	58	62
Leek Town	42	16	13	13	56	47	61
Guiseley	42	16	12	14	66	54	60
Bamber Bridge	42	16	12	14	64	53	60
Bridlington Town	42	16	10	16	70	68	58
Prescot Cables	42	16	10	16	63	65	58
Bishop Auckland	42	14	13	15	61	64	55
Ossett Town	42	15	10	17	62	73	52
Rossendale United	42	13	12	17	53	62	51
Colwyn Bay	42	14	9	19	56	82	51
North Ferriby United	42	13	11	18	64	70	50
Chorley	42	13	10	19	54	70	49
Stocksbridge Park Steels	42	12	12	18	57	69	48
Belper Town	42	9	15	18	44	58	42
Kendal Town	42	11	7	24	53	79	40
Kidsgrove Athletic	42	10	9	23	45	67	39

2004-2005

Premier Division

Hyde United	42	25	13	4	80	43	88
Workington	42	26	7	9	73	30	85
Farsley Celtic	42	25	8	9	81	41	83
Whitby Town	42	23	11	8	65	49	80
Prescot Cables	42	21	8	13	63	54	71
Burscough	42	21	7	14	93	74	70
Leek Town	42	16	15	11	63	52	63
Witton Albion	42	15	17	10	56	44	62
Radcliffe Borough	42	16	14	12	60	60	62
Guiseley	42	16	13	13	70	64	61
Matlock Town	42	14	13	15	59	67	55
Blyth Spartans	42	13	13	16	53	55	52
Wakefield & Emley	42	14	10	18	60	67	52
Lincoln United	42	15	4	23	53	66	49
Marine	42	10	18	14	53	60	48
Ossett Town	42	11	13	18	53	62	46
Gateshead	42	11	12	19	61	84	45
Frickley Athletic	42	10	14	18	44	57	44
Bishop Auckland	42	11	7	24	51	74	40
Bridlington Town	42	7	14	21	43	66	35
Bamber Bridge	42	9	7	26	48	92	34
Spennymoor United	42	9	10	23	44	65	25

Spennymoor United had 12 points deducted.

Division One

North Ferriby United	42	25	8	9	83	49	83
Ilkeston Town	42	24	9	9	64	40	81
AFC Telford United	42	23	11	8	78	44	80
Willenhall Town	42	22	12	8	71	46	78
Kendal Town	42	21	8	13	89	69	71
Eastwood Town	42	20	9	13	73	54	69
Mossley	42	20	6	16	81	56	66
Brigg Town	42	15	19	8	59	46	64
Gresley Rovers	42	17	12	13	57	53	63
Kidsgrove Athletic	42	15	15	12	60	55	60
Woodley Sports	42	16	11	15	68	74	59
Ossett Albion	42	15	13	14	83	74	58
Colwyn Bay	42	14	13	15	54	62	55
Stocksbridge PS	42	15	9	18	58	58	51
Shepshed Dynamo	42	13	11	18	53	75	50
Chorley	42	13	9	20	62	69	48
Belper Town	42	13	8	21	57	66	47
Spalding United	42	13	8	21	57	69	47
Clitheroe	42	12	10	20	47	57	46
Warrington Town	42	11	13	18	45	59	46
Rossendale United	42	10	10	22	64	87	40
Rocester	42	0	6	36	31	132	6

Stocksbridge Park Steels had 3 points deducted.

FORMATION AND SUMMARY

Even after the formation of the Birmingham League in 1889 there were still a large number of clubs in the Birmingham area who were not attached to any league. The Birmingham F.A. already had two cup competitions – the Senior Cup and the Junior Cup – and so it was logical to have a league for both classes of clubs. Thus in 1892 the Birmingham & District Junior League was formed with eight of the area's leading junior clubs who were Aston St. James, Bournbrook, Bournville, Ellen Street Victoria, Hamstead, Kings Heath Albion, Park Mills and Soho Villa. These eight were all from Birmingham itself but the league soon expanded its area of coverage and by 1908 its status had grown to the extent that it changed its name to the Birmingham Combination. For many years the Combination acted as an unofficial second division to the Birmingham League and many of the area's leading clubs played in the Birmingham Combination, including future Football League clubs Hereford United and Cheltenham Town. In the 1930s the strength of the Combination had increased to the level where it equalled that of the Birmingham League and when that league suffered a crisis, the Combination briefly became the stronger of the two. The Birmingham League recovered after the war and during the 1952-53 season it suggested a merger between the two but the Combination refused. Six of the Combination's best clubs then moved across to the League and it was the Combination's turn to suggest a merger but with six new members, there was now no advantage in that for the League. A year later all but one of the remaining Combination clubs also resigned to join the League leaving the Combination with no alternative but to close down.

CHANGES TO THE LEAGUE

1893   Aston St. James, Bournbrook, Ellen Street Victoria, Hamstead and Kings Heath Albion left. Calthorpe Rovers, Causeway Green Villa, Coles Farm Unity, Coombs Wood, Lozells and Oldbury Town joined. Redditch Excelsior also joined, this being their first league. League increased to 10 clubs.

1894   Oldbury Town left and joined the Birmingham League and Bournville, Calthorpe Rovers and Coles Farm Unity also left. Bournbrook, Ellen Street Victoria, Kings Heath Albion, Smethwick Wesleyan Rovers and Windsor Street Gas joined. League increased to 11 clubs.

1895   Coombs Wood and Ellen Street Victoria left. Bournville, Calthorpe Rovers and Harborne joined. League increased to 12 clubs.

1896   Kings Heath Albion left. League reduced to 11 clubs.

1897   Bournville changed their name to Bournville Athletic. Causeway Green Villa left and joined the West Midland League and Windsor Street Gas also left. Bromsgrove Rovers and Evesham Wanderers joined from the Studley & District League and Kings Norton Metal Workers joined from the Redditch Junior League. League increased to 12 clubs.

1898   Evesham Wanderers and Lozells left. Coombs Wood joined from West Midland League, Redditch Town joined from the Studley & District League. Leamington Town and Warwick United also joined. League increased to 14 clubs.

1899   Redditch Town disbanded and Calthorpe Rovers and Park Mills also left. Oldbury Town joined from the Walsall & District League, Eadie's (Redditch) joined from the Redditch League and Windsor Street Gas also joined.

1899-1900   Coombs Wood withdrew during the season and their record was deleted.

1900   Eadie's (Redditch) left and joined the Redditch League and Harborne, Smethwick Wesleyan Rovers, Warwick United and Windsor Street Gas also left. Foleshill Great Heath and Smethwick Town joined. League reduced to 10 clubs.

1901   Langley St. Michaels, Selly Oak St. Marys and Witton Shell Department joined. Smethwick Town left. League increased to 12 clubs.

1902   Coombs Wood Tube Works joined. League increased to 13 clubs.

1902-03   Witton Shell Department withdrew during the season and their record was expunged.

1903   Brades Park and Saltley Gas joined. League increased to 14 clubs.

1904   Saltley Gas changed their name to Birmingham Gas. Selly Oak St. Marys left. Erdington joined.

1905   Redditch Excelsior disbanded and a new club called Redditch was formed and took their place. Leamington Town left to join the Coventry & North Warwickshire League, Oldbury Town left and joined the Walsall & District League and Brades Park also left. Cradley Heath St. Lukes joined from the West Midland League and Churchfield and Rowley United also joined.

1906   Nuneaton Town joined from the Coventry & North Warwickshire League, Oldbury Town joined from the Walsall & District League and Brades Park also joined. Foleshill Great Heath left and joined the Coventry & North Warwickshire League and Birmingham Gas, Churchfield and Soho Villa also left. League reduced to 13 clubs.

1907   Kings Norton Metal Workers and Oldbury Town left. Bilston United, Darlaston, Wednesbury Old Athletic and Willenhall Pickwick joined from Walsall & District League and Stirchley United also joined. League increased to 16 clubs.

1908   The League changed it's name to the Birmingham Combination. Brades Park and Erdington left. Hednesford Town and Willenhall Swifts joined from the Walsall & District League.

1909   Rowley United left. Cannock Town and Wellington St. Georges joined. League increased to 17 clubs.

1909-10   Langley St. Michaels withdrew during the season and their record was expunged.

1910   Wednesbury Old Athletic left and joined the Birmingham League. Birmingham Trams joined.

1911   Darlaston and Willenhall Swifts left and joined the Birmingham League and Stirchley United also left. Halesowen joined from the Birmingham League and Atherstone Town and Dudley Phoenix also joined.

1912   Wellington St. George's disbanded. Stafford Rangers joined from the Birmingham League.

1913   Coombs Wood Tube Works and Dudley Phoenix left. Bloxwich Strollers and Tamworth Castle joined.

1914   Halesowen left. Hinckley United joined from the Leicestershire Senior League.

1919   When the league re-formed after the war Hednesford Town and Nuneaton Town joined the Birmingham League instead and Willenhall Pickwick merged with Willenhall Swifts of the Birmingham League to form Willenhall who continued in the Birmingham League. Bournbrook did not rejoin. Rugby Town joined from the Coventry & North Warwickshire League and Burton All Saints, Halesowen and Talbot Stead also joined. Redditch changed name to Redditch Town.

1920   Dudley Bean and Oakengates Town joined. League increased to 18 clubs.

1921   Bilston United, Burton All Saints, Cannock Town, Redditch Town, Stafford Rangers and Tamworth Castle all left and joined the Birmingham League. Dudley Bean also left. Leamington Town, Newhall Swifts, Round Oak, West Birmingham and Wolseley Athletic joined. League reduced to 16 clubs.

1922   Cradley Heath St. Lukes left and joined the Birmingham League, Talbot Stead left and joined the Walsall Senior League and West Birmingham also left. Wellington St. George's joined from the Walsall Senior League and Foleshill Great Heath also joined. League reduced to 15 clubs.

1923   Oakengates Town left and joined the Birmingham League and Newhall Swifts also left. Lichfield City, Sunbeam Motors and Walsall Wood joined from the Walsall Senior League, Tamworth Castle joined from the Birmingham League and Walsall Reserves also joined. League increased to 18 clubs.

1924   Wellington St. George's left and joined the Birmingham League and Round Oak also left. Hereford United joined as a new club and Wednesbury Old Athletic joined from the Birmingham League.

1924-25   In December 1924, Nuneaton Town Reserves took over the fixtures of Wednesbury Old Athletic who disbanded and had drawn 1 and lost 11 of the 12 games they had played.

1925   Lichfield City and Wolseley Athletic left. Gresley Rovers joined from Central Alliance. Dudley Bean also joined.

1926   Nuneaton Town joined from Southern League, replacing their reserves. Walsall Wood left. Evesham Town joined.

1927   Dudley Bean and Foleshill Great Heath left. Market Harborough Town joined from the Northamptonshire League and Walsall LMS also joined.

1928   Hereford United left and joined the Birmingham League, Tamworth Castle disbanded and Walsall Reserves also left. Birmingham "A", Cannock Town and Darlaston joined from the Birmingham League.

1929   Sunbeam Motors left. Redditch joined from the Birmingham League.

1932   Bloxwich Strollers left and joined the Walsall & District League and Walsall LMS also left. Cheltenham Town joined from the Gloucestershire Northern Senior League, Dudley Town joined from the Worcestershire Combination and Wolverhampton Wanderers "A" also joined. League increased to 19 clubs.

1933   Cannock Town and Nuneaton Town left and joined the Birmingham League, Gresley Rovers left and joined the Central Combination and Market Harborough Town left and joined the United Counties League. Tamworth joined as a new club, Walsall Reserves joined from the Birmingham League and West Bromwich Albion "A" also joined. League reduced to 18 clubs.

1934   Birmingham "A" left and Rugby Town disbanded. Market Harborough Town joined from the Northamptonshire League. League reduced to 17 clubs.

1935   Cheltenham Town joined the Southern League while continuing in the Birmingham Combination. Dudley Town left and joined the Birmingham League and Market Harborough Town disbanded. Gloucester City joined from the Gloucestershire Northern Senior League, Banbury Spencer joined from the Oxfordshire Senior League, Shirley Town joined from the Birmingham Suburban League and Aston Villa "A" also joined. League increased to 19 clubs.

1936   Birmingham "A" joined. League increased to 20 clubs.

1937   Leamington Town replaced by Coventry City "A". It is believed that Coventry took over the Leamington club wholesale and ran it as their nursery side.

1938   Birmingham Trams changed their name to Birmingham City Transport. Shirley Town changed their name to Solihull Town. Evesham Town left. Nuneaton Borough joined from the Central Amateur League.

1939   Bournville Athletic left and joined the Central Amateur League and Stourbridge joined from the Birmingham League but the Combination closed down upon the declaration of war. An emergency version operated later in the season but then closed down from 1940-45.

1945   When the league resumed after the war, Gloucester City joined the Southern League instead and Halesowen Town joined the Birmingham League instead. Solihull Town did not re-form. Aston Villa "A", Cheltenham Town Reserves, Hinckley United, Redditch and West Bromwich Albion "A" did not rejoin. Birmingham changed their name to Birmingham City. Dudley Town, Hednesford, Kidderminster Harriers and Worcester City Reserves joined from the Birmingham League and Moor Green joined from the Central Amateur League. League resumed with 17 clubs.

1946   Birmingham City "A" left. Redditch and West Bromwich Albion "A" rejoined after a season of inactivity and Stafford Rangers joined after a season of inactivity having been pre-war members of the Birmingham League. League increased to 19 clubs.

1947   Kidderminster Harriers and Worcester City Reserves left and joined the Birmingham League. Bedworth Town joined as a new club and Hinckley United rejoined having re-formed as Hinckley Athletic. Birmingham City "A" also joined. League increased to 20 clubs.

1948   Coventry City "A" left. Bilston joined from the Walsall Senior League.

1949   Birmingham City "A" left. Lockheed (Leamington) joined from the Central Amateur League.

1950   Birmingham City Transport left to join the Birmingham Works League and Wolverhampton Wanderers "A" also left. Rugby Town joined from the United Counties League and Sutton Town joined from the Walsall Senior League.

1952   Nuneaton Borough left and joined the Birmingham League and Stafford Rangers left and joined the Cheshire League.

1953   Bromsgrove Rovers, Dudley Town, Hednesford, Redditch, Stourbridge and Walsall Reserves all left and joined the Birmingham League. Birch Coppice joined from the Tamworth & Trent Valley League and Gresley Rovers joined from the Central Alliance.

1954   All remaining clubs left and joined the Birmingham League with the exception of West Bromwich Albion "A" who joined the Warwickshire Combination.

TABLE NOTES

The Birmingham Combination tables as published contained a number of errors and inconsistencies, particularly in the early years when end of season tables were rarely published. Considerable research has been done to produce the tables shown which are subject to the comments below.

1892-93   No published tables have been found at any point during this season; the table given has been compiled using all results found. The missing games may not have been played as they would not have affected the destiny of the championship.

1893-94   Several tables were published during the season but often contained obvious errors and no end of season table has been found. The table has been compiled after correcting errors and adding in missing and late season results as found. The missing games were probably not played.

1895-96   No end of season table was found and tables published during the season often showed inconsistencies. The table given has been compiled using results found and has been calculated using the best available information. Only 21 of Bournbrook's 22 results were found, the missing game being away to Lozells. As all of Smethwick Wesleyan Rovers' results have been found and it is known that Bournbrook were declared champions, Bournbrook must have won their missing game to finish above Smethwick. The missing game has therefore been included in the table as a win for Bournbrook and a defeat for Lozells but without any additions to the clubs' goals for and goals against records. The missing games are believed to have been played but the results have remained elusive.

1905-06   Total goals for 14 more than total goals against.

1908-09   Total goals for 5 less than total goals against.

1909-10   Total goals for 1 less than total goals against.

1910-11   Total goals for 1 more than total goals against.

1911-12   Total goals for 2 less than total goals against.

1913-14   Total goals for 1 less than total goals against.

1925-26   Total goals for 1 less than total goals against.

1926-27   Total goals for 10 more than total goals against.

1927-28   Total goals for 5 less than total goals against.

1928-29   Total goals for 7 more than total goals against.

1930-31   Total goals for 2 less than total goals against.

1931-32   Total goals for 6 less than total goals against.

1948-49   Total goals for 1 more than total goals against.

1952-53   Total goals for 1 more than total goals against.

BIRMINGHAM & DISTRICT JUNIOR LEAGUE

1892-93

Soho Villa	13	10	1	2	47	19	21
Bournville	14	8	3	3	29	20	19
Park Mills	13	7	2	4	48	20	16
Hamstead	11	7	0	4	41	25	14
Bournbrook	14	5	0	9	31	58	10
Aston St. James	11	4	1	6	18	30	9
Kings Heath Albion	12	2	1	9	12	29	5
Ellen Street Victoria	10	2	0	8	12	37	4

1893-94

Coombs Wood	18	12	4	2	50	21	28
Oldbury Town	18	11	3	4	45	30	25
Lozells	18	9	3	6	48	40	21
Coles Farm Unity	17	8	3	6	42	35	19
Bournville	16	7	4	5	40	30	18
Redditch Excelsior	18	7	3	8	48	50	17
Causeway Green Villa	18	7	2	9	36	45	16
Park Mills	16	7	0	9	33	37	14
Soho Villa	18	3	4	11	33	44	10
Calthorpe Rovers	17	2	2	13	25	68	6

1894-95

Lozells	20	17	1	2	63	28	35
Coombs Wood #	20	15	3	2	83	25	31
Smethwick Wesleyan Rovers	20	10	3	7	47	38	23
Soho Villa	20	10	3	7	47	57	23
Bournbrook #	20	11	0	9	61	49	20
Windsor Street Gas	20	7	5	8	31	41	19
Park Mills	20	8	1	11	51	52	17
Redditch Excelsior	20	7	1	12	40	46	15
Causeway Green Villa	20	6	2	12	46	60	14
Kings Heath Albion	20	7	0	13	39	53	14
Ellen Street Victoria	20	2	1	17	24	83	5

Coombs Wood and Bournbrook each had two points deducted for fielding ineligible players.

1895-96

Bournbrook	22	15	4	3	69	24	34
Smethwick Wesleyan Rovers	22	16	2	4	63	34	34
Windsor Street Gas	22	13	3	6	48	41	29
Redditch Excelsior	22	9	5	8	46	39	23
Soho Villa	21	11	1	9	58	47	23
Causeway Green Villa	22	9	4	9	56	40	22
Lozells	21	10	2	9	47	45	22
Park Mills	19	8	4	7	42	41	20
Bournville	21	7	2	12	43	63	16
Calthorpe Rovers	22	6	2	14	51	61	14
Kings Heath Albion	21	5	2	14	27	69	12
Harborne	19	1	3	15	20	66	5

1896-97

Bournbrook	20	14	3	3	54	22	31
Soho Villa	20	14	2	4	59	27	30
Bournville	20	11	5	4	63	30	27
Smethwick Wesleyan Rovers	20	10	7	3	51	27	27
Lozells	20	12	3	5	48	34	27
Calthorpe Rovers	20	8	2	10	41	65	18
Windsor Street Gas	20	7	3	10	25	41	17
Redditch Excelsior	20	7	2	11	40	44	16
Harborne	20	4	7	9	33	42	15
Causeway Green Villa	20	4	2	14	25	55	10
Park Mills	20	0	2	18	21	73	2

1897-98

Bournville Athletic	22	20	1	1	93	23	41
Bournbrook	22	15	2	5	52	23	32
Redditch Excelsior	22	13	3	6	52	33	29
Soho Villa	22	12	3	7	46	37	27
Evesham Wanderers	22	11	2	9	61	49	24
Kings Norton Metal Workers	22	11	0	11	36	45	22
Harborne	22	8	5	9	46	45	21
Smethwick Wesleyan Rovers	22	6	5	11	35	42	17
Park Mills	22	7	3	12	51	62	17
Bromsgrove Rovers	22	7	3	12	27	43	17
Calthorpe Rovers	22	4	2	16	32	80	10
Lozells	22	2	3	17	24	73	7

1898-99

Bournville Athletic	26	24	1	1	115	26	49
Coombs Wood	26	16	2	8	53	33	34
Warwick United	26	14	4	8	58	41	32
Park Mills	26	13	3	10	76	60	29
Kings Norton Metal Workers	26	11	7	8	51	42	29
Soho Villa	26	14	1	11	52	49	29
Bournbrook	26	13	1	12	60	52	27
Bromsgrove Rovers	26	11	4	11	34	44	26
Redditch Excelsior	26	10	4	12	51	70	24
Leamington Town	26	8	6	12	60	64	22
Harborne	26	7	6	13	43	55	20
Calthorpe Rovers	26	8	2	16	35	60	18
Redditch Town	26	4	6	16	45	73	14
Smethwick Wesleyan Rovers	26	4	3	19	37	101	11

1899-1900

Bournville Athletic	24	16	4	4	103	38	36
Leamington Town	24	17	2	5	71	35	36
Oldbury Town	24	15	2	7	79	37	32
Warwick United	24	14	3	7	68	39	31
Bromsgrove Rovers	24	12	4	8	48	43	28
Redditch Excelsior	24	11	4	9	66	53	26
Soho Villa	24	11	2	11	56	63	24
Smethwick Wesleyan Rovers	24	10	2	12	50	63	22
Kings Norton Metal Workers	24	10	1	13	57	64	21
Windsor Street Gas	24	7	3	14	47	64	17
Bournbrook	24	6	4	14	50	74	16
Eadie's (Redditch)	24	5	2	17	39	99	12
Harborne	24	4	3	17	26	88	11

Coombs Wood withdrew during the season. Their record was deleted.

1900-1901

Bournville Athletic	18	14	1	3	71	20	29
Oldbury Town	18	11	3	4	59	30	25
Leamington Town	18	8	5	5	27	23	21
Redditch Excelsior	18	9	2	7	39	42	20
Foleshill Great Heath	18	8	3	7	36	30	19
Bournbrook	18	7	2	9	31	41	16
Kings Norton Metal Workers	17	3	7	7	32	31	13
Soho Villa	17	6	1	10	34	52	13
Bromsgrove Rovers	18	5	3	10	24	54	13
Smethwick Town	18	3	3	12	17	44	9

Soho Villa failed to send a team to Kings Norton on 30th April 1901.

1901-1902

Bournville Athletic	22	15	3	4	63	41	33
Langley St. Michaels	22	13	4	5	55	33	30
Soho Villa	22	14	2	6	65	41	30
Foleshill Great Heath	22	13	2	7	56	33	28
Kings Norton Metal Workers	22	11	5	6	49	35	27
Bournbrook	22	6	6	10	47	42	18
Leamington Town	22	7	4	11	43	49	18
Oldbury Town	22	6	6	10	39	45	18
Witton Shell Department	22	7	4	11	28	35	18
Bromsgrove Rovers	22	7	3	12	28	58	17
Redditch Excelsior	22	7	2	13	40	60	16
Selly Oak St. Marys	22	3	5	14	30	67	11

1902-1903

Bournville Athletic	22	16	3	3	64	25	35
Soho Villa	22	11	6	5	72	31	28
Langley St. Michaels	22	11	4	7	39	28	26
Leamington Town	22	11	4	7	45	36	26
Coombs Wood Tube Works	22	8	9	5	33	28	25
Foleshill Great Heath	22	8	7	7	45	41	23
Redditch Excelsior	22	8	5	9	46	53	21
Selly Oak St. Marys	22	7	6	9	53	73	20
Oldbury Town	22	6	7	9	28	36	19
Bromsgrove Rovers	22	8	2	12	44	48	18
Bournbrook	22	7	2	13	27	49	16
Kings Norton Metal Workers	22	2	3	17	26	77	7

Witton Shell Department withdrew during the season and their record was expunged.

1903-1904

Foleshill Great Heath	26	17	4	5	76	47	38
Soho Villa	26	16	5	5	60	42	37
Bournville Athletic	26	16	3	7	68	33	35
Langley St. Michaels	26	13	6	7	61	34	32
Coombs Wood Tube Works	26	14	4	8	67	54	32
Leamington Town	26	12	7	7	52	46	31
Brades Park	26	14	2	10	68	49	30
Saltley Gas	26	11	5	10	61	52	27
Bournbrook	26	10	4	12	52	51	24
Oldbury Town	26	9	5	12	42	51	23
Redditch Excelsior	26	10	2	14	50	64	22
Bromsgrove Rovers	26	4	6	16	34	58	14
Selly Oak St. Marys	26	2	6	18	31	98	10
Kings Norton Metal Workers	26	3	3	20	33	76	9

1904-1905

Coombs Wood Tube Works	26	18	3	5	69	36	39
Bromsgrove Rovers	26	15	3	8	62	42	33
Oldbury Town	26	14	5	7	53	45	33
Soho Villa	26	13	4	9	54	43	30
Foleshill Great Heath	26	12	6	8	56	45	30
Langley St. Michaels	26	11	5	10	67	56	27
Erdington	26	12	2	12	62	56	26
Kings Norton Metal Workers	26	9	7	10	42	47	25
Bournbrook	26	9	7	10	51	60	25
Bournville Athletic	26	9	6	11	54	61	24
Birmingham Gas	26	7	9	10	35	43	23
Leamington Town	26	8	6	12	34	45	22
Brades Park	26	8	5	13	49	59	21
Redditch Excelsior	26	1	4	21	36	86	6

1905-1906

Coombs Wood Tube Works	26	16	4	6	73	33	36
Bournbrook	26	15	6	5	63	42	36
Cradley Heath St. Lukes	26	16	4	6	76	53	36
Erdington	26	16	2	8	79	58	34
Redditch	26	15	3	8	86	58	33
Rowley United	26	12	6	8	77	61	30
Bournville Athletic	26	10	6	10	59	72	26
Kings Norton Metal Workers	26	10	4	12	61	57	24
Langley St. Michaels	26	7	10	9	62	65	24
Bromsgrove Rovers	26	9	4	13	75	83	22
Soho Villa	26	7	5	14	35	62	19
Churchfield	26	5	8	13	39	65	18
Foleshill Great Heath	26	5	3	18	42	64	13
Birmingham Gas	26	4	5	17	41	81	13

1906-1907

Nuneaton Town	24	17	4	3	86	39	38
Redditch	24	17	1	6	76	37	35
Cradley Heath St. Lukes	24	13	6	5	67	32	32
Kings Norton Metal Workers	24	13	5	6	62	46	31
Coombs Wood Tube Works	24	10	8	6	50	42	28
Bromsgrove Rovers	24	12	2	10	68	60	26
Rowley United	24	9	4	11	56	70	22
Erdington	24	8	4	12	70	70	20
Langley St. Michaels	24	8	4	12	57	64	20
Brades Park	24	7	5	12	45	89	19
Bournbrook	24	6	5	13	53	61	17
Bournville Athletic	24	7	3	14	45	67	17
Oldbury Town	24	1	5	18	29	87	7

1907-1908

Darlaston	30	21	6	3	83	32	48
Bilston United	30	22	3	5	89	35	47
Cradley Heath St. Lukes	30	19	5	6	102	47	43
Nuneaton Town	30	16	4	10	93	65	36
Willenhall Pickwick	30	16	3	11	71	51	35
Wednesbury Old Athletic	30	15	4	11	67	60	34
Coombs Wood Tube Works	30	12	5	13	70	64	29
Stirchley United	30	12	4	14	62	70	28
Redditch	30	11	6	13	63	73	28
Bournbrook	30	8	10	12	61	84	26
Langley St. Michaels	30	9	6	15	54	76	24
Bromsgrove Rovers	30	10	4	16	46	71	24
Erdington	30	8	6	16	58	77	22
Rowley United	30	7	7	16	69	89	21
Brades Park	30	6	8	16	45	84	20
Bournville Athletic	30	4	7	19	44	99	15

THE BIRMINGHAM COMBINATION

1908-1909

Willenhall Pickwick	30	20	6	4	129	54	46
Cradley Heath St. Lukes	30	20	3	7	91	52	43
Darlaston	30	20	1	9	104	46	41
Wednesbury Old Athletic	30	16	6	8	80	54	38
Bilston United	30	15	6	9	78	63	36
Redditch	30	15	5	10	68	52	35
Bournbrook	30	14	3	13	59	83	31
Willenhall Swifts	30	13	4	13	56	49	30
Hednesford Town	30	14	1	15	63	74	29
Nuneaton Town	30	12	3	15	81	62	27
Stirchley United	30	12	3	15	75	95	27
Bromsgrove Rovers	30	11	2	17	50	94	24
Coombs Wood Tube Works	30	9	4	17	87	99	22
Rowley United	30	8	4	18	53	87	20
Langley St. Michaels	30	5	6	19	33	94	16
Bournville Athletic	30	6	3	21	50	104	15

1909-1910

Hednesford Town	30	24	3	3	93	39	51
Cradley Heath St. Lukes	30	21	6	3	80	41	48
Wednesbury Old Athletic	30	18	4	8	76	44	40
Darlaston	30	16	7	7	78	60	39
Coombs Wood Tube Works	30	16	6	8	85	48	38
Willenhall Pickwick	30	15	5	10	82	51	35
Nuneaton Town	30	14	7	9	79	53	35
Bilston United	30	11	8	11	66	62	30
Cannock Town	30	12	4	14	68	69	28
Willenhall Swifts	30	12	2	16	71	69	26
Bromsgrove Rovers	30	9	5	16	65	70	23
Wellington St. Georges	30	8	7	15	62	78	23
Redditch	30	9	4	17	63	71	22
Bournbrook	30	7	3	20	64	128	17
Stirchley United	30	5	3	22	48	129	13
Bournville Athletic	30	4	4	22	43	112	12

Langley St. Michaels withdrew during the season and their record was expunged.

1910-1911

Darlaston	30	25	0	5	115	52	50
Nuneaton Town	30	22	0	8	93	44	44
Willenhall Swifts	30	19	4	7	86	42	42
Hednesford Town	30	16	6	8	85	42	38
Willenhall Pickwick	30	18	2	10	86	49	38
Redditch	30	16	4	10	95	64	36
Birmingham Trams	30	16	4	10	71	50	36
Cannock Town	30	16	3	11	61	54	35
Cradley Heath St. Lukes	29	13	2	14	74	72	28
Coombs Wood Tube Works	30	13	2	15	62	81	28
Stirchley United	29	9	7	13	58	84	25
Bilston United	30	8	7	15	70	77	23
Bromsgrove Rovers	30	7	4	19	59	96	18
Wellington St. Georges	30	7	4	19	52	91	18
Bournbrook	30	6	1	23	41	116	13
Bournville Athletic	30	1	4	25	30	123	6

Stirchley United failed to appear for their game at Cradley Heath and the match was not played.

1911-1912

Cradley Heath St. Lukes	30	21	2	7	99	50	44
Atherstone Town	30	16	8	6	72	41	40
Birmingham Trams	30	18	4	8	58	37	40
Willenhall Pickwick	30	18	3	9	66	43	39
Bournbrook	30	19	0	11	85	61	38
Hednesford Town	30	14	7	9	73	42	35
Nuneaton Town	30	15	5	10	77	57	35
Bilston United	30	15	3	12	64	55	33
Redditch	30	14	3	13	63	56	31
Bromsgrove Rovers	30	11	5	14	51	53	27
Coombs Wood Tube Works	30	11	4	15	48	52	26
Bournville Athletic	30	10	4	16	40	62	24
Cannock Town	30	9	5	16	51	81	23
Wellington St. Georges	30	9	1	20	56	105	19
Dudley Phoenix	30	7	4	19	41	89	18
Halesowen	30	2	4	24	37	99	8

1912-1913

Stafford Rangers	30	23	4	3	91	27	50
Hednesford Town	30	23	2	5	81	28	48
Nuneaton Town	30	16	6	8	71	44	38
Redditch	30	15	5	10	77	59	35
Bilston United	30	14	6	10	62	58	34
Cradley Heath St. Lukes	30	13	5	12	64	57	31
Atherstone Town	30	13	5	12	73	69	31
Cannock Town	30	13	5	12	62	70	31
Willenhall Pickwick	30	9	11	10	71	60	29
Bournville Athletic	30	11	4	15	52	65	26
Birmingham Trams	30	10	5	15	58	63	25
Dudley Phoenix	30	9	6	15	66	75	24
Bournbrook	30	10	4	16	53	76	24
Coombs Wood Tube Works	30	8	5	17	41	73	21
Bromsgrove Rovers	30	7	6	17	41	66	20
Halesowen	30	6	1	23	32	105	13

1913-1914

Redditch	30	22	2	6	105	46	46
Stafford Rangers	30	19	6	5	85	48	44
Hednesford Town	30	17	8	5	64	30	42
Bournbrook	30	15	6	9	57	39	36
Nuneaton Town	30	15	6	9	61	43	36
Willenhall Pickwick	30	15	6	9	61	52	36
Bilston United	30	15	5	10	63	43	35
Bloxwich Strollers	30	15	1	14	65	73	31
Tamworth Castle	30	11	8	11	60	61	30
Birmingham Trams	30	10	7	13	51	49	27
Cradley Heath St. Lukes	30	12	3	15	62	65	27
Bournville Athletic	30	9	8	13	46	56	26
Atherstone Town	30	11	4	15	56	70	26
Bromsgrove Rovers	30	11	3	16	43	61	25
Halesowen	30	2	4	24	29	107	8
Cannock Town	30	1	3	26	44	110	5

1914-1915

Nuneaton Town	30	20	5	5	79	41	45
Redditch	30	18	6	6	80	39	42
Cradley Heath St. Lukes	30	16	5	9	73	45	37
Hinckley United	30	14	8	8	74	57	36
Stafford Rangers	30	14	7	9	75	53	35
Bloxwich Strollers	30	14	7	9	69	49	35
Hednesford Town	30	14	6	10	65	42	34
Birmingham Trams	30	13	8	9	63	44	34
Willenhall Pickwick	30	13	5	12	57	55	31
Bilston United	30	14	2	14	55	51	30
Atherstone Town	30	11	5	14	51	69	27
Bournville Athletic	30	8	9	13	57	69	25
Tamworth Castle	30	9	3	18	50	81	21
Cannock Town	30	10	1	19	34	80	21
Bournbrook	30	7	5	18	36	72	19
Bromsgrove Rovers	30	3	2	25	45	116	8

1919-1920

Cradley Heath St. Lukes	30	21	5	4	105	34	47
Stafford Rangers	30	18	4	8	72	44	40
Tamworth Castle	30	16	5	9	60	44	37
Rugby Town	30	14	8	8	73	45	36
Redditch Town	30	16	4	10	65	57	36
Burton All Saints	30	15	4	11	77	66	34
Bloxwich Strollers	30	13	7	10	63	52	33
Halesowen	30	11	7	12	60	51	29
Bilston United	30	12	4	14	55	60	28
Cannock Town	30	12	4	14	54	61	28
Hinckley United	30	11	5	14	67	84	27
Talbot Stead	30	10	7	13	57	74	27
Bournville Athletic	30	7	9	14	53	67	23
Atherstone Town	30	9	1	20	54	87	19
Birmingham Trams	30	5	8	17	37	79	18
Bromsgrove Rovers	30	6	6	18	36	83	18

1920-1921

Cannock Town	34	21	4	9	72	48	46
Talbot Stead	34	21	3	10	65	46	45
Rugby Town	34	18	7	9	77	41	43
Bilston United	34	19	5	10	87	55	43
Redditch Town	34	18	6	10	75	44	42
Cradley Heath St. Lukes	34	16	7	11	85	44	39
Oakengates Town	34	15	8	11	76	74	38
Burton All Saints	34	14	10	10	62	62	38
Stafford Rangers	34	13	10	11	69	56	36
Atherstone Town	34	15	6	13	70	58	36
Bloxwich Strollers	34	11	11	12	56	63	33
Tamworth Castle	34	10	12	12	56	70	32
Bromsgrove Rovers	34	12	7	15	63	84	31
Halesowen	34	12	5	17	71	76	29
Hinckley United	34	10	5	19	67	86	25
Dudley Bean	34	9	6	19	64	99	24
Birmingham Trams	34	7	7	20	53	82	21
Bournville Athletic	34	4	3	27	31	111	11

1921-1922

Cradley Heath St. Lukes	30	20	7	3	90	36	47
Rugby Town	30	18	7	5	76	36	43
Oakengates Town	30	16	4	10	69	49	36
Leamington Town	30	14	8	8	58	42	36
Hinckley United	30	15	6	9	83	63	36
Bromsgrove Rovers	30	13	8	9	56	36	34
Halesowen	30	15	4	11	82	59	34
Newhall Swifts	30	15	4	11	76	61	34
Birmingham Trams	30	12	3	15	67	71	27
West Birmingham	30	9	6	15	59	74	24
Atherstone Town	30	8	8	14	50	77	24
Bournville Athletic	30	7	9	14	49	68	23
Bloxwich Strollers	30	8	6	16	42	67	22
Talbot Stead	30	9	4	17	40	89	22
Wolseley Athletic	30	7	5	18	53	90	19
Round Oak	30	7	5	18	42	74	19

1922-1923

	P	W	D	L	F	A	Pts
Oakengates Town	28	15	7	6	85	42	37
Bloxwich Strollers	28	16	5	7	61	48	37
Hinckley United	28	16	4	8	76	56	36
Halesowen	28	15	6	7	73	54	36
Birmingham Trams	28	15	4	9	66	55	34
Wellington St. Georg'es	28	14	3	11	66	45	31
Bromsgrove Rovers	28	11	7	10	55	52	29
Round Oak	28	10	8	10	63	58	28
Foleshill Great Heath	28	11	5	12	55	49	27
Rugby Town	28	11	5	12	56	53	27
Wolseley Athletic	28	10	4	14	35	68	24
Leamington Town	28	7	7	14	52	67	21
Bournville Athletic	28	5	10	13	41	68	20
Atherstone Town	28	6	5	17	55	68	17
Newhall Swifts	28	7	2	19	34	90	16

1923-1924

	P	W	D	L	F	A	Pts
Hinckley United	34	27	1	6	130	62	55
Walsall Reserves	34	21	8	5	94	32	50
Wellington St. Georg'es	34	19	5	10	91	44	43
Sunbeam Motors	34	17	7	10	82	61	41
Halesowen	34	16	7	11	75	49	39
Wolseley Athletic	34	14	11	9	78	54	39
Bloxwich Strollers	34	17	2	15	74	66	36
Foleshill Great Heath	34	14	7	13	58	72	35
Round Oak	34	15	4	15	65	66	34
Bromsgrove Rovers	34	13	7	14	50	62	33
Birmingham Trams	34	14	5	15	66	76	33
Walsall Wood	34	15	2	17	68	74	32
Lichfield City	34	13	5	16	41	58	31
Rugby Town	34	11	6	17	54	73	28
Tamworth Castle	34	10	8	16	62	91	28
Leamington Town	34	10	3	21	51	85	23
Bournville Athletic	34	9	2	23	47	91	20
Atherstone Town	34	4	4	26	48	118	12

1924-1925

	P	W	D	L	F	A	Pts
Bloxwich Strollers	34	26	4	4	96	40	56
Walsall Reserves	34	20	8	6	93	27	48
Hinckley United	34	21	4	9	101	56	46
Halesowen	34	20	4	10	86	53	44
Leamington Town	34	17	10	7	71	44	44
Sunbeam Motors	34	16	8	10	83	68	40
Bromsgrove Rovers	34	17	5	12	74	58	39
Birmingham Trams	34	14	8	12	61	51	36
Rugby Town	34	16	3	15	88	73	35
Bournville Athletic	34	13	7	14	74	75	33
Hereford United	34	12	8	14	71	70	32
Walsall Wood	34	13	6	15	64	74	32
Atherstone Town	34	11	7	16	68	90	29
Lichfield City	34	13	1	20	45	86	27
Tamworth Castle	34	5	12	17	56	95	22
Foleshill Great Heath	34	7	6	21	53	95	20
Wolseley Athletic	34	7	1	26	50	105	15
Nuneaton Town Reserves #	34	4	6	24	40	114	14

\# In December 1924, Nuneaton Town Reserves took over the fixtures of Wednesbury Old Athletic whose record was: P 12, W 0, D 1, L 11.

1925-1926

	P	W	D	L	F	A	Pts
Leamington Town	34	24	4	6	114	48	52
Rugby Town	34	23	4	7	96	47	50
Hinckley United	34	22	6	6	122	62	50
Hereford United	34	20	4	10	96	65	44
Dudley Bean	34	17	8	9	87	61	42
Halesowen	34	18	4	12	82	70	40
Gresley Rovers	34	17	3	14	79	76	37
Bournville Athletic	34	16	4	14	91	82	36
Walsall Reserves	34	13	8	13	71	63	34
Tamworth Castle	34	12	9	13	85	102	33
Nuneaton Town Reserves	34	14	4	16	80	81	32
Bloxwich Strollers	34	13	4	17	83	106	30
Birmingham Trams	34	11	7	16	85	94	29
Atherstone Town	34	11	4	19	70	82	26
Walsall Wood	34	11	1	22	52	102	23
Bromsgrove Rovers	34	9	4	21	60	77	22
Sunbeam Motors	34	6	5	23	59	125	17
Foleshill Great Heath	34	3	9	22	66	136	15

1926-1927

	P	W	D	L	F	A	Pts
Hinckley United	34	25	3	6	136	49	53
Walsall Reserves	34	25	2	7	100	48	52
Leamington Town	34	22	4	8	99	53	48
Tamworth Castle	34	20	5	9	84	78	45
Bloxwich Strollers	34	21	2	11	108	77	44
Hereford United	34	20	2	12	113	64	42
Nuneaton Town	34	19	2	13	93	69	40
Sunbeam Motors	34	15	2	17	85	101	32
Evesham Town	34	13	4	17	84	89	30
Bournville Athletic	34	12	5	17	85	91	29
Rugby Town	34	12	5	17	70	85	29
Gresley Rovers	34	14	0	20	93	118	28
Atherstone Town	34	12	3	19	72	84	27
Bromsgrove Rovers	34	10	6	18	57	91	26
Birmingham Trams	34	8	7	19	71	104	23
Foleshill Great Heath	34	9	4	21	53	109	22
Dudley Bean	34	7	7	20	55	85	21
Halesowen	34	9	3	22	56	109	21

1927-1928

	P	W	D	L	F	A	Pts
Walsall Reserves	34	22	3	9	97	63	47
Bloxwich Strollers	34	20	3	11	81	64	43
Hereford United	34	19	4	11	104	62	42
Halesowen	34	20	2	12	89	76	42
Market Harborough Town	34	18	5	11	93	67	41
Leamington Town	34	19	3	12	83	69	41
Evesham Town	34	16	8	10	66	55	40
Gresley Rovers	34	16	4	14	79	71	36
Hinckley United	34	15	5	14	84	75	35
Sunbeam Motors	34	16	1	17	106	99	33
Birmingham Trams	34	14	5	15	79	81	33
Bromsgrove Rovers	34	13	6	15	83	80	32
Atherstone Town	34	13	4	17	72	76	30
Walsall LMS	34	13	4	17	80	94	30
Nuneaton Town	34	11	4	19	75	90	26
Rugby Town	34	11	0	23	73	131	22
Bournville Athletic	34	6	8	20	69	106	20
Tamworth Castle	34	6	7	21	81	135	19

1928-1929

	P	W	D	L	F	A	Pts
Nuneaton Town	34	24	4	6	100	46	52
Leamington Town	34	23	4	7	110	54	50
Market Harborough Town	34	20	3	11	97	65	43
Evesham Town	34	17	7	10	79	53	41
Darlaston	34	17	7	10	107	77	41
Gresley Rovers	34	16	8	10	83	62	40
Birmingham "A"	34	14	9	11	93	76	37
Rugby Town	34	15	7	12	78	72	37
Hinckley United	34	17	3	14	96	91	37
Bromsgrove Rovers	34	16	4	14	95	90	36
Bloxwich Strollers	34	14	6	14	82	75	34
Bournville Athletic	34	13	4	17	63	84	30
Halesowen	34	11	5	18	69	102	27
Birmingham Trams	34	7	11	16	64	88	25
Sunbeam Motors	34	9	6	19	50	97	24
Cannock Town	34	8	6	20	57	92	22
Walsall LMS	34	8	5	21	43	89	21
Atherstone Town	34	6	3	25	64	122	15

1929-1930

	P	W	D	L	F	A	Pts
Market Harborough Town	34	24	6	4	128	53	54
Birmingham "A"	34	24	5	5	112	45	53
Evesham Town	34	21	3	10	101	61	45
Darlaston	34	19	6	9	93	66	44
Redditch	34	18	7	9	99	69	43
Nuneaton Town	34	17	7	10	103	61	41
Rugby Town	34	17	4	13	92	82	38
Bloxwich Strollers	34	15	6	13	78	76	36
Leamington Town	34	15	5	14	83	69	35
Gresley Rovers	34	13	5	16	62	66	31
Atherstone Town	34	11	5	18	64	74	27
Walsall LMS	34	9	7	18	60	90	25
Bromsgrove Rovers	34	11	3	20	60	93	25
Hinckley United	34	11	3	20	78	128	25
Bournville Athletic	34	9	7	18	59	101	25
Birmingham Trams	34	9	6	19	62	87	24
Halesowen	34	10	4	20	67	95	24
Cannock Town	34	6	5	23	54	119	17

1930-1931

Nuneaton Town	34	24	4	6	124	61	52
Evesham Town	34	22	5	7	101	60	49
Hinckley United	34	20	5	9	124	68	45
Market Harborough Town	34	18	6	10	108	66	42
Redditch	34	18	5	11	100	58	41
Birmingham "A"	34	16	8	10	95	66	40
Darlaston	34	15	9	10	112	70	39
Gresley Rovers	34	17	4	13	86	81	38
Walsall LMS	34	15	8	11	89	86	38
Atherstone Town	34	16	4	14	127	105	36
Cannock Town	34	15	6	13	92	80	36
Leamington Town	34	14	5	15	90	97	33
Birmingham Trams	34	10	7	17	73	96	27
Bromsgrove Rovers	34	12	3	19	73	104	27
Bournville Athletic	34	10	5	19	71	109	25
Halesowen	34	10	5	19	80	134	25
Rugby Town	34	5	1	28	64	169	11
Bloxwich Strollers	34	2	4	28	59	160	8

1931-1932

Birmingham "A"	34	27	3	4	120	41	57
Nuneaton Town	34	26	3	5	137	56	55
Redditch	34	23	2	9	147	65	48
Darlaston	34	19	3	12	105	74	41
Market Harborough Town	34	18	2	14	96	90	38
Atherstone Town	34	15	6	13	120	79	36
Birmingham Trams	34	17	2	15	73	105	36
Hinckley United	34	15	3	16	81	82	33
Halesowen Town	34	14	5	15	79	102	33
Bromsgrove Rovers	34	14	2	18	87	106	30
Bloxwich Strollers	34	14	2	18	70	113	30
Cannock Town	34	11	6	17	80	94	28
Walsall LMS	34	13	2	19	72	92	28
Evesham Town	34	10	6	18	73	90	26
Leamington Town	34	10	4	20	81	112	24
Gresley Rovers	34	8	8	18	69	101	24
Bournville Athletic	34	9	5	20	59	101	23
Rugby Town	34	8	6	20	51	103	22

1932-1933

Redditch	36	28	1	7	124	61	57
Birmingham "A"	36	26	4	6	132	46	56
Cheltenham Town	36	20	7	9	93	61	47
Nuneaton Town	36	18	9	9	107	68	45
Wolverhampton Wanderers "A"	36	17	9	10	103	53	43
Atherstone Town	36	18	7	11	106	74	43
Cannock Town	36	19	4	13	99	79	42
Market Harborough Town	36	16	3	17	95	87	35
Dudley Town	36	16	3	17	86	91	35
Halesowen Town	36	15	5	16	96	103	35
Rugby Town	36	14	6	16	64	89	34
Evesham Town	36	16	1	19	76	92	33
Hinckley United	36	14	3	19	98	110	31
Gresley Rovers	36	13	3	20	71	91	29
Bournville Athletic	36	12	5	19	72	115	29
Leamington Town	36	12	3	21	72	122	27
Darlaston	36	6	11	19	80	122	23
Birmingham Trams	36	9	3	24	64	115	21
Bromsgrove Rovers	36	7	5	24	74	133	19

1933-1934

Dudley Town	34	23	6	5	93	35	52
Hinckley United	34	23	2	9	102	61	48
Wolverhampton Wanderers "A"	34	22	3	9	131	54	47
Bromsgrove Rovers	34	20	3	11	93	72	43
Cheltenham Town	34	17	8	9	81	53	42
Walsall Reserves	34	18	5	11	84	56	41
West Bromwich Albion "A"	34	19	2	13	109	73	40
Birmingham "A"	34	18	3	13	111	95	39
Darlaston	34	15	6	13	96	84	36
Redditch	34	15	4	15	82	91	34
Atherstone Town	34	15	4	15	73	87	34
Leamington Town	34	14	4	16	87	84	32
Bournville Athletic	34	10	5	19	74	113	25
Rugby Town	34	9	5	20	52	95	23
Halesowen Town	34	9	4	21	73	136	22
Tamworth	34	8	4	22	77	112	20
Birmingham Trams	34	8	2	24	72	130	18
Evesham Town	34	6	4	24	66	125	16

1934-1935

Wolverhampton Wanderers "A"	32	27	1	4	127	39	55
Dudley Town	32	20	4	8	69	41	44
West Bromwich Albion "A"	32	18	6	8	83	57	42
Walsall Reserves	32	17	5	10	94	58	39
Leamington Town	32	17	5	10	73	58	39
Tamworth	32	16	5	11	88	58	37
Bromsgrove Rovers	32	14	7	11	81	72	35
Birmingham Trams	32	13	8	11	57	49	34
Darlaston	32	13	6	13	78	67	32
Cheltenham Town	32	14	4	14	70	61	32
Atherstone Town	32	12	3	17	69	93	27
Hinckley United	32	10	4	18	66	83	24
Market Harborough Town	32	9	5	18	56	91	23
Bournville Athletic	32	8	6	18	58	95	22
Halesowen Town	32	9	2	21	53	98	20
Redditch	32	9	2	21	53	107	20
Evesham Town	32	8	3	21	58	106	19

1935-1936

Aston Villa "A"	36	25	3	8	126	54	53
West Bromwich Albion "A"	36	25	3	8	119	71	53
Wolverhampton Wanderers "A"	36	23	4	9	99	58	50
Gloucester City	36	21	6	9	99	62	48
Tamworth	36	22	2	12	118	65	46
Walsall Reserves	36	21	3	12	98	57	45
Cheltenham Town Reserves	36	19	6	11	79	61	44
Darlaston	36	16	8	12	86	70	40
Banbury Spencer	36	16	5	15	88	90	37
Birmingham Trams	36	13	9	14	66	64	35
Shirley Town	36	14	4	18	86	94	32
Halesowen Town	36	14	3	19	88	115	31
Evesham Town	36	13	5	18	73	107	31
Leamington Town	36	12	6	18	65	84	30
Atherstone Town	36	10	7	19	82	93	27
Bromsgrove Rovers	36	9	7	20	66	100	25
Redditch	36	8	8	20	66	108	24
Hinckley United	36	9	5	22	60	133	23
Bournville Athletic	36	2	6	28	50	127	10

1936-1937

Team	P	W	D	L	F	A	Pts
Walsall Reserves	38	29	2	7	144	50	60
West Bromwich Albion "A"	38	27	5	6	110	43	59
Banbury Spencer	38	22	5	11	96	88	49
Wolverhampton Wanderers "A"	38	20	7	11	105	58	47
Tamworth	38	21	5	12	124	85	47
Cheltenham Town Reserves	38	18	10	10	99	63	46
Aston Villa "A"	38	20	6	12	85	55	46
Birmingham Trams	38	19	6	13	100	83	44
Darlaston	38	19	5	14	102	59	43
Shirley Town	38	17	6	15	99	83	40
Redditch	38	15	6	17	87	96	36
Gloucester City	38	13	6	19	69	81	32
Halesowen Town	38	13	5	20	69	88	31
Evesham Town	38	12	7	19	76	113	31
Atherstone Town	38	12	5	21	85	127	29
Birmingham "A"	38	11	5	22	63	83	27
Bromsgrove Rovers	38	10	6	22	61	135	26
Hinckley United	38	10	4	24	73	146	24
Leamington Town	38	9	5	24	44	88	23
Bournville Athletic	38	8	4	26	63	130	20

1937-1938

Team	P	W	D	L	F	A	Pts
Darlaston	38	31	2	5	135	34	64
Aston Villa "A"	38	29	3	6	145	47	61
West Bromwich Albion "A"	38	19	13	6	96	51	51
Tamworth	38	20	8	10	119	71	48
Birmingham "A"	38	21	5	12	86	68	47
Coventry City "A"	38	19	6	13	98	57	44
Banbury Spencer	38	19	6	13	105	68	44
Walsall Reserves	38	18	8	12	107	71	44
Evesham Town	38	18	5	15	75	89	41
Shirley Town	38	17	6	15	81	82	40
Birmingham Trams	38	17	6	15	63	79	40
Wolverhampton Wanderers "A"	38	16	7	15	101	66	39
Gloucester City	38	15	8	15	96	85	38
Atherstone Town	38	13	10	15	77	104	36
Cheltenham Town Reserves	38	11	11	16	67	97	33
Redditch	38	12	3	23	81	111	27
Halesowen Town	38	6	5	27	63	137	17
Bromsgrove Rovers	38	5	7	26	49	135	17
Hinckley United	38	6	3	29	49	144	15
Bournville Athletic	38	4	6	28	43	140	14

1938-1939

Team	P	W	D	L	F	A	Pts
Aston Villa "A"	38	26	8	4	130	38	60
Walsall Reserves	38	27	5	6	129	54	59
Birmingham "A"	38	24	4	10	124	48	52
Darlaston	38	26	0	12	120	52	52
Tamworth	38	22	7	9	112	64	51
West Bromwich Albion "A"	38	22	5	11	101	52	49
Wolverhampton Wanderers "A"	38	22	4	12	101	63	48
Gloucester City	38	16	12	10	73	61	44
Coventry City "A"	38	20	3	15	112	86	43
Birmingham City Transport	38	19	5	14	91	86	43
Redditch	38	14	9	15	74	74	37
Cheltenham Town Reserves	38	17	1	20	91	110	35
Solihull Town	38	14	4	20	68	83	32
Banbury Spencer	38	11	8	19	68	87	30
Hinckley United	38	9	10	19	77	116	28
Halesowen Town	38	8	7	23	77	137	23
Nuneaton Borough	38	9	4	25	66	127	22
Atherstone Town	38	9	2	27	74	170	20
Bromsgrove Rovers	38	6	6	26	62	128	18
Bournville Athletic	38	4	6	28	51	165	14

1939-1940

Team	P	W	D	L	F	A	Pts
Solihull Town "A"	16	13	2	1	89	28	28
Stourbridge	18	13	2	3	73	37	28
Darlaston	18	10	5	3	65	31	25
Bromsgrove Rovers	18	10	2	6	57	42	22
Nuneaton Borough	18	6	7	5	47	42	19
Tamworth	18	8	3	7	54	60	19
Sutton Town	18	5	2	11	26	55	12
Redditch	16	4	1	11	36	53	9
Solihull Town "B"	16	4	1	11	34	56	9
Wolverhampton Wanderers "A"	16	0	1	15	19	96	1

1945-1946

Team	P	W	D	L	F	A	Pts
Darlaston	32	22	4	6	117	62	48
Nuneaton Borough	32	19	4	9	113	58	42
Bromsgrove Rovers	32	19	4	9	103	91	42
Atherstone Town	32	18	4	10	91	64	40
Dudley Town	32	17	6	9	92	65	40
Kidderminster Harriers	32	15	6	11	75	57	36
Birmingham City "A"	32	16	4	12	83	65	36
Stourbridge	32	17	2	13	90	78	36
Coventry City "A"	32	12	5	15	73	80	29
Moor Green	32	13	3	16	85	94	29
Walsall Reserves	32	11	6	15	63	82	28
Wolverhampton Wanderers "A"	32	11	5	16	83	93	27
Banbury Spencer	32	10	7	15	56	79	27
Worcester City Reserves	32	12	1	19	76	102	25
Hednesford	32	9	6	17	65	89	24
Tamworth	32	9	5	18	76	108	23
Birmingham City Transport	32	4	4	24	43	117	12

1946-1947

Team	P	W	D	L	F	A	Pts
Bromsgrove Rovers	36	23	4	9	105	57	50
Walsall Reserves	36	22	3	11	95	71	47
Darlaston	36	21	3	12	116	70	45
Nuneaton Borough	36	19	4	13	84	64	42
Atherstone Town	36	18	6	12	85	73	42
Tamworth	36	18	5	13	88	68	41
Stafford Rangers	36	18	5	13	81	70	41
Dudley Town	36	18	5	13	76	71	41
Stourbridge	36	16	7	13	72	75	39
Banbury Spencer	36	15	6	15	86	65	36
Kidderminster Harriers	36	16	4	16	104	84	36
Wolverhampton Wanderers "A"	36	16	4	16	72	67	36
Redditch	36	17	2	17	83	96	36
West Bromwich Albion "A"	36	14	5	17	83	90	33
Moor Green	36	13	5	18	71	108	31
Hednesford	36	12	4	20	85	103	28
Worcester City Reserves	36	10	4	22	68	99	24
Birmingham City Transport	36	5	8	23	51	107	18
Coventry City "A"	36	6	6	24	56	123	18

1947-1948

Team	P	W	D	L	F	A	Pts
Atherstone Town	38	30	1	7	109	40	61
Banbury Spencer	38	29	3	6	106	42	61
Bedworth Town	38	24	6	8	102	65	54
Tamworth	38	24	5	9	96	63	53
Bromsgrove Rovers	38	21	8	9	101	67	50
Nuneaton Borough	38	18	8	12	94	66	44
Darlaston	38	19	6	13	91	74	44
Dudley Town	38	17	8	13	69	56	42
West Bromwich Albion "A"	38	18	5	15	86	88	41
Stourbridge	38	16	8	14	86	66	40
Walsall Reserves	38	15	9	14	76	74	39
Wolverhampton Wanderers "A"	38	12	12	14	68	75	36
Stafford Rangers	38	14	6	18	68	88	34
Hednesford	38	14	4	20	86	97	32
Birmingham City "A"	38	8	11	19	57	79	27
Redditch	38	11	4	23	64	88	26
Birmingham City Transport	38	7	9	22	59	108	23
Moor Green	38	6	8	24	55	112	20
Hinckley Athletic	38	7	5	26	61	112	19
Coventry City "A"	36	6	6	24	56	123	18

1948-1949

Bedworth Town	38	30	5	3	129	38	65
Nuneaton Borough	38	23	9	6	92	44	55
Stourbridge	38	22	9	7	104	55	53
Bromsgrove Rovers	38	23	6	9	109	57	52
Hednesford	38	21	9	8	99	64	51
Tamworth	38	19	10	9	96	57	48
Walsall Reserves	38	20	7	11	88	65	47
West Bromwich Albion "A"	38	16	9	13	100	84	41
Wolverhampton Wanderers "A"	38	15	11	12	73	71	41
Banbury Spencer	38	15	10	13	75	68	40
Redditch	38	13	10	15	63	88	36
Stafford Rangers	38	14	7	17	66	74	35
Bilston	38	13	7	18	62	85	33
Darlaston	38	11	8	19	66	88	30
Dudley Town	38	9	11	18	54	75	29
Hinckley Athletic	38	10	9	19	62	97	29
Atherstone Town	38	10	7	21	82	96	27
Birmingham City "A"	38	7	7	24	56	86	21
Moor Green	38	7	7	24	58	111	21
Birmingham City Transport	38	1	4	33	40	170	6

1949-1950

Bedworth Town	38	28	6	4	111	43	62
Bromsgrove Rovers	38	25	9	4	98	42	59
Nuneaton Borough	38	24	9	5	92	40	57
Atherstone Town	38	24	5	9	79	51	53
Walsall Reserves	38	20	5	13	88	60	45
Hinckley Athletic	38	19	7	12	71	49	45
Tamworth	38	16	12	10	80	61	44
Banbury Spencer	38	19	5	14	63	52	43
Stourbridge	38	18	3	17	81	75	39
Dudley Town	38	16	7	15	57	72	39
Moor Green	38	13	7	18	62	73	33
Bilston	38	14	3	21	63	73	31
Hednesford	38	12	7	19	65	84	31
Stafford Rangers	38	10	11	17	53	71	31
Wolverhampton Wanderers "A"	38	11	8	19	61	68	30
Darlaston	38	12	6	20	71	93	30
Redditch	38	13	3	22	63	69	29
West Bromwich Albion "A"	38	7	14	17	54	62	28
Lockheed (Leamington)	38	10	4	24	49	96	24
Birmingham City Transport	38	2	3	33	34	161	7

1950-1951

Hednesford	38	24	8	6	112	53	56
Nuneaton Borough	38	26	3	9	112	65	55
Redditch	38	20	11	7	87	43	51
Stourbridge	38	23	5	10	82	55	51
Walsall Reserves	38	18	9	11	85	55	45
Stafford Rangers	38	21	3	14	82	56	45
Bromsgrove Rovers	38	16	9	13	76	66	41
Bedworth Town	38	18	4	16	59	77	40
Lockheed (Leamington)	38	17	2	19	65	67	36
Tamworth	38	16	3	19	92	98	35
Sutton Town	38	13	9	16	51	78	35
Banbury Spencer	38	13	8	17	64	75	34
Atherstone Town	38	12	9	17	83	81	33
Hinckley Athletic	38	14	5	19	64	74	33
Darlaston	38	14	5	19	67	80	33
Rugby Town	38	12	8	18	57	87	32
Dudley Town	38	11	7	20	59	68	29
Moor Green	38	9	11	18	61	92	29
Bilston	38	12	5	21	60	96	29
West Bromwich Albion "A"	38	6	6	26	39	91	18

1951-1952

Stourbridge	38	28	6	4	99	49	62
Redditch	38	24	8	6	112	58	56
Hednesford	38	23	5	10	92	48	51
Nuneaton Borough	38	22	7	9	109	75	51
Bromsgrove Rovers	38	19	4	15	73	62	42
Tamworth	38	18	6	14	92	91	42
Stafford Rangers	38	16	9	13	83	72	41
Walsall Reserves	38	18	4	16	100	89	40
Lockheed (Leamington)	38	16	7	15	80	71	39
Dudley Town	38	15	7	16	67	74	37
Moor Green	38	14	7	17	71	80	35
Hinckley Athletic	38	16	3	19	60	84	35
Darlaston	38	15	4	19	77	84	34
Rugby Town	38	13	7	18	69	73	33
Banbury Spencer	38	13	7	18	76	87	33
West Bromwich Albion "A"	38	12	7	19	64	74	31
Bilston	38	11	9	18	74	111	31
Bedworth Town	38	12	6	20	89	88	30
Atherstone Town	38	11	3	24	64	103	25
Sutton Town	38	4	4	30	40	118	12

1952-1953

Redditch	34	21	7	6	84	60	49
Hednesford	34	20	6	8	81	46	46
Stourbridge	34	19	3	12	71	57	41
Rugby Town	34	16	8	10	64	38	40
Bilston	34	16	6	12	75	61	38
Atherstone Town	34	14	9	11	85	75	37
Dudley Town	34	17	2	15	67	71	36
Moor Green	34	16	4	14	64	70	36
Bromsgrove Rovers	34	12	11	11	65	79	35
Hinckley Athletic	34	14	6	14	67	69	34
Walsall Reserves	34	11	11	12	56	57	33
Darlaston	34	14	3	17	53	59	31
Banbury Spencer	34	12	6	16	73	65	30
Tamworth	34	11	8	15	55	64	30
Lockheed (Leamington)	34	10	6	18	56	68	26
Sutton Town	34	9	6	19	44	84	24
West Bromwich Albion "A"	34	10	3	21	54	72	23
Bedworth Town	34	9	5	20	49	67	23

1953-1954

Rugby Town	26	17	3	6	64	35	37
Bilston	26	14	6	6	67	37	34
Atherstone Town	26	13	7	6	60	42	33
Banbury Spencer	26	14	4	8	49	36	32
Lockheed (Leamington)	26	13	5	8	50	27	31
Hinckley Athletic	26	9	10	7	41	39	28
Tamworth	26	11	5	10	53	48	27
Bedworth Town	26	10	6	10	45	54	26
Gresley Rovers	26	10	4	12	65	58	24
West Bromwich Albion "A"	26	10	4	12	46	50	24
Darlaston	26	9	5	12	42	47	23
Birch Coppice	26	6	9	11	37	57	21
Moor Green	26	5	5	16	32	61	15
Sutton Town	26	3	3	20	32	92	9

FORMATION AND SUMMARY

The formation of the Football League in 1888 was highly successful and the following year several more leagues were formed in areas where there were already a significant number of established clubs. In the Birmingham district three of its major clubs – Aston Villa, West Bromwich Albion and Wolverhampton Wanderers – had been founder members of the Football League and three more – Birmingham St. George's, Walsall Town Swifts (later just Walsall) and Small Heath (later Birmingham City) became founder members of the Football Alliance in 1889. This was a nationally based league that became the Second Division of the Football League in 1892.

There were still many more established clubs in the region around Birmingham and so a meeting was called at the Grand Hotel in Birmingham on May 31st 1889 to form the Birmingham & District League. Of the 17 clubs who were invited, 13 sent representatives but it was decided to start with a 12-team league. The 12 selected were: Aston Victoria, Great Bridge Unity, Hednesford Town, Ironbridge, Kidderminster Harriers, Kidderminster Olympic, Langley Green Victoria, Oldbury Town, Smethwick Carriage Works, Unity Gas Department, Wellington St. George's and Willenhall Pickwick. The 13th club who attended the meeting but were not admitted to the league was Worcester Rovers.

It took a few seasons for the league to become properly established but it then became one of the strongest semi-professional competitions outside of the Football League itself with perhaps only the Midland League, Southern League and later the Cheshire League being stronger. It was soon attracting clubs from as far afield as Bristol and North Wales but in the late 1930s the wide spread of the league became something of a disadvantage. A number of clubs resigned, citing the long and expensive journeys as their main reason while some of the stronger clubs moved to other competitions where less travelling was required. As a result the Birmingham League became severely weakened.

The League re-established itself after the Second World War and in 1954 it formed a Second Division after taking over the clubs from the rival Birmingham Combination. The expansion of the Southern League in 1958 attracted some of the stronger Birmingham League clubs and in an effort to widen its appeal, the league decided to expel all remaining reserve and "A" teams and revert to one division. It also changed it's name to the West Midlands Regional League in 1962 and soon afterwards re-formed a Second Division. However there was still a constant drip of its better clubs to the Southern League which continually weakened the league. With the formation of what is now known as the Football Conference in 1979, the WMRL dropped another level in status and with more Southern League expansions and the formation of the Midland Football Alliance above it in 1994, the league is now just a shadow of its former self. However the WMRL is still functioning in 2005 after 116 years of life and so jointly with the Northern League, it can make the proud claim of being the second oldest league in the world.

CHANGES TO THE LEAGUE

1890   Kidderminster Olympic and Kidderminster Harriers merged, left the Birmingham League and joined the Midland League as Kidderminster. Their reserves joined the Birmingham League as Kidderminster Rovers. Aston Victoria changed their name to County Victoria and moved to the Warwickshire County Cricket Ground at Edgbaston following the demise of Warwick County who were the football section of the county cricket club. Ironbridge and Wellington St. George's left and joined the Shropshire & District League and Great Bridge Unity, Unity Gas Department and Willenhall Pickwick also left. Brierley Hill Alliance, Burton Alma, Stourbridge and Wednesbury Old Athletic joined. League reduced to 10 clubs.

1891   Kidderminster folded in March 1891 and their reserves – Kidderminster Rovers – withdrew from the league. Kidderminster Harriers and Kidderminster Olympic both reformed and joined the league for the 1891-92 season but Olympic folded before the start of the season. County Victoria changed name back to Aston Victoria. Wednesbury Old Athletic left and joined the Midland League and Burton Alma and Hednesford Town also left. Great Bridge Unity and Redditch Town joined. League reduced to 9 clubs.

1892   Great Bridge Unity and Oldbury Town both folded during the 1891-92 season and were unable to complete their fixtures. Aston Victoria disbanded at the end of the season and Langley Green Victoria also left. Wolverhampton Wanderers Reserves joined from the Shropshire & District League and Aston Villa Reserves, Halesowen, Old Hill Wanderers and West Bromwich Albion Reserves also joined. League increased to 10 clubs.

1893   Stafford Rangers joined from the Shropshire & District League and Berwick Rangers, Small Heath Reserves and Worcester Rovers also joined. League increased to 14 clubs.

1894   Oldbury Town joined from the Birmingham Junior League and Singers (Coventry) also joined. Smethwick Carriage Works changed their name to Smethwick. League increased to 16 clubs.

1895   Old Hill Wanderers disbanded and Smethwick left. Hereford Thistle joined from the Western League and Shrewsbury Town joined from the Shropshire & District League.

1896   Stafford Rangers and Hereford Town joined from the Shropshire League.

1897   Oldbury Town and Redditch Town left. Bristol Eastville Rovers and Bristol St. George's joined while continuing to play in the Western League.

1898   Dudley joined as a new club and Wellington Town joined from the Shropshire & District League. Singers (Coventry) changed their name to Coventry City. League increased to 18 clubs.

1899   Bristol Eastville Rovers left and were replaced by their reserves. Bristol St. George's disbanded and Hereford Thistle also left. Wellington St. George's joined from the Shropshire & District League and Walsall Reserves also joined.

1900   Wellington St. George's and Worcester Rovers both resigned during the 1899-1900 season and their records were expunged. Bristol Rovers Reserves and Walsall Reserves also left. Stafford Rangers and Stoke Reserves joined from the North Staffordshire & District League, Ironbridge joined from the Shropshire & District League and Ruabon Druids joined from The Combination.

1901   Wellington Town left. Crewe Alexandra joined from the Lancashire League.

1902   Hereford Town left and Wellington Town joined from The Combination. Worcester City took over Berwick Rangers fixtures.

1903   Ironbridge disbanded and Walsall joined from the Midland League.

1904   Ruabon Druids left. Burslem Port Vale Reserves joined from the North Staffordshire & District League.

1905   Halesowen left. Wrexham joined from The Combination. Small Heath changed their name to Birmingham.

1906   Wellington Town left and joined the Walsall & District League, changing places with Halesowen.

1907   Burslem Port Vale disbanded. Burton United joined from the Football League Division Two.

1908   Coventry City left. Stoke dropped out of the Football League and placed their first team in the Birmingham League instead of their reserves. Wellington Town joined from Walsall & District League.

1910   Burton United disbanded and were replaced by Wednesbury Old Athletic from the Birmingham Combination.

1911   Crewe Alexandra and Halesowen left. Stoke withdrew their first team so that they could concentrate on their Southern League fixtures and placed their reserves in the Birmingham League. Darlaston and Willenhall Swifts joined from the Birmingham Combination.

1912   Stafford Rangers left and joined the Birmingham Combination. Coventry City Reserves joined.

1915   Dudley disbanded.

1919   Aston Villa Reserves left. Hednesford Town and Nuneaton Town joined from the Birmingham Combination. Willenhall Swifts merged with Willenhall Pickwick from the Birmingham Combination to form Willenhall.

1921   Walsall, Wrexham and the reserves of Birmingham, Stoke, West Bromwich Albion and Wolverhampton Wanderers left. Bilston United, Burton All Saints, Cannock Town, Redditch, Stafford Rangers and Tamworth Castle all joined from the Birmingham Combination.

1922   Coventry City Reserves left. Cradley Heath joined from the Birmingham Combination.

1923   Tamworth Castle left and joined the Birmingham Combination, swapping with Oakengates Town.

1924   Burton All Saints changed their name to Burton Town. Nuneaton Town and Wednesbury Old Athletic left. Oswestry Town joined from the Welsh National League. Wellington St. George's joined from Birmingham Combination.

1928   Cannock Town and Darlaston both left and joined the Birmingham Combination, swapping places with Hereford United and Walsall Reserves.

1929   Redditch left. Kettering Town Reserves joined while continuing in the Northamptonshire League.

1930   Willenhall disbanded. West Bromwich Albion "A" joined. Kettering Town joined from the Southern League taking the place of their reserves.

1931   Kettering Town, Wellington St. Georges and West Bromwich Albion "A" all left. Colwyn Bay United, Rhyl Athletic and Wrexham Reserves joined from the North Wales Combination.

1932   Bilston United disbanded and Bangor City joined from the North Wales Combination.

1933   Walsall Reserves left to join the Birmingham Combination. Cannock Town and Nuneaton Town joined from the Birmingham Combination and Port Vale Reserves joined from the Cheshire League. League increased to 20 clubs.

1934   Port Vale Reserves returned to the Cheshire League. League reduced to 19 clubs.

1935   Burton Town left and joined the Midland League. Cardiff City Reserves joined while continuing in the Western League and Dudley Town joined from the Birmingham Combination. League increased to 20 clubs.

1936   Rhyl Athletic left and joined the Cheshire League. Bristol Rovers Reserves joined while continuing in the Western League. League increased to 20 clubs.

1936-37   Cannock Town resigned during the season and their record was expunged.

1937   Shrewsbury Town, Nuneaton Town, Bristol Rovers Reserves and Colwyn Bay United left. League reduced to 15 clubs.

1937-38   Hednesford Town resigned during the season and their record was expunged.

1938   Oakengates Town disbanded. Bangor City, Cardiff City Reserves, Worcester City, Wellington Town and

Wrexham Reserves all left. Hednesford Town were re-formed as Hednesford and rejoined the league and Shrewsbury Town Reserves joined from the Midland Midweek League. League reduced to 10 clubs and so it was decided to split the season into two with clubs competing for the Keys Cup up to the end of December and for the League Cup from the start of January.

1938-39   Dudley Town and Brierley Hill Alliance both resigned during the season and their fixtures were taken over by Vono Sports and Revo Sports respectively.

1939   Kidderminster Harriers, Stourbridge, Hereford United and Vono Sports left. Kidderminster and Hereford were replaced by their reserves. Burton Town Reserves, R.A.F. Cosford, R.A.F. Hednesford, Stoke City "A" and Worcester City Reserves joined. League increased to 13 clubs.

1939-45   When war was declared on 3rd September, the original 1939-40 competition was abandoned. After a few weeks an emergency competition was set up which ran for the 1939-40, 1940-41 and 1941-42 seasons. The clubs who took part in at least one season of emergency football were Aston Villa (first team), Birmingham Reserves, Burton Town, Hednesford, Kidderminster Harriers, R.A.F. Bridgnorth, R.A.F. Cosford, R.A.F. Hednesford, R.A.F. Lichfield, Revo Electric (formerly Revo Sports), Stafford Rangers, Wellington Town, West Bromwich Albion Reserves, Wolverhampton Wanderers Reserves and Worcester City.

1945   With the league unable to restart, Dudley Town, Hednesford and Worcester City Reserves joined the Birmingham Combination.

1946   When the league resumed after the war, pre-war members Hereford United Reserves, Oswestry Town and Shrewsbury Town Reserves were joined by Aston Villa "A", Halesowen Town, Kettering Town, Walsall "A" and the reserves of Cheltenham Town, Gloucester City and Wellington Town to form a 10 club competition. Stafford Rangers joined the Birmingham Combination. Brierley Hill Alliance and Cradley Heath were not ready to resume.

1947   Cheltenham Town Reserves left. Kidderminster Harriers and Worcester City Reserves joined from the Birmingham Combination, Lye Town joined from the Central Amateur League and Cradley Heath and Wolverhampton Wanderers "A" also joined. League increased to 14 clubs.

1948   Kidderminster Harriers joined the Southern League and were replaced by their reserves. Brush Sports joined from the United Counties League and Brierley Hill Alliance, Leicester City "A" and Stoke City "A" also joined. League increased to 18 clubs.

1949   Leicester City "A" left. Boldmere St. Michaels and Whitwick Colliery joined from the Central Amateur League, Whitwick had also been members of the Central Alliance. League increased to 19 clubs.

1950   Kettering Town left and joined the Southern League. Burton Albion joined as a new club.

1951   Gloucester City Reserves left and joined the Western League. League reduced to 18 clubs.

1952   Stoke City "A" left. Nuneaton Borough joined from the Birmingham Combination and Bloxwich Strollers joined from the Staffordshire County League (South). League increased to 19 clubs.

1953   Bromsgrove Rovers, Dudley Town, Hednesford, Redditch, Stourbridge and Walsall Reserves joined from the Birmingham Combination. Walsall "A" moved to the Staffordshire County League (South). League increased to 24 clubs.

1954   Atherstone Town, Banbury Spencer, Bedworth Town, Bilston, Birch Coppice, Darlaston, Gresley Rovers, Hinckley Athletic, Lockheed (Leamington), Moor Green, Rugby Town, Sutton Town and Tamworth all joined from the Birmingham Combination, Leek Town joined from the Manchester League, Symingtons joined from the United Counties League and Cheltenham Town Reserves also joined. League increased to 40 clubs and separated into two divisions, Northern and Southern.

1955   The top 10 clubs in each of the Northern and Southern Divisions moved into the new Division One and the remaining clubs moved into the new Division Two with the exception of Birch Coppice who joined the Warwickshire Combination and Symingtons who disbanded. They were replaced by Evesham United from the Worcestershire Combination and West Bromwich Albion "A" from the Warwickshire Combination.

1955-56   Division Two: Bloxwich Strollers resigned during the season and their record was expunged. They are believed to have joined the Bloxwich Combination in 1956-57.

1956   Stoke City "A" joined.

1956-57   Division Two: Leek Town resigned during the season and their record was expunged.

1957   Whitwick Colliery left after finishing in a relegation position and joined the Leicestershire Senior League. Kidderminster Harriers disbanded their reserves side. Stratford Town joined from the Worcestershire Combination and Birmingham City "A" and Coventry City "A" joined from the Warwickshire Combination.

1958   Burton Albion and Nuneaton Borough left as did Rugby Town (who finished in a relegation position). Division One reduced to 18 clubs. Leicester City "A" joined from the Leicestershire Senior League.

1959   Hinckley Athletic left and joined the Southern League despite finishing in a relegation position. Gresley Rovers, Oswestry Town and Shrewsbury Town Reserves left. Division Two reduced to 16 clubs.

1960   League to be for first teams only. Brush Sports, Walsall Reserves and the "A" teams of Aston Villa, Birmingham City, Coventry City, Leicester City, Stoke City, West Bromwich Albion and Wolverhampton Wanderers, Cheltenham Town, Hereford United, Wellington Town and Worcester City all left. Kidderminster Harriers joined from the Southern League. League reduced to a single division of 22 clubs.

1961   Cradley Heath disbanded. League reduced to 21 clubs.

1962   League changed name to West Midlands (Regional) League. Evesham United left. League reduced to 20 clubs.

1963   Boldmere St. Michaels left to join the Worcestershire Combination and Lockheed (Leamington) left to join the Midland League. Lower Gornal Athletic joined from the Worcestershire Combination. League reduced to 19 clubs.

1964   Stratford Town changed their name to Stratford Town Amateurs and Sutton Town changed their name to Sutton Coldfield Town. Walsall Reserves joined from the Midland Intermediate League. League increased to 20 clubs.

1965   Banbury Spencer changed their name to Banbury United. Moor Green and Sutton Coldfield Town left. The remaining 18 clubs were joined by Cinderford Town from the Warwickshire Combination and Port Vale Reserves and Wolverhampton Wanderers "A" from the Midland Intermediate League to form a new 21 club Premier Division. A new 11 club Division One was formed by Wrockwardine Wood who joined from the Shropshire County League and 10 reserve sides – Nuneaton Borough and Wellington Town from the Warwickshire Combination, Bilston, Dudley Town and Hednesford from the Staffordshire County League (South) and Kidderminster Harriers, Lower Gornal Athletic and Stourbridge from the Worcestershire Combination plus Atherstone Town and Stafford Rangers.

1966   Premier Division: Banbury United and Walsall Reserves left. Boston United joined from the United Counties League, Shrewsbury Town Reserves joined from the Football Combination and Coventry City "A" also joined. Division increased to 22 clubs. Division One: The reserves of Atherstone Town, Dudley Town, Nuneaton Borough, Stafford Rangers and Wellington Town all left. These clubs dispensed with professional Saturday reserve teams and introduced a first team squad instead with fringe players taking part in mid-week games in various new Floodlit Leagues that were formed. Sankey of Wellington joined from the Shropshire County League, Tividale joined from the Warwickshire and West Midland Alliance, Tamworth Reserves joined from the Staffordshire County League (South) and Darlaston Reserves also joined. Division reduced to 10 clubs.

1967   Premier Division: Shrewsbury Town Reserves left. Hinckley Athletic joined from the Southern League. Division One: Lower Gornal Athletic Reserves left. Baddesley Colliery and Stratford Town Amateurs Reserves joined from the Warwickshire and West Midlands Alliance, Bedworth Town Reserves, Coventry Amateurs, Hereford United Reserves and Warwick Saltisford Rovers (a merger of Saltisford Rovers and Warwick Town) joined from the Warwickshire Combination, Tipton Town joined from the Wolverhampton Amateur League, Warley joined as a new club and Stewarts & Lloyds and Dudley Town Reserves also joined. Division increased to 19 clubs.

1968   Premier Division: Bedworth Town disbanded and a new club called Bedworth United were formed to replace them in the Premier Division. Boston United, Coventry City "A" and Port Vale Reserves left. Eastwood (Hanley) joined from the Manchester League. Division reduced to 20 clubs. Division One: Sankey of Wellington changed their name to G.K.N. Sankey. Warley, Hednesford Reserves and Tamworth Reserves left. Brereton Social and Oxley joined from the Staffordshire County League (South), Warley County Borough joined from the Birmingham A.F.A. and the reserves of Brierley Hill Alliance, Halesowen Town and Lye Town joined from the Worcestershire Combination. Division increased to 22 clubs.

1969   Premier Division: Cinderford Town left. Division reduced to 19 clubs. Division One: The reserves of Hereford United, Stourbridge and Stratford Town Amateurs left. Division reduced to 19 clubs.

1970   Premier Division: Stratford Town Amateurs left. Wellingborough Town joined from the Metropolitan League. Division One: Stewarts & Lloyds changed their name to B.S.C. (Bilston). Warwick Saltisford Rovers changed their name to Racing Football Club (Warwick). Wrockwardine Wood and the reserves of Bedworth United, Brierley Hill Alliance, Darlaston, Dudley Town, Lye Town and Kidderminster Harriers left. Solihull Amateurs joined from the Midland Combination, Wellingborough Town Reserves joined from the United Counties League and Rowley United and the reserves of Atherstone Town, Burton Albion and Worcester City also joined. Division reduced to 18 clubs.

1970-71   Division One: Atherstone Town Reserves withdrew during the season and their record was expunged.

1971   Premier Division: Redditch changed their name to Redditch United. Stourbridge and Wellingborough Town left. Warley joined from the Midland League and G.K.N. Sankey became the first club to be promoted from Division One. Division One: Wellingborough Town Reserves left. Armitage joined from the Staffordshire County League (South). B.S.C. (Bilston) changed name to Springvale. Division reduced to 16 clubs.

1971-72   Division One: Solihull Amateurs were expelled during the season for breaches of the rules and their record was expunged.

1972   Premier Division: Lower Gornal Athletic changed their name to Gornal Athletic. Atherstone Town, Bedworth United, Bromsgrove Rovers, Kidderminster Harriers, Redditch United and Tamworth all left. Hednesford left and joined the Midland League, swapping leagues with Heanor Town. Hereford United Reserves also joined. Brereton Social and Warley County Borough promoted from Division One. Division reduced to 16 clubs. Division One: Racing F.C. (Warwick), Baddesley Colliery and Burton Albion Reserves left. West Shirley Athletic joined from the Midland Combination having changed their name from Westphalians. Chasetown joined from the Staffordshire County League (South). G.K.N. Sankey Reserves, Langley Celtic and Telford United Reserves also joined. Division reduced to 15 clubs.

1973   Premier Division: Wolverhampton Wanderers "A" left and joined the Midland Combination, swapping leagues with Alvechurch. Tividale and Coventry Amateurs promoted from Division One. Warley were demoted to Division One. Division increased to 17 clubs. Division One: Staffordshire and Stoke Police and the reserves of Bromsgrove Rovers, Nuneaton Borough, Stourbridge and Tamworth joined. Division increased to 19 clubs.

1974   Premier Division: Coventry Amateurs changed their name to Coventry Sporting. G.K.N. Sankey and Hereford United Reserves left. Heanor Town left to join the Midland League, swapping leagues with Hednesford Town. Armitage promoted from Division One. Division reduced to 16 clubs. Division One: Staffordshire and Stoke police changed their name to Staffordshire Police. West Shirley Athletic changed their name to Shirley Town. G.K.N. Sankey Reserves left. Ledbury Town, Hednesford Town Reserves and Stafford Rangers Reserves joined. Division reduced to 20 clubs.

1975   Premier Division: Gresley Rovers joined from the East Midlands Regional League and V.S. Rugby joined from the United Counties League. Staffordshire Police promoted from Division One. Division increased to 19 clubs. Division One: Langley Celtic changed their name to Langley. Stafford Rangers Reserves, Stourbridge Reserves and Tamworth Reserves left. Willenhall Town joined from the Staffordshire Premier League and Oldswinford, V.S. Rugby Reserves and Kidderminster Harriers Reserves also joined. Division increased to 21 clubs.

1976   Premier Division: Walsall Reserves joined. Willenhall Town were promoted from Division One. Division increased to 21 clubs. Division One: Warley disbanded. Oxley merged with Whitmore Old Boys from the Midland Combination and continued in the WMRL as Wolverhampton United. Wednesfield Social joined from the Wolverhampton & District Amateur League, Shifnal Town joined from the Shropshire County League, Lichfield joined from the Staffordshire County League (South) and Burntwood Institute, Causeway Green, Coventry Sporting Reserves, Donnington Wood, G.K.N. Sankey and Redditch United Reserves also joined. Division increased to 29 clubs which were split into two sections, A and B.

1977   Premier Division: Warley County Borough disbanded and Walsall Reserves also left. Division reduced to 19 clubs. Division One: The two sections were split into a 16 club Division One and a 14 club Division Two. Division One was comprised the top eight from Section A and the top seven from Section B, plus Lichfield who had finished 10th in Section B. The remaining 13 clubs went into Division Two with the exception of Bilston Reserves and V.S. Rugby Reserves who left. Division Two expanded to 14 clubs with three new clubs – Albrighton United, Brereton Town and Staffs South End.

1978   Goal difference instead of goal average used to decide precedence of clubs having the same number of points. Premier Division: Alvechurch and Eastwood (Hanley) left. Ledbury Town and Wednesfield Social promoted from Division One. Staffordshire Police relegated to Division One. Division reduced to 18 clubs. Division One: Rowley United disbanded. Rushall Olympic joined from the Staffordshire County League (South). The reserves of Atherstone Town, Nuneaton Borough and Worcester City were promoted from Division Two. Division increased to 18 clubs. Division Two: Redditch United Reserves left. Westfields joined from the Worcester & District League, Brewood joined from the Wolverhampton Amateur League, Ludlow Town joined from the Kidderminster League and Bridgnorth Sports and reserves of Alvechurch, Dudley Town, Tividale and Willenhall Town joined. Division increased to 18 clubs.

1979   Premier Division: Blakenall, Malvern Town and Sutton Coldfield Town all joined from the Midland Combination. Shifnal Town promoted from Division One. Division increased to 22 clubs. Division One: Cheltenham Town Reserves left. Atherstone Town disbanded and their reserves left but a new club called Atherstone United was formed and they took the place of Atherstone Town Reserves. Alvechurch Reserves, Ludlow Town and Willenhall Town Reserves were promoted from Division Two. Division increased to 19 clubs. Division Two: Langley disbanded. Stourport Swifts joined from the Worcester & District League and the reserves of Ledbury Town, Lye Town, Malvern Town, Oswestry Town and Stourbridge also joined. Division increased to 20 clubs.

1980   Premier Division: Gornal Athletic relegated to Division One. Rushall Olympic promoted from Division One. Division One: Brewood, Hednesford Town Reserves and Staffs South End promoted from Division Two. Division increased to 22 clubs. Division Two: Dales United joined from the Herefordshire League, Tamworth Reserves joined from Midland Combination. Great Wyrley and Cheltenham Town Reserves also joined. Division increased to 21 clubs.

1981   Premier Division: Brierley Hill Alliance disbanded. Oldswinford promoted from Division One. Division One : Alvechurch Reserves left. G.K.N. Sankey relegated to Division Two. Bromsgrove Rovers Reserves promoted from Division Two. Division reduced to 20 clubs. Division Two: Brereton Town and the reserves of Kidderminster Harriers, Oswestry Town, Stourbridge and Tividale left. Northpark United joined from the Staffordshire County League (South) and Bilston United, Dowty Ashchurch and Stafford Rangers Reserves also joined. Division reduced to 20 clubs.

1981-82   Division Two: Bridgnorth Sports resigned during the season and their record was expunged.

1982   Premier Division: Dudley Town, Sutton Coldfield Town and Willenhall Town left. Darlaston relegated to Division One. Atherstone United and Wolverhampton United promoted from Division One. Division reduced to 20 clubs. Division One: Staffordshire Police, Burntwood Institute, Causeway Green and the reserves of Bromsgrove Rovers, Telford United and Worcester City all left. Bilston United, Cheltenham Town Reserves, G.K.N. Sankey and Northpark United promoted from Division Two. Division reduced to 17 clubs. Division Two: The reserves of Ledbury Town, Lye Town and Tamworth left. Pelsall Villa and Harrisons joined from the Staffordshire County League (South), Newport Town, Oldswinford Reserves and Wolverhampton Casuals also joined. Division reduced to 17 clubs.

1983   Premier Division: Bilston changed their name to Bilston Town. Coventry Sporting and V.S. Rugby promoted to the Southern League. Ledbury Town disbanded. Cradley Town joined from the Midland Combination. Chasetown, G.K.N. Sankey promoted from Division One. Division One: Staffs South End left. Donnington Wood relegated to Division Two. Dudley Town Reserves, Great Wyrley and Harrisons promoted from Division Two. Division reduced to 16 clubs. Division Two: Albrighton United disbanded and Coventry Sporting Reserves and Stafford Rangers Reserves also left. Aero Lucas and Atherstone United Reserves joined. Division reduced to 14 clubs.

1984   Premier Division: Hednesford Town promoted to the Southern League from which Tamworth were relegated. Tipton Town promoted from Division One. Cradley Town relegated to Division One. Division One: Cheltenham Town Reserves, Hednesford Town Reserves and Willenhall Town Reserves left. Halesowen Town Reserves, Newport Town, Pelsall Villa, Westfields and Wolverhampton Casuals promoted from Division Two. Division increased to 18 clubs. Division Two: Springvale changed their name to Springvale-Tranco. Halesowen Harriers joined from Sunday football (Birmingham Festival League), Ettingshall Holy Trinity joined from the Staffordshire County League (South) and Bloxwich Town, Broseley Athletic, Harrisons Reserves, Jamaica City, Minworth and Stuarts Athletic also joined. Division increased to 17 clubs.

1985   Premier Division: Bilston Town promoted to the Southern League. Harrisons promoted from Division One. Division One: Ettingshall Holy Trinity and Halesowen Harriers promoted from Division Two. Dudley Town disbanded their reserves. Division Two: Dales United, Malvern Town Reserves and Minworth left. Albright & Wilson, Chasetown Reserves, Clancey Halesowen, Metal Box Sports, Millfields and Wednesbury Town joined. Division increased to 18 clubs.

1986   Premier Division: Halesowen Town promoted to the Southern League from which Oldbury United were relegated. Shifnal Town left. Halesowen Harriers promoted from Division One. Division One: Shirley Town left. Lichfield relegated to Division Two. Aero Lucas, Broseley Athletic, Metal Box Sports, Springvale-Tranco and Stourport Swifts promoted from Division Two. Division increased to 20 clubs. Division Two: Hednesford Progressive joined from the Staffordshire Senior League and Hinton and the reserves of Brewood, Gresley Rovers, Tamworth and Wolverhampton Casuals also joined. Division increased to 20 clubs.

1986-87   Division Two: Wednesbury Town were expelled during the season and their record was expunged.

1987   Premier Division: Atherstone United promoted to the Southern League and Armitage disbanded. Westfields promoted from Division One. Division reduced to 18 clubs. Division One: Halesowen Town Reserves, Metal Box Sports and Northpark United left. Rocester joined from the Staffordshire Senior League. Broseley Athletic demoted to Division Two. Hednesford Progressive were promoted from Division Two and changed their name to Cannock Chase. Donnington Wood and Millfields also promoted. Division reduced to 19 clubs. Division Two: Atherstone United Reserves, Bloxwich Town, Dowty Ashchurch, Jamaica City, Oldswinford Reserves and Stuarts Athletic left. Lye Town Reserves joined from the Kidderminster League, Mitchells & Butlers joined from the Birmingham Works League and Claregate United, Gornal Sports, Malvern Town Reserves, Moxley Rangers and Springvale-Tranco Reserves also joined. Division reduced to 18 clubs.

1987-88   Brereton Social resigned during the season and their record was expunged. They later took the place of their reserves in the Staffordshire County League (South).

1988   Three points to be awarded for a win. Premier Division: Tamworth were promoted to the Southern League from which Paget Rangers were relegated. G.K.N. Sankey disbanded. Hinckley Town joined from the Central Midlands League. Wolverhampton United relegated to Division One. Millfields, Rocester, Stourport Swifts and Wolverhampton Casuals promoted from Division One. Division increased to 21 clubs. Division One: Chasetown Reserves and Hinton promoted from Division Two. Division reduced to 18 clubs. Division Two: Brewood Reserves, Claregate United and Springvale-Tranco Reserves left. Hill Top Rangers joined from Mercian F.A., GEC Blackheath joined from Birmingham Works League and Hinckley Town Reserves and Rocester Reserves also joined. Division reduced to 17 clubs.

1989   Premier Division: Wednesfield Social changed name to Wednesfield. Division One: Bilston United disbanded and Aero Lucas also left. Division reduced to 16 clubs. Division Two: Tamworth Reserves left. Wem Town joined from the Shropshire County League. Clancey Halesowen changed name to Clancey Dudley.

1990   Premier Division: Millfields changed name to West Bromwich Town. Hinckley Town were promoted to the

Southern League and Harrisons disbanded. Ilkeston Town joined from the Central Midlands League. Darlaston and Pelsall Villa promoted from Division One. Division increased to 22 clubs. Division One: Brewood left and Springvale-Tranco disbanded. Nuneaton Borough Reserves relegated to Division Two. Broseley Athletic, Hill Top Rangers, Lichfield, Moxley Rangers and Wem Town promoted from Division Two. Division Two: Harrisons Reserves disbanded. GEC Blackheath changed name to Blackheath Motors. Cheslyn Hay joined from the Staffordshire County League (South), Bloxwich Strollers joined from the Midland Combination and the reserves of Oldbury United, Paget Rangers and Rushall Olympic also joined.

1990-91   Division One: Hinton resigned during the season and their record was expunged. They later joined the Herefordshire County League.

1991   Premier Division: Willenhall Town relegated from the Southern League. Darlaston, Ilkeston Town, Tipton Town, Tividale and Wolverhampton Casuals demoted to Division One from which Cradley Town were promoted. Division reduced to 19 clubs. Division One: Newport Town left. Chasetown Reserves relegated to Division Two. Knypersley Victoria joined from the Staffordshire Senior League. Clancy Dudley and Oldbury United Reserves promoted from Division Two. Division increased to 20 clubs. Division Two: Hinckley Town Reserves, Gresley Rovers Reserves and Paget Rangers Reserves left. K Chell joined as a new club, Manders joined, probably from the Wolverhampton Works League, Alvechurch Reserves joined from the Midland Combination Reserve Division, Park Rangers joined from the Staffordshire County League (South) and the reserves of Cradley Town, Halesowen Harriers and Oldswinford also joined. Division increased to 20 clubs.

1992   Premier Division: Gresley Rovers promoted to the Southern League. Alvechurch disbanded after finishing in a Southern League relegation position but joined the WMRL after reforming as Alvechurch Sports. Malvern Town relegated to Division One from which Ilkeston Town were promoted. Division One: Gornal Sports promoted from Division Two. Broseley Athletic and Clancey Dudley left. Division reduced to 19 clubs. Division Two: K Chell and the reserves of Alvechurch, Malvern Town and Nuneaton Borough all left. Hinckley Athletic Reserves and Tividale Reserves joined. Blackheath Motors changed name to Blackheath Electrodrives. Division reduced to 17 clubs.

1993   Premier Division: Oldswinford changed their name to Brierley Hill Town. Darlaston and Knypersley Victoria promoted from Division One. Division increased to 21 clubs. Division One: Gornal Sports changed name to Bilston United. Stafford Town and Walsall Wood joined from the Staffordshire Senior League. Division One to be for first teams only while Division Two was disbanded and a new Reserve Division was formed. As a result Bloxwich Strollers, Manders and Cheslyn Hay promoted from Division Two and Oldbury United Reserves moved to the new Reserve Division. Division increased to 21 clubs. Division Two/Reserve Division: Albright & Wilson, Blackheath Electrodrives, Mitchells & Butlers and Park Rangers all left. Oldswinford (renamed Brierley Hill Town) withdrew their reserves. The reserves of Moxley Rangers, Pelsall Villa and Walsall Wood joined making a reserve division of 13 members.

1993-94   Premier Division: Alvechurch Sports folded in mid-season and their record was expunged.

1994   Premier Division: Brierley Hill Town, Chasetown, Halesowen Harriers, Hinckley Athletic, Knypersley Victoria, Oldbury United, Paget Rangers, Rocester, Rushall Olympic and Willenhall Town left to become founder members of the Midland Football Alliance. Ilkeston Town promoted to the Southern League. West Bromwich Town disbanded. Division became all floodlit and so Bilston United, Bloxwich Strollers, Ettingshall Holy Trinity, Gornal Athletic, Hill Top Rangers, Ludlow Town, Malvern Town, Manders, Stafford Town, Tividale and Walsall Wood were promoted from Division One. Division reduced to 19 clubs. Division One: Merged with Division Two. Lichfield changed name to Lichfield City. Cheslyn Hay and Wolverhampton Casuals Reserves left. Donnington Wood disbanded. The reserves of Halesowen Harriers, Lye Town, Moxley Rangers and Walsall Wood left. Morda United joined from the Mid-Wales League, Goodyear joined from the Wolverhampton Works League and Gornal Athletic Reserves also joined. Division reduced to 19 clubs.

1995   Premier Division: Blakenall promoted to the Midland Football Alliance from which Brierley Hill Town were relegated. Manders disbanded. Bilston United relegated to Division One. Lichfield City and Wolverhampton Casuals promoted from Division One. Division One: Wem Town and the reserves of Cradley Town, Darlaston and Pelsall Villa left. Bandon joined from the Kidderminster League and Brereton Social joined as a new club, having reformed. Bromyard Town joined from the Herefordshire League and Mahal, Pershore Town Reserves and Sikh Hunters also joined. Division increased to 21 clubs.

1996   Premier Division: Lichfield City disbanded as a senior club and changed to Sunday football. Pelsall Villa promoted to the Midland Football Alliance. Wolverhampton United promoted from Division One. Darlaston changed name to Darlaston Town. Division reduced to 18 clubs. Division One: Moxley Rangers and Goodyear disbanded. Hinckley Athletic Reserves and Rocester Reserves left. Division split into two sections, North and South. Brereton Social, Cannock Chase, Chasetown Reserves, Great Wyrley, Morda United, Rushall Olympic Reserves and Sikh Hunters were placed in the North section which was made up to 13 clubs with six new members: Blakenall Reserves, Brereton Town, Corestone Services, Heath Hayes, Sporting Khalsa and Wolverhampton Casuals Reserves. Bandon, Bilston United, Bromyard Town, Gornal Athletic Reserves, Mahal, Oldbury United Reserves, Pershore Town Reserves, Tipton Town and

Tividale Reserves were placed in the South section which was made up to 14 clubs with five new members: Bustleholme, Cradley Town Reserves, Kington Town, Leominster Town and Smethwick Rangers.

1997   Premier Division: Wednesfield promoted to the Midland Football Alliance. Hill Top Rangers disbanded. Bustleholme and Kington Town promoted from Division One (South). Division One (North): Sporting Khalsa, Chasetown Reserves and Rushall Olympic Reserves left. Bandon transferred from South section. Lawson Mardon Star (formerly Star Aluminium), Lucas Flight Controls, Newport Town and Walsall Wood Reserves joined. Division increased to 15 clubs. Division One (South): Bilston United and Oldbury United Reserves left. Birmingham College of Food, Halesowen Harriers Reserves, Hinton, Malvern Town Reserves and Wellington joined.

1998   Premier Division: Stourport Swifts promoted to the Midland Football Alliance and Bloxwich Strollers disbanded. Dudley Town joined after re-forming. Bandon and Lawson Mardon Star (who changed their name to Star) promoted from Division One (North). Smethwick Rangers and Tipton Town promoted from Division One (South). Division increased to 21 clubs. Division One (North): Blakenall Reserves and Brereton Town left. Little Drayton Rangers, Sedgley White Lions, Shifnal Town Reserves, Wolverhampton Town and Wyrley Rangers joined. Sikh Hunters transferred to Division One (South). Division One (South): Birmingham College of Food and Gornal Athletic Reserves left. Borgfield Celtic joined as a new club, Causeway United joined from the Birmingham A.F.A. and Lye Town Reserves also joined.

1999   Premier Division: Cradley Town promoted to the Midland Football Alliance. Wolverhampton United relegated to Division One (North). Heath Hayes and Little Drayton Rangers promoted from Division One (North). Causeway United promoted from Division One (South). Division increased to 22 clubs. Division One (North): Brereton Social disbanded and Wolverhampton Casuals Reserves, Wolverhampton Town and Wyrley Rangers also left. Shawbury United joined from the Shropshire County League and Heath Hayes Reserves also joined. Borgfield Celtic transferred from Division One (South). Division reduced to 13 clubs. Division One (South): The reserves of Halesowen Harriers, Lye Town and Tividale left. Bewdley Town joined from the Kidderminster League, Ledbury Town joined from the Midland Combination and Chaddesley Corbett also joined. Division reduced to 12 clubs.

2000   Premier Division: Smethwick Rangers changed their name to Warley Rangers. Stafford Town promoted to the Midland Football Alliance and Bandon disbanded. Shawbury United promoted from Division One (North). Bromyard Town and Wellington promoted from Division One (South). Division increased to 23 clubs. Division One (North): Borgfield Celtic and Cannock Chase disbanded and Corestone Services also left. Brereton Social joined after re-forming, Ounsdale joined from the Kidderminster League and Chasetown Reserves, Eccleshall Reserves and Wolverhampton Sports GNST also joined. Sedgley White Lions transferred to Division One (South). Sikh Hunters transferred from Division One (South). Lucas Flight Controls changed name to Lucas Sports. Division increased to 14 clubs. Division One (South): Cradley Town Reserves left. Brintons Athletic joined from the Kidderminster League and Bustleholme Reserves and Lye Town Reserves also joined.

2001   Premier Division: Ludlow Town promoted to the Midland Football Alliance. Warley Rangers changed name back to Smethwick Rangers. Brierley Hill Town merged with West Hagley and continued as Brierley & Hagley Alliance. Wolverhampton United promoted from Division One (North). Ledbury Town promoted from Division One (South). Division increased to 24 clubs. Division One (North): Chasetown Reserves and Shifnal Town Reserves left. Wrockwardine Wood joined from the Bridgnorth League, Shenstone Pathfinders joined from the Birmingham A.F.A. and Darlaston Town Reserves, Marston Wolves and Wyrley Rangers also joined. Division increased to 16 clubs. Division One (South): Pershore Town Reserves left. Wyre Forest joined as a new club having re-formed and Bridgnorth Town Reserves, Ludlow Town Reserves and Malvern Rangers also joined. Division increased to 14 clubs.

2002   Premier Division: Causeway United were promoted to the Midland Football Alliance. Star left. Darlaston Town demoted to Division One (North). Sedgley White Lions promoted from Division One (South). Smethwick Rangers changed name to Smethwick Sikh Temple. Division reduced to 22 clubs. Division One (North): Eccleshall Reserves left. Darlaston Town Reserves were replaced by their demoted first team and Ounsdale disbanded. Bilston Town joined having resigned from the Southern League for financial reasons, Riverway Stafford joined from the Wolverhampton Combination, Ashbourne United joined from the Midland Regional Alliance and Shelfield Sports and Wednesbury Town also joined. Division increased to 19 clubs. Division One (South): Brintons Athletic and Wyre Forest merged to form Wyre Forest Brintons. Blackheath Town joined as a new club and Ledbury Town Reserves also joined.

2002-03   Division One (North): Shelfield Sports withdrew during the season and their record was expunged.

2003   Premier Division: Westfields promoted to the Midland Alliance from which Wednesfield were relegated. Sedgley White Lions changed their name to Coseley Town. Walsall Wood relegated to Division One (North) and Gornal Athletic to Division One (South). Newport Town promoted from Division One (North). Little Drayton Rangers changed name to Market Drayton Town. Division reduced to 21 teams. Division One (North): Marston Wolves, Walsall Wood Reserves and Wrockwardine Wood left. Bilston Town transferred to Division One (South), swapping with Mahal.

Bilbrook joined from youth football and Eccleshall A.F.C. also joined. Lucas Sports changed name to Goodrich. Division increased to 17 clubs. Division One (South): Lye Town Reserves left. Tenbury United joined from the Kidderminster League and Cradley Town Reserves also joined. Division increased to 16 clubs.

2003-04   Premier Division: Newport Town resigned during the season and their record was expunged. Division One (North): Wolverhampton Sports GNST resigned during the season and their record was expunged.

2004   Premier Division: Malvern Town promoted to the Midland Alliance from which Pelsall Villa were relegated. Wolverhampton United demoted to Division One. Goodrich promoted from Division One (North) and Gornal Athletic from Division One (South). Division increased to 21 clubs. Division One (North) and (South) replaced by Divisions One and Two. Division One consisted of 19 clubs, made up of the nine who finished between 2nd and 10th in Division One (North), the eight who finished between 2nd and 9th in Division One (South) plus Stafford Town who moved down from the Midland Alliance and demoted Wolverhampton United. Division Two consisted of 17 clubs, made up of the last three from Division One (North), the four who finished between 12th and 15th in Division One (South) and 10 new clubs: Bromyard Town Reserves from the Herefordshire League, Brereton Town, Cresswell Wanderers from youth football, Darlaston Town Reserves, Dudley United who were a new club, Ellesmere Rangers from the Shropshire County League, Kington Town Reserves, Parkfields Leisure and Sporting Khalsa from Sunday football and Wednesfield Reserves. Heath Hayes Reserves, Morda United and Sikh Hunters left from Division One (North). Leominster Town left Division One (South) to join the Herefordshire League and Ledbury Town Reserves and Wyre Forest Brintons also left.

TABLE NOTES

The Birmingham League tables as published contained a number of errors. Additional research has succeeded in correcting all but those noted below.

1978-79   Division One: Total goals for 5 less than total goals against.

1999-2000 Division One (South): Table given assumes Bewdley won 4-0 away to Mahal on 4th December 1999, whereas one report gave the score as 5-0.

BIRMINGHAM & DISTRICT LEAGUE

1889-1890

Kidderminster Olympic	21	19	2	0	84	9	40
Kidderminster Harriers	21	13	2	6	75	38	28
Oldbury Town	21	11	4	6	43	33	26
Smethwick Carriage Works	21	11	3	7	72	46	25
Langley Green Victoria	21	9	7	5	52	40	25
Hednesford Town	19	7	3	9	50	72	17
Wellington St. George's	20	6	5	9	39	57	17
Aston Victoria	20	7	1	12	53	64	15
Unity Gas Department	21	5	5	11	34	66	15
Willenhall Pickwick	21	5	4	12	44	78	14
Ironbridge	22	5	3	14	46	65	13
Great Bridge Unity	20	6	1	13	41	65	13

As the fixtures were not completed, no champions were declared. Two games were ordered to be replayed but the replays never took place. Those two games are not included in the table above but the original results were:
Kidderminster Olympic 12 Aston Victoria 0
Great Bridge Unity 3 Kidderminster Harriers 2

1890-1891

Brierley Hill Alliance	17	9	5	3	41	23	23
Oldbury Town	15	8	2	5	31	35	18
Hednesford Town	13	8	1	4	46	15	17
Stourbridge	15	8	1	6	30	33	17
Langley Green Victoria	13	6	3	4	32	24	15
Wednesbury Old Athletic	11	6	1	4	37	22	13
Smethwick Carriage Works	16	6	1	9	35	47	13
Burton Alma	15	4	2	9	21	37	10
County Victoria	15	4	1	10	26	41	9
Kidderminster Rovers	12	3	1	8	13	35	7

As the fixtures were not completed, no champions were declared.
The table excludes: Wednesbury Old Athletic 9 Hednesford Town 0. This game was played as a friendly after the referee ruled the pitch unfit.
Kidderminster Rovers folded and withdrew in March.

1891-1892

Brierley Hill Alliance	15	12	2	1	56	8	26
Stourbridge	15	10	2	3	39	17	22
Aston Victoria	16	9	3	4	47	22	21
Smethwick Carriage Works	16	5	5	6	27	29	15
Kidderminster Harriers	15	5	4	6	25	30	14
Redditch Town	13	5	2	6	21	31	12
Langley Green Victoria	15	3	3	9	27	42	9
Oldbury Town	13	1	5	7	8	37	7
Great Bridge Unity	12	1	2	9	10	44	4

All fixtures were not completed as both Great Bridge Unity and Oldbury Town folded during the season. No champions were declared.

1892-1893

Wolverhampton Wanderers Res.	18	15	1	2	66	12	31
Aston Villa Reserves	18	15	1	2	81	18	31
Brierley Hill Alliance	18	11	1	6	38	23	23
West Bromwich Albion Reserves	18	8	5	5	33	25	21
Stourbridge	18	9	2	7	42	36	20
Old Hill Wanderers	18	7	4	7	34	43	18
Kidderminster Harriers	18	5	6	7	33	41	16
Redditch Town	18	4	2	12	23	53	10
Smethwick Carriage Works	18	3	2	13	20	69	8
Halesowen	18	0	2	16	14	64	2

1893-1894

Old Hill Wanderers	26	19	2	5	70	30	40
Aston Villa Reserves	26	16	5	5	76	46	37
Wolverhampton Wanderers Res.	26	14	5	7	66	39	33
Stourbridge	26	13	6	7	46	36	32
Halesowen	26	12	6	8	63	48	30
Brierley Hill Alliance	26	12	5	9	67	42	29
Small Heath Reserves	26	13	3	10	65	55	29
West Bromwich Albion Reserves	26	10	6	10	53	43	26
Worcester Rovers	26	10	4	12	53	61	24
Berwick Rangers	26	9	3	14	43	76	21
Smethwick Carriage Works	26	7	5	14	38	55	19
Stafford Rangers	26	5	6	15	38	70	16
Redditch Town	26	4	7	15	37	68	15
Kidderminster Harriers	26	6	1	19	36	82	13

1894-1895

Team	P	W	D	L	F	A	Pts
Aston Villa Reserves	30	26	3	1	133	35	55
West Bromwich Albion Reserves	30	23	4	3	100	49	50
Stourbridge	30	21	3	6	93	44	45
Wolverhampton Wanderers Res.	30	20	4	6	106	46	44
Berwick Rangers	30	14	9	7	51	41	37
Small Heath Reserves	30	16	4	10	118	65	36
Oldbury Town	30	13	3	14	64	64	29
Worcester Rovers	30	11	5	14	72	72	27
Brierley Hill Alliance	30	12	3	15	53	65	27
Old Hill Wanderers	30	11	5	14	44	65	27
Kidderminster Harriers	30	10	6	14	64	74	26
Redditch Town	30	12	0	18	64	96	24
Singers (Coventry)	30	7	5	18	46	91	19
Halesowen	30	4	5	21	45	102	13
Stafford Rangers	30	5	2	23	45	106	12
Smethwick	30	3	3	24	26	109	9

1895-1896

Team	P	W	D	L	F	A	Pts
Aston Villa Reserves	30	21	6	3	84	29	48
Small Heath Reserves	30	21	5	4	100	35	47
Wolverhampton Wanderers Res.	30	20	4	6	98	35	44
West Bromwich Albion Reserves	30	18	5	7	100	46	41
Stourbridge	30	15	6	9	50	30	36
Berwick Rangers	30	15	3	12	57	51	33
Hereford Thistle	30	15	3	12	61	62	33
Kidderminster Harriers	30	11	7	12	44	41	29
Halesowen	30	13	3	14	64	80	29
Worcester Rovers	30	12	4	14	51	55	28
Brierley Hill Alliance	30	9	5	16	40	59	23
Shrewsbury Town	30	8	5	17	46	98	21
Singers (Coventry)	30	9	2	19	36	68	20
Redditch Town	30	7	5	18	45	90	19
Oldbury Town	30	6	6	18	41	86	18
Stafford Rangers	30	5	1	24	35	87	11

1896-1897

Team	P	W	D	L	F	A	Pts
Hereford Thistle	30	23	3	4	82	25	49
Wolverhampton Wanderers Res.	30	20	4	6	77	29	44
Small Heath Reserves	30	15	8	7	76	43	38
Berwick Rangers	30	14	6	10	51	41	34
Hereford Town	30	14	5	11	60	47	33
Brierley Hill Alliance	30	14	5	11	53	52	33
Aston Villa Reserves	30	12	8	10	49	40	32
Worcester Rovers	30	10	10	10	56	65	30
Stourbridge	30	10	9	11	63	52	29
Kidderminster Harriers	30	10	8	12	52	45	28
West Bromwich Albion Reserves	30	11	4	15	56	68	26
Shrewsbury Town	30	11	3	16	58	67	25
Singers (Coventry)	30	10	5	15	45	63	25
Halesowen	30	11	3	16	49	91	25
Oldbury Town	30	6	7	17	34	60	19
Redditch Town	30	3	4	23	49	122	10

1897-1898

Team	P	W	D	L	F	A	Pts
Wolverhampton Wanderers Res.	30	21	8	1	93	16	50
Aston Villa Reserves	30	19	6	5	107	36	44
Bristol Eastville Rovers	30	20	4	6	84	34	44
Worcester Rovers	30	20	2	8	64	43	42
Small Heath Reserves	30	17	7	6	83	49	41
Bristol St. George's	30	12	6	12	50	45	30
Singers (Coventry)	30	13	3	14	50	59	29
Hereford Thistle	30	11	5	14	55	62	27
Stourbridge	30	11	5	14	45	65	27
Berwick Rangers	30	11	3	16	53	63	25
Shrewsbury Town	30	10	3	17	44	65	23
West Bromwich Albion Reserves	30	11	1	18	56	88	23
Hereford Town	30	9	5	16	33	64	23
Halesowen	30	8	6	16	58	81	22
Brierley Hill Alliance	30	6	4	20	43	83	16
Kidderminster Harriers	30	6	2	22	31	96	14

1898-1899

Team	P	W	D	L	F	A	Pts
Wolverhampton Wanderers Res.	34	29	2	3	118	19	60
Aston Villa Reserves	34	26	5	3	142	45	57
Stourbridge	34	21	5	8	85	54	47
Bristol Eastville Rovers	34	20	5	9	132	49	45
Small Heath Reserves	34	18	5	11	88	64	41
Bristol St. George's	34	17	5	12	87	69	39
Coventry City	34	13	7	14	57	63	33
West Bromwich Albion Reserves	34	14	5	15	65	81	33
Brierley Hill Alliance	34	14	4	16	57	82	32
Halesowen	34	13	2	19	70	84	28
Wellington Town	34	11	6	17	44	82	28
Hereford Town	34	10	7	17	41	63	27
Shrewsbury Town	34	10	6	18	65	90	26
Dudley	34	10	6	18	51	88	26
Kidderminster Harriers	34	11	4	19	45	85	26
Hereford Thistle	34	10	5	19	49	94	25
Worcester Rovers	34	8	5	21	48	89	21
Berwick Rangers	34	7	4	23	52	95	18

1899-1900

Team	P	W	D	L	F	A	Pts
Aston Villa Reserves	30	21	7	2	93	37	49
Wolverhampton Wanderers Res.	30	20	3	7	73	30	43
Dudley	30	19	4	7	93	43	42
Small Heath Reserves	30	16	4	10	63	49	36
West Bromwich Albion Reserves	30	14	4	12	69	57	32
Hereford Town	30	12	8	10	47	42	32
Stourbridge	30	11	9	10	73	59	31
Wellington Town	30	11	7	12	59	50	29
Bristol Rovers Reserves	30	11	6	13	50	63	28
Kidderminster Harriers	30	11	6	13	47	74	28
Halesowen	30	11	5	14	69	59	27
Brierley Hill Alliance	30	10	6	14	50	66	26
Walsall Reserves	30	9	6	15	51	81	24
Shrewsbury Town	30	9	3	18	40	73	21
Berwick Rangers	30	7	3	20	41	82	17
Coventry City	30	6	3	21	47	100	15

Wellington St. George's and Worcester Rovers resigned during the season and their records were expunged.

1900-1901

Team	P	W	D	L	F	A	Pts
Wolverhampton Wanderers Res.	34	29	3	2	107	18	61
Aston Villa Reserves	34	23	6	5	116	37	52
Stourbridge	34	17	8	9	68	52	42
Stoke Reserves	34	17	5	12	80	51	39
West Bromwich Albion Reserves	34	16	6	12	83	62	38
Stafford Rangers	34	16	6	12	57	49	38
Halesowen	34	16	6	12	82	71	38
Dudley	34	17	2	15	71	65	36
Small Heath Reserves	34	12	9	13	73	57	33
Brierley Hill Alliance	34	12	8	14	64	80	32
Hereford Town	34	13	6	15	46	61	32
Ruabon Druids	34	11	9	14	61	62	31
Berwick Rangers	34	12	6	16	48	53	30
Coventry City	34	10	6	18	63	102	26
Ironbridge	34	10	4	20	58	85	24
Wellington Town	34	9	5	20	50	89	23
Kidderminster Harriers	34	9	2	23	44	110	20
Shrewsbury Town	34	7	3	24	29	96	17

1901-1902

Team	P	W	D	L	F	A	Pts
West Bromwich Albion Reserves	34	26	2	6	126	32	54
Stourbridge	34	21	4	9	77	46	46
Crewe Alexandra	34	20	4	10	93	54	44
Aston Villa Reserves	34	18	6	10	91	49	42
Small Heath Reserves	34	19	4	11	79	45	42
Dudley	34	20	2	12	76	76	42
Wolverhampton Wanderers Res.	34	17	6	11	74	50	40
Stafford Rangers	34	18	2	14	85	68	38
Stoke Reserves	34	15	6	13	50	45	36
Ironbridge	34	15	3	16	61	67	33
Shrewsbury Town	34	14	4	16	57	80	32
Brierley Hill Alliance	34	13	4	17	75	82	30
Ruabon Druids	34	12	4	18	54	82	28
Halesowen	34	11	5	18	54	94	27
Berwick Rangers	34	11	4	19	59	71	26
Coventry City	34	7	6	21	42	97	20
Hereford Town	34	6	6	22	31	75	18
Kidderminster Harriers	34	5	4	25	38	109	14

1902-1903

Aston Villa Reserves	34	21	9	4	96	30	51
Crewe Alexandra	34	22	2	10	92	51	46
West Bromwich Albion Reserves	34	19	7	8	68	37	45
Stourbridge	34	18	5	11	81	49	41
Wolverhampton Wanderers Res.	34	17	6	11	81	61	40
Shrewsbury Town	34	13	11	10	60	44	37
Coventry City	34	15	6	13	75	67	36
Small Heath Reserves	34	14	8	12	67	61	36
Stafford Rangers	34	16	3	15	67	62	35
Stoke Reserves	34	14	6	14	63	45	34
Ruabon Druids	34	13	5	16	48	58	31
Dudley	34	13	5	16	56	77	31
Kidderminster Harriers	34	12	6	16	70	68	30
Halesowen	34	11	7	16	52	72	29
Worcester City & Berwick Rangers	34	12	2	20	40	67	26
Wellington Town	34	10	5	19	66	101	25
Brierley Hill Alliance	34	10	4	20	51	75	24
Ironbridge	34	4	7	23	35	143	15

1903-1904

Aston Villa Reserves	34	24	4	6	117	33	52
Stoke Reserves	34	21	6	7	89	55	48
Wellington Town	34	18	7	9	75	57	43
Crewe Alexandra	34	17	7	10	57	57	41
Small Heath Reserves	34	17	6	11	82	59	40
West Bromwich Albion Reserves	34	15	7	12	73	50	37
Wolverhampton Wanderers Res.	34	16	5	13	71	69	37
Stourbridge	34	13	10	11	80	58	36
Stafford Rangers	34	13	9	12	65	59	35
Shrewsbury Town	34	14	6	14	51	48	34
Coventry City	34	12	7	15	53	58	31
Kidderminster Harriers	34	12	6	16	57	66	30
Walsall	34	11	7	16	45	65	29
Halesowen	34	9	7	18	45	81	25
Worcester City	34	7	11	16	39	91	25
Ruabon Druids	34	10	4	20	63	78	24
Brierley Hill Alliance	34	7	10	17	47	77	24
Dudley	34	7	7	20	39	87	21

1904-1905

Aston Villa Reserves	34	23	4	7	109	34	50
Stoke Reserves	34	20	5	9	68	33	45
Kidderminster Harriers	34	17	10	7	54	32	44
Wolverhampton Wanderers Res.	34	17	9	8	66	39	43
Small Heath Reserves	34	19	4	11	75	59	42
Crewe Alexandra	34	16	9	9	53	44	41
Stafford Rangers	34	15	6	13	49	49	36
Brierley Hill Alliance	34	15	4	15	59	53	34
Worcester City	34	15	4	15	44	53	34
Dudley	34	13	6	15	55	62	32
Wellington Town	34	13	5	16	51	59	31
Burslem Port Vale Reserves	34	9	12	13	57	62	30
Stourbridge	34	13	3	18	43	56	29
Walsall	34	11	6	17	44	77	28
West Bromwich Albion Reserves	34	11	5	18	48	79	27
Shrewsbury Town	34	10	4	20	42	63	24
Coventry City	34	9	4	21	51	82	22
Halesowen	34	7	6	21	45	77	20

1905-1906

Aston Villa Reserves	34	24	5	5	121	46	53
Wolverhampton Wanderers Res.	34	22	5	7	81	43	49
West Bromwich Albion Reserves	34	21	6	7	106	51	48
Crewe Alexandra	34	16	12	6	58	39	44
Birmingham Reserves	34	16	7	11	91	58	39
Wrexham	34	17	5	12	72	55	39
Stourbridge	34	15	6	13	68	49	36
Stoke Reserves	34	14	7	13	71	60	35
Brierley Hill Alliance	34	15	5	14	74	70	35
Shrewsbury Town	34	15	3	16	57	84	33
Coventry City	34	13	6	15	64	61	32
Dudley	34	11	10	13	53	56	32
Kidderminster Harriers	34	12	6	16	42	51	30
Stafford Rangers	34	10	8	16	44	52	28
Worcester City	34	7	7	20	53	91	21
Walsall	34	7	6	21	42	89	20
Wellington Town	34	9	2	23	47	134	20
Burslem Port Vale Reserves	34	8	2	24	47	102	18

1906-1907

Aston Villa Reserves	34	23	4	7	102	44	50
Birmingham Reserves	34	19	5	10	84	47	43
Kidderminster Harriers	34	18	7	9	69	44	43
West Bromwich Albion Reserves	34	18	6	10	78	50	42
Wolverhampton Wanderers Res.	34	16	7	11	55	48	39
Brierley Hill Alliance	34	17	3	14	66	61	37
Coventry City	34	16	4	14	70	58	36
Crewe Alexandra	34	15	4	15	58	56	34
Stoke Reserves	34	13	8	13	62	64	34
Wrexham	34	14	6	14	68	76	34
Stourbridge	34	13	6	15	60	63	32
Halesowen	34	14	4	16	63	72	32
Walsall	34	14	4	16	58	79	32
Worcester City	34	12	5	17	69	75	29
Dudley	34	10	6	18	58	75	26
Stafford Rangers	34	10	6	18	56	89	26
Burslem Port Vale Reserves	34	8	8	18	53	83	24
Shrewsbury Town	34	7	5	22	61	106	19

1907-1908

Aston Villa Reserves	34	23	5	6	92	36	51
Crewe Alexandra	34	20	7	7	80	41	47
West Bromwich Albion Reserves	34	19	5	10	86	54	43
Coventry City	34	18	3	13	97	64	39
Shrewsbury Town	34	16	7	11	67	65	39
Wrexham	34	14	9	11	51	56	37
Kidderminster Harriers	34	16	5	13	55	64	37
Worcester City	34	17	2	15	76	56	36
Stafford Rangers	34	16	3	15	57	68	35
Walsall	34	15	3	16	67	72	33
Stoke Reserves	34	12	9	13	53	57	33
Dudley	34	14	4	16	57	68	32
Burton United	34	14	3	17	51	50	31
Birmingham Reserves	34	12	7	15	54	63	31
Halesowen	34	14	2	18	55	62	30
Brierley Hill Alliance	34	7	9	18	43	81	23
Wolverhampton Wanderers Res.	34	8	6	20	53	76	22
Stourbridge	34	5	3	26	31	92	13

1908-1909

Aston Villa Reserves	34	24	6	4	118	36	54
Crewe Alexandra	34	24	4	6	99	42	52
Wolverhampton Wanderers Res.	34	21	6	7	71	46	48
West Bromwich Albion Reserves	34	18	6	10	85	43	42
Brierley Hill Alliance	34	14	8	12	57	54	36
Shrewsbury Town	34	11	13	10	51	48	35
Kidderminster Harriers	34	13	6	15	58	85	32
Stoke	34	13	5	16	71	64	31
Worcester City	34	14	3	17	71	70	31
Stafford Rangers	34	11	9	14	51	63	31
Wrexham	34	14	3	17	60	76	31
Birmingham Reserves	34	11	7	16	53	73	29
Burton United	34	13	3	18	48	75	29
Stourbridge	34	9	10	15	49	57	28
Walsall	34	10	8	16	47	56	28
Wellington Town	34	11	5	18	60	86	27
Halesowen	34	11	4	19	42	83	26
Dudley	34	10	2	22	55	89	22

1909-1910

Aston Villa Reserves	34	25	4	5	98	36	54
Crewe Alexandra	34	23	3	8	117	56	49
Wolverhampton Wanderers Res.	34	22	5	7	74	46	49
Brierley Hill Alliance	34	19	8	7	79	49	46
Walsall	34	18	7	9	66	44	43
Birmingham Reserves	34	17	7	10	73	60	41
Stoke	34	15	7	12	82	52	37
West Bromwich Albion Reserves	34	16	5	13	76	65	37
Stourbridge	34	15	3	16	78	74	33
Wrexham	34	13	7	14	61	62	33
Shrewsbury Town	34	13	5	16	48	63	31
Worcester City	34	10	9	15	65	69	29
Wellington Town	34	10	7	17	48	76	27
Kidderminster Harriers	34	9	6	19	52	83	24
Dudley	34	9	5	20	65	87	23
Stafford Rangers	34	9	5	20	48	80	23
Halesowen	34	8	3	23	44	90	19
Burton United	34	6	2	26	36	121	14

1910-1911

Team	P	W	D	L	F	A	Pts
Stoke	34	24	2	8	95	48	50
Aston Villa Reserves	34	22	4	8	97	41	48
Walsall	34	20	6	8	60	44	46
Wrexham	34	17	7	10	74	52	41
Crewe Alexandra	34	16	8	10	85	61	40
Stourbridge	34	16	6	12	82	54	38
Worcester City	34	17	4	13	77	79	38
Wellington Town	34	15	7	12	65	62	37
West Bromwich Albion Reserves	34	13	8	13	54	58	34
Dudley	34	13	7	14	56	67	33
Shrewsbury Town	34	14	4	16	61	74	32
Wednesbury Old Athletic	34	14	2	18	61	82	30
Wolverhampton Wanderers Res.	34	12	5	17	69	75	29
Brierley Hill Alliance	34	10	9	15	63	75	29
Birmingham Reserves	34	11	4	19	73	92	26
Stafford Rangers	34	11	4	19	45	73	26
Kidderminster Harriers	34	6	8	20	37	66	20
Halesowen	34	6	3	25	48	99	15

1911-1912

Team	P	W	D	L	F	A	Pts
Aston Villa Reserves	34	24	5	5	111	56	53
Darlaston	34	19	8	7	69	45	46
Worcester City	34	20	3	11	80	49	43
Walsall	34	17	7	10	56	34	41
West Bromwich Albion Reserves	34	17	6	11	75	55	40
Wrexham	34	15	10	9	62	52	40
Wolverhampton Wanderers Res.	34	17	3	14	75	58	37
Kidderminster Harriers	34	15	6	13	55	53	36
Stoke Reserves	34	11	12	11	51	52	34
Dudley	34	14	5	15	66	62	33
Birmingham Reserves	34	13	6	15	60	68	32
Wednesbury Old Athletic	34	13	6	15	55	65	32
Brierley Hill Alliance	34	12	5	17	57	68	29
Willenhall Swifts	34	11	4	19	52	68	26
Wellington Town	34	8	10	16	43	60	26
Stourbridge	34	11	4	19	58	91	26
Shrewsbury Town	34	9	3	22	44	76	21
Stafford Rangers	34	7	3	24	38	95	17

1912-1913

Team	P	W	D	L	F	A	Pts
West Bromwich Albion Reserves	34	21	5	8	86	32	47
Coventry City Reserves	34	19	6	9	62	41	44
Worcester City	34	20	3	11	64	53	43
Willenhall Swifts	34	19	4	11	71	58	42
Birmingham Reserves	34	16	9	9	99	60	41
Wrexham	34	16	4	14	58	48	36
Walsall	34	15	5	14	60	54	35
Wellington Town	34	15	5	14	74	74	35
Dudley	34	15	4	15	53	75	34
Shrewsbury Town	34	14	5	15	59	50	33
Brierley Hill Alliance	34	12	9	13	55	61	33
Aston Villa Reserves	34	15	2	17	62	72	32
Wednesbury Old Athletic	34	13	3	18	63	71	29
Stoke Reserves	34	13	3	18	58	75	29
Darlaston	34	12	4	18	57	72	28
Wolverhampton Wanderers Res.	34	10	6	18	61	88	26
Kidderminster Harriers	34	9	5	20	39	63	23
Stourbridge	34	8	6	20	55	89	22

1913-1914

Team	P	W	D	L	F	A	Pts
Worcester City	34	20	8	6	93	33	48
Shrewsbury Town	34	21	5	8	76	48	47
Aston Villa Reserves	34	20	5	9	71	44	45
Stoke Reserves	34	17	7	10	73	46	41
Birmingham Reserves	34	18	3	13	79	51	39
Wolverhampton Wanderers Res.	34	16	6	12	64	56	38
Wrexham	34	15	8	11	46	47	38
Dudley	34	15	5	14	66	70	35
Stourbridge	34	12	10	12	59	48	34
Walsall	34	13	8	13	48	61	34
West Bromwich Albion Reserves	34	11	11	12	67	46	33
Kidderminster Harriers	34	11	8	15	61	85	30
Brierley Hill Alliance	34	12	5	17	43	76	29
Wednesbury Old Athletic	34	11	5	18	43	56	27
Darlaston	34	9	8	17	47	64	26
Coventry City Reserves	34	9	7	18	56	83	25
Willenhall Swifts	34	10	4	20	51	80	24
Wellington Town	34	7	5	22	48	97	19

1914-1915

Team	P	W	D	L	F	A	Pts
Birmingham Reserves	34	26	1	7	160	39	53
West Bromwich Albion Reserves	34	23	5	6	88	39	51
Walsall	34	21	5	8	66	44	47
Darlaston	34	19	4	11	83	47	42
Wolverhampton Wanderers Res.	34	19	3	12	84	73	41
Wrexham	34	16	8	10	63	49	40
Brierley Hill Alliance	34	16	8	10	55	52	40
Stoke Reserves	34	17	5	12	80	52	39
Aston Villa Reserves	34	15	8	11	96	65	38
Dudley	34	15	5	14	71	68	35
Stourbridge	34	12	9	13	68	65	33
Shrewsbury Town	34	12	6	16	62	69	30
Kidderminster Harriers	34	9	6	19	61	95	24
Worcester City	34	9	3	22	39	81	21
Wellington Town	34	9	3	22	44	98	21
Willenhall Swifts	34	6	9	19	37	88	21
Coventry City Reserves	34	8	4	22	52	115	20
Wednesbury Old Athletic	34	7	2	25	34	104	16

1919-1920

Team	P	W	D	L	F	A	Pts
West Bromwich Albion Reserves	34	18	9	7	61	45	45
Wellington Town	34	18	5	11	94	66	41
Wrexham	34	17	5	12	73	45	39
Coventry City Reserves	34	18	3	13	88	57	39
Hednesford Town	34	15	9	10	82	64	39
Birmingham Reserves	34	18	2	14	78	57	38
Stourbridge	34	16	5	13	77	78	37
Nuneaton Town	34	16	4	14	70	66	36
Wolverhampton Wanderers Res.	34	16	4	14	74	85	36
Darlaston	34	15	4	15	63	55	34
Willenhall	34	14	5	15	86	84	33
Stoke Reserves	34	14	4	16	73	68	32
Worcester City	34	12	6	16	62	69	30
Shrewsbury Town	34	14	2	18	59	95	30
Kidderminster Harriers	34	11	7	16	55	76	29
Walsall	34	11	6	17	53	62	28
Wednesbury Old Athletic	34	11	5	18	42	72	27
Brierley Hill Alliance	34	7	5	22	42	88	19

1920-1921

Team	P	W	D	L	F	A	Pts
Wellington Town	34	26	1	7	84	25	53
Birmingham Reserves	34	24	5	5	91	35	53
Wrexham	34	22	5	7	77	32	49
Hednesford Town	34	18	9	7	74	53	45
Walsall	34	18	6	10	68	47	42
Shrewsbury Town	34	17	4	13	69	55	38
West Bromwich Albion Reserves	34	15	7	12	46	41	37
Willenhall	34	16	5	13	63	73	37
Coventry City Reserves	34	12	9	13	56	57	33
Stourbridge	34	12	7	15	61	61	31
Nuneaton Town	34	11	9	14	54	61	31
Stoke Reserves	34	11	6	17	46	62	28
Darlaston	34	8	9	17	38	61	25
Brierley Hill Alliance	34	10	5	19	38	65	25
Wolverhampton Wanderers Res.	34	8	8	18	56	70	24
Kidderminster Harriers	34	8	7	19	46	67	23
Worcester City	34	8	4	22	44	93	20
Wednesbury Old Athletic	34	6	6	22	33	86	18

1921-1922

Team	P	W	D	L	F	A	Pts
Willenhall	34	23	7	4	86	44	53
Wellington Town	34	22	5	7	102	34	49
Hednesford Town	34	20	5	9	89	39	45
Nuneaton Town	34	19	6	9	77	47	44
Shrewsbury Town	34	14	12	8	71	54	40
Bilston United	34	17	6	11	84	68	40
Darlaston	34	15	8	11	55	36	38
Worcester City	34	14	5	15	61	61	33
Burton All Saints	34	12	9	13	42	45	33
Cannock Town	34	14	4	16	67	71	32
Stourbridge	34	11	9	14	49	62	31
Brierley Hill Alliance	34	13	5	16	48	76	31
Stafford Rangers	34	12	6	16	74	66	30
Coventry City Reserves	34	10	10	14	54	61	30
Kidderminster Harriers	34	13	2	19	40	82	28
Tamworth Castle	34	5	10	19	28	66	20
Redditch	34	7	4	23	36	78	18
Wednesbury Old Athletic	34	6	5	23	32	105	17

1922-1923

	P	W	D	L	F	A	Pts
Shrewsbury Town	34	23	4	7	82	41	50
Bilston United	34	22	3	9	100	46	47
Nuneaton Town	34	20	5	9	77	45	45
Worcester City	34	18	7	9	64	50	43
Willenhall	34	16	9	9	76	44	41
Stourbridge	34	18	5	11	66	46	41
Wellington Town	34	18	2	14	63	47	38
Darlaston	34	16	6	12	61	50	38
Cradley Heath	34	12	13	9	60	52	37
Burton All Saints	34	13	8	13	58	50	34
Redditch	34	15	3	16	59	65	33
Hednesford Town	34	11	9	14	55	63	31
Stafford Rangers	34	10	8	16	65	72	28
Brierley Hill Alliance	34	11	3	20	46	80	25
Cannock Town	34	7	9	18	42	79	23
Kidderminster Harriers	34	8	6	20	37	71	22
Wednesbury Old Athletic	34	7	6	21	41	94	20
Tamworth Castle	34	5	6	23	41	98	16

1923-1924

	P	W	D	L	F	A	Pts
Stourbridge	34	22	8	4	70	21	52
Shrewsbury Town	34	21	3	10	78	43	45
Willenhall	34	20	4	10	77	47	44
Wellington Town	34	18	6	10	76	42	42
Worcester City	34	16	9	9	61	46	41
Burton All Saints	34	17	4	13	76	54	38
Cradley Heath	34	16	6	12	66	47	38
Redditch	34	16	3	15	56	57	35
Hednesford Town	34	15	5	14	60	67	35
Oakengates Town	34	13	6	15	64	71	32
Darlaston	34	11	10	13	47	64	32
Bilston United	34	13	5	16	55	63	31
Nuneaton Town	34	13	3	18	62	64	29
Cannock Town	34	11	7	16	57	73	29
Kidderminster Harriers	34	12	5	17	44	60	29
Stafford Rangers	34	11	5	18	48	71	27
Brierley Hill Alliance	34	8	7	19	38	81	23
Wednesbury Old Athletic	34	3	4	27	34	98	10

1924-1925

	P	W	D	L	F	A	Pts
Worcester City	34	18	10	6	74	35	46
Kidderminster Harriers	34	21	4	9	71	37	46
Stourbridge	34	18	7	9	94	43	43
Cradley Heath	34	16	10	8	63	35	42
Wellington Town	34	16	9	9	72	44	41
Burton Town	34	17	6	11	79	46	40
Brierley Hill Alliance	34	18	4	12	53	52	40
Redditch	34	16	6	12	75	60	38
Shrewsbury Town	34	16	5	13	75	46	37
Oswestry Town	34	15	7	12	80	57	37
Wellington St. George's	34	14	7	13	60	59	35
Willenhall	34	14	6	14	64	53	34
Stafford Rangers	34	12	8	14	52	65	32
Oakengates Town	34	9	11	14	50	69	29
Bilston United	34	9	6	19	49	79	24
Cannock Town	34	8	2	24	34	108	18
Darlaston	34	5	6	23	38	115	16
Hednesford Town	34	4	6	24	46	126	14

1925-1926

	P	W	D	L	F	A	Pts
Cradley Heath	34	24	5	5	100	38	53
Stourbridge	34	15	13	6	66	45	43
Wellington Town	34	17	7	10	86	44	41
Willenhall	34	18	5	11	70	60	41
Shrewsbury Town	34	17	4	13	76	59	38
Kidderminster Harriers	34	16	5	13	75	68	37
Oakengates Town	34	17	2	15	73	90	36
Brierley Hill Alliance	34	14	7	13	62	53	35
Bilston United	34	12	11	11	65	68	35
Oswestry Town	34	13	7	14	77	79	33
Worcester City	34	12	8	14	58	53	32
Burton Town	34	14	3	17	87	78	31
Darlaston	34	12	7	15	63	72	31
Wellington St. George's	34	12	6	16	77	86	30
Stafford Rangers	34	12	5	17	79	91	29
Cannock Town	34	9	10	15	68	80	28
Redditch	34	11	5	18	72	97	27
Hednesford Town	34	5	2	27	47	140	12

1926-1927

	P	W	D	L	F	A	Pts
Stafford Rangers	34	22	6	6	108	50	50
Burton Town	34	22	5	7	86	40	49
Kidderminster Harriers	34	19	7	8	79	49	45
Cradley Heath	34	17	9	8	79	42	43
Stourbridge	34	17	5	12	95	65	39
Brierley Hill Alliance	34	16	5	13	84	80	37
Wellington Town	34	16	4	14	76	65	36
Bilston United	34	16	4	14	64	73	36
Worcester City	34	14	6	14	68	67	34
Oakengates Town	34	13	6	15	58	70	32
Wellington St. George's	34	14	4	16	67	90	32
Willenhall	34	13	5	16	77	72	31
Shrewsbury Town	34	13	4	17	73	79	30
Cannock Town	34	12	5	17	51	73	29
Redditch	34	10	6	18	69	75	26
Hednesford Town	34	11	3	20	73	103	25
Darlaston	34	9	3	22	62	112	21
Oswestry Town	34	5	7	22	68	132	17

1927-1928

	P	W	D	L	F	A	Pts
Burton Town	34	25	3	6	107	40	53
Wellington Town	34	25	3	6	109	50	53
Stafford Rangers	34	24	2	8	127	71	50
Shrewsbury Town	34	20	4	10	119	71	44
Brierley Hill Alliance	34	20	1	13	90	81	41
Stourbridge	34	17	5	12	74	68	39
Willenhall	34	17	4	13	77	64	38
Cradley Heath	34	16	5	13	79	62	37
Oswestry Town	34	14	5	15	102	110	33
Kidderminster Harriers	34	10	11	13	57	74	31
Wellington St. George's	34	13	4	17	77	85	30
Bilston United	34	10	8	16	59	85	28
Hednesford Town	34	11	5	18	80	116	27
Oakengates Town	34	10	5	19	74	86	25
Redditch	34	9	7	18	66	107	25
Worcester City	34	9	6	19	57	76	24
Cannock Town	34	8	8	18	55	87	24
Darlaston	34	4	2	28	43	119	10

1928-1929

	P	W	D	L	F	A	Pts
Worcester City	34	25	1	8	102	48	51
Stafford Rangers	34	21	7	6	93	42	49
Oswestry Town	34	22	4	8	126	69	48
Wellington Town	34	16	11	7	92	44	43
Shrewsbury Town	34	19	3	12	97	69	41
Walsall Reserves	34	18	3	13	75	64	39
Cradley Heath	34	15	8	11	82	61	38
Willenhall	34	17	3	14	81	77	37
Burton Town	34	13	10	11	77	79	36
Bilston United	34	14	8	12	78	103	36
Hereford United	34	14	7	13	86	61	35
Kidderminster Harriers	34	12	10	12	78	76	34
Brierley Hill Alliance	34	10	10	14	56	69	30
Hednesford Town	34	12	4	18	69	88	28
Stourbridge	34	10	2	22	70	114	22
Oakengates Town	34	6	6	22	54	117	18
Redditch	34	5	6	23	54	113	16
Wellington St. George's	34	2	7	25	42	118	11

1929-1930

	P	W	D	L	F	A	Pts
Worcester City	34	26	3	5	153	40	55
Stafford Rangers	34	22	3	9	100	61	47
Cradley Heath	34	20	2	12	105	49	42
Shrewsbury Town	34	19	4	11	78	55	42
Brierley Hill Alliance	34	19	4	11	82	65	42
Burton Town	34	19	2	13	90	59	40
Kidderminster Harriers	34	16	6	12	68	70	38
Oakengates Town	34	16	4	14	70	76	36
Oswestry Town	34	15	5	14	103	87	35
Kettering Town Reserves	34	14	7	13	63	58	35
Walsall Reserves	34	14	4	16	71	74	32
Wellington Town	34	12	6	16	63	74	30
Hereford United	34	11	7	16	79	83	29
Willenhall	34	12	4	18	70	110	28
Stourbridge	34	13	1	20	84	122	27
Hednesford Town	34	12	1	21	78	108	25
Bilston United	34	5	5	24	35	112	15
Wellington St. George's	34	5	4	25	46	135	14

1930-1931

Cradley Heath	34	23	3	8	91	50	49
Oakengates Town	34	21	7	6	92	52	49
Stafford Rangers	34	18	11	5	114	56	47
Burton Town	34	18	6	10	112	61	42
Worcester City	34	18	5	11	106	59	41
Brierley Hill Alliance	34	17	7	10	81	54	41
Walsall Reserves	34	17	7	10	77	75	41
Wellington Town	34	18	3	13	82	76	39
Shrewsbury Town	34	14	5	15	76	79	33
Kidderminster Harriers	34	12	8	14	73	72	32
Kettering Town	34	11	8	15	72	83	30
Hereford United	34	11	8	15	55	75	30
Hednesford Town	34	11	5	18	71	92	27
Oswestry Town	34	12	3	19	83	111	27
Bilston United	34	10	4	20	59	84	24
Stourbridge	34	7	9	18	71	113	23
West Bromwich Albion "A"	34	6	7	21	47	97	19
Wellington St. George's	34	7	4	23	60	133	18

1931-1932

Cradley Heath	34	21	5	8	93	46	47
Worcester City	34	21	5	8	118	62	47
Oakengates Town	34	19	5	10	83	61	43
Burton Town	34	18	5	11	94	69	41
Rhyl Athletic	34	18	2	14	94	79	38
Colwyn Bay United	34	16	5	13	79	78	37
Hereford United	34	16	4	14	75	70	36
Brierley Hill Alliance	34	15	5	14	65	71	35
Stafford Rangers	34	13	7	14	54	56	33
Shrewsbury Town	34	13	7	14	64	82	33
Stourbridge	34	11	9	14	59	69	31
Kidderminster Harriers	34	13	4	17	67	66	30
Wellington Town	34	12	6	16	67	80	30
Bilston United	34	12	6	16	48	89	30
Wrexham Reserves	34	11	5	18	60	70	27
Oswestry Town	34	12	3	19	71	91	27
Walsall Reserves	34	10	6	18	58	70	26
Hednesford Town	34	8	5	21	58	98	21

1932-1933

Wrexham Reserves	34	22	6	6	91	49	50
Worcester City	34	21	3	10	108	52	45
Wellington Town	34	19	6	9	85	53	44
Hereford United	34	18	7	9	78	58	43
Bangor City	34	15	7	12	76	59	37
Brierley Hill Alliance	34	14	9	11	82	71	37
Burton Town	34	16	4	14	92	64	36
Shrewsbury Town	34	15	6	13	70	62	36
Cradley Heath	34	14	8	12	78	71	36
Hednesford Town	34	16	3	15	90	76	35
Rhyl Athletic	34	16	3	15	68	72	35
Stourbridge	34	11	10	13	77	82	32
Colwyn Bay United	34	12	5	17	65	99	29
Kidderminster Harriers	34	10	5	19	65	87	25
Oswestry Town	34	10	5	19	64	101	25
Oakengates Town	34	10	5	19	47	93	25
Stafford Rangers	34	9	6	19	64	89	24
Walsall Reserves	34	7	4	23	48	110	18

1933-1934

Wrexham Reserves	38	27	3	8	131	52	57
Worcester City	38	24	3	11	118	62	51
Kidderminster Harriers	38	23	5	10	115	75	51
Port Vale Reserves	38	22	7	9	91	67	51
Hereford United	38	23	4	11	97	61	50
Burton Town	38	22	5	11	103	51	49
Rhyl Athletic	37	20	6	11	82	61	46
Nuneaton Town	38	21	3	14	80	65	45
Bangor City	38	20	4	14	84	62	44
Shrewsbury Town	38	18	6	14	89	77	42
Hednesford Town	37	16	7	14	92	71	39
Brierley Hill Alliance	38	17	3	18	89	76	37
Wellington Town	38	15	5	18	88	106	35
Stourbridge	38	14	3	21	84	89	31
Stafford Rangers	38	9	8	21	65	118	26
Oswestry Town	38	11	3	24	79	117	25
Cannock Town	38	10	4	24	62	110	24
Colwyn Bay United	38	10	4	24	63	126	24
Cradley Heath	38	8	5	25	51	109	21
Oakengates Town	38	4	2	32	44	152	10

Hednesford Town vs Rhyl Athletic was not played.

1934-1935

Wellington Town	36	26	4	6	131	51	56
Kidderminster Harriers	36	25	2	9	100	49	52
Nuneaton Town	36	23	6	7	85	44	52
Shrewsbury Town	36	21	6	9	81	43	48
Wrexham Reserves	36	23	1	12	117	68	47
Worcester City	36	20	7	9	90	60	47
Burton Town	36	19	4	13	102	59	42
Stourbridge	36	17	7	12	100	72	41
Hereford United	36	14	9	13	88	79	37
Cradley Heath	36	17	2	17	76	98	36
Hednesford Town	36	13	9	14	59	80	35
Colwyn Bay United	36	12	6	18	69	96	30
Oswestry Town	36	13	2	21	59	80	28
Bangor City	36	10	7	19	62	100	27
Stafford Rangers	36	8	6	22	58	90	22
Brierley Hill Alliance	36	9	4	23	49	83	22
Rhyl Athletic	36	8	6	22	59	115	22
Oakengates Town	36	8	5	23	60	112	21
Cannock Town	36	9	1	26	54	120	19

1935-1936

Wellington Town	38	29	3	6	129	37	61
Brierley Hill Alliance	38	28	2	8	128	70	58
Shrewsbury Town	38	26	1	11	124	70	53
Kidderminster Harriers	38	24	5	9	104	66	53
Worcester City	38	19	11	8	104	68	49
Cardiff City Reserves	38	21	5	12	102	69	47
Wrexham Reserves	38	19	5	14	92	77	43
Dudley Town	38	17	7	14	91	72	41
Hednesford Town	38	17	4	17	80	82	38
Hereford United	38	15	4	19	77	81	34
Stafford Rangers	38	15	4	19	84	90	34
Bangor City	38	15	4	19	83	97	34
Stourbridge	38	15	3	20	110	111	33
Rhyl Athletic	38	10	11	17	80	81	31
Oswestry Town	38	13	5	20	71	97	31
Nuneaton Town	38	14	2	22	66	84	30
Cradley Heath	38	9	9	20	69	114	27
Oakengates Town	38	10	5	23	73	115	25
Cannock Town	38	8	4	26	56	161	20
Colwyn Bay United	38	6	6	26	52	133	18

1936-1937

Bristol Rovers Reserves	36	24	8	4	127	44	56
Shrewsbury Town	36	23	4	9	133	64	50
Brierley Hill Alliance	36	22	4	10	106	59	48
Wellington Town	36	20	7	9	114	55	47
Cardiff City Reserves	36	21	2	13	87	57	44
Stafford Rangers	35	19	3	13	68	65	41
Kidderminster Harriers	35	18	4	13	90	54	40
Bangor City	36	18	3	15	80	81	39
Dudley Town	36	16	6	14	63	61	38
Worcester City	36	15	6	15	70	66	36
Stourbridge	36	15	5	16	95	77	35
Hereford United	36	15	4	17	61	82	34
Wrexham Reserves	36	13	6	17	73	85	32
Cradley Heath	36	13	3	20	71	85	29
Oswestry Town	36	12	3	21	62	100	27
Hednesford Town	36	10	4	22	56	113	24
Nuneaton Town	36	9	5	22	65	115	23
Oakengates Town	36	10	1	25	62	148	21
Colwyn Bay United	36	7	4	25	51	123	18

Cannock Town resigned during the season. Their record was expunged. Stafford Rangers vs Kidderminster Harriers was abandoned with two minutes remaining when many of the crowd invaded the pitch when Kidderminster were leading 2-1. The score was not included in the final table, nor was the game replayed. Stafford's ground was closed for three weeks at the start of the next season as a punishment.

1937-1938

Kidderminster Harriers	26	17	9	0	60	22	43
Stourbridge	26	18	2	6	64	37	38
Brierley Hill Alliance	26	17	2	7	72	34	36
Oswestry Town	26	16	2	8	65	46	34
Wellington Town	26	12	6	8	55	41	30
Cardiff City Reserves	26	13	3	10	62	48	29
Worcester City	26	11	3	12	50	53	25
Bangor City	26	10	5	11	42	57	25
Hereford United	26	8	7	11	40	44	23
Oakengates Town	26	8	6	12	41	59	22
Dudley Town	26	8	2	16	44	66	18
Wrexham Reserves	26	6	6	14	38	64	18
Stafford Rangers	26	5	5	16	41	58	15
Cradley Heath	26	2	4	20	29	74	8

Hednesford Town resigned during the season and their record was
expunged.

1938-1939

Keys Cup

Kidderminster Harriers	18	16	1	1	70	14	33
Stourbridge	18	10	6	2	60	34	26
Oswestry Town	18	10	0	8	46	43	20
Brierley Hill Alliance & Revo Sports	18	8	1	9	42	40	17
Cradley Heath	18	7	3	8	34	41	17
Stafford Rangers	18	7	2	9	29	44	16
Dudley Town and Vono Sports	18	6	3	9	37	53	15
Shrewsbury Town Reserves	18	7	0	11	34	49	14
Hereford United	18	6	1	11	39	47	13
Hednesford	18	4	1	13	34	60	9

Brierley Hill Alliance resigned during the season and their fixtures were
taken over by Revo Sports.
Dudley Town resigned during the season and their fixtures were taken
over by Vono Sports.

League Cup

Kidderminster Harriers	18	14	2	2	57	18	30
Stourbridge	18	13	2	3	65	28	28
Oswestry Town	18	11	1	6	42	43	23
Shrewsbury Town Reserves	18	9	3	6	47	28	21
Hereford United	18	7	2	9	28	29	16
Vono Sports	18	6	4	8	38	40	16
Stafford Rangers	18	8	0	10	30	45	16
Cradley Heath	18	7	0	11	34	38	14
Hednesford	18	5	3	10	34	54	13
Revo Sports	18	1	1	16	13	65	3

1946-1947

Halesowen Town	18	12	4	2	56	27	28
Wellington Town Reserves	18	12	1	5	64	26	25
Aston Villa "A"	18	10	3	5	41	36	23
Shrewsbury Town Reserves	18	11	0	7	56	44	22
Kettering Town	18	10	1	7	58	42	21
Hereford United Reserves	18	7	5	6	45	44	19
Oswestry Town	18	7	2	9	48	51	16
Cheltenham Town Reserves	18	4	3	11	35	51	11
Walsall "A"	18	3	2	13	22	61	8
Gloucester City Reserves	18	2	3	13	31	74	7

1947-1948

Kettering Town	26	20	1	5	83	33	41
Kidderminster Harriers	26	15	5	6	72	43	35
Oswestry Town	26	16	2	8	63	46	34
Halesowen Town	26	14	5	7	65	46	33
Wellington Town Reserves	26	12	5	9	74	51	29
Wolverhampton Wanderers "A"	26	14	1	11	52	53	29
Cradley Heath	26	13	2	11	58	62	28
Lye Town	26	10	5	11	56	57	25
Worcester City Reserves	26	10	3	13	49	49	23
Aston Villa "A"	26	8	6	12	46	53	22
Shrewsbury Town Reserves	26	9	3	14	55	65	21
Hereford United Reserves	26	9	2	15	60	70	20
Walsall "A"	26	7	2	17	39	74	16
Gloucester City Reserves	26	3	2	21	29	99	8

1948-1949

Worcester City Reserves	34	23	6	5	85	38	52
Kettering Town	34	24	3	7	91	38	51
Brush Sports	34	23	5	6	111	50	51
Brierley Hill Alliance	34	22	5	7	84	53	49
Lye Town	34	20	3	11	96	69	43
Wellington Town Reserves	34	18	4	12	89	74	40
Halesowen Town	34	15	7	12	78	53	37
Shrewsbury Town Reserves	34	13	8	13	81	72	34
Cradley Heath	34	12	5	17	52	70	29
Oswestry Town	34	7	14	13	48	73	28
Kidderminster Harriers Reserves	34	12	4	18	55	76	28
Wolverhampton Wanderers "A"	34	10	7	17	59	62	27
Gloucester City Reserves	34	12	3	19	50	98	27
Hereford United Reserves	34	11	4	19	62	74	26
Stoke City "A"	34	11	3	20	45	83	25
Aston Villa "A"	34	8	9	17	57	68	25
Walsall "A"	34	7	10	17	47	87	24
Leicester City "A"	34	7	2	25	37	104	16

1949-1950

Hereford United Reserves	36	24	5	7	92	39	53
Brierley Hill Alliance	36	22	7	7	77	51	51
Brush Sports	36	20	9	7	93	53	49
Wolverhampton Wanderers "A"	36	20	8	8	66	53	48
Cradley Heath	36	19	9	8	81	49	47
Oswestry Town	36	19	9	10	86	58	43
Shrewsbury Town Reserves	36	16	6	14	75	68	38
Lye Town	36	15	8	13	86	79	38
Halesowen Town	36	15	7	14	66	58	37
Whitwick Colliery	36	17	2	17	76	72	36
Gloucester City Reserves	36	14	6	16	74	82	36
Aston Villa "A"	36	14	7	15	50	44	35
Kettering Town	36	15	4	17	84	70	34
Boldmere St. Michaels	36	12	8	16	36	63	32
Kidderminster Harriers Reserves	36	12	4	20	48	66	28
Worcester City Reserves	36	9	6	21	47	76	24
Wellington Town Reserves	36	8	5	23	41	86	21
Walsall "A"	36	7	4	25	40	101	18
Stoke City "A"	36	5	6	25	41	91	16

1950-1951

Brierley Hill Alliance	36	28	3	5	129	49	59
Hereford United Reserves	36	24	3	9	91	31	51
Boldmere St. Michaels	36	19	11	6	75	47	49
Brush Sports	36	20	7	9	77	42	47
Shrewsbury Town Reserves	36	18	8	10	82	60	44
Cradley Heath	36	17	8	11	73	44	42
Oswestry Town	36	18	3	15	83	72	39
Halesowen Town	36	15	7	14	66	76	37
Aston Villa "A"	36	14	6	16	54	45	34
Whitwick Colliery	36	14	5	17	79	97	33
Wellington Town Reserves	36	14	3	19	81	84	31
Gloucester City Reserves	36	14	3	19	58	80	31
Stoke City "A"	36	12	7	17	46	71	31
Kidderminster Harriers Reserves	36	13	3	20	64	89	29
Walsall "A"	36	9	9	18	54	98	27
Burton Albion	36	10	6	20	63	97	26
Worcester City Reserves	36	11	4	21	51	99	26
Wolverhampton Wanderers "A"	36	9	6	21	75	86	24
Lye Town	36	9	6	21	57	91	24

1951-1952

Brierley Hill Alliance	34	24	5	5	115	36	53
Hereford United Reserves	34	20	7	7	87	61	47
Oswestry Town	34	21	4	9	93	50	46
Lye Town	34	18	6	10	78	56	42
Burton Albion	34	17	7	10	81	62	41
Halesowen Town	34	18	2	14	70	60	38
Wolverhampton Wanderers "A"	34	14	8	12	75	67	36
Kidderminster Harriers Reserves	34	14	7	13	72	70	35
Boldmere St. Michaels	34	16	3	15	64	87	35
Worcester City Reserves	34	12	9	13	68	65	33
Aston Villa "A"	34	14	5	15	55	53	33
Brush Sports	34	12	8	14	65	68	32
Shrewsbury Town Reserves	34	14	3	17	62	61	31
Whitwick Colliery	34	11	4	19	77	100	26
Cradley Heath	34	8	9	17	63	85	25
Stoke City "A"	34	10	4	20	49	70	24
Wellington Town Reserves	34	9	6	19	47	79	24
Walsall "A"	34	4	3	27	37	128	11

1952-1953

Oswestry Town	36	27	5	4	95	40	59
Kidderminster Harriers Reserves	36	24	3	9	91	45	51
Brierley Hill Alliance	36	21	7	8	117	53	49
Burton Albion	36	20	8	8	95	45	48
Nuneaton Borough	36	19	5	12	81	50	43
Hereford United Reserves	36	15	13	8	79	61	43
Brush Sports	36	19	5	12	76	62	43
Halesowen Town	36	18	6	12	97	74	42
Shrewsbury Town Reserves	36	17	7	12	89	73	41
Worcester City Reserves	36	17	4	15	93	87	38
Lye Town	36	14	8	14	79	90	36
Wolverhampton Wanderers "A"	36	13	6	17	69	73	32
Wellington Town Reserves	36	12	5	19	61	92	29
Bloxwich Strollers	36	10	6	20	51	96	26
Cradley Heath	36	9	7	20	63	94	25
Aston Villa "A"	36	10	5	21	60	93	25
Whitwick Colliery	36	8	6	22	86	126	22
Boldmere St. Michaels	36	8	1	27	47	123	17
Walsall "A"	36	5	5	26	43	95	15

1953-1954

Wolverhampton Wanderers "A"	46	33	5	8	158	57	71
Burton Albion	46	31	6	9	120	58	68
Brierley Hill Alliance	46	29	5	12	138	72	63
Nuneaton Borough	46	27	8	11	129	59	62
Kidderminster Harriers Reserves	46	27	8	11	100	73	62
Hednesford	46	25	7	14	122	81	57
Hereford United Reserves	46	23	10	13	124	74	56
Redditch	46	26	4	16	109	76	56
Oswestry Town	46	24	6	16	122	82	54
Bromsgrove Rovers	46	25	4	17	125	98	54
Stourbridge	46	25	3	18	89	68	53
Worcester City Reserves	46	22	5	19	116	119	49
Halesowen Town	46	19	8	19	99	104	46
Shrewsbury Town Reserves	46	17	11	18	98	86	45
Lye Town	46	17	9	20	89	96	43
Brush Sports	46	15	11	20	98	101	41
Aston Villa "A"	46	16	6	24	91	126	38
Walsall Reserves	46	14	7	25	66	112	35
Cradley Heath	46	10	11	25	64	114	31
Wellington Town Reserves	46	10	9	27	76	126	29
Whitwick Colliery	46	9	9	28	110	169	27
Bloxwich Strollers	46	8	11	27	58	138	27
Boldmere St. Michaels	46	5	9	32	70	194	19
Dudley Town	46	4	10	32	56	144	18

1954-1955

Southern Division

Redditch	38	27	6	5	110	41	60
Lockheed (Leamington)	38	24	7	7	122	54	55
Brierley Hill Alliance	38	23	7	8	105	61	53
Banbury Spencer	38	20	11	7	84	42	51
Rugby Town	38	21	7	10	91	54	49
Worcester City Reserves	38	22	4	12	103	60	48
Stourbridge	38	21	6	11	86	56	48
Bromsgrove Rovers	38	18	8	12	77	56	44
Halesowen Town	38	20	4	14	100	84	44
Lye Town	38	18	4	16	76	72	40
Kidderminster Harriers Reserves	38	17	5	16	79	83	39
Cheltenham Town Reserves	38	17	3	18	67	87	37
Moor Green	38	15	4	19	74	78	34
Cradley Heath	38	9	9	20	70	83	27
Hereford United Reserves	38	11	5	22	73	97	27
Symingtons	38	11	5	22	64	97	27
Aston Villa "A"	38	8	5	25	56	108	21
Sutton Town	38	7	6	25	53	117	20
Dudley Town	38	6	7	25	54	125	19
Boldmere St. Michaels	38	5	7	26	41	130	17

Northern Division

Nuneaton Borough	38	26	7	5	112	43	59
Wolverhampton Wanderers "A"	38	24	2	12	106	65	50
Burton Albion	38	23	3	12	100	50	49
Shrewsbury Town Reserves	38	20	6	12	103	68	46
Brush Sports	38	19	7	12	90	57	45
Walsall Reserves	38	20	5	13	83	71	45
Bedworth Town	38	20	4	14	95	59	44
Bilston	38	17	10	11	86	65	44
Hinckley Athletic	38	18	7	13	89	77	43
Whitwick Colliery	38	18	6	14	95	70	42
Oswestry Town	38	17	6	15	84	72	40
Gresley Rovers	38	13	11	14	66	70	37
Hednesford	38	14	8	16	72	79	36
Atherstone Town	38	15	5	18	88	101	35
Tamworth	38	13	8	17	67	75	34
Leek Town	38	10	9	19	64	94	29
Darlaston	38	8	8	22	57	110	24
Wellington Town Reserves	38	8	5	25	59	123	21
Birch Coppice	38	6	8	24	47	99	20
Bloxwich Strollers	38	7	3	28	47	162	17

1955-1956

Division One

Nuneaton Borough	38	24	8	6	109	55	56
Stourbridge	38	24	5	9	85	48	53
Banbury Spencer	38	23	6	9	68	40	52
Lockheed (Leamington)	38	21	6	11	96	60	48
Burton Albion	38	20	7	11	82	48	47
Brierley Hill Alliance	38	18	8	12	91	81	44
Brush Sports	38	20	4	14	58	56	44
Bedworth Town	38	16	7	15	74	60	39
Wolverhampton Wanderers "A"	38	17	5	16	70	60	39
Bromsgrove Rovers	38	14	10	14	74	67	38
Halesowen Town	38	15	6	17	75	74	36
Walsall Reserves	38	13	9	16	66	68	35
Shrewsbury Town Reserves	38	13	7	18	84	87	33
Rugby Town	38	12	9	17	72	86	33
Worcester City Reserves	38	14	4	20	65	95	32
Whitwick Colliery	38	10	11	17	62	87	31
Bilston	38	10	8	20	53	100	28
Hinckley Athletic	38	12	3	23	75	83	27
Redditch	38	7	10	21	50	101	24
Lye Town	38	7	7	24	50	103	21

Division Two

Tamworth	36	26	5	5	107	46	57
Atherstone Town	36	26	4	6	126	57	56
Aston Villa "A"	36	22	6	8	100	49	50
Oswestry Town	36	22	5	9	90	55	49
Gresley Rovers	36	21	5	10	78	50	47
Cradley Heath	36	18	8	10	75	47	44
West Bromwich Albion "A"	36	18	6	12	85	61	42
Hereford United Reserves	36	17	3	16	98	84	37
Evesham United	36	14	7	15	88	79	35
Hednesford	36	15	5	16	68	81	35
Cheltenham Town Reserves	36	15	4	17	82	71	34
Moor Green	36	15	3	18	78	96	33
Wellington Town Reserves	36	11	5	20	72	102	27
Darlaston	36	10	6	20	48	66	26
Kidderminster Harriers Reserves	36	11	4	21	79	112	26
Boldmere St. Michaels	36	11	2	23	66	100	24
Dudley Town	36	8	6	22	50	101	22
Leek Town	36	8	5	23	48	111	21
Sutton Town	36	7	5	24	56	126	19

Bloxwich Strollers resigned during the season and their record was expunged.

1956-1957

Division One

Walsall Reserves	38	23	8	7	95	48	54
Bromsgrove Rovers	38	22	7	9	93	61	51
Tamworth	38	20	9	9	94	62	49
Burton Albion	38	17	11	10	98	74	45
Rugby Town	38	19	7	12	80	68	45
Lockheed (Leamington)	38	16	10	12	84	65	42
Banbury Spencer	38	17	7	14	87	71	41
Aston Villa "A"	38	17	7	14	93	79	41
Bedworth Town	38	16	8	14	85	75	40
Brierley Hill Alliance	38	18	3	17	62	77	39
Wolverhampton Wanderers "A"	38	16	6	16	84	79	38
Atherstone Town	38	16	5	17	100	99	37
Worcester City Reserves	38	14	7	17	82	107	35
Nuneaton Borough	38	14	6	18	76	75	34
Stourbridge	38	13	8	17	66	68	34
Shrewsbury Town Reserves	38	13	7	18	74	90	33
Oswestry Town	38	12	8	18	71	86	32
Halesowen Town	38	10	9	19	74	96	29
Brush Sports	38	10	7	21	59	80	27
Whitwick Colliery	38	6	2	30	42	139	14

Division Two

Bilston	36	27	7	2	103	30	61
Hereford United Reserves	36	24	3	9	96	52	51
Hinckley Athletic	36	21	6	9	97	53	48
Gresley Rovers	36	20	8	8	75	42	48
Evesham United	36	19	8	9	88	47	46
Cradley Heath	36	18	4	14	65	58	40
Redditch	36	15	9	12	68	60	39
West Bromwich Albion "A"	36	16	7	13	71	65	39
Lye Town	36	16	5	15	72	76	37
Darlaston	36	16	4	16	69	69	36
Hednesford	36	14	6	16	74	84	34
Stoke City "A"	36	13	7	16	55	63	33
Wellington Town Reserves	36	11	9	16	71	76	31
Boldmere St. Michaels	36	12	6	18	55	71	30
Moor Green	36	12	6	18	54	74	30
Cheltenham Town Reserves	36	11	6	19	74	77	28
Dudley Town	36	9	7	20	56	91	25
Kidderminster Harriers Reserves	36	7	4	25	43	106	18
Sutton Town	36	1	8	27	35	127	10

Leek Town resigned during the season and their record was expunged.

1957-1958

Division One

Wolverhampton Wanderers "A"	38	24	6	8	116	64	54
Walsall Reserves	38	24	4	10	83	60	52
Brierley Hill Alliance	38	22	6	10	82	61	50
Bilston	38	21	1	16	85	65	43
Bromsgrove Rovers	38	19	5	14	85	65	43
Stourbridge	38	17	9	12	67	63	43
Lockheed (Leamington)	38	17	7	14	73	52	41
Shrewsbury Town Reserves	38	17	7	14	85	71	41
Banbury Spencer	38	18	4	16	76	63	40
Hereford United Reserves	38	15	8	15	63	59	38
Burton Albion	38	14	8	16	60	65	36
Tamworth	38	14	7	17	57	57	35
Nuneaton Borough	38	13	7	18	68	79	33
Hinckley Athletic	38	14	5	19	69	81	33
Bedworth Town	38	12	9	17	61	78	33
Aston Villa "A"	38	13	7	18	68	92	33
Worcester City Reserves	38	13	7	18	48	68	33
Rugby Town	38	12	8	18	50	70	32
Gresley Rovers	38	10	5	23	59	100	25
Atherstone Town	38	8	6	24	46	88	22

Division Two

Oswestry Town	38	28	5	5	134	43	61
Brush Sports	38	24	10	4	73	37	58
Halesowen Town	38	26	5	7	119	56	57
West Bromwich Albion "A"	38	23	4	11	107	56	50
Evesham United	38	22	6	10	92	51	50
Hednesford	38	20	8	10	106	73	48
Cradley Heath	38	21	5	12	90	56	47
Birmingham City "A"	38	18	7	13	84	69	43
Cheltenham Town Reserves	38	16	9	13	80	76	41
Lye Town	38	19	3	16	87	84	41
Wellington Town Reserves	38	15	9	14	64	65	39
Moor Green	38	14	10	14	63	71	38
Stoke City "A"	38	16	5	17	80	73	37
Sutton Town	38	14	7	17	65	74	35
Stratford Town	38	13	3	22	62	99	29
Darlaston	38	12	5	21	64	103	29
Boldmere St. Michaels	38	8	6	24	43	86	22
Coventry City "A"	38	5	3	30	45	116	13
Redditch	38	4	3	31	40	117	11
Dudley Town	38	5	1	32	45	138	11

1958-1959

Division One

Wolverhampton Wanderers "A"	34	26	7	1	91	40	59
Oswestry Town	34	22	4	8	96	58	48
Brierley Hill Alliance	34	20	4	10	85	50	44
Bromsgrove Rovers	34	15	10	9	62	56	40
Tamworth	34	15	8	11	51	58	38
Lockheed (Leamington)	34	15	7	12	85	59	37
Banbury Spencer	34	15	6	13	59	55	36
Walsall Reserves	34	15	4	15	66	68	34
Brush Sports	34	14	6	14	54	61	34
Bilston	34	12	7	15	57	66	31
Hereford United Reserves	34	11	9	14	53	74	31
Bedworth Town	34	12	6	16	55	56	30
Shrewsbury Town Reserves	34	11	7	16	54	54	29
West Bromwich Albion "A"	34	11	6	17	77	75	28
Stourbridge	34	11	3	20	67	90	25
Halesowen Town	34	10	5	19	79	112	25
Aston Villa "A"	34	9	6	19	63	86	24
Hinckley Athletic	34	7	5	22	55	91	19

Division Two

Birmingham City "A"	38	31	3	4	114	35	65
Leicester City "A"	38	26	6	6	118	32	58
Atherstone Town	38	25	7	6	118	52	57
Stoke City "A"	38	25	7	6	102	51	57
Cheltenham Town Reserves	38	26	3	9	122	50	55
Evesham United	38	22	6	10	85	53	50
Sutton Town	38	17	8	13	74	76	42
Hednesford	38	18	4	16	72	73	40
Redditch	38	16	7	15	80	85	39
Worcester City Reserves	38	18	3	17	82	89	39
Cradley Heath	38	15	4	19	62	73	34
Lye Town	38	13	7	18	84	83	33
Moor Green	38	10	12	16	55	76	32
Wellington Town Reserves	38	11	9	18	66	106	31
Boldmere St. Michaels	38	10	6	22	61	96	26
Gresley Rovers	38	11	3	24	72	109	25
Stratford Town	38	9	5	24	51	103	23
Coventry City "A"	38	9	4	25	47	98	22
Darlaston	38	7	7	24	48	102	21
Dudley Town	38	2	7	29	46	117	11

1959-1960

Division One

Bromsgrove Rovers	34	23	8	3	94	36	54
Birmingham City "A"	34	22	6	6	90	50	50
Wolverhampton Wanderers "A"	34	20	4	10	75	39	44
Bilston	34	17	6	11	82	77	40
Walsall Reserves	34	13	12	9	54	37	38
Brierley Hill Alliance	34	17	3	14	59	48	37
Leicester City "A"	34	15	6	13	75	70	36
Tamworth	34	15	4	15	55	52	34
Brush Sports	34	15	4	15	54	63	34
Atherstone Town	34	15	3	16	80	75	33
Lockheed (Leamington)	34	15	3	16	59	58	33
Hereford United Reserves	34	14	5	15	64	75	33
Halesowen Town	34	15	1	18	63	84	31
Banbury Spencer	34	10	7	17	60	71	27
West Bromwich Albion "A"	34	9	6	19	53	75	24
Stoke City "A"	34	7	8	19	48	76	22
Stourbridge	34	10	2	22	47	82	22
Bedworth Town	34	7	6	21	44	88	20

Division Two

Aston Villa "A"	30	21	3	6	104	52	45
Cheltenham Town Reserves	30	19	6	5	103	44	44
Sutton Town	30	17	3	10	61	47	37
Redditch	30	16	3	11	79	53	35
Worcester City Reserves	30	13	8	9	77	60	34
Evesham United	30	14	5	11	43	49	33
Stratford Town	30	14	4	12	55	40	32
Hednesford	30	14	4	12	64	60	32
Cradley Heath	30	12	6	12	66	63	30
Moor Green	30	12	4	14	52	53	28
Wellington Town Reserves	30	12	3	15	54	55	27
Lye Town	30	9	8	13	58	55	26
Boldmere St. Michaels	30	9	6	15	47	62	24
Coventry City "A"	30	11	2	17	53	83	24
Dudley Town	30	9	6	15	45	76	24
Darlaston	30	1	3	26	22	131	5

1960-1961

Bilston	42	33	5	4	149	51	71
Bromsgrove Rovers	42	30	7	5	140	48	67
Lockheed (Leamington)	42	29	4	9	125	46	62
Redditch	42	28	5	9	113	54	61
Brierley Hill Alliance	42	24	12	6	87	36	60
Kidderminster Harriers	42	23	7	12	99	58	53
Stourbridge	42	21	8	13	119	64	50
Atherstone Town	42	20	8	14	97	80	48
Tamworth	42	20	7	15	86	71	47
Banbury Spencer	42	21	5	16	108	92	47
Halesowen Town	42	20	6	16	106	90	46
Stratford Town	42	18	6	18	85	85	42
Sutton Town	42	19	1	22	88	82	39
Evesham United	42	16	3	23	76	89	35
Moor Green	42	14	6	22	76	99	34
Bedworth Town	42	14	5	23	78	96	33
Hednesford	42	13	5	24	73	123	31
Lye Town	42	11	7	24	65	112	29
Cradley Heath	42	8	9	25	73	143	25
Boldmere St. Michaels	42	7	5	30	49	118	19
Dudley Town	42	6	5	31	50	152	17
Darlaston	42	4	0	38	46	199	8

1961-1962

Lockheed (Leamington)	40	31	5	4	124	37	67
Brierley Hill Alliance	40	27	8	5	96	37	62
Bromsgrove Rovers	40	27	5	8	117	56	59
Bilston	40	24	6	10	135	62	54
Kidderminster Harriers	40	24	6	10	102	58	54
Tamworth	40	21	7	12	91	63	49
Redditch	40	21	7	12	89	67	49
Sutton Town	40	21	7	12	104	79	49
Halesowen Town	40	21	6	13	97	75	48
Banbury Spencer	40	18	8	14	107	84	44
Stourbridge	40	18	6	16	84	70	42
Stratford Town	40	17	7	16	82	73	41
Darlaston	40	14	7	19	70	93	35
Moor Green	40	13	8	19	67	79	34
Atherstone Town	40	12	9	19	70	97	33
Bedworth Town	40	11	6	23	61	86	28
Lye Town	40	10	6	24	45	89	26
Evesham United	40	8	5	27	74	132	21
Boldmere St. Michaels	40	9	3	28	59	126	21
Hednesford	40	6	4	30	58	155	16
Dudley Town	40	3	2	35	45	159	8

WEST MIDLANDS REGIONAL LEAGUE

1962-1963

Lockheed (Leamington)	38	28	7	3	119	40	63
Stourbridge	38	26	6	6	98	38	58
Hednesford	38	22	7	9	97	62	51
Halesowen Town	38	23	3	12	97	53	49
Atherstone Town	38	23	3	12	95	57	49
Kidderminster Harriers	38	20	8	10	88	53	48
Bromsgrove Rovers	38	21	5	12	95	52	47
Brierley Hill Alliance	38	17	10	11	70	62	44
Dudley Town	38	19	6	13	72	71	44
Stratford Town	38	15	12	11	52	48	42
Tamworth	38	15	8	15	69	69	38
Darlaston	38	15	4	19	80	71	34
Banbury Spencer	38	15	4	19	86	86	34
Bilston	38	14	6	18	78	95	34
Moor Green	38	11	9	18	59	95	31
Lye Town	38	11	5	22	56	99	27
Bedworth Town	38	9	4	25	61	88	22
Redditch	38	6	9	23	44	95	21
Boldmere St. Michaels	38	4	5	29	39	133	13
Sutton Town	38	4	3	31	45	133	11

1963-1964

Tamworth	36	29	2	5	88	35	60
Kidderminster Harriers	36	24	3	9	108	45	51
Halesowen Town	36	22	5	9	105	52	49
Bromsgrove Rovers	36	19	9	8	94	55	47
Dudley Town	36	19	7	10	90	63	45
Stourbridge	36	18	7	11	76	61	43
Hednesford	36	18	7	11	77	63	43
Bilston	36	14	11	11	70	60	39
Banbury Spencer	36	16	6	14	69	69	38
Atherstone Town	36	12	12	12	73	67	36
Brierley Hill Alliance	36	14	8	14	47	49	36
Lower Gornal Athletic	36	12	10	14	60	69	34
Lye Town	36	12	7	17	60	71	31
Darlaston	36	12	7	17	67	84	31
Stratford Town	36	11	7	18	48	78	29
Redditch	36	10	7	19	44	75	27
Moor Green	36	7	7	22	44	90	21
Bedworth Town	36	3	8	25	36	106	14
Sutton Town	36	2	6	28	41	101	10

1964-1965

Kidderminster Harriers	38	30	6	2	124	37	66
Halesowen Town	38	26	4	8	107	52	56
Dudley Town	38	27	1	10	103	42	55
Lower Gornal Athletic	38	23	6	9	74	50	52
Tamworth	38	24	4	10	101	69	52
Brierley Hill Alliance	38	23	4	11	87	58	50
Stourbridge	38	18	10	10	81	56	46
Bromsgrove Rovers	38	19	8	11	76	60	46
Walsall Reserves	38	21	4	13	75	61	46
Bilston	38	18	4	16	75	67	40
Hednesford	38	16	6	16	75	61	38
Redditch	38	13	8	17	55	56	34
Stratford Town Amateurs	38	10	9	19	68	80	29
Lye Town	38	11	4	23	64	104	26
Banbury Spencer	38	11	3	24	79	99	25
Darlaston	38	8	9	21	69	112	25
Atherstone Town	38	8	4	26	59	121	20
Bedworth Town	38	8	3	27	39	95	19
Moor Green	38	7	4	27	44	108	18
Sutton Coldfield Town	38	4	9	25	53	120	17

1965-1966

Premier Division

Tamworth	40	29	7	4	123	51	65
Walsall Reserves	40	24	8	8	84	40	56
Banbury United	40	23	9	8	91	55	55
Kidderminster Harriers	40	22	8	10	85	54	52
Dudley Town	40	21	8	11	84	46	50
Hednesford	40	22	3	15	87	61	47
Bilston	40	19	9	12	71	60	47
Halesowen Town	40	21	4	15	97	76	46
Redditch	40	14	16	10	75	60	44
Port Vale Reserves	40	19	6	15	90	73	44
Stourbridge	40	16	9	15	73	69	41
Bromsgrove Rovers	40	16	8	16	73	76	40
Lower Gornal Athletic	40	15	9	16	76	73	39
Wolverhampton Wanderers "A"	40	13	10	17	77	73	36
Atherstone Town	40	13	10	17	82	97	36
Brierley Hill Alliance	40	13	10	17	75	91	36
Stratford Town Amateurs	40	12	6	22	58	88	30
Cinderford Town	40	10	5	25	54	81	25
Darlaston	40	6	6	28	58	123	18
Bedworth Town	40	6	6	28	41	126	18
Lye Town	40	6	3	31	53	134	15

Division One

Wrockwardine Wood	20	15	3	2	56	25	33
Hednesford Reserves	20	11	6	3	48	34	28
Nuneaton Borough Reserves	20	11	2	7	50	46	24
Kidderminster Harriers Reserves	20	9	4	7	38	30	22
Lower Gornal Athletic Reserves	20	9	4	7	49	45	22
Stourbridge Reserves	20	8	5	7	39	39	21
Wellington Town Reserves	20	6	4	10	45	51	16
Bilston Reserves	20	6	3	11	31	47	15
Stafford Rangers Reserves	20	6	2	12	38	47	14
Atherstone Town Reserves	20	5	3	12	42	60	13
Dudley Town Reserves	20	4	4	12	42	54	12

1966-1967

Premier Division

Boston United	42	32	6	4	139	42	70
Kidderminster Harriers	42	31	5	6	123	61	67
Darlaston	42	22	14	6	80	44	58
Stourbridge	42	24	8	10	97	62	56
Tamworth	42	22	9	11	90	59	53
Halesowen Town	42	22	8	12	94	66	52
Dudley Town	42	22	7	13	70	50	51
Bromsgrove Rovers	42	22	5	15	74	70	49
Bilston	42	20	7	15	88	94	47
Stratford Town Amateurs	42	17	12	13	70	69	46
Atherstone Town	42	17	7	18	75	82	41
Lower Gornal Athletic	42	17	6	19	73	66	40
Brierley Hill Alliance	42	15	8	19	66	75	38
Hednesford	42	14	7	21	65	87	35
Coventry City "A"	42	12	10	20	72	78	34
Port Vale Reserves	42	11	9	22	65	93	31
Cinderford Town	42	12	6	24	65	92	30
Redditch	42	9	10	23	36	81	28
Shrewsbury Town Reserves	42	11	5	26	66	98	27
Bedworth Town	42	10	7	25	50	95	27
Wolverhampton Wanderers "A"	42	6	13	23	38	74	25
Lye Town	42	7	5	30	48	106	19

Division One

Tamworth Reserves	36	26	5	5	91	39	57
Sankey of Wellington	36	24	7	5	97	44	55
Wrockwardine Wood	36	22	6	8	99	53	50
Hednesford Reserves	36	20	9	7	83	60	49
Bilston Reserves	36	11	10	15	65	75	32
Stourbridge Reserves	36	11	8	17	62	79	30
Kidderminster Harriers Reserves	36	8	8	20	57	76	24
Tividale	36	7	9	20	72	102	23
Darlaston Reserves	36	7	7	22	55	103	21
Lower Gornal Athletic Reserves	36	6	7	23	39	89	19

1967-1968

Premier Division

Boston United	42	24	14	4	91	44	62
Tamworth	42	25	11	6	101	44	61
Kidderminster Harriers	42	26	9	7	102	45	61
Dudley Town	42	22	10	10	73	48	54
Hednesford	42	22	8	12	101	63	52
Halesowen Town	42	22	6	14	93	65	50
Redditch	42	18	14	10	64	45	50
Bromsgrove Rovers	42	19	11	12	69	56	49
Atherstone Town	42	17	10	15	66	64	44
Bilston	42	15	14	13	60	59	44
Lye Town	42	17	9	16	61	76	43
Stratford Town Amateurs	42	15	10	17	58	59	40
Stourbridge	42	14	10	18	60	69	38
Cinderford Town	42	12	13	17	61	61	37
Darlaston	42	13	11	18	51	55	37
Lower Gornal Athletic	42	13	10	19	50	68	36
Brierley Hill Alliance	42	13	9	20	61	84	35
Bedworth Town	42	12	7	23	42	81	31
Coventry City "A"	42	10	10	22	46	77	30
Port Vale Reserves	42	9	9	24	52	99	27
Wolverhampton Wanderers "A"	42	11	5	26	39	82	27
Hinckley Athletic	42	4	8	30	25	82	16

Division One

Warley	36	27	5	4	120	29	59
Wrockwardine Wood	36	25	6	5	95	40	56
Kidderminster Harriers Reserves	36	20	6	10	78	48	46
Coventry Amateurs	36	19	7	10	86	44	45
Sankey of Wellington	36	20	5	11	85	50	45
Baddesley Colliery	36	16	8	12	86	73	40
Hereford United Reserves	36	13	11	12	74	76	37
Tipton Town	36	14	9	13	56	72	37
Warwick Saltisford Rovers	36	12	12	12	64	65	36
Dudley Town Reserves	36	10	14	12	58	69	34
Stewarts & Lloyds	36	13	7	16	63	81	33
Stourbridge Reserves	36	14	4	18	77	86	32
Darlaston Reserves	36	11	10	15	56	70	32
Tamworth Reserves	36	12	5	19	76	71	29
Tividale	36	11	7	18	64	74	29
Bilston Reserves	36	10	7	19	47	79	27
Hednesford Reserves	36	9	8	19	61	92	26
Stratford Town Amateurs Reserves	36	11	4	21	58	92	26
Bedworth Town Reserves	36	3	9	24	45	138	15

1968-1969

Premier Division

Kidderminster Harriers	38	32	4	2	123	25	68
Tamworth	38	27	5	6	109	41	59
Hednesford	38	26	7	5	98	43	59
Bromsgrove Rovers	38	24	5	9	90	46	53
Atherstone Town	38	22	6	10	76	53	50
Halesowen Town	38	20	8	10	88	53	48
Cinderford Town	38	18	7	13	81	74	43
Redditch	38	17	8	13	72	52	42
Stourbridge	38	16	9	13	67	68	41
Dudley Town	38	13	14	11	45	39	40
Eastwood (Hanley)	38	13	9	16	59	70	35
Lower Gornal Athletic	38	13	8	17	47	62	34
Brierley Hill Alliance	38	12	6	20	51	85	30
Bilston	38	10	9	19	51	79	29
Lye Town	38	9	8	21	56	83	26
Darlaston	38	10	4	24	42	70	24
Bedworth United	38	8	8	22	42	80	24
Stratford Town Amateurs	38	8	6	24	37	73	22
Wolverhampton Wanderers "A"	38	8	4	26	35	91	20
Hinckley Athletic	38	4	5	29	37	119	13

Division One

Wrockwardine Wood	42	29	10	3	111	35	68
Brereton Social	42	29	6	7	116	47	64
Warwick Saltisford Rovers	42	27	5	10	86	55	59
Tividale	42	23	11	8	95	52	57
Coventry Amateurs	42	25	6	11	100	53	56
Kidderminster Harriers Reserves	42	20	11	11	61	40	51
Oxley	42	20	11	11	100	66	51
Baddesley Colliery	42	21	8	13	85	61	50
G.K.N. Sankey	42	20	7	15	98	71	47
Stourbridge Reserves	42	17	10	15	74	61	44
Tipton Town	42	17	7	18	67	76	41
Stewarts & Lloyds	42	18	4	20	71	85	40
Halesowen Town Reserves	42	14	10	18	58	83	38
Brierley Hill Alliance Reserves	42	15	7	20	88	97	37
Lye Town Reserves	42	14	7	21	52	88	35
Bilston Reserves	42	12	8	22	83	94	32
Hereford United Reserves	42	10	12	20	62	78	32
Warley County Borough	42	11	8	23	56	90	30
Dudley Town Reserves	42	10	9	23	63	90	29
Darlaston Reserves	42	11	7	24	60	107	29
Bedworth United Reserves	42	7	5	30	46	116	19
Stratford Town Amateurs Reserves	42	4	7	31	44	131	15

1969-1970

Premier Division

Kidderminster Harriers	36	26	7	3	115	34	59
Bromsgrove Rovers	36	27	2	7	105	32	56
Stourbridge	36	23	9	4	101	37	55
Tamworth	36	23	7	6	101	50	53
Hednesford	36	22	6	8	98	53	50
Atherstone Town	36	20	8	8	68	38	48
Redditch	36	15	9	12	53	60	39
Bedworth United	36	13	11	12	49	51	37
Halesowen Town	36	15	6	15	61	54	36
Bilston	36	12	11	13	53	56	35
Eastwood (Hanley)	36	13	8	15	62	78	34
Lower Gornal Athletic	36	13	7	16	50	65	33
Wolverhampton Wanderers "A"	36	11	8	17	43	63	30
Brierley Hill Alliance	36	8	12	16	37	59	28
Dudley Town	36	8	10	18	41	58	26
Lye Town	36	6	7	23	39	95	19
Darlaston	36	7	3	26	40	108	17
Stratford Town Amateurs	36	7	3	26	30	91	17
Hinckley Athletic	36	5	2	29	30	94	12

Division One

Warley County Borough	36	27	5	4	87	25	59
Coventry Amateurs	36	24	7	5	80	29	55
Wrockwardine Wood	36	20	13	3	67	33	53
Baddesley Colliery	36	22	8	6	83	35	52
G.K.N. Sankey	36	21	8	7	72	25	50
Brereton Social	36	18	8	10	78	51	44
Stewarts & Lloyds	36	17	9	10	53	52	43
Warwick Saltisford Rovers	36	17	7	12	88	47	41
Tividale	36	17	5	14	80	58	39
Tipton Town	36	13	8	15	70	67	34
Halesowen Town Reserves	36	14	6	16	79	80	34
Kidderminster Harriers Reserves	36	12	10	14	56	62	34
Bilston Reserves	36	12	9	15	60	57	33
Oxley	36	9	8	19	55	81	26
Lye Town Reserves	36	8	6	22	48	93	22
Bedworth United Reserves	36	6	9	21	34	71	21
Dudley Town Reserves	36	6	7	23	43	105	19
Brierley Hill Alliance Reserves	36	5	4	27	32	98	14
Darlaston Reserves	36	2	7	27	26	122	11

1970-1971

Premier Division

Kidderminster Harriers	36	26	6	4	90	31	58
Bilston	36	23	8	5	62	17	54
Welingborough Town	36	23	7	6	92	39	53
Tamworth	36	23	6	7	80	41	52
Bromsgrove Rovers	36	20	10	6	89	35	50
Stourbridge	36	22	4	10	79	40	48
Atherstone Town	36	18	10	8	68	34	46
Bedworth United	36	15	11	10	57	47	41
Eastwood (Hanley)	36	10	13	13	40	48	33
Hednesford	36	12	7	17	51	47	31
Halesowen Town	36	11	8	17	54	63	30
Dudley Town	36	10	9	17	37	49	29
Wolverhampton Wanderers "A"	36	9	8	19	39	66	26
Lye Town	36	7	12	17	31	57	26
Redditch	36	8	9	19	43	70	25
Lower Gornal Athletic	36	9	7	20	33	72	25
Darlaston	36	10	4	22	37	91	24
Brierley Hill Alliance	36	5	12	19	29	56	22
Hinckley Athletic	36	4	3	29	22	130	11

Division One

Brereton Social	32	24	1	7	66	27	49
Warley County Borough	32	20	6	6	69	26	46
G.K.N. Sankey	32	20	6	6	72	32	46
Baddesley Colliery	32	19	8	5	70	36	46
Coventry Amateurs	32	16	8	8	65	36	40
Racing F.C. (Warwick)	32	19	2	11	62	36	40
Rowley United	32	15	7	10	58	48	37
Tipton Town	32	13	5	14	54	74	31
Worcester City Reserves	32	12	6	14	47	51	30
Tividale	32	12	5	15	44	53	29
Solihull Amateurs	32	11	6	15	41	58	28
Oxley	32	10	5	17	43	61	25
Bilston Reserves	32	8	9	15	40	58	25
Wellingborough Town Reserves	32	8	8	16	39	50	24
Burton Albion Reserves	32	9	4	19	43	58	22
B.S.C. Bilston	32	6	8	18	36	59	20
Halesowen Town Reserves	32	2	2	28	21	107	6

Atherstone Town Reserves withdrew and their record was expunged.

1971-1972

Premier Division

Tamworth	36	25	7	4	81	38	57
Atherstone Town	36	24	7	5	74	32	55
Kidderminster Harriers	36	23	7	6	84	32	53
Bromsgrove Rovers	36	22	8	6	74	39	52
Bilston	36	16	9	11	63	37	41
Redditch United	36	17	6	13	75	59	40
Lye Town	36	14	10	12	52	46	38
Hednesford	36	16	6	14	65	59	38
Dudley Town	36	13	12	11	37	36	38
Bedworth United	36	14	8	14	72	64	36
Eastwood (Hanley)	36	13	9	14	51	58	35
Lower Gornal Athletic	36	13	6	17	47	60	32
G.K.N. Sankey	36	10	10	16	38	63	30
Warley	36	13	3	20	56	75	29
Brierley Hill Alliance	36	11	6	19	47	58	28
Wolverhampton Wanderers "A"	36	7	11	18	35	68	25
Darlaston	36	6	11	19	34	68	23
Halesowen Town	36	3	12	21	41	77	18
Hinckley Athletic	36	4	8	24	26	83	16

Division One

Warley County Borough	28	17	7	4	82	28	41
Brereton Social	28	15	9	4	44	25	39
Worcester City Reserves	28	15	7	6	40	24	37
Racing F.C. (Warwick)	28	15	6	7	49	20	36
Armitage	28	12	11	5	53	34	35
Tividale	28	14	6	8	63	27	34
Bilston Reserves	28	11	9	8	42	36	31
Baddesley Colliery	28	10	7	11	31	34	27
Oxley	28	11	4	13	52	53	26
Coventry Amateurs	28	7	12	9	23	28	26
Springvale	28	8	6	14	41	51	22
Rowley United	28	9	3	16	40	56	21
Tipton Town	28	6	6	16	23	47	18
Halesowen Town Reserves	28	5	6	17	30	87	16
Burton Albion Reserves	28	4	3	21	23	86	11

Solihull Amateurs were expelled and their record was expunged.

1972-1973

Premier Division

Bilston	30	21	7	2	71	25	49
Heanor Town	30	16	8	6	53	35	40
Brereton Social	30	15	9	6	49	23	39
Darlaston	30	12	11	7	58	34	35
Brierley Hill Alliance	30	15	5	10	49	46	35
Wolverhampton Wanderers "A"	30	14	6	10	54	44	34
Eastwood (Hanley)	30	14	5	11	57	54	33
Hereford United Reserves	30	13	5	12	40	39	31
Lye Town	30	13	4	13	54	46	30
Warley County Borough	30	9	11	10	38	44	29
Warley	30	6	12	12	46	49	24
G.K.N. Sankey	30	8	8	14	29	43	24
Gornal Athletic	30	8	7	15	25	53	23
Halesowen Town	30	7	5	18	38	69	19
Dudley Town	30	6	6	18	32	56	18
Hinckley Athletic	30	5	7	18	31	64	17

Division One

Tividale	28	22	3	3	90	24	47
Coventry Amateurs	28	17	5	6	58	26	39
Chasetown	28	15	3	10	52	38	33
Armitage	28	13	7	8	41	31	33
Oxley	28	14	4	10	50	46	32
Rowley United	28	13	5	10	42	38	31
Langley Celtic	28	14	3	11	53	48	31
Telford United Reserves	28	11	7	10	35	39	29
Worcester City Reserves	28	9	6	13	50	59	24
Tipton Town	28	8	8	12	37	49	24
G.K.N. Sankey Reserves	28	10	4	14	35	47	24
West Shirley Athletic	28	9	5	14	28	44	23
Springvale	28	7	4	17	34	52	18
Bilston Reserves	28	6	4	18	49	71	16
Halesowen Town Reserves	28	5	6	17	38	80	16

1973-1974

Premier Division

Alvechurch	32	23	5	4	89	24	51
Bilston	32	25	1	6	75	28	51
Brierley Hill Alliance	32	22	5	5	65	31	49
Brereton Social	32	16	10	6	49	23	42
Lye Town	32	17	8	7	57	31	42
Hereford United Reserves	32	17	5	10	62	43	39
Darlaston	32	13	12	7	40	31	38
Dudley Town	32	16	4	12	49	42	36
Warley County Borough	32	11	9	12	55	50	31
Coventry Amateurs	32	10	10	12	39	41	30
Halesowen Town	32	11	5	16	54	78	27
Tividale	32	7	10	15	39	57	24
Heanor Town	32	11	2	19	34	54	24
Eastwood (Hanley)	32	8	6	18	32	70	22
Hinckley Athletic	32	5	8	19	27	65	18
G.K.N. Sankey	32	2	10	20	9	41	14
Gornal Athletic	32	0	6	26	18	84	6

Division One

Armitage	36	22	9	5	84	39	53
Chasetown	36	21	8	7	88	47	50
Staffordshire and Stoke Police	36	18	13	5	70	39	49
Langley Celtic	36	18	11	7	52	33	47
Worcester City Reserves	36	19	7	10	68	43	45
Telford United Reserves	36	16	11	9	57	33	43
Nuneaton Borough Reserves	36	15	12	9	58	38	42
Tamworth Reserves	36	18	5	13	67	62	41
Stourbridge Reserves	36	16	6	14	52	46	38
Bilston Reserves	36	16	4	16	44	54	36
West Shirley Athletic	36	13	9	14	50	41	35
Tipton Town	36	11	12	13	58	59	34
Bromsgrove Rovers Reserves	36	11	11	14	60	66	33
Springvale	36	11	10	15	44	59	32
Rowley United	36	12	5	19	54	67	29
Oxley	36	10	6	20	70	95	26
Halesowen Town Reserves	36	7	6	23	41	83	20
Warley	36	7	3	26	37	86	17
G.K.N. Sankey Reserves	36	4	6	26	31	95	14

1974-1975

Premier Division

Alvechurch	30	20	8	2	74	30	48
Brierley Hill Alliance	30	16	9	5	56	31	41
Lye Town	30	18	5	7	53	35	41
Brereton Social	30	14	9	7	40	30	37
Bilston	30	11	12	7	53	42	34
Dudley Town	30	12	10	8	47	38	34
Coventry Sporting	30	11	10	9	40	32	32
Darlaston	30	12	8	10	41	37	32
Hednesford Town	30	12	7	11	44	41	31
Eastwood (Hanley)	30	13	4	13	49	53	30
Armitage	30	10	7	13	45	50	27
Tividale	30	9	7	14	40	52	25
Warley County Borough	30	6	7	17	29	52	19
Gornal Athletic	30	6	6	18	26	59	18
Hinckley Athletic	30	5	7	18	29	47	17
Halesowen Town	30	3	8	19	30	67	14

Division One

Staffordshire Police	38	24	10	4	76	33	58
Chasetown	38	23	7	8	67	41	53
Stafford Rangers Reserves	38	21	9	8	82	36	51
Bilston Reserves	38	15	14	9	66	49	44
Worcester City Reserves	38	21	2	15	64	49	44
Rowley United	38	19	5	14	91	60	43
Langley Celtic	38	16	10	12	66	63	42
Nuneaton Borough Reserves	38	12	17	9	56	51	41
Bromsgrove Rovers Reserves	38	15	11	12	65	62	41
Shirley Town	38	15	8	15	56	56	38
Hednesford Town Reserves	38	10	17	11	48	55	37
Stourbridge Reserves	38	13	9	16	51	53	35
Tipton Town	38	14	7	17	78	82	35
Warley	38	14	7	17	51	63	35
Telford United Reserves	38	13	6	19	61	67	32
Springvale	38	10	11	17	44	66	31
Tamworth Reserves	38	12	6	20	59	88	30
Ledbury Town	38	8	8	22	57	100	24
Oxley	38	9	5	24	65	99	23
Halesowen Town Reserves	38	7	9	22	43	73	23

1975-1976

Premier Division

Alvechurch	36	29	3	4	74	20	61
Bilston	36	24	6	6	74	25	54
Dudley Town	36	19	11	6	61	34	49
Tividale	36	21	7	8	75	46	49
Lye Town	36	16	13	7	60	36	45
Darlaston	36	18	9	9	59	42	45
Brereton Social	36	16	7	13	42	34	39
Armitage	36	15	9	12	64	52	39
Hednesford Town	36	12	13	11	61	52	37
Coventry Sporting	36	13	9	14	41	42	35
Eastwood (Hanley)	36	12	10	14	46	45	34
Brierley Hill Alliance	36	14	6	16	53	63	34
Halesowen Town	36	10	9	17	46	59	29
Gresley Rovers	36	8	11	17	51	65	27
V.S. Rugby	36	9	7	20	26	57	25
Gornal Athletic	36	10	5	21	32	71	25
Hinckley Athletic	36	6	9	21	21	69	21
Staffordshire Police	36	7	5	24	39	79	19
Warley County Borough	36	5	7	24	30	64	17

Division One

Willenhall Town	40	32	4	4	115	26	68
Chasetown	40	28	8	4	94	30	64
Oldswinford	40	22	10	8	70	51	54
Warley	40	22	9	9	71	38	53
Bilston Reserves	40	20	12	8	81	40	52
Cheltenham Town Reserves	40	22	7	11	75	50	51
Shirley Town	40	20	8	12	74	49	48
Tipton Town	40	18	7	15	77	65	43
Telford United Reserves	40	17	9	14	61	55	43
Kidderminster Harriers Reserves	40	11	14	15	54	57	36
Nuneaton Borough Reserves	40	12	12	16	51	64	36
Worcester City Reserves	40	12	11	17	55	69	35
V.S. Rugby Reserves	40	13	9	18	42	59	35
Bromsgrove Rovers Reserves	40	12	10	18	52	69	34
Hednesford Town Reserves	40	13	7	20	56	63	33
Ledbury Town	40	10	12	18	63	79	32
Springvale	40	13	5	22	42	61	31
Langley	40	11	9	20	58	94	31
Halesowen Town Reserves	40	10	9	21	45	69	29
Rowley United	40	5	7	28	32	102	17
Oxley	40	4	7	29	30	108	15

1976-1977

Premier Division

Alvechurch	40	29	6	5	74	20	64
Lye Town	40	26	5	9	76	35	57
Hednesford Town	40	22	13	5	59	31	57
Brereton Social	40	20	11	9	69	46	51
Dudley Town	40	18	11	11	65	41	47
V.S. Rugby	40	17	12	11	48	41	46
Tividale	40	15	14	11	47	37	44
Coventry Sporting	40	14	16	10	46	40	44
Armitage	40	15	13	12	67	57	43
Hinckley Athletic	40	14	15	11	59	54	43
Bilston	40	15	11	14	47	48	41
Darlaston	40	16	8	16	49	55	40
Warley County Borough	40	10	18	12	40	48	38
Walsall Reserves	40	11	14	15	49	58	36
Eastwood (Hanley)	40	14	4	22	60	75	32
Willenhall Town	40	11	10	19	52	57	32
Gresley Rovers	40	8	13	19	54	66	29
Brierley Hill Alliance	40	7	15	18	46	78	29
Staffordshire Police	40	7	11	22	37	78	25
Gornal Athletic	40	5	13	22	37	76	23
Halesowen Town	40	5	9	26	46	86	19

Division One – Section A

Wednesfield Social	26	19	3	4	56	20	41
Tipton Town	26	16	7	3	64	25	39
Rowley United	26	17	2	7	55	45	36
Ledbury Town	26	14	4	8	56	32	32
Cheltenham Town Reserves	26	13	5	8	53	38	31
Oldswinford	26	11	7	8	57	42	29
Shirley Town	26	10	6	10	36	45	26
Causeway Green	26	11	3	12	38	42	25
V.S. Rugby Reserves	26	9	6	11	41	46	24
Langley	26	10	4	12	39	45	24
Worcester City Reserves	26	5	7	14	29	52	17
Coventry Sporting Reserves	26	5	4	17	31	57	14
Halesowen Town Reserves	26	4	5	17	38	65	13
Redditch United Reserves	26	4	5	17	30	69	13

Division One – Section B

Wolverhampton United	28	18	7	3	52	24	43
Donnington Wood	28	16	10	2	46	19	42
Telford United Reserves	28	19	4	5	52	25	42
Chasetown	28	14	6	8	43	26	34
G.K.N. Sankey	28	14	6	8	44	31	34
Burntwood Institute	28	11	5	12	40	44	27
Shifnal Town	28	8	10	10	50	48	26
Kidderminster Harriers Reserves	28	11	4	13	46	55	26
Bilston Reserves	28	9	7	12	37	36	25
Lichfield	28	8	9	11	32	35	25
Springvale	28	9	5	14	22	40	23
Nuneaton Borough Reserves	28	9	3	16	33	56	21
Hednesford Town Reserves	28	7	6	15	31	43	20
Atherstone Town Reserves	28	4	8	16	22	42	16
Bromsgrove Rovers Reserves	28	5	6	17	24	50	16

1977-1978

Premier Division

Hednesford Town	36	20	11	5	82	28	51
Alvechurch	36	20	10	6	71	33	50
Bilston	36	19	10	7	68	37	48
Lye Town	36	20	8	8	64	46	48
Willenhall Town	36	20	7	9	76	37	47
Eastwood (Hanley)	36	17	10	9	75	51	44
Tividale	36	16	11	9	46	35	43
Hinckley Athletic	36	16	10	10	54	43	42
Halesowen Town	36	17	7	12	55	40	41
Dudley Town	36	14	13	9	53	42	41
Brereton Social	36	18	5	13	58	50	41
Armitage	36	13	12	11	63	53	38
V.S. Rugby	36	12	9	15	56	49	33
Brierley Hill Alliance	36	11	7	18	40	60	29
Gresley Rovers	36	9	7	20	44	66	25
Coventry Sporting	36	7	10	19	24	67	24
Darlaston	36	7	9	20	35	66	23
Gornal Athletic	36	2	5	29	26	116	9
Staffordshire Police	36	1	5	30	22	93	7

Division One

Chasetown	30	20	7	3	49	20	47
Wednesfield Social	30	19	5	6	60	27	43
Causeway Green	30	11	11	8	38	30	33
Oldswinford	30	12	9	9	46	38	33
Ledbury Town	30	10	12	8	45	36	32
Lichfield	30	13	6	11	48	45	32
Shifnal Town	30	14	4	12	39	39	32
Telford United Reserves	30	12	6	12	52	46	30
Wolverhampton United	30	11	7	12	45	47	29
G.K.N. Sankey	30	8	13	9	33	35	29
Cheltenham Town Reserves	30	13	3	14	53	59	29
Donnington Wood	30	9	8	13	39	46	26
Tipton Town	30	8	10	12	36	44	26
Rowley United	30	8	7	15	39	55	23
Burntwood Institute	30	7	8	15	28	56	22
Shirley Town	30	4	6	20	40	67	14

Division Two

Worcester City Reserves	26	16	5	5	61	30	37
Atherstone Town Reserves	26	15	7	4	43	25	37
Nuneaton Borough Reserves	26	15	5	6	51	27	35
Staffs South End	26	14	5	7	48	27	33
Hednesford Town Reserves	26	14	5	7	53	41	33
Brereton Town	26	14	5	7	46	38	33
Albrighton United	26	10	5	11	35	44	25
Springvale	26	9	5	12	30	34	23
Halesowen Town Reserves	26	8	7	11	33	38	23
Langley	26	9	4	13	45	56	22
Coventry Sporting Reserves	26	9	3	14	28	51	21
Kidderminster Harriers Reserves	26	7	4	15	46	52	18
Bromsgrove Rovers Reserves	26	6	6	14	42	50	18
Redditch United Reserves	26	2	2	22	21	69	6

1978-1979

Premier Division

Willenhall Town	34	23	7	4	82	32	53
Lye Town	34	21	11	2	62	33	53
Dudley Town	34	21	8	5	53	23	50
Hednesford Town	34	19	10	5	59	26	48
Tividale	34	19	6	9	63	40	44
Bilston	34	15	10	9	50	34	40
Brierley Hill Alliance	34	17	5	12	67	47	39
Brereton Social	34	17	5	12	48	40	39
Darlaston	34	15	5	14	52	51	35
Coventry Sporting	34	12	6	16	39	48	30
Hinckley Athletic	34	12	5	17	42	52	29
Ledbury Town	34	10	7	17	57	63	27
V.S. Rugby	34	9	9	16	29	41	27
Wednesfield Social	34	7	12	15	27	45	26
Halesowen Town	34	8	8	18	35	55	24
Armitage	34	7	6	21	44	69	20
Gresley Rovers	34	4	7	23	27	67	15
Gornal Athletic	34	4	5	25	21	91	13

Division One

Shifnal Town	34	20	11	3	83	38	51
Causeway Green	34	18	13	3	58	24	49
Cheltenham Town Reserves	34	18	13	3	47	26	49
Rushall Olympic	34	21	6	7	70	37	48
Donnington Wood	34	17	10	7	60	37	44
G.K.N. Sankey	34	14	10	10	56	40	38
Wolverhampton United	34	15	7	12	45	32	37
Oldswinford	34	14	8	12	45	44	36
Lichfield	34	10	13	11	33	37	33
Nuneaton Borough Reserves	34	10	12	12	43	51	32
Chasetown	34	7	16	11	34	43	30
Atherstone Town Reserves	34	11	7	16	45	58	29
Telford United Reserves	34	11	7	16	52	67	29
Staffordshire Police	34	11	6	17	49	65	28
Worcester City Reserves	34	7	11	16	42	56	25
Tipton Town	34	8	7	19	38	53	23
Shirley Town	34	6	6	22	26	69	18
Burntwood Institute	34	3	7	24	26	80	13

Division Two

Ludlow Town	34	19	8	7	54	39	46
Willenhall Town Reserves	34	17	9	8	68	41	43
Alvechurch Reserves	34	18	6	10	62	41	42
Kidderminster Harriers Reserves	34	18	5	11	70	41	41
Bridgnorth Sports	34	18	5	11	67	44	41
Brereton Town	34	17	7	10	60	50	41
Brewood	34	15	10	9	52	40	40
Staffs South End	34	14	10	10	61	48	38
Halesowen Town Reserves	34	14	8	12	61	64	36
Hednesford Town Reserves	34	11	10	13	45	51	32
Albrighton United	34	12	8	14	51	61	32
Dudley Town Reserves	34	13	5	16	47	50	31
Coventry Sporting Reserves	34	12	6	16	52	65	30
Bromsgrove Rovers Reserves	34	9	10	15	53	67	28
Tividale Reserves	34	11	4	19	44	64	26
Westfields	34	7	10	17	59	76	24
Langley	34	8	7	19	38	63	23
Springvale	34	5	8	21	23	62	18

1979-1980

Premier Division

Sutton Coldfield Town	42	28	11	3	96	39	67
Lye Town	42	30	7	5	73	29	67
Willenhall Town	42	23	11	8	95	45	57
Hednesford Town	42	19	16	7	72	41	54
Brereton Social	42	20	11	11	86	45	51
Brierley Hill Alliance	42	20	11	11	62	49	51
Shifnal Town	42	19	10	13	72	53	48
Dudley Town	42	20	6	16	61	52	46
Coventry Sporting	42	16	10	16	64	67	42
Ledbury Town	42	13	15	14	62	71	41
Malvern Town	42	13	11	18	56	71	37
Halesowen Town	42	13	11	18	52	69	37
Hinckley Athletic	42	12	12	18	40	59	36
Tividale	42	13	9	20	70	75	35
Gresley Rovers	42	10	14	18	49	69	34
Armitage	42	12	9	21	39	55	33
V.S. Rugby	42	11	11	20	43	60	33
Blakenall	42	11	11	20	45	76	33
Wednesfield Social	42	10	12	20	44	66	32
Darlaston	42	9	13	20	42	86	31
Gornal Athletic	42	7	16	19	52	69	30
Bilston	42	8	13	21	50	79	29

Division One

Rushall Olympic	36	28	5	3	79	17	61
Telford United Reserves	36	18	9	9	70	40	45
Oldswinford	36	17	9	10	52	35	43
Chasetown	36	17	8	11	57	43	42
Atherstone United	36	16	10	10	47	39	42
Burntwood Institute	36	15	8	13	54	51	38
Willenhall Town Reserves	36	13	11	12	49	50	37
Causeway Green	36	15	7	14	43	54	37
Tipton Town	36	11	14	11	37	37	36
Donnington Wood	36	13	9	14	46	43	35
Staffordshire Police	36	11	12	13	55	53	34
Wolverhampton United	36	10	13	13	48	57	33
Lichfield	36	9	14	13	36	38	32
Nuneaton Borough Reserves	36	11	10	15	45	61	32
Worcester City Reserves	36	8	14	14	38	54	30
Ludlow Town	36	11	6	19	43	48	28
Shirley Town	36	8	11	17	26	51	27
Alvechurch Reserves	36	6	15	15	42	79	27
G.K.N. Sankey	36	9	7	20	41	58	25

Division Two

Brewood	38	24	8	6	89	37	56
Staffs South End	38	20	8	10	82	58	48
Hednesford Town Reserves	38	21	6	11	65	51	48
Brereton Town	38	20	7	11	72	51	47
Kidderminster Harriers Reserves	38	17	12	9	82	45	46
Oswestry Town Reserves	38	18	10	10	72	51	46
Coventry Sporting Reserves	38	17	11	10	84	60	45
Springvale	38	19	7	12	58	50	45
Westfields	38	18	8	12	58	41	44
Dudley Town Reserves	38	15	11	12	72	65	41
Lye Town Reserves	38	12	15	11	48	53	39
Bromsgrove Rovers Reserves	38	13	12	13	60	64	38
Stourport Swifts	38	13	12	13	59	64	38
Albrighton United	38	14	9	15	66	72	37
Stourbridge Reserves	38	13	10	15	67	53	36
Halesowen Town Reserves	38	17	11	20	47	75	25
Bridgnorth Sports	38	9	7	22	54	89	25
Ledbury Town Reserves	38	8	7	23	62	109	23
Malvern Town Reserves	38	5	9	24	38	91	19
Tividale Reserves	38	2	10	26	40	96	14

Division Two

Bromsgrove Rovers Reserves	40	26	8	6	115	49	60
Stourbridge Reserves	40	24	8	8	91	52	56
Westfields	40	24	8	8	89	60	56
Springvale	40	21	10	9	97	60	52
Brereton Town	40	20	9	11	87	65	49
Halesowen Town Reserves	40	20	8	12	91	74	48
Stourport Swifts	40	15	12	13	56	56	42
Albrighton United	40	16	10	14	67	84	42
Malvern Town Reserves	40	16	8	16	67	70	40
Kidderminster Harriers Reserves	40	15	9	16	83	68	39
Great Wyrley	40	16	7	17	72	67	39
Oswestry Town Reserves	40	14	8	18	68	84	36
Bridgnorth Sports	40	14	8	18	43	60	36
Lye Town Reserves	40	13	9	18	67	74	35
Ledbury Town Reserves	40	15	4	21	71	74	34
Cheltenham Town Reserves	40	14	6	20	72	98	34
Tividale Reserves	40	11	11	18	61	76	33
Coventry Sporting Reserves	40	11	11	18	60	80	33
Dales United	40	12	7	21	57	95	31
Dudley Town Reserves	40	10	8	22	39	56	28
Tamworth Reserves	40	5	7	28	40	91	17

1980-1981

Premier Division

Shifnal Town	42	31	7	4	89	33	69
Lye Town	42	27	9	6	80	36	63
Willenhall Town	42	25	11	6	93	41	61
Brereton Social	42	22	8	12	74	51	52
Hednesford Town	42	20	11	11	73	48	51
Coventry Sporting	42	19	12	11	75	54	50
Ledbury Town	42	19	10	13	74	52	48
Dudley Town	42	19	10	13	55	44	48
Sutton Coldfield Town	42	18	10	14	71	56	46
Bilston	42	18	10	14	78	65	46
Armitage	42	20	5	17	58	59	45
Rushall Olympic	42	15	13	14	50	52	43
Blakenall	42	14	15	13	55	58	43
Darlaston	42	17	5	20	68	95	39
Gresley Rovers	42	13	10	19	46	62	36
Halesowen Town	42	10	15	17	53	67	35
Wednesfield Social	42	11	11	20	52	67	33
V.S. Rugby	42	9	10	23	50	80	28
Tividale	42	5	17	20	35	64	27
Malvern Town	42	9	7	26	56	93	25
Brierley Hill Alliance	42	6	8	28	33	85	20
Hinckley Athletic	42	3	10	29	43	99	16

1981-1982

Premier Division

Shifnal Town	42	26	11	5	82	36	63
Sutton Coldfield Town	42	26	9	7	80	43	61
Halesowen Town	42	24	8	10	84	45	56
Bilston	42	23	8	11	70	49	54
Ledbury Town	42	19	14	9	83	58	52
Rushall Olympic	42	16	18	8	72	54	50
Willenhall Town	42	18	11	13	64	46	47
V.S. Rugby	42	20	7	15	67	51	47
Blakenall	42	20	7	15	59	53	47
Dudley Town	42	17	12	13	61	52	46
Wednesfield Social	42	15	13	14	43	42	43
Lye Town	42	15	12	15	59	49	42
Hednesford Town	42	17	8	17	61	57	42
Coventry Sporting	42	13	11	18	43	54	37
Gresley Rovers	42	13	9	20	50	59	35
Hinckley Athletic	42	12	10	20	43	66	34
Tividale	42	13	6	23	56	82	32
Malvern Town	42	11	10	21	49	78	32
Armitage	42	10	11	21	43	69	31
Oldswinford	42	9	11	22	48	74	29
Brereton Social	42	7	10	25	47	100	24
Darlaston	42	6	8	28	37	84	20

Division One

Oldswinford	42	32	5	5	95	33	69
Chasetown	42	26	11	5	81	25	63
Atherstone United	42	23	13	6	80	33	59
Wolverhampton United	42	26	7	9	80	38	59
Worcester City Reserves	42	24	9	9	83	48	57
Donnington Wood	42	24	6	12	87	68	54
Willenhall Town Reserves	42	21	10	11	64	36	52
Brewood	42	18	10	14	58	58	46
Gornal Athletic	42	16	12	14	59	54	44
Tipton Town	42	19	4	19	73	82	42
Telford United Reserves	42	17	6	19	67	83	40
Causeway Green	42	15	9	18	50	47	39
Ludlow Town	42	15	8	19	71	73	38
Lichfield	42	14	9	19	57	73	37
Staffordshire Police	42	12	12	18	69	86	36
Hednesford Town Reserves	42	11	8	23	58	82	30
Nuneaton Borough Reserves	42	10	9	23	53	74	29
Alvechurch Reserves	42	9	11	22	58	92	29
Shirley Town	42	7	13	22	42	70	27
Staffs South End	42	10	7	25	59	101	27
Burntwood Institute	42	8	9	25	39	82	25
G.K.N. Sankey	42	7	8	27	42	87	22

Division One

Atherstone United	38	23	11	4	79	30	57
Wolverhampton United	38	24	8	6	64	25	56
Chasetown	38	21	13	4	64	29	55
Tipton Town	38	22	8	8	67	31	52
Nuneaton Borough Reserves	38	22	7	9	71	35	51
Brewood	38	18	10	10	55	38	46
Donnington Wood	38	15	14	9	64	45	44
Causeway Green	38	17	7	14	55	49	41
Worcester City Reserves	38	13	10	15	56	59	36
Burntwood Institute	38	12	11	15	51	54	35
Willenhall Town Reserves	38	14	7	17	52	58	35
Bromsgrove Rovers Reserves	38	12	10	16	43	55	34
Staffs South End	38	12	9	17	46	60	33
Ludlow Town	38	13	5	20	38	62	31
Staffordshire Police	38	13	4	21	47	86	30
Gornal Athletic	38	10	9	19	44	72	29
Lichfield	38	9	9	20	53	66	27
Telford United Reserves	38	7	10	21	43	63	24
Shirley Town	38	8	7	23	40	74	23
Hednesford Town Reserves	38	5	11	22	30	71	21

Division Two

G.K.N. Sankey	36	23	6	7	85	38	52
Northpark United	36	20	10	6	74	40	50
Bilston United	36	19	10	7	73	47	48
Lye Town Reserves	36	19	8	9	69	47	46
Cheltenham Town Reserves	36	16	10	10	63	41	42
Stourport Swifts	36	16	10	10	50	38	42
Springvale	36	18	5	13	63	54	41
Westfields	36	17	6	13	78	54	40
Dudley Town Reserves	36	16	7	13	47	38	39
Coventry Sporting Reserves	36	16	7	13	58	57	39
Stafford Rangers Reserves	36	15	6	15	64	58	36
Malvern Town Reserves	36	15	6	15	68	65	36
Ledbury Town Reserves	36	16	4	16	70	88	36
Albrighton United	36	11	7	18	51	62	29
Halesowen Town Reserves	36	10	8	18	49	70	28
Great Wyrley	36	11	4	21	52	79	26
Dales United	36	9	5	22	55	92	23
Dowty Ashchurch	36	8	6	22	41	76	22
Tamworth Reserves	36	2	5	29	27	93	9

Bridgnorth Sports resigned during the season and their record was expunged.

1982-1983

Premier Division

Halesowen Town	38	28	6	4	124	37	62
Hinckley Athletic	38	24	7	7	59	32	55
Hednesford Town	38	22	4	12	64	53	48
Shifnal Town	38	19	9	10	78	48	47
Atherstone United	38	21	5	12	73	46	47
Bilston	38	19	7	12	82	50	45
V.S. Rugby	38	17	10	11	69	36	44
Armitage	38	18	8	12	61	51	44
Gresley Rovers	38	15	11	12	69	52	41
Tividale	38	18	5	15	52	48	41
Wednesfield Social	38	17	7	14	47	47	41
Wolverhampton United	38	14	12	12	50	47	40
Lye Town	38	13	10	15	50	49	36
Rushall Olympic	38	12	8	18	59	66	32
Blakenall	38	8	13	17	45	61	29
Coventry Sporting	38	7	14	17	40	64	28
Oldswinford	38	6	11	21	46	78	23
Brereton Social	38	8	6	24	43	89	22
Ledbury Town	38	6	7	25	45	117	19
Malvern Town	38	6	4	28	40	125	16

Division One

Brewood	32	18	8	6	55	34	44
Chasetown	32	19	6	7	56	36	44
Tipton Town	32	19	5	8	65	39	43
Cheltenham Town Reserves	32	17	5	10	60	39	39
G.K.N. Sankey	32	15	6	11	47	38	36
Willenhall Town Reserves	32	13	10	9	51	46	36
Gornal Athletic	32	9	13	10	41	36	31
Donnington Wood	32	11	9	12	62	59	31
Nuneaton Borough Reserves	32	10	11	11	45	43	31
Northpark United	32	11	9	12	47	52	31
Ludlow Town	32	11	6	15	52	58	28
Shirley Town	32	12	3	17	42	56	27
Bilston United	32	10	6	16	47	67	26
Hednesford Town Reserves	32	8	9	15	39	53	25
Lichfield	32	9	7	16	44	65	25
Staffs South End	32	9	6	17	46	59	24
Darlaston	32	7	9	16	38	57	23

Division Two

Great Wyrley	32	20	7	5	67	30	47
Harrisons	32	19	8	5	53	27	46
Stafford Rangers Reserves	32	18	9	5	75	32	45
Wolverhampton Casuals	32	20	5	7	55	30	45
Dudley Town Reserves	32	19	6	7	70	36	44
Dales United	32	17	5	10	60	48	39
Albrighton United	32	14	9	9	61	48	37
Stourport Swifts	32	16	4	12	57	44	36
Newport Town	32	10	12	10	39	39	32
Halesowen Town Reserves	32	10	10	12	46	52	30
Springvale	32	12	5	15	54	48	29
Westfields	32	10	7	15	55	59	27
Pelsall Villa	32	8	5	19	42	76	21
Oldswinford Reserves	32	6	6	20	38	60	18
Dowty Ashchurch	32	8	2	22	44	70	18
Coventry Sporting Reserves	32	5	7	20	27	83	17
Malvern Town Reserves	32	5	3	24	34	95	13

1983-1984

Premier Division

Halesowen Town	38	32	3	3	112	36	67
Hednesford Town	38	23	10	5	70	34	56
Atherstone United	38	17	11	10	63	44	45
Gresley Rovers	38	17	9	12	68	61	43
Lye Town	38	15	12	11	55	45	42
Wolverhampton United	38	17	7	14	53	55	41
Oldswinford	38	15	11	12	61	64	41
Armitage	38	17	5	16	67	61	39
Shifnal Town	38	13	12	13	59	56	38
Wednesfield Social	38	15	8	15	52	58	38
Tividale	38	12	12	14	53	48	36
Malvern Town	38	14	7	17	64	61	35
Rushall Olympic	38	11	11	16	55	59	33
Hinckley Athletic	38	12	9	17	51	61	33
G.K.N. Sankey	38	13	7	18	54	74	33
Brereton Social	38	10	12	16	46	62	32
Bilston Town	38	10	11	17	44	58	31
Blakenall	38	11	7	20	39	59	29
Chasetown	38	9	8	21	39	81	26
Cradley Town	38	9	4	25	44	72	22

Division One

Tipton Town	30	18	11	1	65	28	47
Gornal Athletic	30	18	8	4	60	29	44
Northpark United	30	19	5	6	73	23	43
Harrisons	30	19	5	6	60	29	43
Cheltenham Town Reserves	30	13	10	7	51	37	36
Brewood	30	14	7	9	49	36	35
Great Wyrley	30	13	6	11	52	44	32
Darlaston	30	14	3	13	49	40	31
Dudley Town Reserves	30	9	9	12	31	43	27
Lichfield	30	10	6	14	34	44	26
Willenhall Town Reserves	30	6	10	14	33	58	22
Nuneaton Borough Reserves	30	8	6	16	31	60	22
Ludlow Town	30	8	4	18	38	64	20
Hednesford Town Reserves	30	5	9	16	36	58	19
Shirley Town	30	3	11	16	27	63	17
Bilston United	30	3	10	17	26	59	16

Division Two

Halesowen Town Reserves	26	16	8	2	54	21	40
Westfields	26	17	5	4	50	21	39
Newport Town	26	17	2	7	54	24	36
Pelsall Villa	26	14	6	6	47	32	34
Donnington Wood	26	13	6	7	52	35	32
Wolverhampton Casuals	26	13	5	8	42	23	31
Springvale	26	14	2	10	43	37	30
Stourport Swifts	26	13	3	10	47	28	29
Dales United	26	11	5	10	44	40	27
Atherstone United Reserves	26	11	3	12	26	29	25
Aero Lucas	26	5	6	15	29	53	16
Oldswinford Reserves	26	2	8	16	28	70	12
Dowty Ashchurch	26	2	3	21	16	71	7
Malvern Town Reserves	26	1	4	21	20	68	6

1984-1985

Premier Division

Halesowen Town	38	28	6	4	96	36	62
Bilston Town	38	24	5	9	84	49	53
Atherstone United	38	20	8	10	64	40	48
Wednesfield Social	38	20	8	10	52	34	48
Tipton Town	38	19	10	9	67	52	48
Tividale	38	19	9	10	53	39	47
Tamworth	38	16	14	8	66	38	46
Gresley Rovers	38	16	8	14	62	56	40
Hinckley Athletic	38	14	10	14	63	59	38
Oldswinford	38	14	7	17	61	61	35
G.K.N. Sankey	38	11	13	14	47	50	35
Lye Town	38	11	12	15	47	47	34
Rushall Olympic	38	12	10	16	57	58	34
Brereton Social	38	12	10	16	58	83	34
Wolverhampton United	38	10	11	17	39	49	31
Chasetown	38	10	11	17	45	65	31
Malvern Town	38	9	12	17	49	57	30
Blakenall	38	7	10	21	40	69	24
Armitage	38	8	7	23	45	95	23
Shifnal Town	38	5	9	24	30	88	19

Division One

Harrisons	34	26	4	4	77	25	56
Wolverhampton Casuals	34	24	5	5	89	37	53
Westfields	34	21	9	4	74	39	51
Brewood	34	21	3	10	60	42	45
Darlaston	34	17	7	10	65	41	41
Newport Town	34	15	7	12	54	43	37
Dudley Town Reserves	34	15	4	15	57	45	34
Halesowen Town Reserves	34	13	8	13	57	52	34
Pelsall Villa	34	11	11	12	46	45	33
Gornal Athletic	34	10	11	13	45	53	31
Northpark United	34	11	8	15	56	58	30
Great Wyrley	34	11	8	15	49	55	30
Nuneaton Borough Reserves	34	11	6	17	34	62	28
Lichfield	34	10	6	18	42	51	26
Cradley Town	34	7	10	17	46	72	24
Ludlow Town	34	8	8	18	54	92	24
Shirley Town	34	9	5	20	39	71	23
Bilston United	34	4	4	26	32	93	12

Division Two

Halesowen Harriers	32	28	1	3	108	21	57
Ettingshall Holy Trinity	32	22	6	4	70	25	50
Springvale-Tranco	32	21	3	8	84	41	45
Broseley Athletic	32	16	11	5	64	36	43
Bloxwich Town	32	16	7	9	57	39	39
Donnington Wood	32	16	6	10	72	51	38
Jamaica City	32	14	8	10	57	44	36
Stourport Swifts	32	14	6	12	68	42	34
Harrisons Reserves	32	12	7	13	54	70	31
Atherstone United Reserves	32	10	10	12	59	61	30
Aero Lucas	32	10	5	17	46	66	25
Dowty Ashchurch	32	9	6	17	33	53	24
Stuarts Athletic	32	6	10	16	42	66	22
Minworth	32	5	11	16	47	81	21
Dales United	32	5	8	19	36	74	18
Malvern Town Reserves	32	6	6	20	36	95	18
Oldswinford Reserves	32	5	3	24	35	103	13

1985-1986

Premier Division

Halesowen Town	38	31	4	3	108	28	66
Gresley Rovers	38	25	9	4	91	29	59
Atherstone United	38	26	7	5	90	48	59
Harrisons	38	22	9	7	82	40	53
Wednesfield Social	38	21	7	10	88	48	49
Lye Town	38	18	11	9	54	39	47
G.K.N. Sankey	38	15	12	11	59	64	42
Hinckley Athletic	38	15	11	12	60	50	41
Tamworth	38	15	8	15	68	52	38
Brereton Social	38	13	11	14	58	54	37
Rushall Olympic	38	14	9	15	63	65	37
Malvern Town	38	13	10	15	51	61	36
Shifnal Town	38	9	10	19	38	76	28
Oldswinford	38	9	9	20	46	68	27
Blakenall	38	9	8	21	38	61	26
Tividale	38	8	10	20	51	83	26
Chasetown	38	7	10	21	40	74	24
Wolverhampton United	38	8	8	22	31	66	24
Tipton Town	38	8	8	22	43	79	24
Armitage	38	7	3	28	44	118	17

Division One

Halesowen Harriers	34	24	7	3	108	26	55
Wolverhampton Casuals	34	21	5	8	62	33	47
Westfields	34	19	7	8	67	32	45
Ettingshall Holy Trinity	34	17	9	8	69	39	43
Newport Town	34	16	9	9	68	46	41
Halesowen Town Reserves	34	14	9	11	50	43	37
Pelsall Villa	34	15	7	12	43	42	37
Great Wyrley	34	13	10	11	61	52	36
Nuneaton Borough Reserves	34	13	8	13	46	56	34
Cradley Town	34	12	9	13	48	62	33
Brewood	34	13	6	15	60	65	32
Darlaston	34	11	9	14	51	58	31
Bilston United	34	10	10	14	52	61	30
Gornal Athletic	34	9	8	17	43	53	26
Ludlow Town	34	8	9	17	51	64	25
Northpark United	34	9	6	19	43	84	24
Lichfield	34	9	2	23	34	81	20
Shirley Town	34	4	8	22	35	94	16

Division Two

Springvale-Tranco	34	25	5	4	80	27	55
Metal Box Sports	34	23	6	5	66	32	52
Broseley Athletic	34	20	8	6	72	32	48
Stourport Swifts	34	16	12	6	60	36	44
Aero Lucas	34	18	6	10	66	45	42
Millfields	34	15	7	12	48	41	37
Atherstone United Reserves	34	15	6	13	80	63	36
Donnington Wood	34	14	8	12	62	59	36
Bloxwich Town	34	12	10	12	49	54	34
Jamaica City	34	13	7	14	64	55	33
Chasetown Reserves	34	12	9	13	58	55	33
Harrisons Reserves	34	12	6	16	61	67	30
Albright & Wilson	34	11	5	18	58	63	27
Wednesbury Town	34	8	8	18	52	73	24
Dowty Ashchurch	34	10	4	20	29	63	24
Oldswinford Reserves	34	7	8	19	32	76	22
Clancey Halesowen	34	8	4	22	40	92	20
Stuarts Athletic	34	3	9	22	46	90	15

1986-1987

Premier Division

	P	W	D	L	F	A	Pts
Atherstone United	38	29	4	5	115	30	62
Oldbury United	38	28	5	5	89	28	61
Wednesfield Social	38	26	5	7	80	32	57
Gresley Rovers	38	23	11	4	73	39	57
Tamworth	38	21	4	13	103	47	46
Malvern Town	38	20	6	12	74	51	46
Halesowen Harriers	38	19	6	13	75	51	44
Hinckley Athletic	38	18	6	14	70	67	42
Chasetown	38	12	15	11	64	63	39
Harrisons	38	15	8	15	60	56	38
G.K.N. Sankey	38	13	12	13	73	69	38
Rushall Olympic	38	13	8	17	60	63	34
Lye Town	38	12	9	17	41	56	33
Brereton Social	38	14	5	19	61	80	33
Tividale	38	12	8	18	54	71	32
Wolverhampton United	38	11	8	19	44	63	30
Oldswinford	38	7	8	23	49	93	22
Tipton Town	38	5	8	25	37	109	18
Armitage	38	5	5	28	37	113	15
Blakenall	38	4	5	29	38	116	13

1987-1988

Premier Division

	P	W	D	L	F	A	Pts
Tamworth	34	27	3	4	98	31	57
Oldbury United	34	25	6	3	91	39	56
Lye Town	34	22	8	4	65	27	52
Gresley Rovers	34	20	10	4	74	36	50
Chasetown	34	22	4	8	74	40	48
Halesowen Harriers	34	18	6	10	66	40	42
Malvern Town	34	15	6	13	59	47	36
Wednesfield Social	34	14	7	13	43	43	35
Rushall Olympic	34	13	7	14	43	44	33
Hinckley Athletic	34	11	9	14	58	58	31
Harrisons	34	13	5	16	54	61	31
Blakenall	34	11	7	16	42	49	29
Tividale	34	11	5	18	40	68	27
Westfields	34	10	6	18	60	64	26
Tipton Town	34	7	9	18	38	56	23
G.K.N. Sankey	34	7	7	20	46	73	21
Wolverhampton United	34	4	4	26	25	88	12
Oldswinford	34	1	1	32	16	128	3

Brereton Social resigned during the season and their record was expunged.

Division One

	P	W	D	L	F	A	Pts
Westfields	38	30	1	7	111	46	61
Wolverhampton Casuals	38	26	5	7	92	58	57
Broseley Athletic	38	23	6	9	88	47	52
Metal Box Sports	38	21	9	8	81	43	51
Springvale-Tranco	38	21	7	10	86	47	49
Newport Town	38	21	5	12	95	64	47
Ettingshall Holy Trinity	38	18	11	9	59	36	47
Great Wyrley	38	18	10	10	75	58	46
Darlaston	38	15	10	13	73	64	40
Pelsall Villa	38	15	8	15	66	83	38
Brewood	38	14	8	16	83	74	36
Ludlow Town	38	14	5	19	64	81	33
Aero Lucas	38	11	9	18	43	65	31
Gornal Athletic	38	11	8	19	61	75	30
Nuneaton Borough Reserves	38	12	6	20	51	69	30
Cradley Town	38	9	10	19	54	74	28
Halesowen Town Reserves	38	9	6	23	44	91	24
Northpark United	38	9	5	24	57	98	23
Stourport Swifts	38	8	5	25	41	88	21
Bilston United	38	5	6	27	38	101	16

Division One

	P	W	D	L	F	A	Pts
Rocester	36	28	6	2	91	27	62
Stourport Swifts	36	22	7	7	79	40	51
Millfields	36	20	11	5	60	38	51
Wolverhampton Casuals	36	20	8	8	74	48	48
Great Wyrley	36	19	8	9	76	48	46
Ettingshall Holy Trinity	36	17	12	7	58	43	46
Newport Town	36	15	11	10	68	46	41
Donnington Wood	36	16	7	13	62	60	39
Nuneaton Borough Reserves	36	13	11	12	53	46	37
Aero Lucas	36	14	5	17	51	62	33
Springvale-Tranco	36	12	7	17	54	53	31
Cradley Town	36	12	7	17	45	62	31
Pelsall Villa	36	12	6	18	61	70	30
Ludlow Town	36	12	6	18	39	57	30
Brewood	36	8	13	15	44	51	29
Bilston United	36	7	10	19	49	79	24
Cannock Chase	36	8	8	20	51	92	24
Gornal Athletic	36	5	8	23	35	83	18
Darlaston	36	4	5	27	43	88	13

Division Two

	P	W	D	L	F	A	Pts
Donnington Wood	36	25	3	8	105	54	53
Millfields	36	22	7	7	77	34	51
Hinton	36	23	5	8	87	55	51
Hednesford Progressive	36	18	11	7	70	50	47
Atherstone United Reserves	36	20	6	10	86	40	46
Albright & Wilson	36	20	5	11	79	53	45
Wolverhampton Casuals Reserves	36	17	11	8	71	46	45
Jamaica City	36	17	4	15	73	65	38
Bloxwich Town	36	17	4	15	60	58	38
Gresley Rovers Reserves	36	15	7	14	69	54	37
Stuarts Athletic	36	15	3	18	68	72	33
Tamworth Reserves	36	13	6	17	61	88	32
Chasetown Reserves	36	12	7	17	67	70	31
Brewood Reserves	36	13	3	20	55	87	29
Lichfield	36	9	6	21	48	76	24
Oldswinford Reserves	36	6	11	19	64	91	23
Clancey Halesowen	37	7	9	20	38	86	23
Dowty Ashchurch	36	7	6	23	41	87	20
Harrisons Reserves	36	6	6	24	50	103	18

Wednesbury Town left the League during the season and their record was expunged.

Division Two

	P	W	D	L	F	A	Pts
Hinton	34	20	10	4	70	24	50
Chasetown Reserves	34	19	9	6	77	37	47
Moxley Rangers	34	18	11	5	54	28	47
Broseley Athletic	34	20	6	8	73	36	46
Malvern Town Reserves	34	18	9	7	64	35	45
Gresley Rovers Reserves	34	16	9	9	56	33	41
Lichfield	34	16	9	9	72	59	41
Tamworth Reserves	34	17	5	12	67	53	39
Gornal Sports	34	16	5	13	77	63	37
Wolverhampton Casuals Reserves	34	15	3	16	53	55	33
Albright & Wilson	34	13	6	15	60	45	32
Mitchells & Butlers	34	12	7	15	65	52	31
Clancey Halesowen	34	12	6	16	58	70	30
Lye Town Reserves	34	11	4	19	46	66	26
Harrisons Reserves	34	7	6	21	39	85	20
Brewood Reserves	34	7	3	24	42	87	17
Claregate United	34	5	6	23	34	101	16
Springvale-Tranco Reserves	34	5	4	25	34	112	14

1988-1989

Premier Division

	P	W	D	L	F	A	Pts
Blakenall	40	25	11	4	81	31	86
Gresley Rovers	40	24	13	3	100	30	85
Halesowen Harriers	40	23	9	8	74	43	78
Paget Rangers	40	23	8	9	91	41	77
Rushall Olympic	40	22	11	7	73	39	77
Oldbury United	40	22	10	8	89	49	76
Hinckley Town	40	23	6	11	96	38	75
Lye Town	40	20	7	13	61	42	67
Chasetown	40	19	9	12	54	48	66
Malvern Town	40	17	12	11	81	47	63
Rocester	40	14	15	11	67	49	57
Harrisons	40	12	10	18	50	71	46
Tividale	40	10	9	21	65	84	39
Hinckley Athletic	40	9	12	19	50	76	39
Wolverhampton Casuals	40	8	13	19	49	86	37
Wednesfield Social	40	9	8	23	33	82	35
Westfields	40	8	9	23	43	97	33
Millfields	40	9	5	26	42	85	32
Oldswinford	40	8	8	24	42	98	32
Tipton Town	40	8	6	26	30	86	30
Stourport Swifts	40	6	11	23	45	94	29

Division One

	P	W	D	L	F	A	Pts
Newport Town	34	24	6	4	71	27	78
Donnington Wood	34	22	6	6	79	43	72
Ettingshall Holy Trinity	34	21	6	7	71	44	69
Darlaston	34	20	8	6	83	42	68
Pelsall Villa	34	19	9	6	64	41	66
Chasetown Reserves	34	16	7	11	68	62	55
Ludlow Town	34	16	6	12	79	50	54
Springvale-Tranco	34	14	5	15	49	49	47
Aero Lucas	34	12	10	12	55	59	46
Hinton	34	13	7	14	56	65	46
Brewood	34	10	11	13	51	60	41
Cradley Town	34	10	8	16	43	61	38
Nuneaton Borough Reserves	34	9	9	16	50	56	36
Cannock Chase	34	10	6	18	52	72	36
Great Wyrley	34	9	4	21	62	76	31
Gornal Athletic	34	8	7	19	51	78	31
Wolverhampton United	34	6	6	22	42	76	24
Bilston United	34	4	5	25	25	90	17

Division Two

	P	W	D	L	F	A	Pts
Broseley Athletic	32	20	5	7	73	44	65
Lichfield	32	19	6	7	72	40	63
Gresley Rovers Reserves	32	18	8	6	80	40	62
Gornal Sports	32	16	9	7	72	45	57
Mitchells & Butlers	32	17	6	9	70	56	57
Lye Town Reserves	32	14	8	10	55	51	50
GEC Blackheath	32	12	10	10	51	64	46
Hill Top Rangers	32	14	4	14	73	69	46
Moxley Rangers	32	13	6	13	46	49	45
Albright & Wilson	32	13	5	14	55	62	44
Clancey Halesowen	32	11	10	11	65	58	43
Hinckley Town Reserves	32	12	6	14	63	67	42
Harrisons Reserves	32	11	6	15	48	59	39
Tamworth Reserves	32	8	5	19	41	63	29
Malvern Town Reserves	32	6	10	16	42	63	28
Rocester Reserves	32	5	6	21	46	80	21
Wolverhampton Casuals Reserves	32	4	8	20	34	76	20

1989-1990

Premier Division

	P	W	D	L	F	A	Pts
Hinckley Town	40	24	10	6	87	30	82
Rocester	40	25	7	8	85	44	82
Gresley Rovers	40	24	8	8	89	42	80
Blakenall	40	24	5	11	78	52	77
Lye Town	40	22	10	8	68	35	76
Hinckley Athletic	40	18	10	12	58	47	64
Wednesfield	40	16	14	10	60	44	62
Oldbury United	40	18	8	14	62	60	62
Halesowen Harriers	40	17	10	13	79	55	61
Chasetown	40	16	12	12	57	36	60
Paget Rangers	40	18	6	16	74	63	60
Harrisons	40	15	11	14	55	54	56
Malvern Town	40	15	10	15	62	62	55
Rushall Olympic	40	15	5	20	65	56	50
Stourport Swifts	40	12	10	18	40	59	46
Wolverhampton Casuals	40	10	9	21	41	80	39
Westfields	40	10	7	23	44	84	37
Oldswinford	40	10	5	25	39	82	35
Tividale	40	8	8	24	42	80	32
Millfields	40	6	9	25	39	90	27
Tipton Town	40	4	12	24	30	99	24

Division One

	P	W	D	L	F	A	Pts
Darlaston	30	23	4	3	81	35	73
Springvale-Tranco	30	19	6	5	82	41	63
Pelsall Villa	30	20	3	7	73	34	63
Newport Town	30	19	3	8	73	46	60
Ludlow Town	30	14	7	9	80	47	49
Donnington Wood	30	13	8	9	57	56	47
Ettingshall Holy Trinity	30	13	6	11	55	47	45
Gornal Athletic	30	12	6	12	60	51	42
Brewood	30	11	8	11	31	38	41
Cannock Chase	30	9	7	14	52	64	34
Great Wyrley	30	9	6	15	52	64	33
Nuneaton Borough Reserves	30	7	8	15	41	69	29
Wolverhampton United	30	7	7	16	37	71	28
Chasetown Reserves	30	7	6	17	43	60	27
Hinton	30	6	8	16	37	59	26
Cradley Town	30	2	5	23	21	93	11

Division Two

	P	W	D	L	F	A	Pts
Hill Top Rangers	32	25	3	4	82	38	78
Broseley Athletic	32	19	7	6	76	39	64
Lichfield	32	19	6	7	84	44	63
Moxley Rangers	32	18	8	6	55	33	62
Wem Town	32	15	10	7	58	34	55
Clancey Dudley	32	16	5	11	69	43	53
Hinckley Town Reserves	32	15	5	12	48	41	50
Gresley Rovers Reserves	32	15	4	13	63	62	49
Gornal Sports	32	14	3	15	61	47	45
Mitchells & Butlers	32	12	8	12	55	51	44
Lye Town Reserves	32	11	8	13	53	56	41
Albright & Wilson	32	10	4	18	47	60	34
Malvern Town Reserves	32	9	4	19	35	70	31
Harrisons Reserves	32	9	4	19	39	77	31
Rocester Reserves	32	9	3	20	47	84	30
GEC Blackheath	32	6	9	17	30	59	27
Wolverhampton Casuals Reserves	32	3	3	26	24	88	12

1990-1991

Premier Division

Gresley Rovers	42	32	5	5	104	36	101
Chasetown	42	24	13	5	79	32	85
Oldbury United	42	23	14	5	75	37	83
Darlaston	42	20	11	11	89	67	71
Hinckley Athletic	42	20	10	12	76	51	70
Wednesfield	42	21	7	14	76	59	70
Ilkeston Town	42	19	12	11	75	49	69
West Bromwich Town	42	19	11	12	76	51	68
Lye Town	42	19	10	13	53	41	67
Halesowen Harriers	42	19	9	14	84	54	66
Rocester	42	18	12	12	72	44	66
Rushall Olympic	42	17	12	13	67	51	63
Stourport Swifts	42	15	13	14	74	56	58
Blakenall	42	14	16	12	56	59	58
Pelsall Villa	42	10	14	18	49	64	44
Wolverhampton Casuals	42	11	10	21	50	98	43
Paget Rangers	42	10	8	24	50	94	38
Oldswinford	42	9	10	23	60	89	37
Tividale	42	9	5	28	45	100	32
Westfields	42	9	11	22	49	87	38
Malvern Town	42	6	7	29	36	106	25
Tipton Town	42	4	8	30	27	97	20

Division One

Cradley Town	28	20	6	2	75	27	66
Ludlow Town	28	17	6	5	53	20	57
Cannock Chase	28	16	4	8	62	47	52
Moxley Rangers	28	15	5	8	37	31	50
Great Wyrley	28	13	5	10	45	38	44
Wolverhampton United	28	12	4	12	38	36	40
Donnington Wood	28	11	7	10	41	39	40
Ettingshall Holy Trinity	28	12	4	12	42	57	40
Newport Town	28	10	6	12	41	40	36
Broseley Athletic	28	9	7	12	34	39	34
Lichfield	28	11	1	16	37	47	34
Wem Town	28	9	5	14	38	46	32
Gornal Athletic	28	7	7	14	30	49	28
Hill Top Rangers	28	7	5	16	45	65	26
Chasetown Reserves	28	3	4	21	25	62	13

Hinton resigned during the season and their record was expunged.

Division Two

Clancey Dudley	32	21	5	6	76	45	68
Oldbury United Reserves	32	20	6	6	57	26	66
Hinckley Town Reserves	32	20	4	8	87	32	64
Mitchells & Butlers	32	19	6	7	57	36	63
Gresley Rovers Reserves	32	18	7	7	78	39	61
Gornal Sports	32	18	6	8	67	33	60
Lye Town Reserves	32	15	9	8	63	43	54
Bloxwich Strollers	32	14	9	9	65	48	51
Rushall Olympic Reserves	32	14	5	13	62	51	47
Cheslyn Hay	32	11	6	15	57	72	39
Rocester Reserves	32	11	5	16	49	88	38
Albright & Wilson	32	9	9	14	60	56	36
Blackheath Motors	32	9	9	14	38	49	36
Paget Rangers Reserves	32	7	6	19	56	85	27
Wolverhampton Casuals Reserves	32	5	7	20	36	88	22
Malvern Town Reserves	32	2	11	19	36	77	17
Nuneaton Borough Reserves	32	1	6	25	22	98	9

1991-1992

Premier Division

Gresley Rovers	36	24	7	5	83	37	79
Paget Rangers	36	20	5	11	81	44	65
Stourport Swifts	36	18	10	8	62	45	64
Blakenall	36	17	10	9	67	49	61
Chasetown	36	17	10	9	73	41	61
Rocester	36	17	8	11	64	52	59
Oldbury United	36	17	7	12	61	47	58
Rushall Olympic	36	16	9	11	61	38	57
Lye Town	36	14	11	11	51	34	53
Halesowen Harriers	36	13	11	12	63	52	50
Willenhall Town	36	14	6	16	56	63	48
Pelsall Villa	36	12	11	13	52	58	47
West Bromwich Town	36	11	11	14	41	60	44
Cradley Town	36	12	7	17	39	56	43
Hinckley Athletic	36	9	7	20	36	56	34
Malvern Town	36	8	9	19	39	79	33
Wednesfield	36	8	8	20	43	69	32
Westfields	36	6	12	18	48	74	30
Oldswinford	36	7	5	24	34	84	26

Division One

Ilkeston Town	38	31	6	1	121	30	99
Darlaston	38	22	11	5	83	34	77
Donnington Wood	38	21	12	5	77	43	75
Gornal Athletic	38	21	8	9	73	41	71
Knypersley Victoria	38	19	9	10	84	54	66
Ettingshall Holy Trinity	38	15	15	8	60	47	60
Hill Top Rangers	38	17	5	16	75	76	56
Cannock Chase	38	16	7	15	68	71	55
Ludlow Town	38	16	5	17	72	71	53
Moxley Rangers	38	14	9	15	32	42	51
Wolverhampton Casuals	38	13	11	14	51	59	50
Lichfield	38	14	5	19	57	50	47
Tipton Town	38	11	12	15	51	62	45
Wem Town	38	10	10	18	63	73	40
Wolverhampton United	38	8	14	16	63	80	38
Tividale	38	10	6	22	46	72	36
Oldbury United Reserves	38	8	11	19	34	68	35
Great Wyrley	38	9	6	23	45	86	33
Clancey Dudley	38	8	8	22	49	90	32
Broseley Athletic	38	8	8	22	38	93	32

Division Two

K Chell	38	28	4	6	128	39	88
Gornal Sports	38	26	8	4	86	32	86
Rushall Olympic Reserves	38	21	8	9	91	54	71
Park Rangers	38	22	5	11	91	68	71
Mitchells & Butlers	38	21	7	10	96	48	70
Manders	38	20	9	9	70	40	69
Lye Town Reserves	38	19	7	12	75	51	64
Albright & Wilson	38	18	6	14	74	56	60
Bloxwich Strollers	38	14	10	14	81	71	52
Oldswinford Reserves	38	16	4	18	79	85	52
Halesowen Harriers Reserves	38	14	6	18	63	65	48
Alvechurch Reserves	38	13	9	16	62	84	48
Chasetown Reserves	38	13	7	18	63	86	46
Cradley Town Reserves	38	12	9	17	74	102	45
Blackheath Motors	38	12	6	20	65	93	42
Malvern Town Reserves	38	10	9	19	63	68	39
Rocester Reserves	38	11	5	22	53	119	38
Wolverhampton Casuals Reserves	38	9	5	24	58	116	32
Cheslyn Hay	38	7	9	22	62	93	30
Nuneaton Borough Reserves	38	4	7	27	50	114	19

1992-1993

Premier Division

Oldbury United	36	24	8	4	80	39	80
Chasetown	36	23	11	2	66	28	80
Paget Rangers	36	21	7	8	84	54	70
Rocester	36	20	9	7	71	41	69
Stourport Swifts	36	19	9	8	69	38	66
Ilkeston Town	36	19	8	9	73	38	65
Rushall Olympic	36	17	7	12	61	53	58
Wednesfield	36	14	10	12	58	47	52
Alvechurch Sports	36	14	5	17	58	65	47
West Bromwich Town	36	13	6	17	55	86	45
Pelsall Villa	36	10	12	14	60	54	42
Blakenall	36	9	13	14	57	75	40
Willenhall Town	36	12	4	20	49	69	40
Hinckley Athletic	36	11	6	19	56	68	39
Halesowen Harriers	36	8	9	19	44	62	33
Cradley Town	36	9	6	21	42	71	33
Oldswinford	36	9	6	21	39	80	33
Westfields	36	8	6	22	56	85	30
Lye Town	36	7	8	21	47	72	29

Division One

Knypersley Victoria	36	26	3	7	105	34	81
Darlaston	36	25	6	5	69	27	81
Lichfield	36	23	6	7	75	42	75
Ettingshall Holy Trinity	36	20	11	5	69	34	71
Gornal Athletic	36	17	8	11	75	52	59
Cannock Chase	36	16	4	16	50	59	52
Wolverhampton United	36	14	7	15	60	69	49
Great Wyrley	36	12	12	12	44	53	48
Tividale	36	14	5	17	76	67	47
Hill Top Rangers	36	13	8	15	58	62	47
Donnington Wood	36	12	11	13	67	77	47
Malvern Town	36	12	10	14	56	71	46
Oldbury United Reserves	36	10	13	13	52	67	43
Moxley Rangers	36	11	11	14	48	53	44
Ludlow Town	36	10	9	17	55	78	39
Wolverhampton Casuals	36	11	5	20	57	72	38
Tipton Town	36	9	11	16	42	63	38
Gornal Sports	36	7	6	23	42	75	27
Wem Town	36	4	6	26	39	84	18

Division Two

Rushall Olympic Reserves	32	23	4	5	87	42	73
Bloxwich Strollers	32	23	2	7	99	39	71
Chasetown Reserves	32	21	5	6	81	28	68
Rocester Reserves	32	20	6	6	104	49	66
Manders	32	20	5	7	83	40	65
Blackheath Electrodrives	32	17	5	10	69	56	56
Mitchells & Butlers	32	14	9	9	70	53	51
Hinckley Athletic Reserves	32	14	9	9	57	48	51
Lye Town Reserves	32	14	5	13	61	71	47
Albright & Wilson	32	13	5	14	53	62	44
Oldswinford Reserves	32	10	4	18	40	67	34
Halesowen Harriers Reserves	32	9	6	17	49	86	33
Cradley Town Reserves	32	8	4	20	38	68	28
Wolverhampton Casuals Reserves	32	7	5	20	44	87	26
Park Rangers	32	6	5	21	34	80	23
Cheslyn Hay	32	4	6	22	44	87	18
Tividale Reserves	32	5	3	24	38	88	18

1993-1994

Premier Division

Ilkeston Town	38	25	6	7	102	43	81
Stourport Swifts	38	24	7	7	83	37	79
Oldbury United	38	23	9	6	85	42	78
Blakenall	38	23	8	7	78	45	77
Paget Rangers	38	21	5	12	79	43	68
Knypersley Victoria	38	19	8	11	75	60	65
Rocester	38	20	4	14	83	63	64
Hinckley Athletic	38	18	7	13	77	58	61
Chasetown	38	18	6	14	51	57	60
Pelsall Villa	38	16	8	14	70	78	56
Willenhall Town	38	15	8	15	73	60	53
Wednesfield	38	13	11	14	65	63	50
Halesowen Harriers	38	15	5	18	63	66	50
Darlaston	38	12	12	14	61	74	48
Lye Town	38	10	10	18	43	67	40
Brierley Hill Town	38	11	5	22	56	83	38
Rushall Olympic #	38	10	7	21	53	76	34
Westfields	38	7	7	24	58	92	28
Cradley Town	38	4	10	24	42	104	22
West Bromwich Town	38	3	3	32	37	123	12

Rushall Olympic had three points deducted.
Alvechurch Sports folded in mid-season and their record was expunged.

Division One

Stafford Town	40	32	2	6	109	52	98
Gornal Athletic	40	30	4	6	92	35	94
Tividale	40	26	5	9	96	48	83
Ludlow Town	40	21	7	12	70	39	70
Walsall Wood	40	19	10	11	71	40	67
Bloxwich Strollers	40	20	3	17	101	68	63
Wolverhampton United	40	18	8	14	89	70	62
Tipton Town	40	19	5	16	68	67	62
Malvern Town	40	18	8	14	73	74	62
Ettingshall Holy Trinity	40	16	10	14	70	71	58
Wolverhampton Casuals	40	17	5	18	73	63	56
Hill Top Rangers	40	14	11	15	66	72	53
Lichfield #	40	14	12	14	66	60	50
Great Wyrley	40	13	9	18	63	85	48
Cannock Chase	40	12	11	17	60	84	47
Donnington Wood	40	11	10	19	50	54	43
Manders	40	11	10	19	54	70	43
Bilston United	40	11	10	19	54	91	43
Moxley Rangers	40	8	5	27	47	81	29
Wem Town	40	8	5	27	46	116	29
Cheslyn Hay	40	5	4	31	32	110	19

Lichfield had four points deducted.

Reserve Division

Rushall Olympic Reserves	24	22	1	1	75	20	67
Rocester Reserves	24	16	5	3	73	31	53
Lye Town Reserves	24	13	3	8	59	44	42
Hinckley Athletic Reserves	24	10	7	7	50	33	37
Pelsall Villa Reserves	24	9	6	9	50	47	33
Wolverhampton Casuals Reserves	24	9	6	9	41	47	33
Oldbury United Reserves	24	10	3	11	42	49	33
Chasetown Reserves #	24	10	3	11	47	41	30
Halesowen Harriers Reserves	24	7	8	9	43	53	29
Walsall Wood Reserves	24	8	1	15	33	52	25
Tividale Reserves	24	6	5	13	33	47	23
Cradley Town Reserves	24	4	8	12	28	47	20
Moxley Rangers Reserves	24	2	4	18	15	78	10

Chasetown Reserves had three points deducted.

1994-1995

Premier Division

Pelsall Villa	36	28	3	5	83	31	87
Blakenall	36	27	4	5	101	22	85
Stourport Swifts	36	25	7	4	91	29	82
Stafford Town	36	21	5	10	85	53	68
Westfields	36	19	6	11	76	53	63
Walsall Wood	36	18	8	10	84	57	62
Darlaston	36	17	5	14	71	60	56
Bloxwich Strollers	36	15	5	16	50	60	50
Lye Town	36	15	4	17	67	59	49
Wednesfield	36	15	4	17	63	72	49
Gornal Athletic	36	12	10	14	53	54	46
Manders	36	13	6	17	58	83	45
Ludlow Town	36	10	14	12	43	52	44
Tividale	36	13	3	20	49	69	42
Cradley Town #	36	11	7	18	46	71	37
Ettingshall Holy Trinity	36	9	6	21	63	78	33
Hill Top Rangers	36	8	4	24	46	98	28
Bilston United	36	6	5	25	39	106	23
Malvern Town	36	5	4	27	31	89	19

Cradley Town had three points deducted.

Division One

Wolverhampton Casuals	38	29	2	7	126	53	89
Lichfield City	38	25	6	7	107	37	81
Morda United	38	24	4	10	92	45	76
Wem Town	38	20	5	13	69	60	65
Moxley Rangers	38	20	4	14	85	73	64
Rocester Reserves #	38	18	10	10	91	66	61
Rushall Olympic Reserves	38	18	6	14	65	65	60
Tipton Town	38	18	5	15	80	52	59
Goodyear	38	17	8	13	81	68	59
Great Wyrley	38	15	11	12	85	56	56
Chasetown Reserves	38	15	11	12	73	59	56
Pelsall Villa Reserves	38	13	11	14	74	80	50
Hinckley Athletic Reserves	38	14	6	18	97	99	48
Oldbury United Reserves #	38	14	7	17	77	71	46
Wolverhampton United	38	12	9	17	71	95	45
Tividale Reserves *	38	10	10	18	45	67	39
Cannock Chase	38	10	7	21	57	98	37
Gornal Athletic Reserves	38	7	10	21	49	91	31
Cradley Town Reserves	38	8	5	25	57	93	29
Darlaston Reserves	38	3	3	32	31	184	12

Oldbury United Reserves and Rocester Reserves both had three points deducted.
* Tividale Reserves had one point deducted.

1995-1996

Premier Division

Wednesfield	36	28	6	2	95	30	90
Pelsall Villa	36	27	5	4	97	30	86
Lye Town	36	20	11	5	80	34	71
Stafford Town	36	19	10	7	79	35	67
Stourport Swifts	36	19	10	7	74	50	67
Bloxwich Strollers	36	17	9	10	67	50	60
Walsall Wood	36	16	8	12	61	42	56
Gornal Athletic	36	16	7	13	55	42	55
Westfields	36	16	6	14	86	73	54
Ludlow Town	36	14	9	13	68	71	51
Ettingshall Holy Trinity	36	11	9	16	62	80	42
Tividale	36	10	9	17	65	80	39
Lichfield City	36	9	10	17	43	65	37
Malvern Town	36	9	9	18	34	67	36
Brierley Hill Town	36	10	4	22	49	73	34
Cradley Town	36	8	7	21	55	82	31
Wolverhampton Casuals	36	9	4	23	53	108	31
Darlaston	36	5	11	20	40	86	26
Hill Top Rangers	36	4	6	26	34	99	18

Division One

Goodyear	40	27	6	7	110	45	87
Wolverhampton United	40	27	3	10	85	50	84
Rocester Reserves	40	24	10	6	109	46	82
Morda United	40	26	4	10	87	54	82
Chasetown Reserves	40	23	6	11	92	69	75
Bandon	40	22	7	11	94	57	73
Tipton Town	40	21	10	9	78	41	73
Rushall Olympic Reserves	40	21	4	15	98	70	67
Bilston United	40	17	10	13	92	84	61
Brereton Social	40	14	12	14	65	62	54
Moxley Rangers	40	16	8	16	70	64	56
Bromyard Town	40	16	5	19	70	67	53
Hinckley Athletic Reserves	40	15	4	21	71	84	49
Gornal Athletic Reserves	40	13	5	22	42	91	44
Great Wyrley	40	13	4	23	55	103	43
Mahal	40	12	6	22	61	89	42
Oldbury United Reserves	40	11	7	22	68	87	40
Pershore Town Reserves	40	10	7	23	47	82	37
Tividale Reserves	40	10	6	24	51	92	36
Cannock Chase	40	7	9	24	54	97	30
Sikh Hunters	40	6	5	29	50	115	23

1996-1997

Premier Division

Wednesfield	34	26	5	3	103	25	83
Stourport Swifts	34	24	5	5	103	34	77
Bloxwich Strollers	34	23	7	4	84	29	76
Lye Town	34	20	6	8	82	40	66
Brierley Hill Town	34	20	5	9	83	44	65
Stafford Town	34	17	9	8	57	40	60
Wolverhampton Casuals	34	17	7	10	72	69	58
Gornal Athletic	34	15	8	11	55	48	53
Ludlow Town	34	15	7	12	63	57	52
Westfields	34	13	8	13	50	53	47
Tividale	34	12	8	14	53	78	44
Darlaston Town	34	10	9	15	49	60	39
Ettingshall Holy Trinity	34	8	7	19	42	81	31
Cradley Town	34	7	6	21	51	83	27
Malvern Town	34	6	8	20	47	70	26
Walsall Wood	34	6	6	22	35	72	24
Wolverhampton United	34	5	7	22	34	102	22
Hill Top Rangers	34	2	2	30	27	105	8

Division One (North)

Great Wyrley	24	20	1	3	66	20	61
Blakenall Reserves	24	17	3	4	71	19	54
Brereton Town	24	15	5	4	61	31	50
Brereton Social	24	11	5	8	65	47	38
Morda United	24	11	4	9	50	45	37
Cannock Chase	24	11	3	10	56	57	36
Heath Hayes	24	9	5	10	38	49	32
Sikh Hunters	24	8	4	12	62	72	28
Corestone Services	24	7	7	10	36	59	28
Wolverhampton Casuals Reserves	24	8	3	13	45	75	27
Rushall Olympic Reserves	24	7	2	15	32	55	23
Chasetown Reserves	24	6	2	16	43	54	20
Sporting Khalsa	24	2	4	18	24	66	10

Division One (South)

Kington Town	26	22	2	2	91	35	68
Bustleholme	26	16	4	6	62	32	52
Bandon	26	15	3	8	70	31	48
Smethwick Rangers	26	14	5	7	50	35	47
Bromyard Town	26	14	2	10	63	43	44
Leominster Town	26	12	4	10	70	58	40
Tipton Town	26	12	4	10	58	55	40
Bilston United	26	11	4	11	57	52	37
Oldbury United Reserves	26	10	7	9	44	42	37
Mahal	26	10	6	10	51	44	36
Cradley Town Reserves	26	6	4	16	43	73	22
Tividale Reserves	26	5	4	17	31	81	19
Pershore Town Reserves	26	3	6	17	28	78	15
Gornal Athletic Reserves	26	1	7	18	27	86	10

1997-1998

Premier Division

Lye Town	34	26	6	2	91	35	84
Stourport Swifts	34	23	6	5	101	34	75
Brierley Hill Town	34	21	5	8	64	34	68
Kington Town	34	21	3	10	97	67	66
Bloxwich Strollers	34	18	4	12	81	49	58
Malvern Town	34	17	4	13	73	59	55
Wolverhampton Casuals	34	15	6	13	64	52	51
Gornal Athletic	34	15	5	14	56	50	50
Darlaston Town	34	15	3	16	78	70	48
Tividale #	34	15	6	13	64	57	48
Ludlow Town	34	14	3	17	58	71	45
Stafford Town	34	12	7	15	49	57	43
Walsall Wood	34	11	7	16	49	64	40
Westfields	34	11	5	18	57	69	38
Bustleholme	34	11	3	20	48	76	36
Cradley Town	34	9	5	20	54	80	32
Ettingshall Holy Trinity	34	5	7	22	37	100	22
Wolverhampton United	34	2	5	27	19	116	11

Tividale had 3 points deducted.

1998-1999

Premier Division

Kington Town	40	32	3	5	120	39	99
Cradley Town	40	28	3	9	98	40	87
Stafford Town	40	27	5	8	89	38	86
Wolverhampton Casuals	40	24	5	11	99	72	77
Smethwick Rangers	40	21	8	11	88	52	71
Darlaston Town	40	21	7	12	81	63	70
Bandon	40	19	7	14	72	53	64
Malvern Town	40	16	12	12	76	62	60
Tipton Town	40	17	6	17	62	75	57
Bustleholme	40	16	7	17	63	71	55
Gornal Athletic	40	14	11	15	68	65	53
Lye Town	40	12	15	13	56	54	51
Star	40	14	8	18	55	63	50
Dudley Town	40	11	13	16	52	67	46
Tividale	40	12	9	19	55	69	45
Brierley Hill Town	40	11	12	17	57	74	45
Westfields	40	9	15	16	57	69	42
Ludlow Town	40	12	5	23	46	82	41
Ettingshall Holy Trinity	40	10	9	21	62	87	39
Walsall Wood	40	5	7	28	43	99	22
Wolverhampton United	40	1	9	30	33	138	12

Division One (North)

Bandon	28	20	6	2	86	31	66
Lawson Mardon Star	28	19	3	6	100	48	60
Blakenall Reserves	28	17	4	7	78	33	55
Brereton Social	28	14	7	7	60	43	49
Heath Hayes	28	15	2	11	62	55	47
Great Wyrley #	28	14	5	9	55	37	44
Morda United	28	13	5	10	47	47	44
Brereton Town *	28	13	4	11	63	61	42
Newport Town	28	11	8	9	64	45	41
Sikh Hunters	28	10	4	14	46	53	34
Lucas Flight Controls	28	8	7	13	60	72	31
Wolverhampton Casuals Reserves	28	9	4	15	51	79	31
Corestone Services	28	6	2	20	37	78	20
Cannock Chase	28	6	2	20	40	102	20
Walsall Wood Reserves	28	3	1	24	33	98	10

Great Wyrley had 3 points deducted.
* Brereton Town had 1 point deducted.

Division One (North)

Heath Hayes	28	19	5	4	75	28	62
Little Drayton Rangers #	28	19	6	3	74	24	60
Lucas Flight Controls	28	18	4	6	91	37	58
Great Wyrley	28	17	5	6	75	35	56
Brereton Social	28	16	8	4	83	48	56
Newport Town	28	17	5	6	62	40	56
Cannock Chase	28	14	7	7	63	43	49
Sedgley White Lions	28	11	7	10	44	38	40
Morda United	28	9	3	16	55	72	30
Shifnal Town Reserves	28	9	2	17	42	66	29
Wolverhampton Casuals Reserves	28	8	4	16	53	79	28
Wyrley Rangers	28	6	5	17	39	92	23
Wolverhampton Town	28	3	7	18	35	71	16
Corestone Services	28	2	8	18	37	105	14
Walsall Wood Reserves *	28	2	4	22	25	75	9

Little Drayton Rangers had 3 points deducted.
* Walsall Wood Reserves had 1 point deducted.

Division One (South)

Smethwick Rangers	26	18	5	3	75	32	59
Tipton Town	26	18	4	4	71	26	58
Leominster Town	26	15	4	7	68	44	49
Halesowen Harriers Reserves	26	12	7	7	54	35	43
Bromyard Town	26	11	6	9	62	47	39
Tividale Reserves #	26	11	7	8	38	36	37
Wellington	26	11	4	11	45	53	37
Cradley Town Reserves	26	10	6	10	52	40	36
Birmingham College of Food	26	11	3	12	55	48	36
Malvern Town Reserves	26	9	8	9	38	52	35
Mahal	26	10	2	14	54	62	32
Pershore Town Reserves	26	3	7	16	28	94	16
Hinton	26	4	3	19	33	67	15
Gornal Athletic Reserves	26	2	8	16	18	55	14

Tividale Reserves had 3 points deducted.

Division One (South)

Wellington	26	22	1	3	115	17	67
Causeway United	26	21	1	4	75	24	64
Leominster Town	26	13	5	8	57	48	44
Bromyard Town	26	13	3	10	43	34	42
Tividale Reserves	26	12	4	10	48	49	40
Sikh Hunters	26	12	3	11	68	70	39
Halesowen Harriers Reserves	26	11	4	11	59	51	37
Malvern Town Reserves	26	9	7	10	45	54	34
Cradley Town Reserves	26	10	2	14	43	50	32
Hinton	26	10	2	14	53	68	32
Pershore Town Reserves	26	9	4	13	28	50	31
Mahal	26	7	5	14	42	67	26
Lye Town Reserves	26	8	1	17	44	91	25
Borgfield Celtic	26	3	2	21	36	83	11

1999-2000

Premier Division

Stafford Town	42	35	4	3	113	31	109
Causeway United	42	34	2	6	88	35	104
Darlaston Town	42	30	5	7	115	64	95
Bandon	42	26	7	9	83	46	85
Wolverhampton Casuals	42	25	6	11	99	54	81
Kington Town #	42	25	3	14	88	68	72
Tividale	42	19	9	14	66	58	66
Heath Hayes	42	19	4	19	64	66	61
Malvern Town	42	17	7	18	73	56	58
Little Drayton Rangers	42	16	10	16	64	66	58
Lye Town	42	15	9	18	65	66	54
Dudley Town	42	13	13	16	53	59	52
Gornal Athletic	42	14	4	24	58	75	46
Tipton Town	42	12	9	21	61	87	45
Smethwick Rangers	42	12	8	22	67	95	44
Ettingshall Holy Trinity	42	11	10	21	53	91	43
Ludlow Town	42	10	11	21	52	75	41
Brierley Hill Town	42	11	8	23	50	73	41
Bustleholme	42	10	9	23	69	95	39
Westfields	42	9	9	24	56	89	36
Walsall Wood	42	8	10	24	55	99	34
Star	42	8	9	25	37	81	33

Kington Town had 6 points deducted

2000-2001

Premier Division

Ludlow Town	44	34	9	1	100	35	111
Smethwick Rangers	44	29	7	8	129	54	94
Little Drayton Rangers	44	27	7	10	91	53	88
Darlaston Town	44	24	7	13	111	76	79
Causeway United	44	22	11	11	78	47	77
Shawbury United	44	22	6	16	77	59	72
Malvern Town #	44	19	16	9	83	67	72
Kington Town	44	19	9	16	92	78	66
Lye Town	44	18	12	14	68	63	66
Wolverhampton Casuals	44	17	12	15	82	67	63
Wellington	44	19	6	19	69	75	63
Tividale	44	16	11	17	72	74	59
Star	44	15	12	17	77	69	57
Westfields	44	14	14	16	60	63	56
Heath Hayes	44	15	8	21	63	74	53
Bustleholme	44	15	6	23	79	91	51
Ettingshall Holy Trinity	44	14	9	21	58	80	51
Dudley Town	44	13	8	23	48	72	47
Bromyard Town	44	10	10	24	51	97	40
Walsall Wood	44	9	10	25	54	78	37
Gornal Athletic	44	10	7	27	59	105	37
Brierley Hill Town	44	10	7	27	48	125	37
Tipton Town	44	10	6	28	61	108	36

Malvern Town had 1 point deducted

Division One (North)

Shawbury United	24	18	3	3	75	19	57
Wolverhampton United	24	16	2	6	55	23	50
Great Wyrley	24	16	2	6	57	31	50
Sedgley White Lions	24	13	8	3	48	18	47
Cannock Chase	24	15	2	7	67	46	47
Newport Town	24	13	4	7	44	28	43
Lucas Flight Controls	24	8	5	11	58	50	29
Shifnal Town Reserves	24	8	5	11	45	55	29
Morda United	24	8	1	15	40	61	25
Walsall Wood Reserves	24	6	5	13	35	59	23
Borgfield Celtic	24	4	5	15	38	75	17
Heath Hayes Reserves	24	3	5	16	28	71	14
Corestone Services #	24	1	7	16	28	82	10

Corestone Services had 1 point deducted.

Division One (North)

Wolverhampton United	26	23	0	3	101	27	69
Ounsdale	26	22	1	3	85	21	67
Brereton Social	26	18	1	7	63	29	55
Newport Town	26	14	4	8	60	47	46
Lucas Sports	26	13	6	7	80	46	45
Great Wyrley #	26	14	2	10	65	50	38
Eccleshall Reserves	26	10	5	11	37	37	35
Morda United	26	10	2	14	29	62	32
Walsall Wood Reserves †	26	8	5	13	41	64	25
Sikh Hunters	26	8	1	17	45	71	25
Shifnal Town Reserves *	26	7	3	16	39	67	23
Heath Hayes Reserves	26	5	5	16	34	72	20
Wolverhampton Sports GNST	26	5	4	17	30	74	19
Chasetown Reserves	26	2	7	17	31	73	13

Great Wyrley had 6 points deducted.
† Walsall Wood Reserves had 4 points deducted.
* Shifnal Town Reserves had 1 point deducted.

Division One (South)

Bromyard Town	22	17	2	3	75	27	53
Wellington	22	16	4	2	65	21	52
Ledbury Town	22	14	2	6	65	35	44
Sikh Hunters	22	9	4	9	57	51	31
Hinton	22	10	1	11	41	52	31
Malvern Town Reserves	22	8	6	8	36	37	30
Leominster Town	22	8	3	11	41	53	27
Chaddesley Corbett	22	8	2	12	47	53	26
Bewdley Town	22	7	5	10	41	48	26
Pershore Town Reserves	22	7	3	12	46	65	24
Cradley Town Reserves #	22	7	3	12	40	62	21
Mahal	22	3	1	18	26	76	10

Cradley Town Reserves had 3 points deducted.

Division One (South)

Ledbury Town *	22	16	2	4	99	37	49
Brintons Athletic	22	14	4	4	66	40	46
Sedgley White Lions	22	13	2	7	61	29	41
Chaddesley Corbett	22	11	6	5	55	39	39
Bewdley Town	22	12	2	8	58	37	38
Mahal	22	11	0	11	50	57	33
Hinton	22	8	6	8	36	47	30
Bustleholme Reserves	22	7	4	11	41	44	25
Malvern Town Reserves #	22	9	1	12	37	55	25
Leominster Town	22	5	4	13	39	66	19
Lye Town Reserves	22	5	1	16	29	74	16
Pershore Town Reserves	22	4	2	16	19	65	14

Malvern Town Reserves had 3 points deducted.
* Ledbury Town had 1 point deducted.

2001-2002

Premier Division

	P	W	D	L	F	A	Pts
Causeway United	46	29	12	5	107	55	99
Tividale #	46	27	10	9	94	57	88
Wolverhampton Casuals	46	26	8	12	89	69	86
Little Drayton Rangers	46	24	13	9	98	54	85
Westfields	46	24	9	13	89	53	81
Ledbury Town	46	26	3	17	103	85	81
Star	46	24	8	14	91	65	80
Kington Town	46	20	14	12	76	42	74
Malvern Town	46	20	11	15	87	57	71
Heath Hayes	46	19	13	14	60	54	70
Tipton Town	46	19	12	15	76	50	69
Brierley & Hagley Alliance	46	18	15	13	74	60	69
Wellington	46	18	11	17	63	69	65
Lye Town	46	16	15	15	59	47	63
Ettingshall Holy Trinity	46	16	13	17	66	73	61
Bustleholme	46	16	10	20	80	92	58
Wolverhampton United	46	15	11	20	79	81	56
Shawbury United	46	13	14	19	69	83	53
Darlaston Town	46	13	12	21	69	99	51
Bromyard Town	46	11	10	25	73	97	43
Gornal Athletic	46	7	15	24	54	113	36
Smethwick Rangers	46	11	3	32	70	147	36
Walsall Wood	46	7	12	27	52	96	33
Dudley Town	46	3	6	37	42	122	15

Tividale had 3 points deducted

2002-2003

Premier Division

	P	W	D	L	F	A	Pts
Westfields	42	32	6	4	119	30	102
Kington Town	42	31	6	5	121	51	99
Tipton Town	42	27	8	7	95	40	89
Little Drayton Rangers	42	26	5	11	113	66	83
Tividale	42	22	10	10	104	53	76
Malvern Town	42	22	9	11	96	49	75
Shawbury United	42	21	9	12	86	68	72
Lye Town	42	19	7	16	69	64	64
Ledbury Town	42	18	9	15	90	75	63
Brierley & Hagley Alliance	42	17	11	14	74	73	62
Wellington	42	16	10	16	59	69	58
Heath Hayes	42	15	12	15	72	75	57
Wolverhampton Casuals	42	17	5	20	71	91	56
Wolverhampton United	42	15	8	19	66	73	53
Smethwick Sikh Temple	42	11	11	20	58	83	44
Sedgley White Lions	42	11	9	22	48	74	42
Ettingshall Holy Trinity	42	12	5	25	65	92	41
Bustleholme	42	11	7	24	69	93	40
Bromyard Town	42	11	2	29	61	125	35
Dudley Town	42	7	9	26	46	112	30
Walsall Wood	42	6	11	25	48	109	29
Gornal Athletic	42	7	7	28	41	106	28

Division One (North)

	P	W	D	L	F	A	Pts
Ounsdale	30	24	5	1	101	15	77
Great Wyrley #	30	24	4	2	127	33	73
Brereton Social	30	22	5	3	83	31	71
Newport Town	30	16	5	9	69	48	53
Sikh Hunters	30	15	5	10	79	63	50
Morda United	30	13	9	8	43	36	48
Marston Wolves	30	13	8	9	58	45	47
Wrockwardine Wood	30	13	6	11	80	49	45
Shenstone Pathfinders	30	11	8	11	54	60	41
Lucas Sports	30	10	8	12	58	63	38
Wyrley Rangers	30	9	6	15	56	70	33
Eccleshall Reserves	30	9	5	16	43	60	32
Heath Hayes Reserves	30	7	8	15	50	70	29
Darlaston Town Reserves	30	4	4	22	35	88	16
Wolverhampton Sports GNST	30	3	4	23	24	106	13
Walsall Wood Reserves	30	1	2	27	20	143	5

Great Wyrley had 3 points deducted.

Division One (North)

	P	W	D	L	F	A	Pts
Newport Town	34	29	3	2	105	28	90
Bilston Town	34	28	4	2	125	29	88
Lucas Sports	34	25	3	6	124	51	78
Brereton Social	34	18	7	9	87	58	61
Ashbourne United	34	18	5	11	106	69	59
Morda United	34	16	5	13	65	57	53
Darlaston Town	34	14	8	12	76	75	50
Marston Wolves	34	14	6	14	65	58	48
Great Wyrley	34	13	7	14	84	69	46
Sikh Hunters	34	12	9	13	81	73	45
Heath Hayes Reserves	34	12	6	16	55	72	42
Wrockwardine Wood	34	10	7	17	45	77	37
Wednesbury Town	34	10	5	19	68	85	35
Shenstone Pathfinders	34	9	8	17	50	81	35
Riverway Stafford	34	9	7	18	52	91	34
Wyrley Rangers	34	10	3	21	42	82	33
Wolverhampton Sports GNST	34	9	4	21	51	101	31
Walsall Wood Reserves	34	0	3	31	23	148	3

Shelfield Sports withdrew during the season and their record was expunged.

Division One (South)

	P	W	D	L	F	A	Pts
Sedgley White Lions	26	22	3	1	77	18	69
Bewdley Town	26	15	3	8	56	31	48
Hinton	26	13	7	6	54	44	46
Leominster Town	26	13	4	9	49	38	43
Wyre Forest	26	10	10	6	44	34	40
Brintons Athletic	26	12	3	11	41	47	39
Bridgnorth Town Reserves	26	11	5	10	50	45	38
Ludlow Town Reserves	26	11	4	11	62	50	37
Chaddesley Corbett	26	10	1	15	56	61	31
Mahal	26	8	4	14	37	50	28
Malvern Town Reserves	26	8	4	14	38	54	28
Lye Town Reserves	26	6	8	12	35	54	26
Malvern Rangers	26	7	4	15	47	63	25
Bustleholme Reserves	26	5	2	19	32	89	17

Division One (South)

	P	W	D	L	F	A	Pts
Bewdley Town	26	19	5	2	83	31	62
Hinton	26	17	1	8	74	42	52
Blackheath Town	26	14	8	4	65	36	50
Bridgnorth Town Reserves	26	14	6	6	58	34	48
Mahal	26	13	5	8	55	46	44
Chaddesley Corbett	26	12	6	8	50	37	42
Ludlow Town Reserves	26	10	8	8	61	51	38
Wyre Forest Brintons	26	11	3	12	58	60	36
Lye Town Reserves	26	10	5	11	36	38	35
Malvern Town Reserves	26	8	6	12	52	62	30
Bustleholme Reserves	26	5	5	16	38	70	20
Ledbury Town Reserves	26	5	4	17	38	76	19
Leominster Town	26	4	5	17	36	74	17
Malvern Rangers	26	4	5	17	33	80	17

2003-2004

Premier Division

Malvern Town	38	29	3	6	138	38	90
Tipton Town	38	26	8	4	105	36	86
Kington Town	38	26	2	10	100	62	80
Shawbury United	38	21	10	7	73	56	73
Ledbury Town	38	22	6	10	96	60	72
Heath Hayes	38	20	6	12	81	48	66
Market Drayton Town	38	19	8	11	69	54	65
Tividale	38	18	8	12	81	55	62
Wellington	38	18	8	12	74	54	62
Lye Town	38	19	5	14	62	52	62
Bromyard Town	38	17	4	17	78	66	55
Brierley & Hagley Alliance	38	14	7	17	59	68	49
Bustleholme	38	13	3	22	76	85	42
Dudley Town	38	11	9	18	65	81	42
Ettingshall Holy Trinity	38	12	4	22	58	94	40
Wolverhampton United	38	12	3	23	63	116	39
Smethwick Sikh Temple	38	11	5	22	65	93	38
Wednesfield	38	11	4	23	49	125	37
Wolverhampton Casuals	38	7	2	29	51	106	23
Coseley Town	38	0	3	35	23	117	3

Newport Town resigned during the season and their record was expunged.

Division One (North)

Goodrich	30	24	0	6	73	39	72
Darlaston Town	30	23	2	5	101	42	71
Riverway Stafford	30	21	4	5	101	44	67
Great Wyrley	30	19	7	4	89	26	64
Wyrley Rangers	30	20	4	6	69	40	64
Eccleshall A.F.C.	30	17	4	9	58	32	55
Walsall Wood	30	14	5	11	59	53	47
Brereton Social	30	10	7	13	54	56	37
Wednesbury Town	30	11	3	16	51	73	36
Ashbourne United	30	9	4	17	47	62	31
Morda United	30	8	6	16	55	78	30
Sikh Hunters	30	8	5	17	38	65	29
Heath Hayes Reserves	30	8	4	18	40	74	28
Shenstone Pathfinders	30	5	4	21	32	83	19
Mahal	30	4	6	20	47	93	18
Bilbrook	30	4	5	21	30	84	17

Wolverhampton Sports GNST resigned during the season and their record was expunged.

Division One (South)

Gornal Athletic	30	24	2	4	72	12	74
Bridgnorth Town Reserves	30	20	6	4	79	32	66
Bilston Town #	30	21	4	5	88	35	64
Bewdley Town	30	17	4	9	67	40	55
Blackheath Town	30	15	4	11	53	42	49
Tenbury United	30	15	3	12	57	62	48
Malvern Town Reserves	30	12	6	12	48	44	42
Hinton	30	12	3	15	60	55	39
Ludlow Town Reserves	30	9	7	14	38	50	34
Leominster Town	30	10	3	17	48	76	33
Wyre Forest Brintons	30	9	6	15	40	68	33
Bustleholme Reserves	30	8	8	14	51	52	32
Cradley Town Reserves	30	9	5	16	52	68	32
Malvern Rangers	30	8	7	15	36	65	31
Chaddesley Corbett	30	6	8	16	38	58	26
Ledbury Town Reserves	30	4	6	20	20	88	18

Bilston Town had 3 points deducted.

2004-2005

Premier Division

Tipton Town	38	31	3	4	111	19	96
Market Drayton Town	38	23	6	9	76	47	75
Shawbury United	38	20	7	11	59	45	67
Ledbury Town	38	18	7	13	81	60	61
Wellington	38	18	6	14	84	65	60
Heath Hayes	38	18	6	14	67	54	60
Bromyard Town	38	16	8	14	67	62	56
Lye Town	38	16	8	14	63	59	56
Bustleholme	38	15	10	13	90	67	55
Gornal Athletic	38	15	9	14	55	47	54
Wolverhampton Casuals	38	15	9	14	67	73	54
Dudley Town	38	14	11	13	64	63	53
Kington Town	38	13	11	14	72	90	50
Smethwick Sikh Temple	38	15	4	19	60	71	49
Pelsall Villa	38	13	8	17	73	86	47
Tividale	38	12	10	16	56	69	46
Goodrich	38	11	11	16	40	60	44
Brierley & Hagley Alliance	38	7	9	22	46	86	30
Coseley Town	38	6	10	22	48	96	28
Wednesfield	38	4	7	27	49	109	19

Ettingshall Holy Trinity resigned and folded during April. Their record was expunged when it read: 35　5　5　25　34　89　20

Division One

Great Wyrley	36	29	6	1	131	31	93
Bewdley Town	36	27	5	4	107	36	86
Wyrley Rangers	36	22	4	10	80	52	70
Riverway Stafford	36	20	5	11	93	64	65
Hinton	36	17	9	10	82	66	60
Walsall Wood	36	19	2	15	81	55	59
Stafford Town	36	16	8	12	71	59	56
Blackheath Town	36	16	8	12	58	49	56
Ashbourne United *	36	17	6	13	57	49	56
Malvern Town Reserves	36	14	8	14	66	56	50
Darlaston Town	36	15	5	16	64	77	50
Brereton Social	36	13	9	14	75	65	48
Eccleshall A.F.C.	36	13	7	16	62	78	46
Tenbury United	36	11	12	13	58	59	45
Bridgnorth Town Reserves	36	7	13	16	47	75	34
Wednesbury Town	36	8	6	22	55	97	30
Bilston Town	36	8	5	23	62	95	29
Ludlow Town Reserves	36	5	6	25	31	98	21
Wolverhampton United	36	2	2	32	41	160	8

* Ashbourne United had 1 point deducted.

Division Two

Parkfields Leisure	32	28	4	0	116	19	88
Cresswell Wanderers	32	25	2	5	91	34	77
Malvern Rangers	32	23	2	7	99	55	71
Ellesmere Rangers	32	21	5	6	108	38	68
Sporting Khalsa	32	18	5	9	85	50	59
Mahal	32	17	2	13	58	57	53
Shenstone Pathfinders	32	15	5	12	79	54	50
Bilbrook	32	14	1	17	63	64	43
Cradley Town Reserves	32	10	7	15	60	72	37
Bustleholme Reserves	32	10	5	17	53	62	35
Brereton Town **	31	11	2	18	55	76	32
Kington Town Reserves *	32	9	5	18	53	82	31
Darlaston Town Reserves	32	8	5	19	65	112	29
Wednesfield Reserves	31	9	2	20	61	120	29
Chaddesley Corbett	32	8	4	20	40	83	28
Dudley United	32	6	6	20	38	94	24
Bromyard Town Reserves	32	7	2	23	44	96	23

* Kington Town Reserves had 1 point deducted.
** Brereton Town had 3 points deducted.

FORMATION AND SUMMARY

Although their roots were very different, the West Midlands Regional League (WMRL) and the Midland Combination had for many years been gradually converging. By the early 1990s their catchment areas and the standard of clubs competing were almost identical and both leagues were at the same level in the non-League pyramid. It made sense for the best clubs in the two competitions to play each other in a stronger league and so in 1994 the Midland Football Alliance was formed. Ten of the top clubs were selected from each of the two older leagues both of which then became feeders to the new competition. The clubs from the Midland Combination were Barwell, Boldmere St. Michaels, Bolehall Swifts, Pershore Town, Sandwell Borough, Shifnal Town, Stapenhill, Stratford Town and West Midlands Police. The tenth club were Shepshed Dynamo who were a quickly formed replacement for Shepshed Albion who had folded with financial difficulties in May 1994. The ten from the West Midlands Regional League were Brierley Hill Town, Chasetown, Halesowen Harriers, Hinckley Athletic, Knypersley Victoria, Oldbury United, Paget Rangers, Rocester, Rushall Olympic and Willenhall Town. The Midland Football Alliance itself became a feeder to the Southern League.

CHANGES TO THE LEAGUE

1995   Paget Rangers were promoted to the Southern League being replaced by relegated Armitage. Brierley Hill Town were relegated to the WMRL being replaced by promoted Blakenall.

1995-96 Armitage resigned on 13th December 1995 while leading the league and their record was expunged.

1996   Shepshed Dynamo were promoted to the Southern League being replaced by relegated Bridgnorth Town. Bolehall Swifts were relegated to the Midland Combination being replaced by promoted Bloxwich Town. Pelsall Villa were promoted from the WMRL.

1997   Hinckley Athletic merged with Hinckley Town and joined the Southern League as Hinckley United. Blakenall were also promoted to the Southern League. These two were replaced by Wednesfield who were promoted from the WMRL and Kings Norton Town who were promoted from the Midland Combination, having changed their name from Richmond Swifts.

1998   Bloxwich Town were promoted to the Southern League. Stourport Swifts were promoted from the WMRL.

1999   Rocester were promoted to the Southern League being replaced by relegated Bloxwich Town. Cradley Town were promoted from the WMRL and Oadby Town were promoted from the Leicestershire Senior League. League increased to 22 clubs.

2000   Kings Norton Town disbanded and Pershore Town were relegated to the Midland Combination. These two were replaced by Stourbridge who were relegated from the Southern League and Stafford Town who were promoted from the WMRL.

2001   Bloxwich Town merged with Blakenall and joined the Southern League as Bloxwich United. Sandwell Borough disbanded. Stourport Swifts were promoted to the Southern League being replaced by two relegated clubs, Bromsgrove Rovers and Paget Rangers. West Midlands Police were relegated to the Midland Combination being replaced by promoted Studley BKL. Ludlow Town were promoted from the WMRL and Quorn were promoted from the Leicestershire Senior League. League increased to 23 clubs.

2001-02 Stapenhill withdrew during the season and their record was expunged.

2002   Bromsgrove Rovers were promoted to the Southern League and Paget Rangers disbanded. Causeway United were promoted from the WMRL and Grosvenor Park were promoted from the Midland Combination. Knypersley Victoria changed their name to Biddulph Victoria. Studley BKL changed their name to Studley. League reduced to 22 clubs.

2003   Halesowen Harriers disbanded. Shifnal Town were relegated to the Midland Combination being replaced by promoted Alvechurch. Wednesfield were relegated to the WMRL being replaced by promoted Westfields. Racing Club Warwick and Rocester were relegated from the Southern League and Coalville Town were promoted from the Leicestershire Senior League. League increased to 24 clubs.

2004   Rocester and Willenhall Town were promoted to the Northern Premier League. Grosvenor Park resigned and moved to Sunday football. Pelsall Villa and Stafford Town were both relegated to the WMRL being replaced by just one promoted club, Malvern Town. Romulus were promoted from the Midland Combination and Loughborough Dynamo were promoted from the Leicestershire Senior League. League reduced to 22 clubs.

1994-95

Team	P	W	D	L	F	A	Pts
Paget Rangers	38	24	9	5	65	32	81
Hinckley Athletic	38	20	9	9	76	49	69
Stratford Town	38	19	9	10	69	46	66
Shepshed Dynamo	38	18	10	10	63	51	64
Halesowen Harriers	38	19	6	13	87	55	63
Shifnal Town	38	16	14	8	65	45	62
Boldmere St. Michaels	38	18	8	12	65	48	62
Oldbury United	38	18	8	12	58	47	62
Knypersley Victoria	38	15	12	11	82	54	57
Willenhall Town	38	15	7	16	55	58	52
West Midlands Police	38	14	8	16	53	51	50
Stapenhill	38	15	5	18	60	80	50
Rocester	38	12	12	14	48	50	48
Sandwell Borough	38	12	12	14	62	69	48
Barwell	38	12	9	17	58	69	45
Pershore Town	38	12	9	17	49	71	45
Chasetown	38	8	13	17	52	72	37
Rushall Olympic	38	9	10	19	60	85	37
Bolehall Swifts	38	9	9	20	45	60	36
Brierley Hill Town	38	3	5	30	27	107	14

1995-96

Team	P	W	D	L	F	A	Pts
Shepshed Dynamo	36	22	10	4	90	37	76
Blakenall	36	19	11	6	60	36	68
Hinckley Athletic	36	21	4	11	78	54	67
Rocester	36	19	9	8	55	50	66
Knypersley Victoria	36	18	8	10	73	43	62
Boldmere St. Michaels	36	18	5	13	73	51	59
Sandwell Borough	36	17	5	14	56	50	56
Willenhall Town	36	16	7	13	52	62	55
Barwell	36	15	6	15	57	53	51
Oldbury United	36	14	8	14	49	41	50
Rushall Olympic	36	15	5	16	57	65	50
Halesowen Harriers	36	13	7	16	54	62	46
Stratford Town	36	12	9	15	56	54	45
Pershore Town	36	12	9	15	58	73	45
West Midlands Police	36	11	11	14	49	55	44
Chasetown	36	10	10	16	44	52	40
Shifnal Town	36	8	9	19	38	60	33
Stapenhill	36	5	6	25	38	87	21
Bolehall Swifts	36	5	5	26	30	82	20

Armitage resigned on 13th December 1995 whilst leading the league and their record was expunged.

1996-97

Team	P	W	D	L	F	A	Pts
Blakenall	38	23	11	4	85	39	80
Hinckley Athletic	38	22	10	6	77	44	76
Boldmere St. Michaels	38	22	7	9	69	41	73
Willenhall Town	38	20	9	9	77	45	69
Barwell	38	17	10	11	65	51	61
Bridgnorth Town	38	18	4	16	76	67	58
Rocester	38	16	9	13	62	53	57
Stratford Town	38	15	10	13	53	48	55
Bloxwich Town	38	16	6	16	63	53	54
Oldbury United	38	14	11	13	50	43	53
Pelsall Villa	38	13	9	16	52	70	48
Knypersley Victoria	38	11	12	15	42	53	45
Stapenhill	38	10	14	14	45	58	44
Shifnal Town	38	11	10	17	45	50	43
West Midlands Police	38	10	11	17	37	60	41
Rushall Olympic	38	10	10	18	40	59	40
Sandwell Borough	38	9	13	16	48	69	40
Chasetown	38	9	12	17	44	65	39
Halesowen Harriers	38	8	12	18	44	67	36
Pershore Town	38	8	6	24	41	80	30

1997-98

Team	P	W	D	L	F	A	Pts
Bloxwich Town	38	28	4	6	77	31	88
Rocester	38	23	7	8	74	36	76
Oldbury United	38	20	11	7	73	43	71
Boldmere St. Michaels	38	19	11	8	54	38	68
Kings Norton Town	38	18	13	7	57	37	67
Barwell	38	16	12	10	68	55	60
Bridgnorth Town	38	15	13	10	64	47	58
West Midlands Police	38	15	12	11	58	42	57
Halesowen Harriers	38	17	5	16	53	63	56
Chasetown	38	14	11	13	57	43	53
Wednesfield	38	14	11	13	56	49	53
Knypersley Victoria	38	11	17	10	52	53	50
Willenhall Town	38	12	13	13	45	44	49
Pelsall Villa	38	10	15	13	66	66	45
Sandwell Borough	38	10	15	13	57	63	45
Rushall Olympic	38	12	8	18	51	57	44
Stapenhill	38	7	12	19	39	74	33
Stratford Town	38	8	7	23	39	70	31
Pershore Town	38	4	6	28	36	97	18
Shifnal Town	38	3	5	30	35	103	14

1998-1999

Team	P	W	D	L	F	A	Pts
Rocester	38	25	7	6	80	36	82
Kings Norton Town	38	25	5	8	65	29	80
Oldbury United	38	19	9	10	67	42	66
Boldmere St. Michaels	38	19	8	11	56	49	65
Barwell	38	17	10	11	69	54	61
Halesowen Harriers	38	17	8	13	65	63	59
Rushall Olympic	38	16	10	12	57	44	58
Shifnal Town	38	16	8	14	59	60	56
West Midlands Police	38	15	10	13	50	52	55
Chasetown	38	12	17	9	48	38	53
Bridgnorth Town	38	14	11	13	44	40	53
Stourport Swifts	38	13	11	14	56	50	50
Knypersley Victoria	38	13	8	17	59	61	47
Willenhall Town	38	13	8	17	51	53	47
Wednesfield	38	12	6	20	63	72	42
Pelsall Villa	38	11	7	20	41	67	40
Stapenhill	38	11	5	22	51	82	38
Sandwell Borough	38	10	7	21	37	65	37
Pershore Town	38	8	11	19	47	64	35
Stratford Town	38	7	8	23	39	83	29

1999-2000

Team	P	W	D	L	F	A	Pts
Oadby Town	42	27	7	8	107	48	88
Stratford Town	42	22	12	8	73	47	78
Willenhall Town	42	20	13	9	77	42	73
Wednesfield	42	21	9	12	71	56	72
Boldmere St. Michaels	42	20	12	10	61	48	72
Stourport Swifts	42	19	13	10	73	57	70
Rushall Olympic	42	20	9	13	75	65	69
Shifnal Town	42	17	16	9	66	50	67
Barwell	42	18	12	12	85	57	66
Oldbury United	42	17	13	12	62	45	64
Chasetown	42	18	7	17	61	62	61
Knypersley Victoria	42	17	10	15	75	71	61
West Midlands Police	42	15	8	19	62	71	53
Bridgnorth Town	42	15	7	20	70	72	52
Halesowen Harriers	42	14	8	20	63	71	50
Sandwell Borough	42	12	13	17	53	69	49
Bloxwich Town	42	11	13	18	57	84	46
Kings Norton Town	42	9	16	17	60	68	43
Cradley Town	42	10	12	20	56	87	42
Pelsall Villa	42	9	10	23	57	88	37
Stapenhill	42	8	6	28	42	91	30
Pershore Town	42	7	6	29	46	103	27

2000-2001

Team	P	W	D	L	F	A	Pts
Stourport Swifts	42	28	9	5	109	38	93
Rushall Olympic	42	28	9	5	98	28	93
Barwell	42	26	11	5	74	35	89
Oadby Town #	42	26	7	9	89	45	82
Stourbridge	42	23	10	9	93	52	79
Stratford Town	42	20	10	12	96	58	70
Boldmere St. Michaels	42	19	13	10	73	49	70
Willenhall Town	42	19	8	15	76	62	65
Bridgnorth Town	42	17	8	17	79	66	59
Chasetown	42	15	10	17	55	78	55
Oldbury United	42	14	11	17	70	71	53
Cradley Town	42	15	4	23	52	80	49
Stafford Town	42	12	12	18	68	83	48
Bloxwich Town	42	14	6	22	54	80	48
Wednesfield	42	14	6	22	60	91	48
Shifnal Town	42	12	11	19	56	75	47
Halesowen Harriers	42	13	7	22	55	73	46
Stapenhill	42	12	8	22	58	91	44
Pelsall Villa	42	12	6	24	60	90	42
Knypersley Victoria #	42	10	10	22	64	100	37
West Midlands Police	42	9	7	26	67	112	34
Sandwell Borough	42	9	7	26	62	111	34

Knypersley Victoria and Oadby Town both had 3 points deducted.

2001-2002

Team	P	W	D	L	F	A	Pts
Stourbridge	42	27	7	8	82	39	88
Bromsgrove Rovers	42	26	9	7	94	41	87
Wednesfield	42	24	9	9	73	39	81
Stratford Town	42	24	7	11	81	49	79
Rushall Olympic	42	22	11	9	81	50	77
Oadby Town	42	21	12	9	78	62	75
Quorn	42	20	10	12	76	55	70
Barwell	42	15	17	10	67	44	62
Studley BKL	42	16	12	14	76	57	60
Ludlow Town	42	15	14	13	58	53	59
Bridgnorth Town	42	18	5	19	74	73	59
Willenhall Town	42	16	9	17	65	62	57
Boldmere St. Michaels	42	15	11	16	43	51	56
Halesowen Harriers	42	16	8	18	56	69	56
Paget Rangers	42	10	19	13	58	55	49
Stafford Town	42	13	6	23	59	88	45
Pelsall Villa	42	10	12	20	39	70	42
Chasetown	42	9	13	20	43	74	40
Shifnal Town	42	9	10	23	36	77	37
Knypersley Victoria	42	10	5	27	51	82	35
Oldbury United	42	7	11	24	39	77	32
Cradley Town	42	5	11	26	36	98	26

Stapenhill withdrew during the season and their record was expunged.

2002-2003

Team	P	W	D	L	F	A	Pts
Stourbridge	42	31	8	3	96	27	101
Rushall Olympic	42	31	6	5	94	37	99
Stratford Town	42	29	6	7	105	38	93
Oadby Town	42	26	7	9	87	52	85
Quorn	42	25	9	8	115	55	84
Willenhall Town	42	23	10	9	91	47	79
Studley	42	24	6	12	97	58	78
Oldbury United	42	22	7	13	88	58	73
Chasetown	42	20	8	14	79	64	68
Grosvenor Park	42	19	10	13	81	58	67
Causeway United	42	18	5	19	70	73	59
Barwell	42	17	7	18	70	68	58
Biddulph Victoria	42	17	6	19	51	69	57
Boldmere St. Michaels	42	16	5	21	59	63	53
Ludlow Town	42	12	8	22	63	76	44
Bridgnorth Town	42	11	9	22	48	79	42
Stafford Town	42	11	8	23	61	93	41
Pelsall Villa	42	10	11	21	64	97	41
Cradley Town	42	8	7	27	43	87	31
Shifnal Town	42	6	7	29	43	93	25
Halesowen Harriers	42	4	6	32	44	107	18
Wednesfield	42	4	0	38	19	169	12

2003-2004

Team	P	W	D	L	F	A	Pts
Rocester	46	28	12	6	96	45	96
Willenhall Town	46	27	13	6	114	49	94
Stratford Town	46	28	8	10	89	45	92
Quorn	46	26	12	8	84	47	90
Studley	46	26	7	13	96	52	85
Oadby Town	46	23	8	15	90	56	77
Chasetown	46	22	11	13	68	50	77
Coalville Town	46	20	12	14	87	61	72
Stourbridge	46	19	15	12	74	52	72
Bridgnorth Town	46	20	12	14	76	66	72
Oldbury United	46	19	14	13	72	55	71
Racing Club Warwick	46	20	9	17	64	63	69
Westfields	46	20	6	20	67	61	66
Rushall Olympic	46	15	16	15	58	55	61
Boldmere St. Michaels	46	17	9	20	76	77	60
Biddulph Victoria	46	16	12	18	66	74	60
Causeway United	46	15	11	20	66	82	56
Barwell	46	15	9	22	63	75	54
Alvechurch	46	12	14	20	67	87	50
Ludlow Town	46	12	11	23	56	84	47
Grosvenor Park	46	9	9	28	53	79	36
Cradley Town	46	8	12	26	60	92	36
Pelsall Villa	46	7	7	32	46	132	28
Stafford Town	46	1	5	40	27	176	8

2004-2005

Team	P	W	D	L	F	A	Pts
Rushall Olympic	42	27	7	8	88	44	88
Chasetown	42	25	6	11	78	45	81
Coalville Town	42	22	11	9	68	38	77
Quorn	42	21	11	10	78	52	74
Malvern Town	42	21	9	12	78	70	72
Westfields	42	18	13	11	61	48	67
Oadby Town	42	18	11	13	64	53	65
Stourbridge	42	19	7	16	84	65	64
Racing Club Warwick	42	19	7	16	79	68	64
Boldmere St. Michaels	42	19	7	16	79	70	64
Stratford Town	42	20	4	18	71	67	64
Romulus	42	17	11	14	74	66	62
Barwell	42	17	10	15	60	60	61
Loughborough Dynamo	42	16	6	20	69	83	54
Alvechurch	42	16	5	21	75	68	53
Causeway United	42	12	9	21	53	68	45
Oldbury United *	42	13	8	21	70	90	44
Studley	42	11	11	20	55	76	44
Cradley Town	42	12	7	23	59	84	43
Biddulph Victoria	42	10	11	21	59	83	41
Ludlow Town	42	12	5	25	55	84	41
Bridgnorth Town	42	7	4	31	38	113	25

* Oldbury United had 3 points deducted.

BACKGROUND AND SUMMARY

Shrewsbury School has a tradition of playing football that goes back for centuries and it was largely because of this tradition that the game became popular in Shropshire much earlier than in virtually every other area of the country. In the late 1860s there were already several clubs playing in Shrewsbury and following the spread of the game throughout the county, the Shropshire F.A. was founded in 1877. The Shropshire Senior Cup was first played for in the 1877-78 season and the only older football competitions anywhere in the world are the Birmingham Senior Cup, the Sheffield & Hallamshire Cup and the oldest of all, the F.A. Cup itself.

When football first began to be played in the growing industrial cities of the North and the Midlands, the earliest clubs often found it difficult to get fixtures against enough local teams of sufficient strength and they therefore had to travel further afield to find worthwhile opponents. Thus it was that the established teams in the tiny towns of Shropshire once played host to some of today's most famous League clubs. Wolverhampton Wanderers started life as St. Luke's and it was under that title that they twice visited Shifnal in the 1879-80 season, and were twice beaten – by Shifnal Mechanics in November and by Shifnal Wanderers in January. Notice that Wolves were not of sufficient status to play Shifnal's top club, Shifnal Town who did however have annual home fixtures with Aston Villa. In the same era Oswestry often beat Everton in their annual home and away fixtures, while the Toffees also came to grief on Boxing Day 1881 when their first XI were thrashed 5-1 by one of Shropshire's weaker sides, Ellesmere.

The legalisation of professionalism in 1885 meant that the best players from rural areas soon gravitated to the large cities where the gate receipts meant that they could pay the best wages (or expenses as they were usually described!) but Shropshire still had enough strong teams left to form one of the earliest county leagues. Only two years after the Football League was formed in 1888, the Shropshire & District League came into being "to help to improve the standard of football in the county". The intended eight founder members were Ironbridge, Ludlow, Newport, Oswestry, Shifnal Town, Shrewsbury Town, St. George's and Wellington Town. However Shifnal were experiencing financial difficulties at the time and just a few days before the start of the season, they withdrew because of a lack of signed-up players. Whitchurch quickly accepted an invitation to replace them.

Of the founder members, Ironbridge and St. George's had already played one season of league football, having been founder members of the Birmingham League a year earlier, but it was not long before the best of the Shropshire League's clubs began to move in the opposite direction and in 1900 the League closed down, its strength having already being significantly diluted. There were a number of attempts to revive it but none of these lasted more than a season or two until today's Shropshire County League was formed in 1950. Today's league though is at a much lower level than the original Shropshire & District League.

CHANGES TO THE LEAGUE

1891   Ludlow and Oswestry left but Nantwich, Stafford Rangers and Wolverhampton Wanderers Reserves joined. League increased to 9 clubs.

1892   Nantwich and Wolverhampton Wanderers Reserves left. Hereford and Newtown joined.

1893   Stafford Rangers left. Market Drayton and Oswestry United joined. League increased to 10 clubs.

1894   Market Drayton left and were replaced by Wrockwardine Wood.

1895   Shrewsbury Town left and joined the Birmingham League and were replaced by Market Drayton.

1896   Hereford left and joined the Birmingham League as Hereford Town. Newtown and Oswestry United also left but Leominster and Wem joined. League reduced to 9 clubs.

1897   Leominster and Whitchurch left. Newtown, Oswestry United and Shrewsbury Town Reserves joined. League increased to 10 clubs.

1898   Wellington Town, Oswestry United, Market Drayton and Shrewsbury Town Reserves all left. Walsall Reserves and Welshpool joined. League reduced to 8 clubs.

1898-99   Wrockwardine Wood were unable to complete their fixtures and their record was expunged.

1899   St. George's, Newtown and Walsall Reserves all left. Bridgnorth, Singleton & Coles and St. Georges United joined from the Wellington & District League and Stafford Christ Church also joined.

1900   Ironbridge and Newport left. Wem only wanted to play cup matches and friendlies and with only Bridgnorth, Singleton & Coles and Welshpool willing to continue, the league was forced to close down.

TABLE NOTES

The Shropshire League tables as published contained a number of errors. Additional research has succeeded in correcting all but those noted below.

1891-92   Total goals for 3 more than total goals against.

1898-99   Total goals for 1 less than total goals against.

1890-1891

Ironbridge #	14	11	0	3	40	12	22
Shrewsbury Town	14	9	1	4	42	21	19
Newport #	14	8	0	6	21	27	16
Wellington Town	14	6	2	6	26	25	14
St. George's	14	6	1	7	35	24	13
Ludlow	14	4	2	8	18	26	10
Whitchurch	14	5	0	9	25	44	10
Oswestry #	14	4	0	10	14	42	8

Oswestry were unable to fulfill two fixtures, with Newport and Ironbridge who were therefore each awarded a win.

1891-1892

Wolverhampton Wanderers Res.	16	15	1	0	89	10	31
Nantwich	16	8	2	6	44	35	18
Stafford Rangers	16	8	2	6	35	31	18
St. George's	16	7	3	6	44	41	17
Ironbridge	16	6	4	6	61	53	16
Shrewsbury Town	16	6	4	6	48	48	16
Newport	16	4	4	8	35	64	12
Wellington Town	16	2	4	10	20	44	8
Whitchurch	16	3	2	11	25	72	8

1892-1893

Newtown	16	8	6	2	72	24	22
Ironbridge	16	9	3	4	41	34	21
St. George's	16	8	4	4	47	38	20
Shrewsbury Town	16	7	6	3	45	37	20
Wellington Town	16	5	7	4	48	35	17
Stafford Rangers	16	7	3	6	31	34	17
Hereford	16	5	4	7	20	35	14
Newport	16	4	3	9	30	43	11
Whitchurch	16	0	2	14	23	77	2

1893-1894

St. George's	18	12	2	4	48	23	26
Newtown	18	12	1	5	68	28	25
Shrewsbury Town	17	11	2	4	60	37	24
Wellington Town	18	6	5	7	40	45	17
Market Drayton	18	7	2	9	34	50	16
Hereford	17	7	1	9	55	44	15
Ironbridge	18	6	3	9	36	51	15
Whitchurch	18	6	3	9	47	65	15
Newport	18	5	3	10	34	51	13
Oswestry United	18	4	4	10	35	63	12

The game between Hereford and Shrewsbury Town was not played.

1894-1895

St. George's	17	12	4	1	44	18	28
Oswestry United	18	10	5	3	53	25	25
Shrewsbury Town	17	8	4	5	42	28	20
Hereford	18	5	8	5	34	25	18
Newtown	17	8	2	7	42	35	18
Wrockwardine Wood	17	6	4	7	30	34	16
Ironbridge	18	6	3	9	38	47	15
Wellington Town	18	4	5	9	45	63	13
Whitchurch	18	4	4	10	30	54	12
Newport	18	4	3	11	21	50	11

Two games were not played.

1895-1896

Hereford	18	14	1	3	69	22	29
Wrockwardine Wood	18	11	4	3	46	21	26
Wellington Town	18	9	5	4	54	37	23
Newtown	18	10	2	6	48	29	22
St. George's	18	9	3	6	53	28	21
Ironbridge	18	8	4	6	49	43	20
Market Drayton	18	6	2	10	31	41	14
Newport	18	5	1	12	29	58	11
Whitchurch	18	3	2	13	19	78	8
Oswestry United	18	3	0	15	30	71	6

1896-1897

Wellington Town	16	12	4	0	55	18	28
Wrockwardine Wood	14	8	3	3	46	15	19
St. George's	14	7	4	3	30	20	18
Newport	16	7	4	5	33	31	18
Ironbridge	16	7	2	7	44	31	16
Market Drayton	14	5	2	7	35	36	12
Whitchurch	14	4	1	9	19	71	9
Wem	16	3	3	10	27	53	9
Leominster	16	3	1	12	32	46	7

Four games were not played.

1897-1898

Wellington Town	18	15	1	2	64	18	31
Newtown	18	13	1	4	64	21	27
Ironbridge	18	10	4	4	48	26	24
St. George's	18	10	2	6	44	32	22
Newport	18	8	5	5	36	35	21
Oswestry United	18	8	1	9	36	40	17
Market Drayton	18	7	2	9	32	45	16
Wrockwardine Wood	18	6	1	11	35	44	13
Shrewsbury Town Reserves	18	2	1	15	19	69	5
Wem	18	1	2	15	19	67	4

1898-1899

Ironbridge	11	7	3	1	32	7	17
Walsall Reserves	12	8	1	3	30	10	17
St. George's	12	8	1	3	30	17	17
Newtown	11	5	2	4	26	16	12
Wem	12	4	2	6	10	21	10
Welshpool	12	3	1	8	19	47	7
Newport	12	0	2	10	3	33	2

Wrockwardine Wood were unable to complete their fixtures and their record was expunged. Ironbridge against Newtown was not played.

1899-1900

Ironbridge	14	12	1	1	56	12	25
Singleton & Coles	13	8	2	3	46	27	18
St. George's United	13	6	3	4	36	29	15
Bridgnorth	14	5	3	6	37	35	13
Newport	14	4	3	7	22	32	11
Stafford Christ Church	13	5	0	8	34	32	10
Wem	14	3	3	8	14	46	9
Welshpool	13	3	1	9	13	45	7

Two games were not played.

Supporters' Guides Series

This top-selling series has been published annually since 1982 and contains 2004/2005 Season's results and tables, Directions, Photographs, Phone numbers, Parking information, Admission details, Disabled information and much more.

THE SUPPORTERS' GUIDE TO PREMIER & FOOTBALL LEAGUE CLUBS 2006

The 22nd edition featuring all Premiership and Football League clubs. *Price £6.99*

THE SUPPORTERS' GUIDE TO NON-LEAGUE FOOTBALL 2006

Following the reorganisation of Non-League Football this 14th edition covers all 66 Step 1 & Step 2 clubs – the Football Conference National, Conference North and Conference South. *Price £6.99*

THE SUPPORTERS' GUIDE TO NON-LEAGUE FOOTBALL 2006 – STEP 3 CLUBS

Following the reorganisation of Non-League Football the 2nd edition of this book features the 66 clubs which feed into the Football Conference. *Price £6.99*

THE SUPPORTERS' GUIDE TO SCOTTISH FOOTBALL 2006

The 14th edition featuring all Scottish Premier League, Scottish League and Highland League clubs. *Price £6.99*

THE SUPPORTERS' GUIDE TO WELSH FOOTBALL GROUNDS 2006

The 10th edition featuring all League of Wales, Cymru Alliance & Welsh Football League Clubs + results, tables & much more. *Price £6.99*

THE SUPPORTERS' GUIDE TO NORTHERN IRISH FOOTBALL 2006

Back after a long absence, this 3rd edition features all Irish Premier League and Irish Football League Clubs + results, tables & much more. *Price £6.99*

THE SUPPORTERS' GUIDE TO EIRCOM FAI CLUBS 2005

Back after a long absence this 3rd edition features all Eircom League Premier and First Division Clubs + 10 years of results, tables & much more. *Price £6.99*

These books are available UK & Surface post free from –

Soccer Books Limited (Dept. SBL)
72 St. Peter's Avenue
Cleethorpes
N.E. Lincolnshire
DN35 8HU